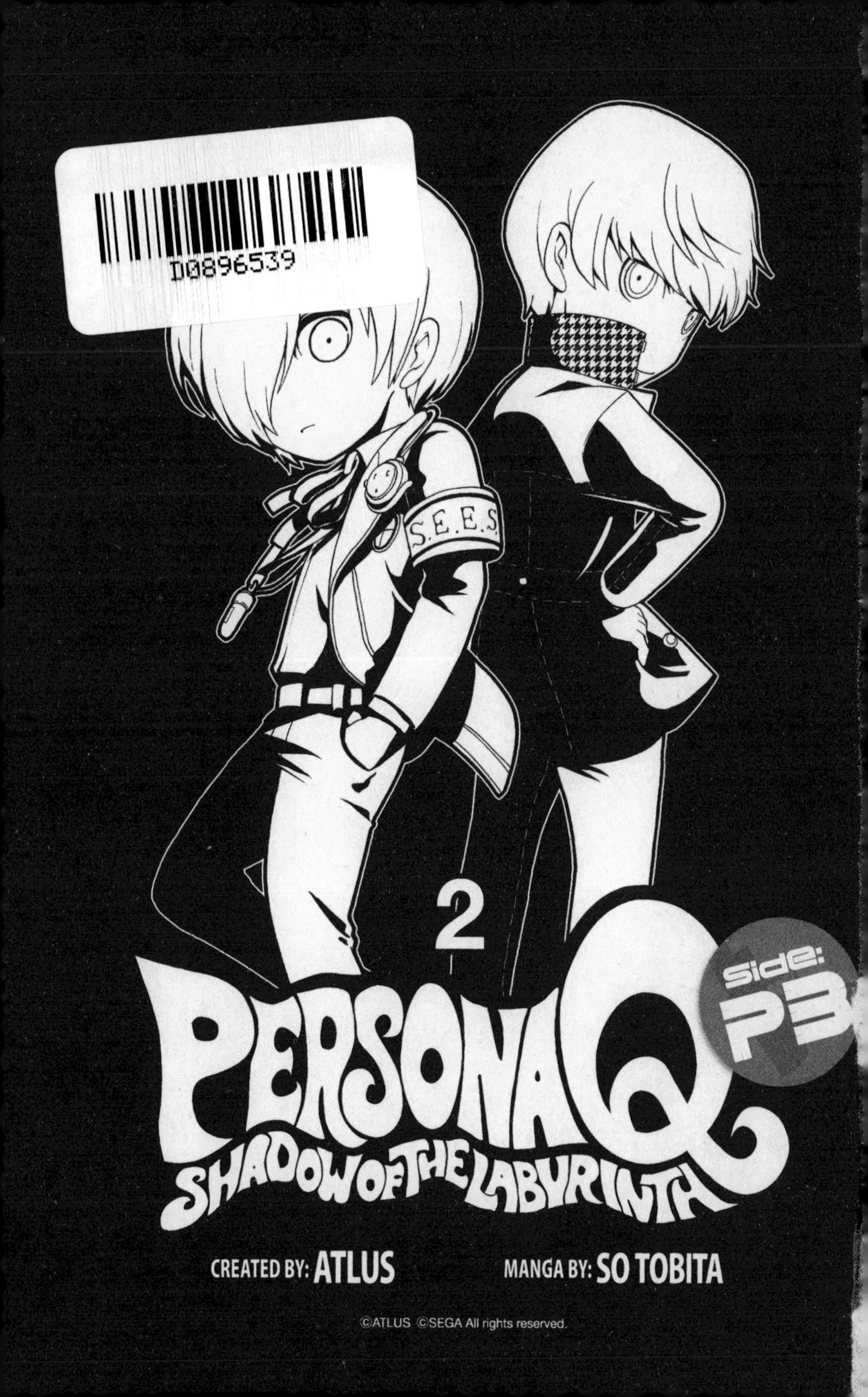
S.E.E.S

2

PERSONA Q
SHADOW OF THE LABYRINTH
Side: P3

CREATED BY: ATLUS

MANGA BY: SO TOBITA

CONTENTS

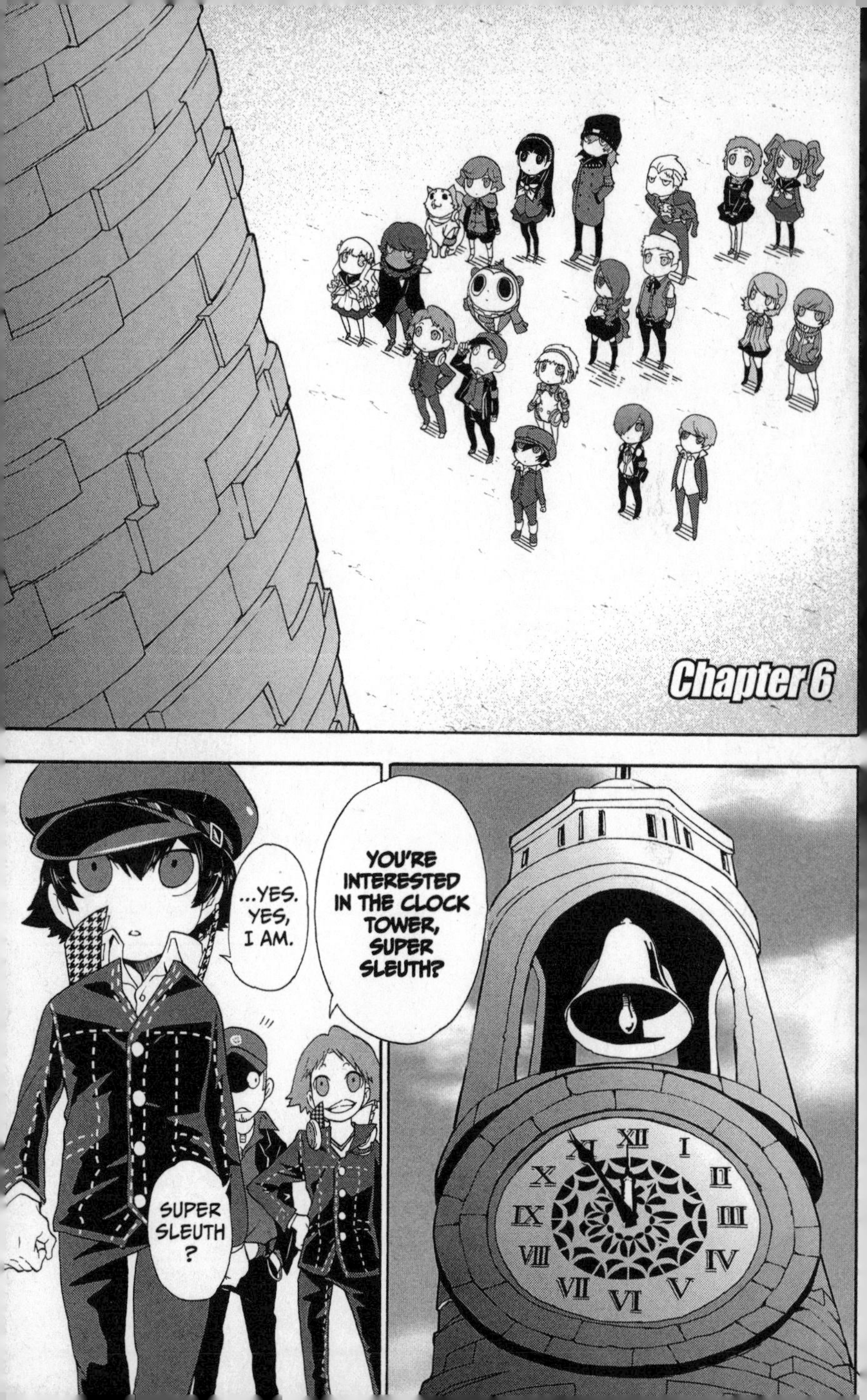
Chapter 6
YOU'RE INTERESTED IN THE CLOCK TOWER, SUPER SLEUTH?
...YES. YES, I AM.
SUPER SLEUTH ?

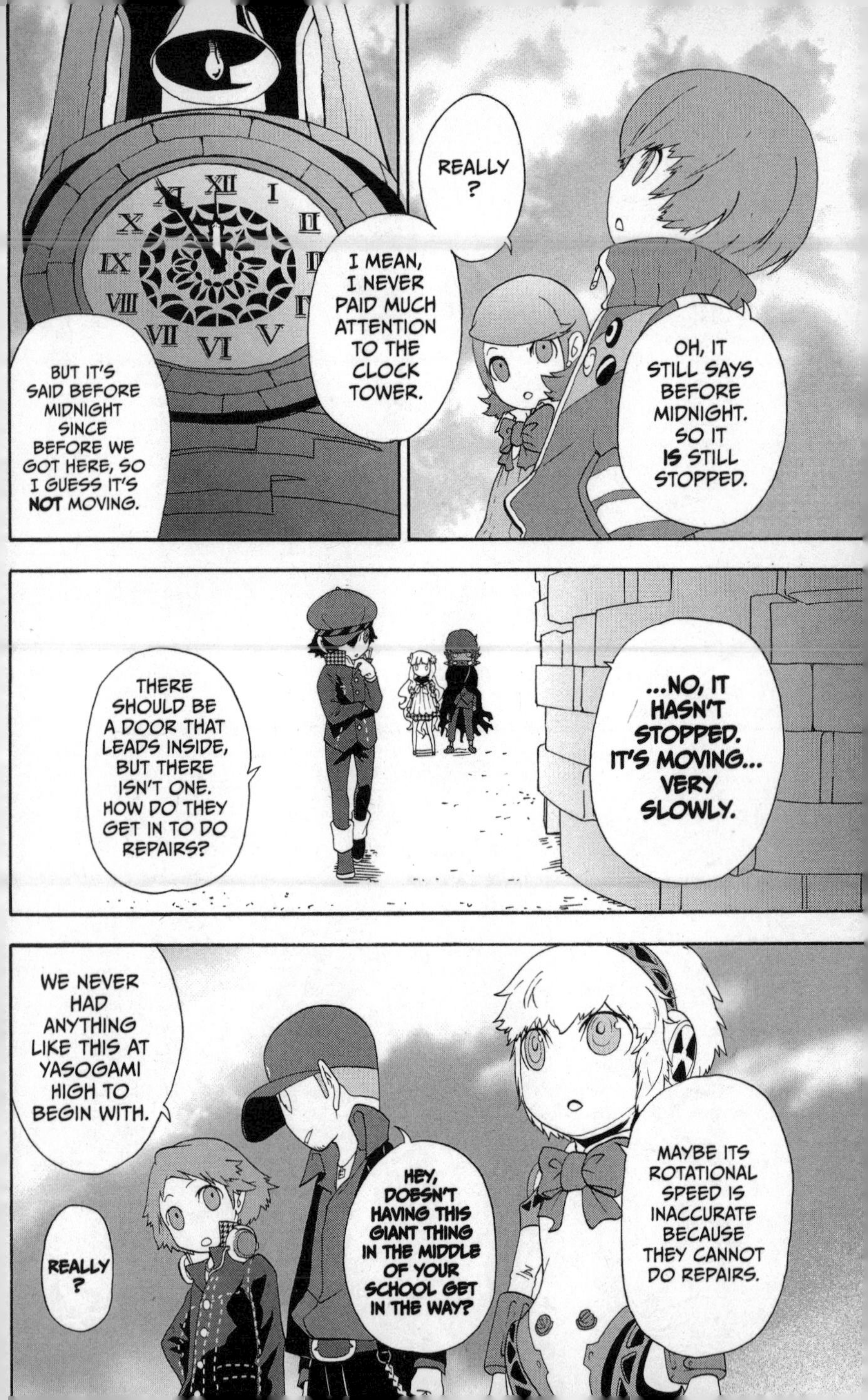
OH, IT STILL SAYS BEFORE MIDNIGHT. SO IT **IS** STILL STOPPED.
REALLY ?
I MEAN, I NEVER PAID MUCH ATTENTION TO THE CLOCK TOWER.
BUT IT'S SAID BEFORE MIDNIGHT SINCE BEFORE WE GOT HERE, SO I GUESS IT'S **NOT** MOVING.
...NO, IT HASN'T STOPPED. IT'S MOVING... VERY SLOWLY.
THERE SHOULD BE A DOOR THAT LEADS INSIDE, BUT THERE ISN'T ONE. HOW DO THEY GET IN TO DO REPAIRS?
MAYBE ITS ROTATIONAL SPEED IS INACCURATE BECAUSE THEY CANNOT DO REPAIRS.
HEY, DOESN'T HAVING THIS GIANT THING IN THE MIDDLE OF YOUR SCHOOL GET IN THE WAY?
WE NEVER HAD ANYTHING LIKE THIS AT YASOGAMI HIGH TO BEGIN WITH.
REALLY ?

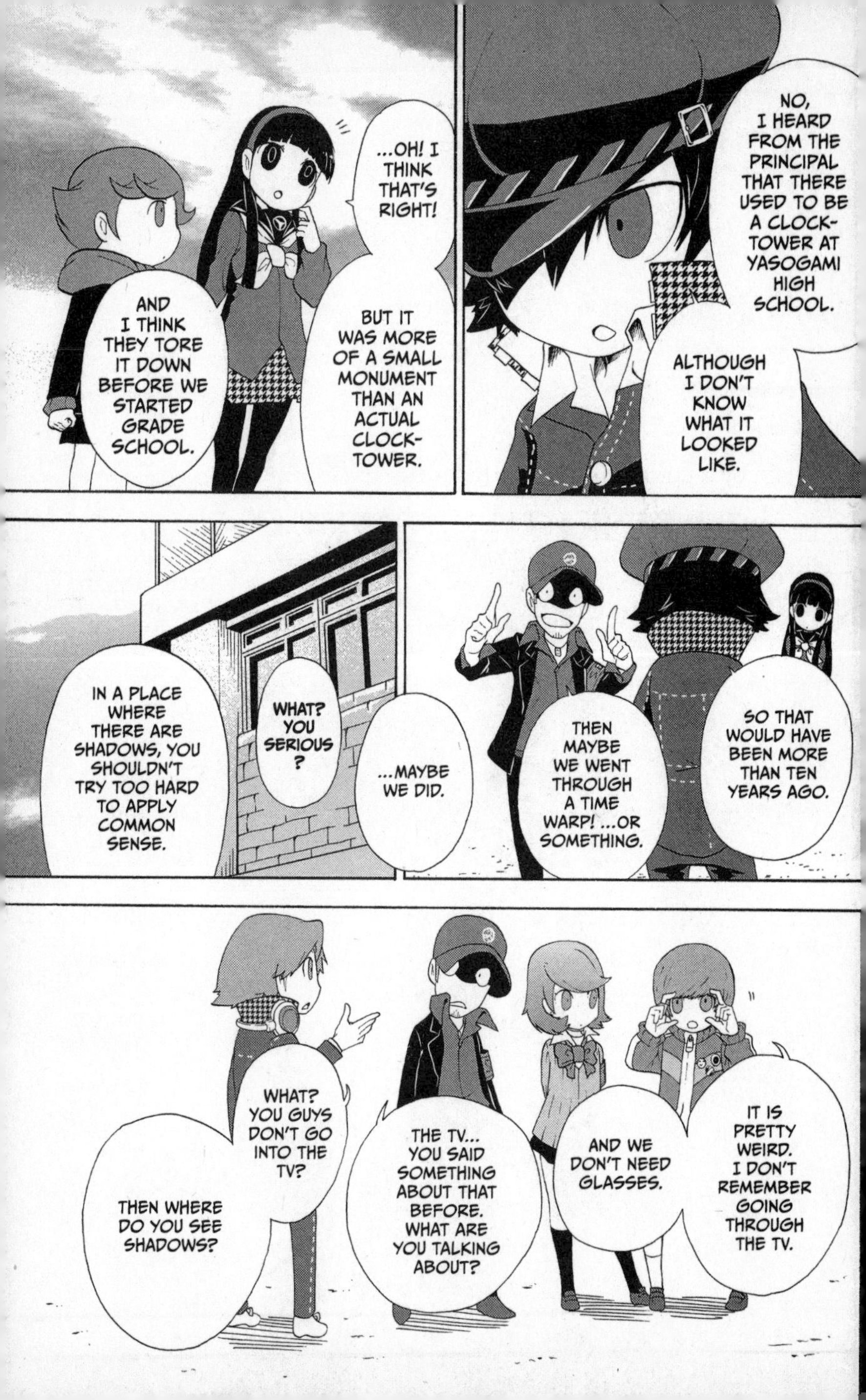
NO, I HEARD FROM THE PRINCIPAL THAT THERE USED TO BE A CLOCK-TOWER AT YASOGAMI HIGH SCHOOL.
ALTHOUGH I DON'T KNOW WHAT IT LOOKED LIKE.
...OH! I THINK THAT'S RIGHT!
BUT IT WAS MORE OF A SMALL MONUMENT THAN AN ACTUAL CLOCK-TOWER.
AND I THINK THEY TORE IT DOWN BEFORE WE STARTED GRADE SCHOOL.
SO THAT WOULD HAVE BEEN MORE THAN TEN YEARS AGO.
THEN MAYBE WE WENT THROUGH A TIME WARP! ...OR SOMETHING.
...MAYBE WE DID.
WHAT? YOU SERIOUS?
IN A PLACE WHERE THERE ARE SHADOWS, YOU SHOULDN'T TRY TOO HARD TO APPLY COMMON SENSE.
IT IS PRETTY WEIRD. I DON'T REMEMBER GOING THROUGH THE TV.
AND WE DON'T NEED GLASSES.
THE TV... YOU SAID SOMETHING ABOUT THAT BEFORE. WHAT ARE YOU TALKING ABOUT?
WHAT? YOU GUYS DON'T GO INTO THE TV?
THEN WHERE DO YOU SEE SHADOWS?

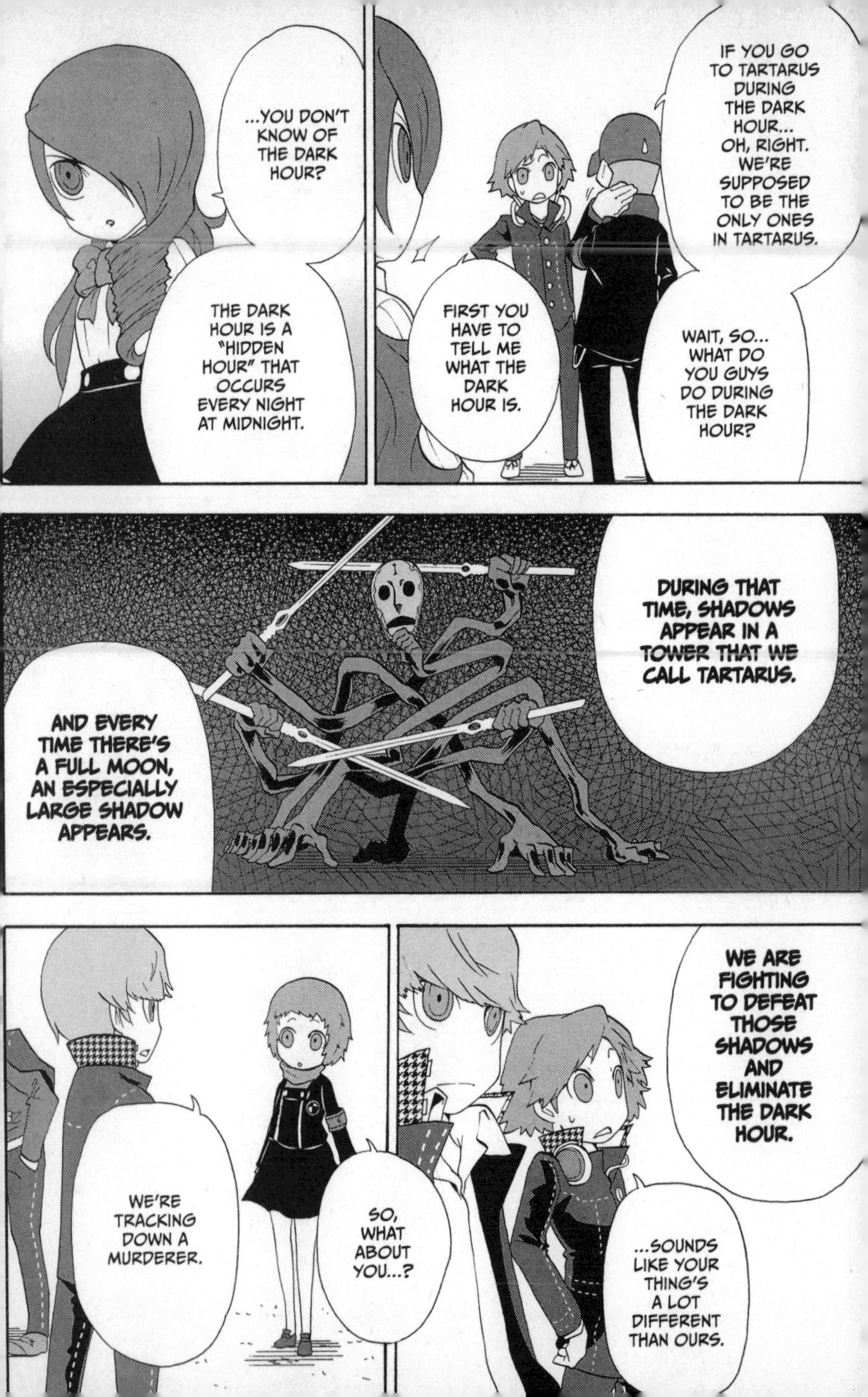
IF YOU GO TO TARTARUS DURING THE DARK HOUR... OH, RIGHT. WE'RE SUPPOSED TO BE THE ONLY ONES IN TARTARUS.
WAIT, SO... WHAT DO YOU GUYS DO DURING THE DARK HOUR?
FIRST YOU HAVE TO TELL ME WHAT THE DARK HOUR IS.
...YOU DON'T KNOW OF THE DARK HOUR?
THE DARK HOUR IS A "HIDDEN HOUR" THAT OCCURS EVERY NIGHT AT MIDNIGHT.
DURING THAT TIME, SHADOWS APPEAR IN A TOWER THAT WE CALL TARTARUS.
AND EVERY TIME THERE'S A FULL MOON, AN ESPECIALLY LARGE SHADOW APPEARS.
WE ARE FIGHTING TO DEFEAT THOSE SHADOWS AND ELIMINATE THE DARK HOUR.
...SOUNDS LIKE YOUR THING'S A LOT DIFFERENT THAN OURS.
SO, WHAT ABOUT YOU...?
WE'RE TRACKING DOWN A MURDERER.

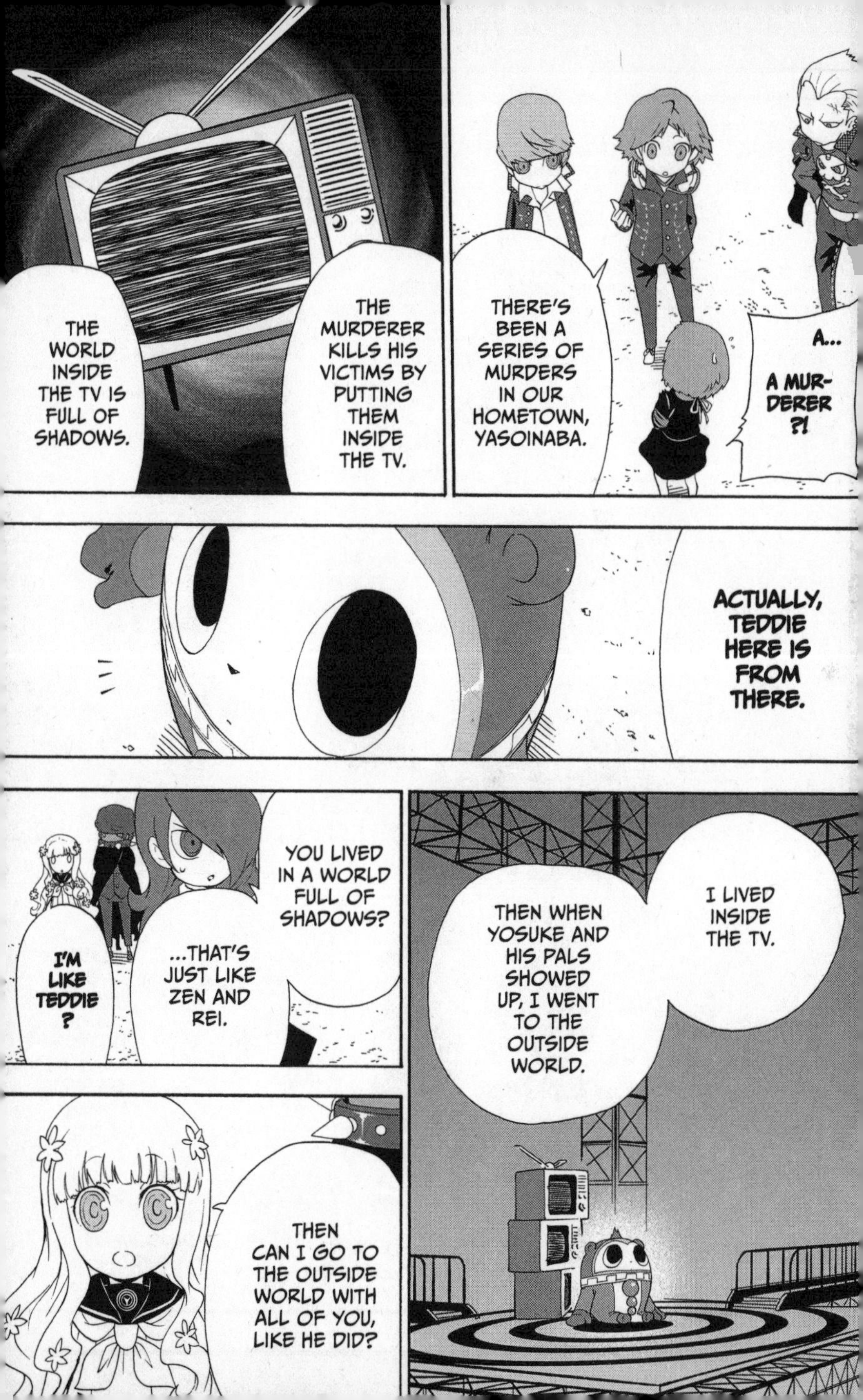
A... A MURDERER?!
THERE'S BEEN A SERIES OF MURDERS IN OUR HOMETOWN, YASOINABA.
THE MURDERER KILLS HIS VICTIMS BY PUTTING THEM INSIDE THE TV.
THE WORLD INSIDE THE TV IS FULL OF SHADOWS.
ACTUALLY, TEDDIE HERE IS FROM THERE.
I LIVED INSIDE THE TV.
THEN WHEN YOSUKE AND HIS PALS SHOWED UP, I WENT TO THE OUTSIDE WORLD.
YOU LIVED IN A WORLD FULL OF SHADOWS?
...THAT'S JUST LIKE ZEN AND REI.
I'M LIKE TEDDIE?
THEN CAN I GO TO THE OUTSIDE WORLD WITH ALL OF YOU, LIKE HE DID?

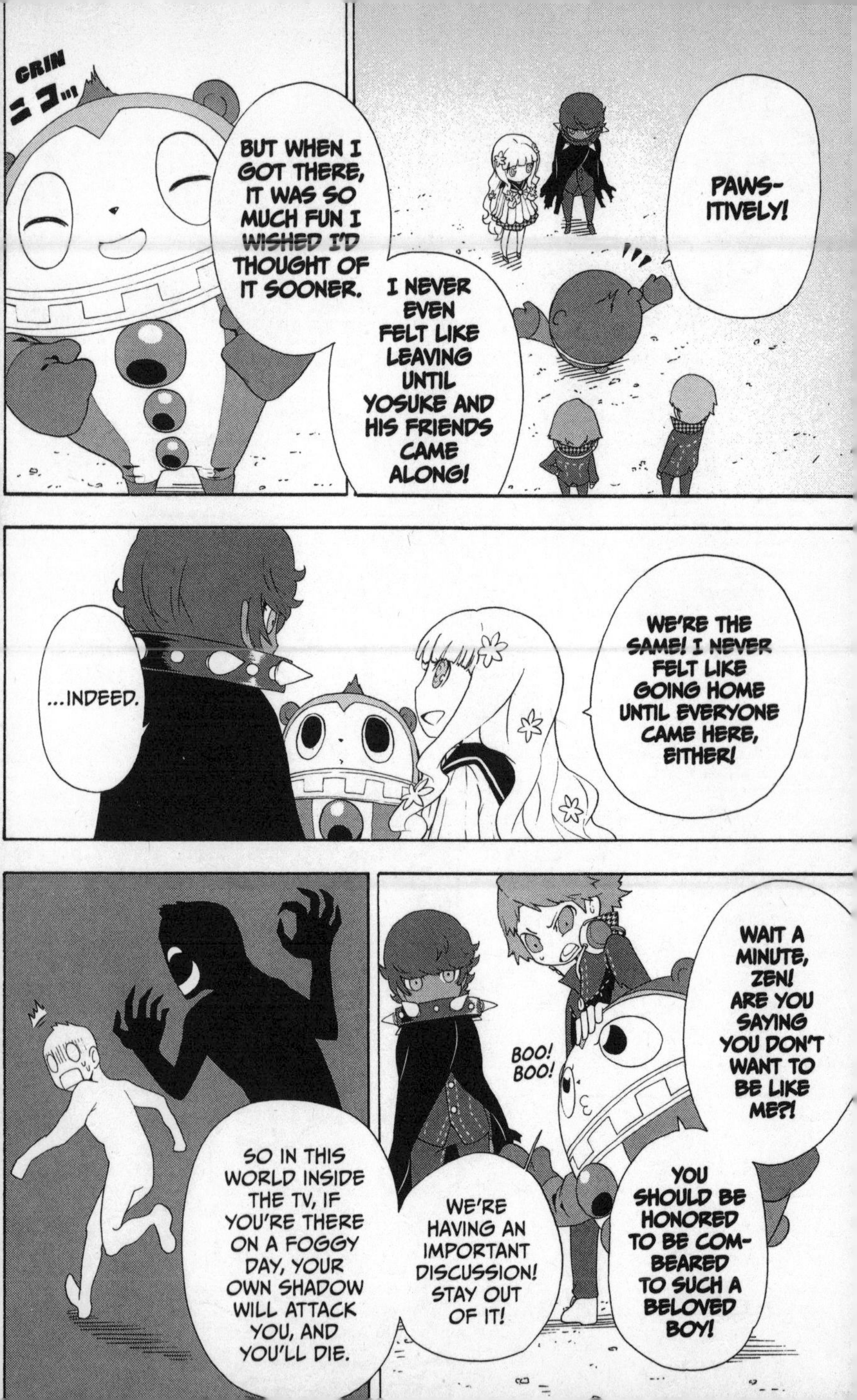
PAWS-ITIVELY!
I NEVER EVEN FELT LIKE LEAVING UNTIL YOSUKE AND HIS FRIENDS CAME ALONG!
GRIN
ニコッ
BUT WHEN I GOT THERE, IT WAS SO MUCH FUN I WISHED I'D THOUGHT OF IT SOONER.
WE'RE THE SAME! I NEVER FELT LIKE GOING HOME UNTIL EVERYONE CAME HERE, EITHER!
...INDEED.
WAIT A MINUTE, ZEN! ARE YOU SAYING YOU DON'T WANT TO BE LIKE ME?!
BOO! BOO!
YOU SHOULD BE HONORED TO BE COM-BEARED TO SUCH A BELOVED BOY!
WE'RE HAVING AN IMPORTANT DISCUSSION! STAY OUT OF IT!
SO IN THIS WORLD INSIDE THE TV, IF YOU'RE THERE ON A FOGGY DAY, YOUR OWN SHADOW WILL ATTACK YOU, AND YOU'LL DIE.

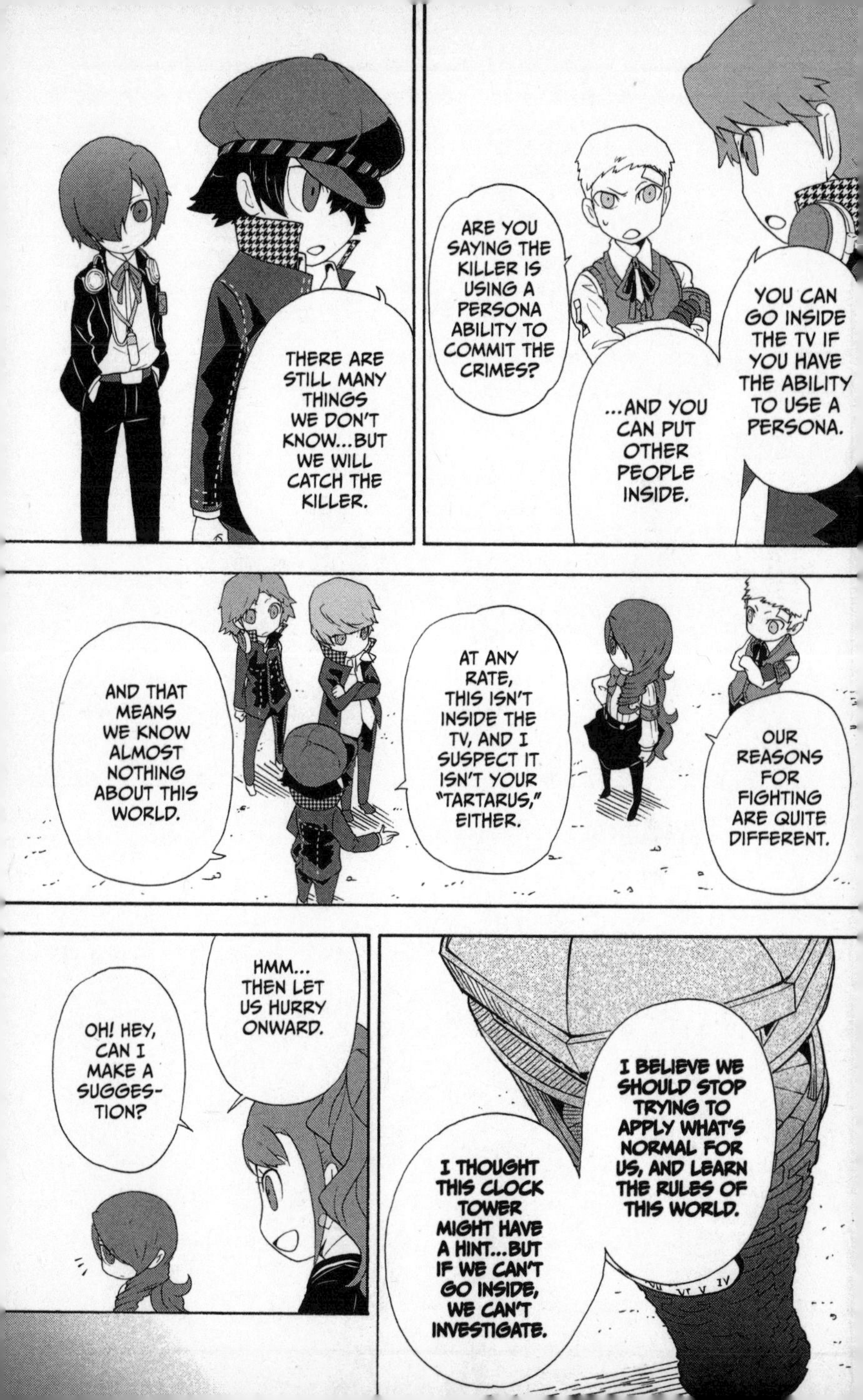
YOU CAN GO INSIDE THE TV IF YOU HAVE THE ABILITY TO USE A PERSONA.
...AND YOU CAN PUT OTHER PEOPLE INSIDE.
ARE YOU SAYING THE KILLER IS USING A PERSONA ABILITY TO COMMIT THE CRIMES?
THERE ARE STILL MANY THINGS WE DON'T KNOW...BUT WE WILL CATCH THE KILLER.
OUR REASONS FOR FIGHTING ARE QUITE DIFFERENT.
AT ANY RATE, THIS ISN'T INSIDE THE TV, AND I SUSPECT IT ISN'T YOUR "TARTARUS," EITHER.
AND THAT MEANS WE KNOW ALMOST NOTHING ABOUT THIS WORLD.
I BELIEVE WE SHOULD STOP TRYING TO APPLY WHAT'S NORMAL FOR US, AND LEARN THE RULES OF THIS WORLD.
I THOUGHT THIS CLOCK TOWER MIGHT HAVE A HINT...BUT IF WE CAN'T GO INSIDE, WE CAN'T INVESTIGATE.
HMM... THEN LET US HURRY ONWARD.
OH! HEY, CAN I MAKE A SUGGES- TION?

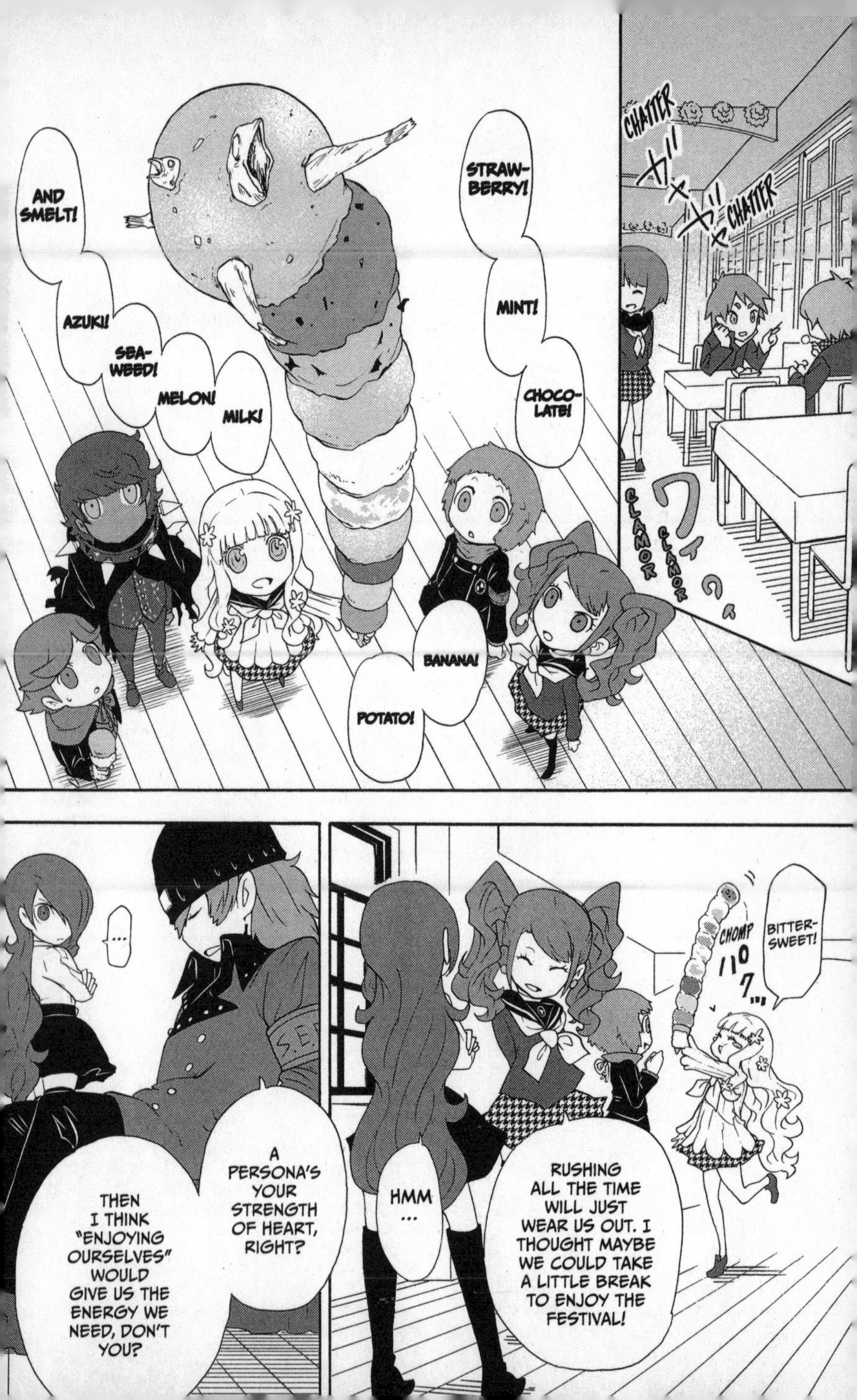

CHATTER
CHATTER
GLAMOR
GLAMOR
STRAW-BERRY!
MINT!
CHOCO-LATE!
BANANA!
POTATO!
MILK!
MELON!
SEA-WEED!
AZUKI!
AND SMELT!
CHOMP
BITTER-SWEET!
RUSHING ALL THE TIME WILL JUST WEAR US OUT. I THOUGHT MAYBE WE COULD TAKE A LITTLE BREAK TO ENJOY THE FESTIVAL!
HMM...
A PERSONA'S YOUR STRENGTH OF HEART, RIGHT?
THEN I THINK "ENJOYING OURSELVES" WOULD GIVE US THE ENERGY WE NEED, DON'T YOU?
...

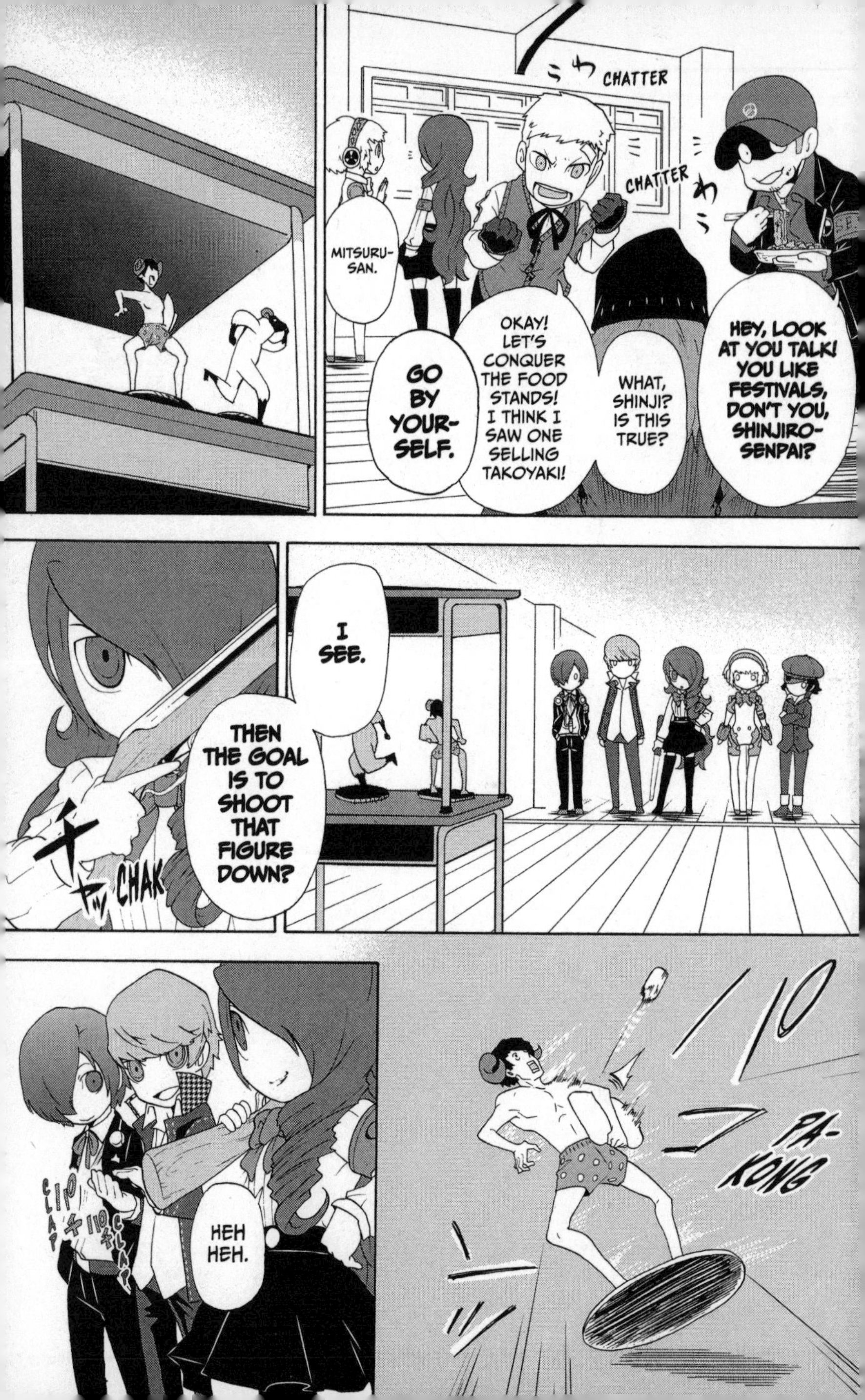
CHATTER
CHATTER
HEY, LOOK AT YOU TALK! YOU LIKE FESTIVALS, DON'T YOU, SHINJIRO-SENPAI?
WHAT, SHINJI? IS THIS TRUE?
OKAY! LET'S CONQUER THE FOOD STANDS! I THINK I SAW ONE SELLING TAKOYAKI!
MITSURU-SAN.
GO BY YOURSELF.
I SEE.
THEN THE GOAL IS TO SHOOT THAT FIGURE DOWN?
CHAK
PA-KONG
CLAP
CLAP
HEH HEH.

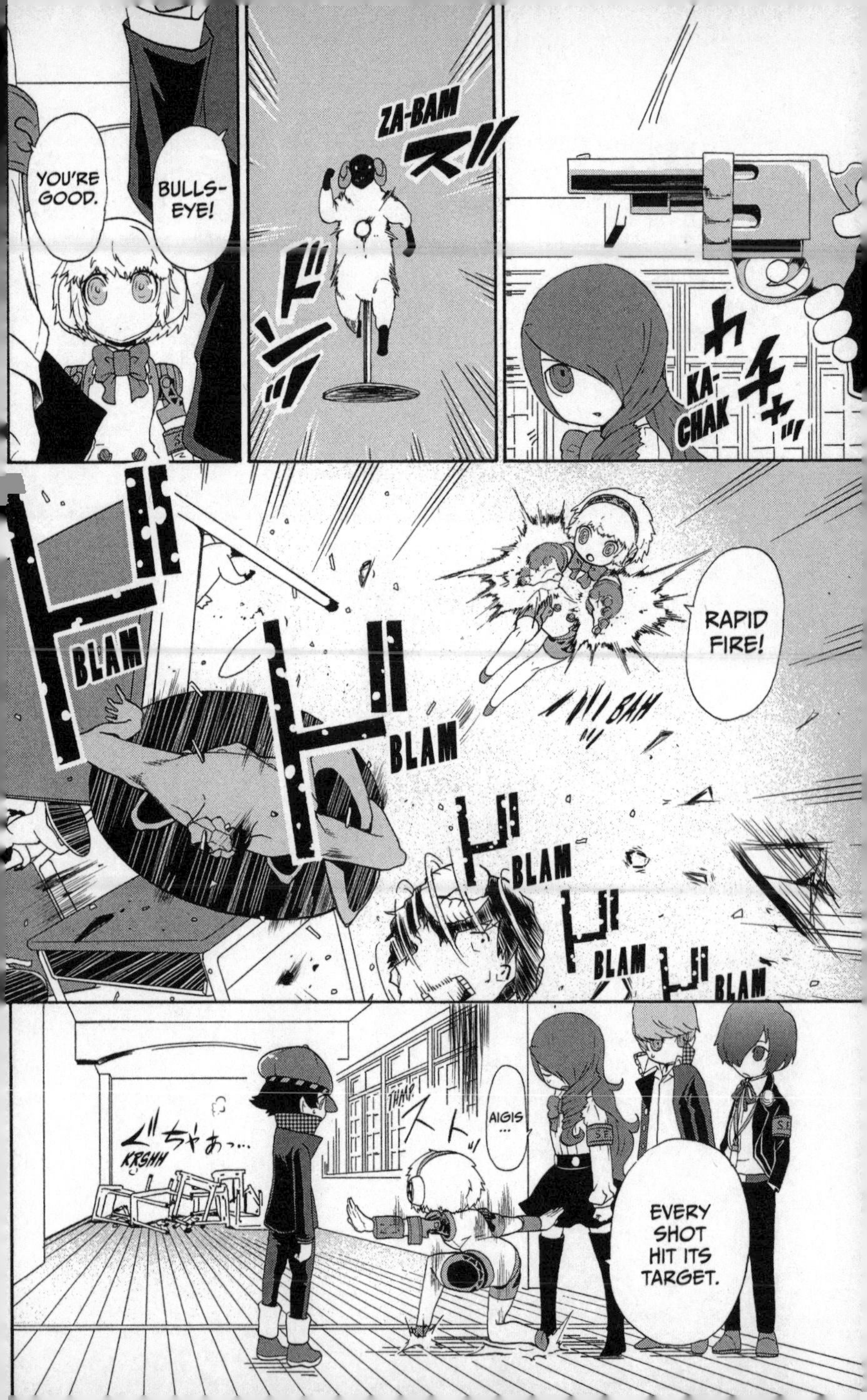
KA-CHAK
カチャッ
ZA-BAM
ズドンッ
BULLS-EYE!
YOU'RE GOOD.
RAPID FIRE!
BAH
BLAM
BLAM
BLAM
BLAM
BLAM
EVERY SHOT HIT ITS TARGET.
AIGIS...
THAP
ストッ
ぐちゃあっ...
KRSHH

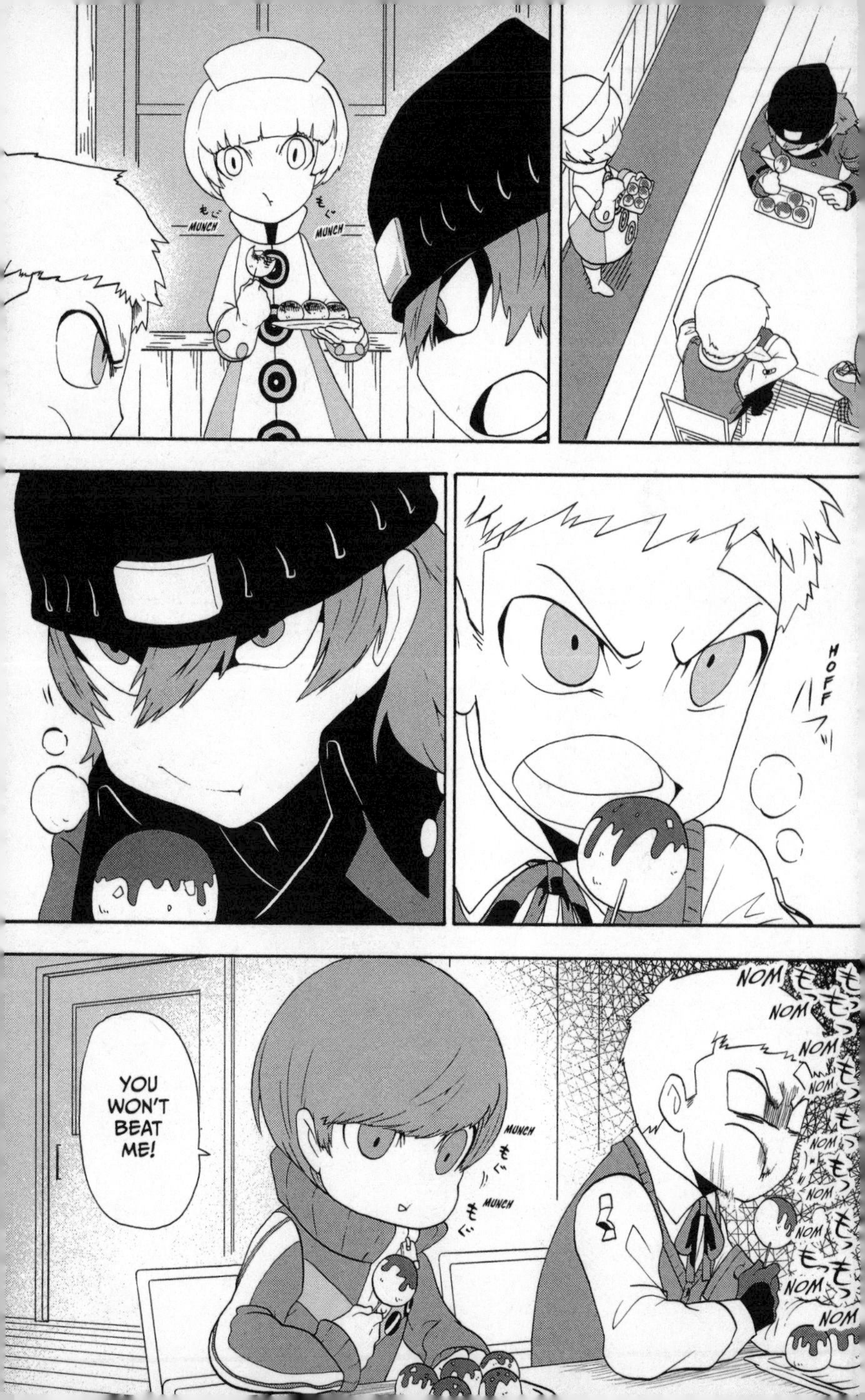
もぐ MUNCH
もぐ MUNCH
HOFF
NOM もっ
NOM もっ
NOM もっ
NOM もっ
NOM もっ
NOM もっ
NOM もっ
NOM もっ
NOM
もぐ MUNCH
もぐ MUNCH
YOU WON'T BEAT ME!

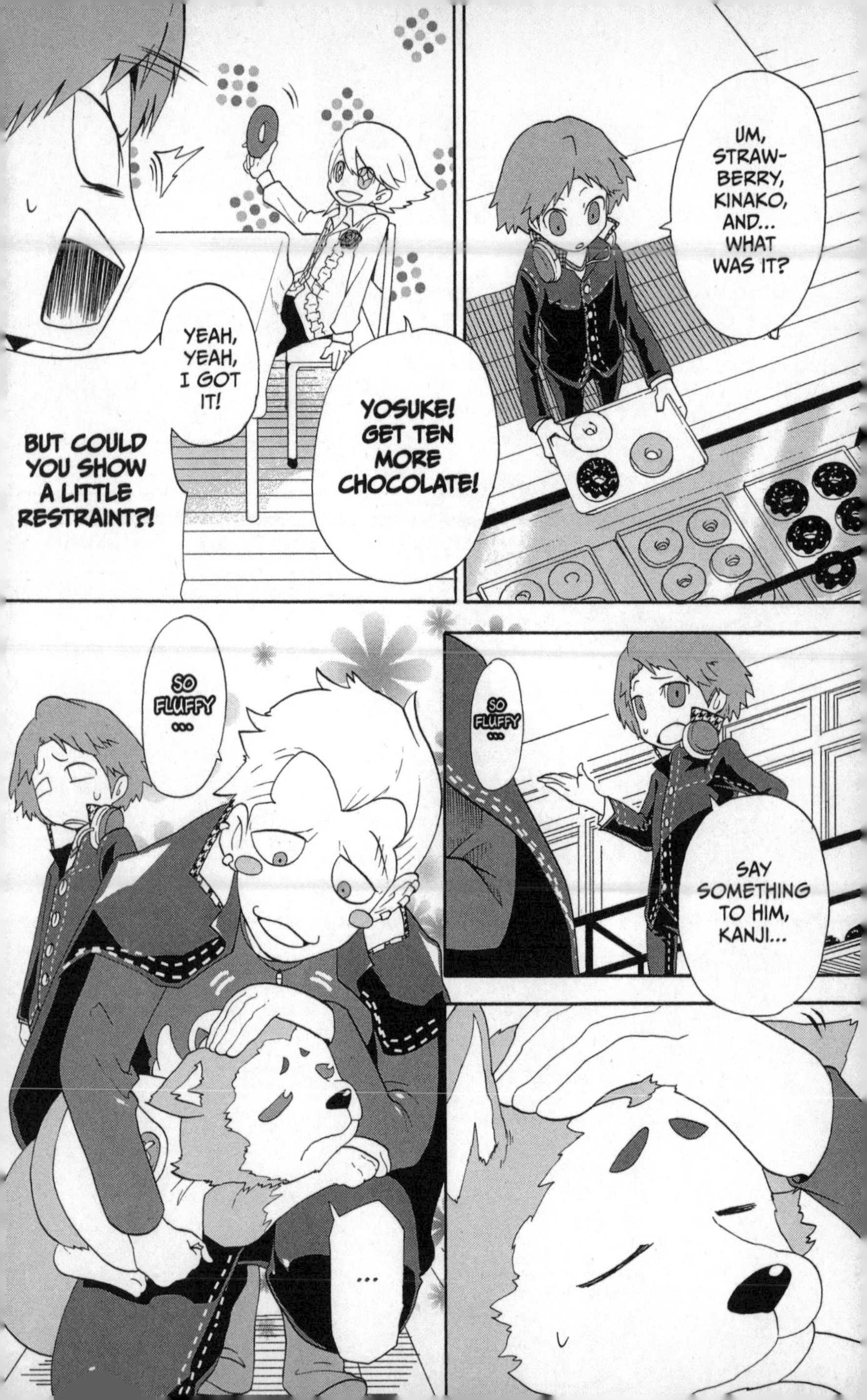
UM, STRAW-BERRY, KINAKO, AND... WHAT WAS IT?
YOSUKE! GET TEN MORE CHOCOLATE!
YEAH, YEAH, I GOT IT!
BUT COULD YOU SHOW A LITTLE RESTRAINT?!
SO FLUFFY...
SAY SOMETHING TO HIM, KANJI...
SO FLUFFY...
...

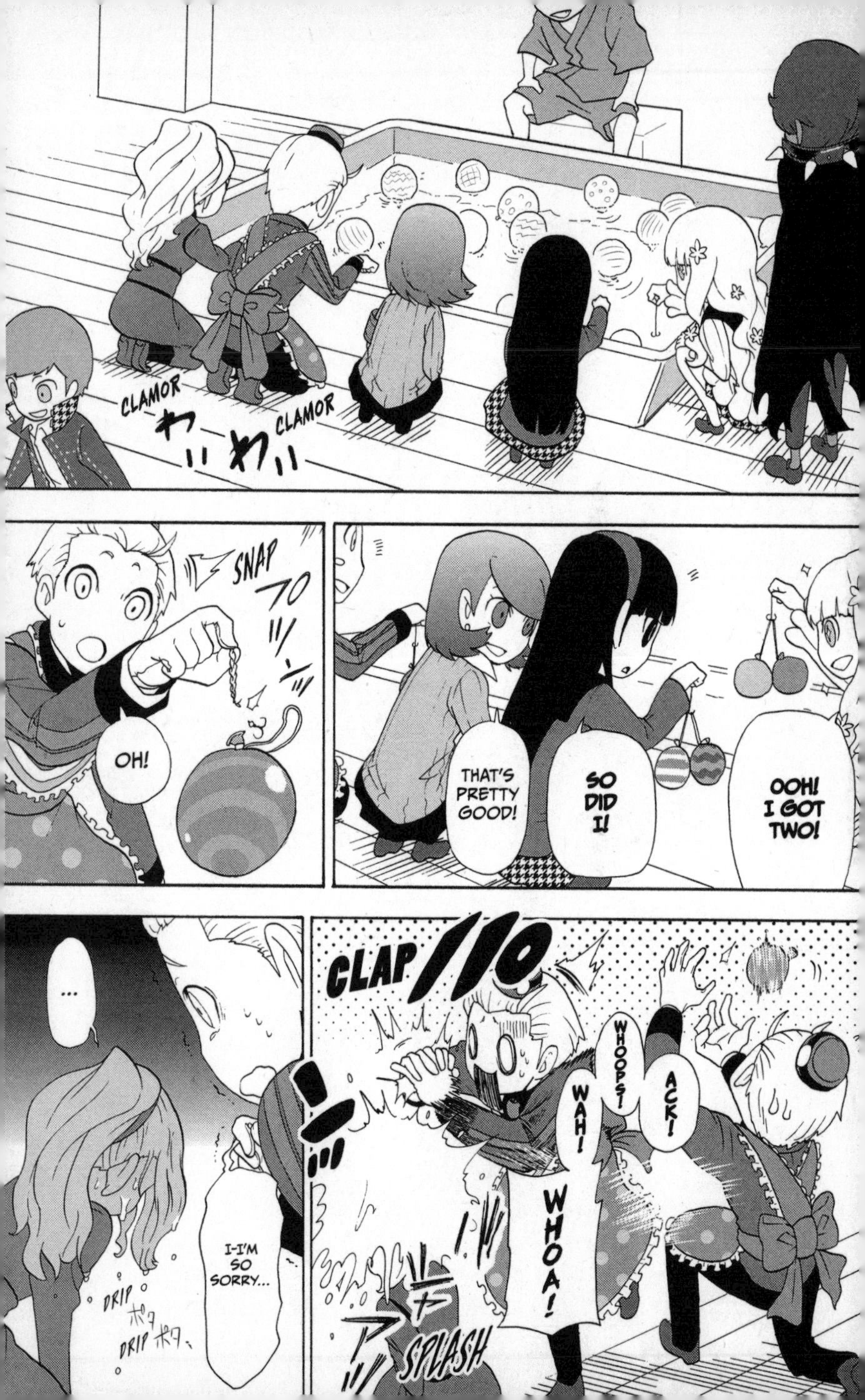
CLAMOR
CLAMOR
わいわい
OOH! I GOT TWO!
SO DID I!
THAT'S PRETTY GOOD!
SNAP
OH!
CLAP
ACK!
WHOOPS!
WAH!
WHOA!
SPLASH
...
I-I'M SO SORRY...
DRIP ポタ
DRIP ポタ

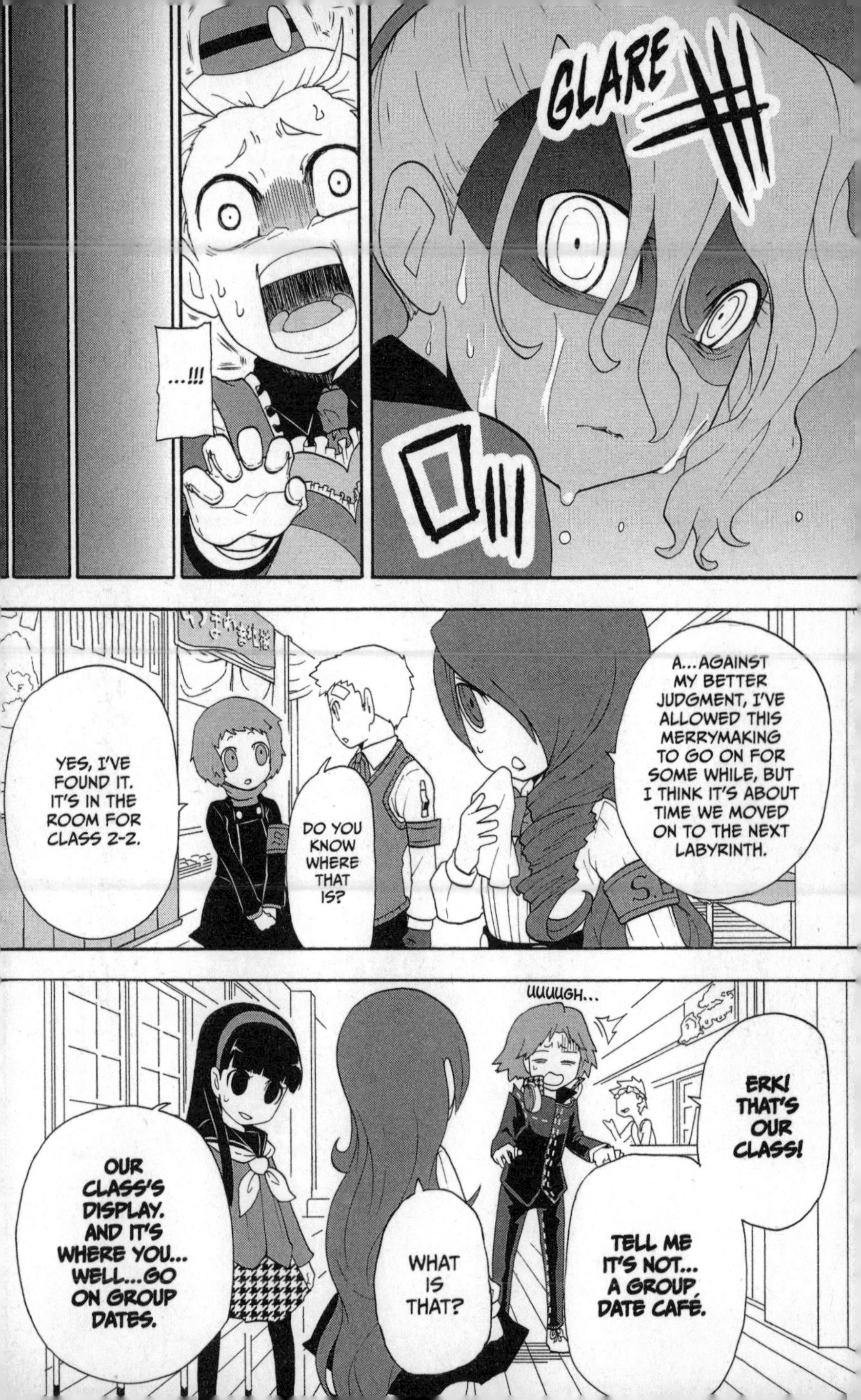
GLARE
...!!!
A...AGAINST MY BETTER JUDGMENT, I'VE ALLOWED THIS MERRYMAKING TO GO ON FOR SOME WHILE, BUT I THINK IT'S ABOUT TIME WE MOVED ON TO THE NEXT LABYRINTH.
DO YOU KNOW WHERE THAT IS?
YES, I'VE FOUND IT. IT'S IN THE ROOM FOR CLASS 2-2.
UUUUGH...
ERK! THAT'S OUR CLASS!
TELL ME IT'S NOT... A GROUP DATE CAFÉ.
WHAT IS THAT?
OUR CLASS'S DISPLAY. AND IT'S WHERE YOU... WELL...GO ON GROUP DATES.

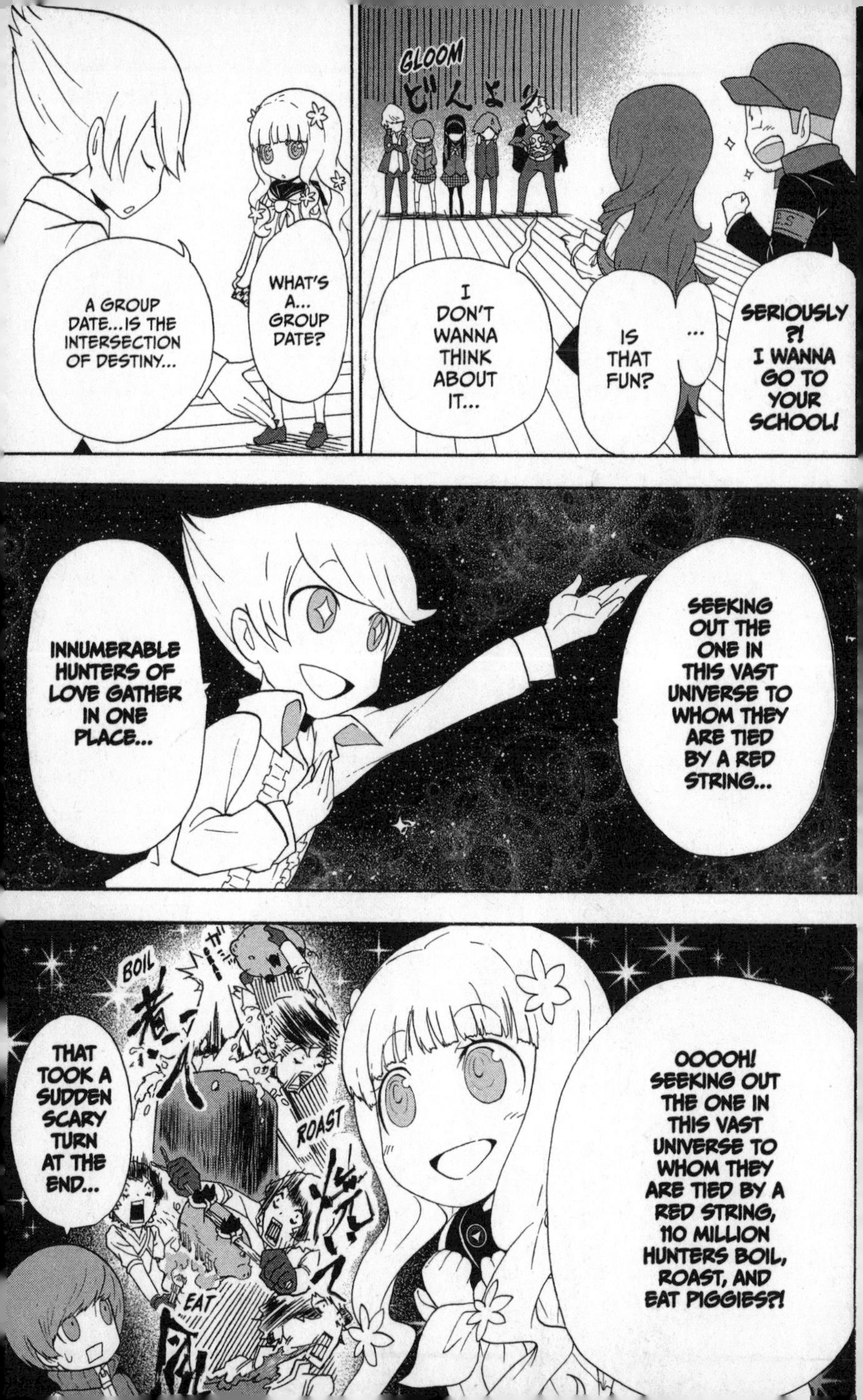
SERIOUSLY?! I WANNA GO TO YOUR SCHOOL!
...
IS THAT FUN?
GLOOM
どんより
I DON'T WANNA THINK ABOUT IT...
WHAT'S A... GROUP DATE?
A GROUP DATE...IS THE INTERSECTION OF DESTINY...
SEEKING OUT THE ONE IN THIS VAST UNIVERSE TO WHOM THEY ARE TIED BY A RED STRING...
INNUMERABLE HUNTERS OF LOVE GATHER IN ONE PLACE...
OOOOH! SEEKING OUT THE ONE IN THIS VAST UNIVERSE TO WHOM THEY ARE TIED BY A RED STRING, 110 MILLION HUNTERS BOIL, ROAST, AND EAT PIGGIES?!
BOIL
ROAST
EAT
THAT TOOK A SUDDEN SCARY TURN AT THE END...

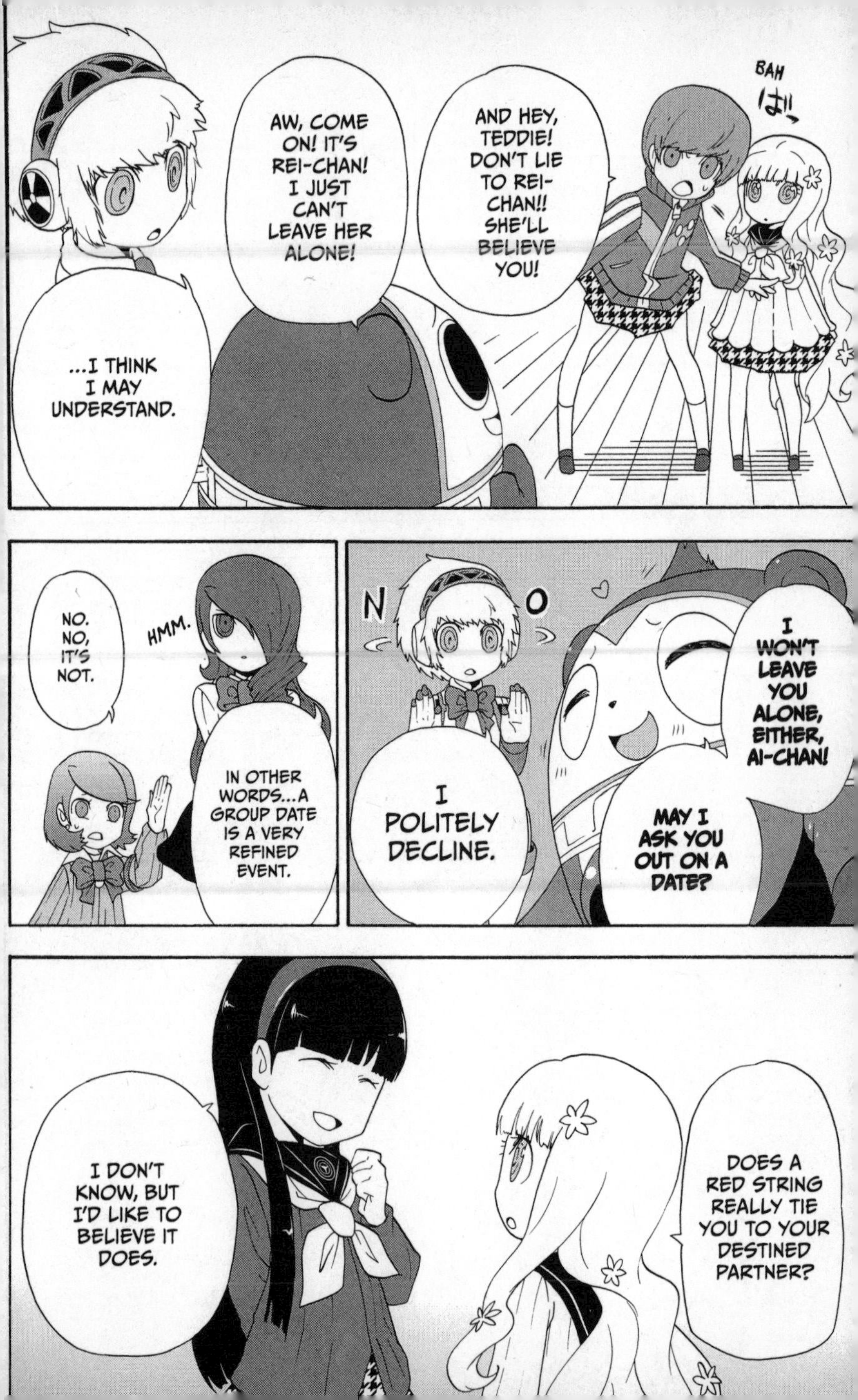
BAH
は!!
AND HEY, TEDDIE! DON'T LIE TO REI-CHAN!! SHE'LL BELIEVE YOU!
AW, COME ON! IT'S REI-CHAN! I JUST CAN'T LEAVE HER ALONE!
...I THINK I MAY UNDERSTAND.
I WON'T LEAVE YOU ALONE, EITHER, AI-CHAN!
MAY I ASK YOU OUT ON A DATE?
N O
I POLITELY DECLINE.
HMM.
NO. NO, IT'S NOT.
IN OTHER WORDS...A GROUP DATE IS A VERY REFINED EVENT.
DOES A RED STRING REALLY TIE YOU TO YOUR DESTINED PARTNER?
I DON'T KNOW, BUT I'D LIKE TO BELIEVE IT DOES.

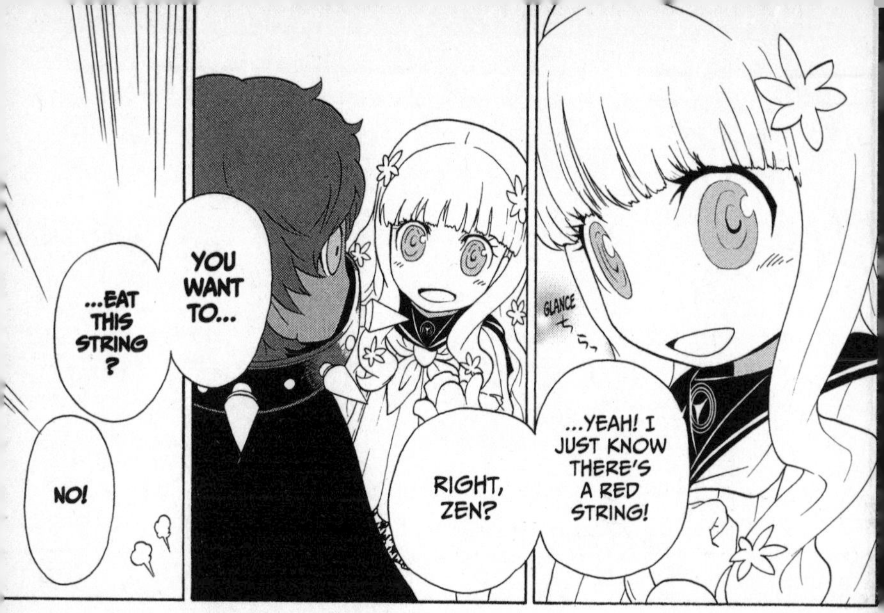
GLANCE
...YEAH! I JUST KNOW THERE'S A RED STRING!
RIGHT, ZEN?
YOU WANT TO...
...EAT THIS STRING?
NO!
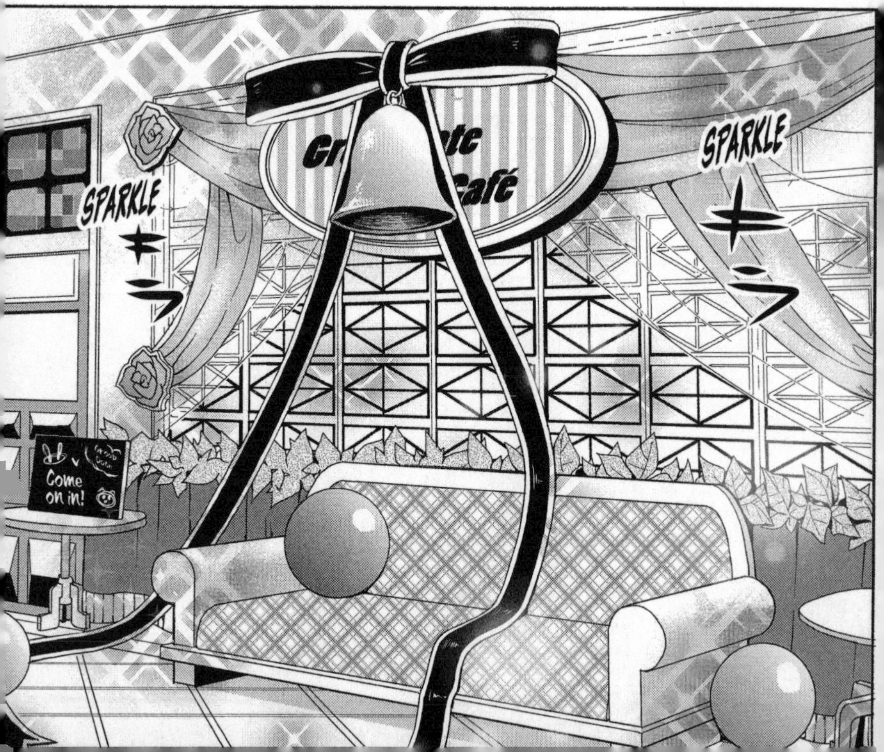
SPARKLE
SPARKLE
Come on in!

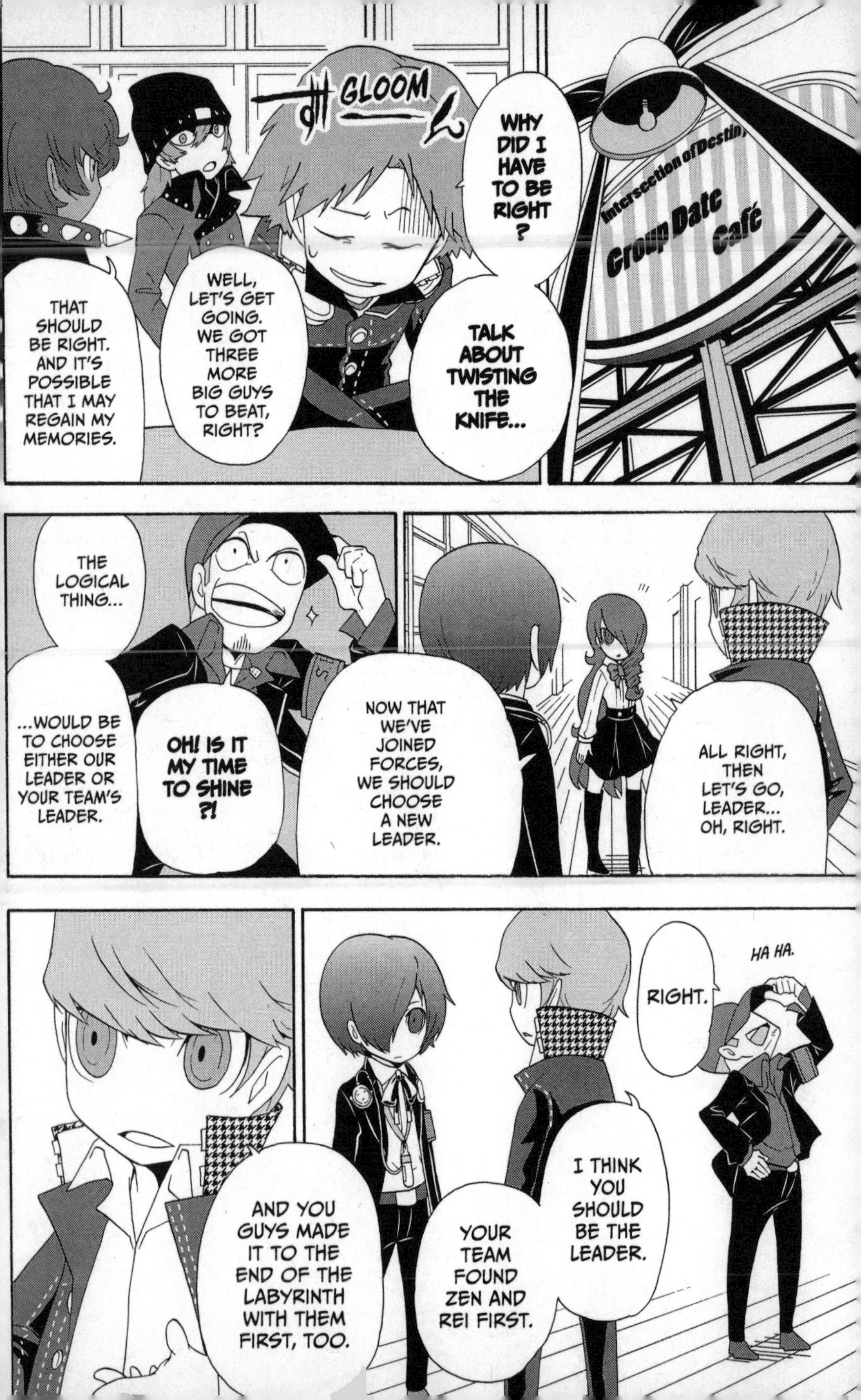
Intersection of Destiny
Group Date Café
WHY DID I HAVE TO BE RIGHT?
GLOOM
TALK ABOUT TWISTING THE KNIFE...
WELL, LET'S GET GOING. WE GOT THREE MORE BIG GUYS TO BEAT, RIGHT?
THAT SHOULD BE RIGHT. AND IT'S POSSIBLE THAT I MAY REGAIN MY MEMORIES.
ALL RIGHT, THEN LET'S GO, LEADER... OH, RIGHT.
NOW THAT WE'VE JOINED FORCES, WE SHOULD CHOOSE A NEW LEADER.
THE LOGICAL THING...
OH! IS IT MY TIME TO SHINE?!
...WOULD BE TO CHOOSE EITHER OUR LEADER OR YOUR TEAM'S LEADER.
HA HA.
RIGHT.
I THINK YOU SHOULD BE THE LEADER.
YOUR TEAM FOUND ZEN AND REI FIRST.
AND YOU GUYS MADE IT TO THE END OF THE LABYRINTH WITH THEM FIRST, TOO.

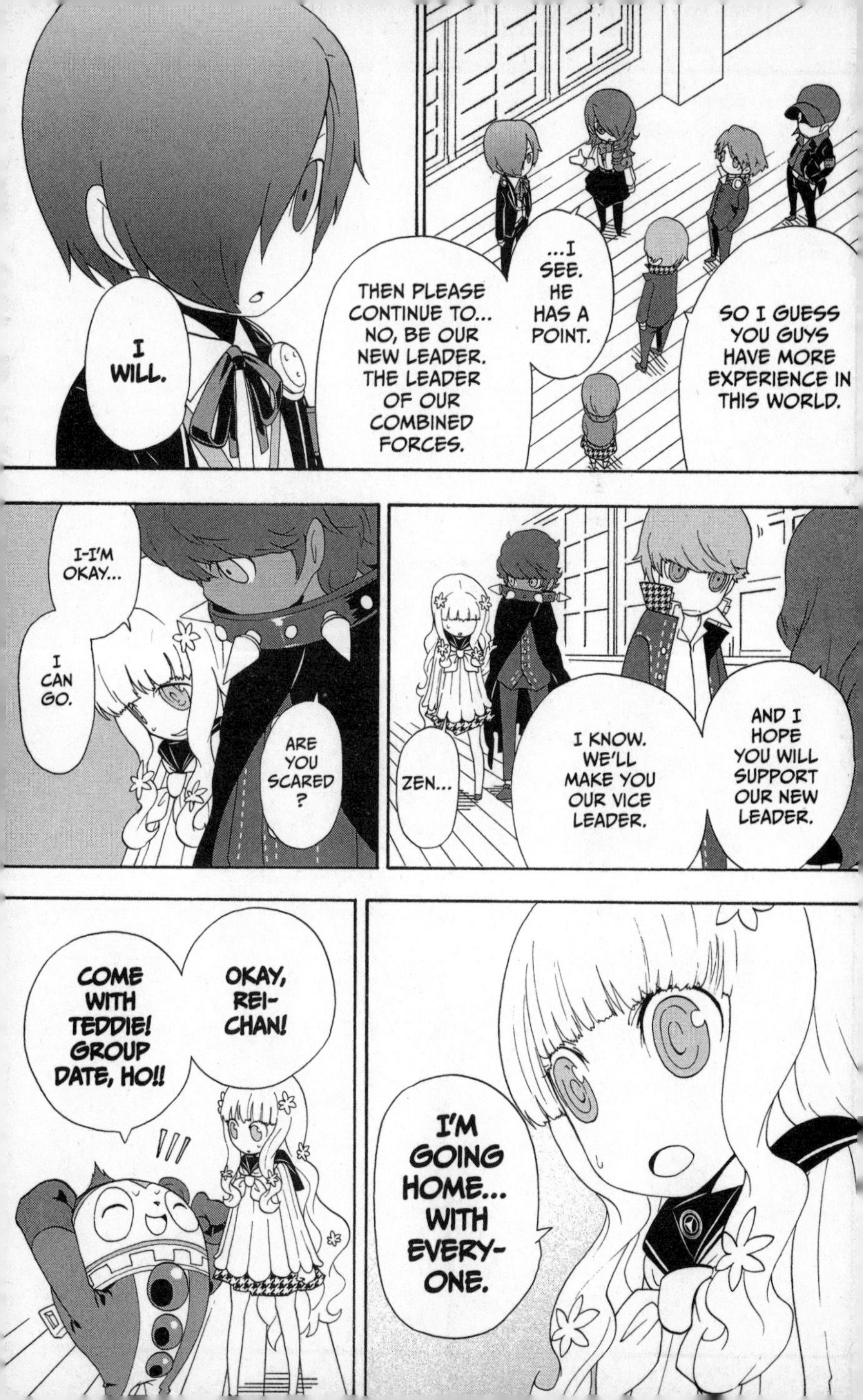
SO I GUESS YOU GUYS HAVE MORE EXPERIENCE IN THIS WORLD.
...I SEE. HE HAS A POINT.
THEN PLEASE CONTINUE TO... NO, BE OUR NEW LEADER. THE LEADER OF OUR COMBINED FORCES.
I WILL.
AND I HOPE YOU WILL SUPPORT OUR NEW LEADER.
I KNOW. WE'LL MAKE YOU OUR VICE LEADER.
ZEN...
ARE YOU SCARED?
I-I'M OKAY...
I CAN GO.
I'M GOING HOME... WITH EVERY-ONE.
OKAY, REI-CHAN!
COME WITH TEDDIE! GROUP DATE, HO!!

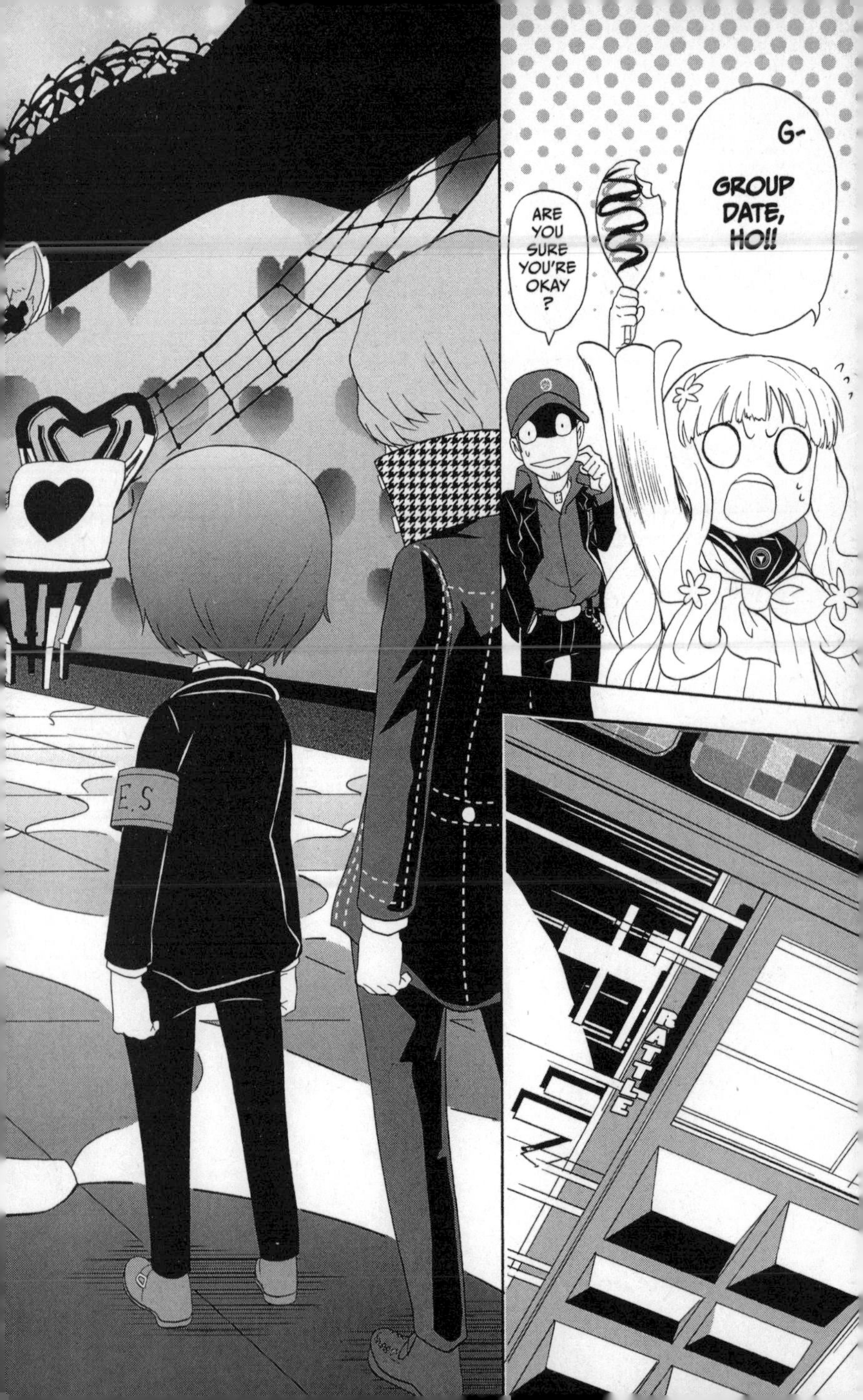
G- GROUP DATE, HO!!
ARE YOU SURE YOU'RE OKAY?
RATTLE

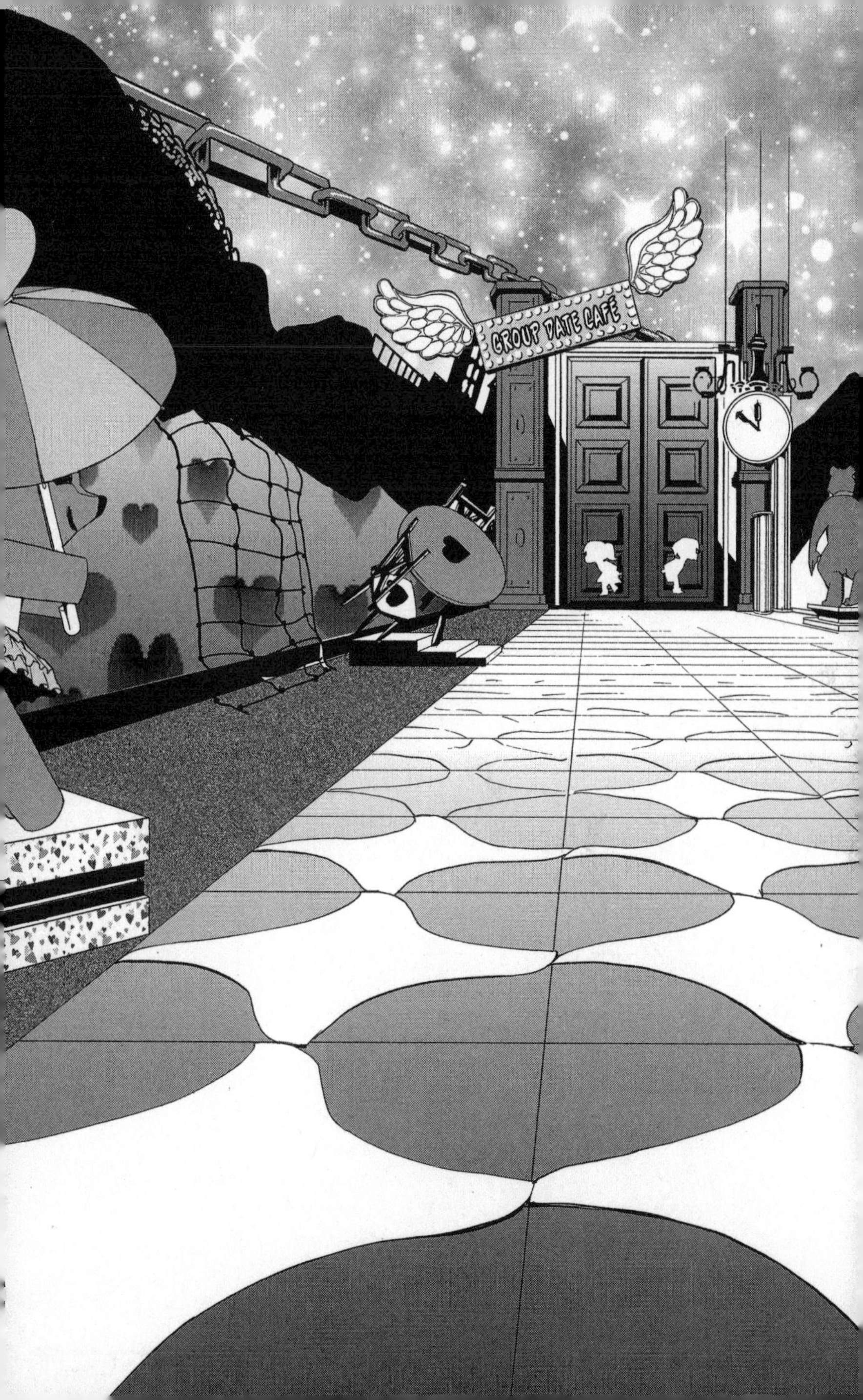
GROUP DATE CAFÉ

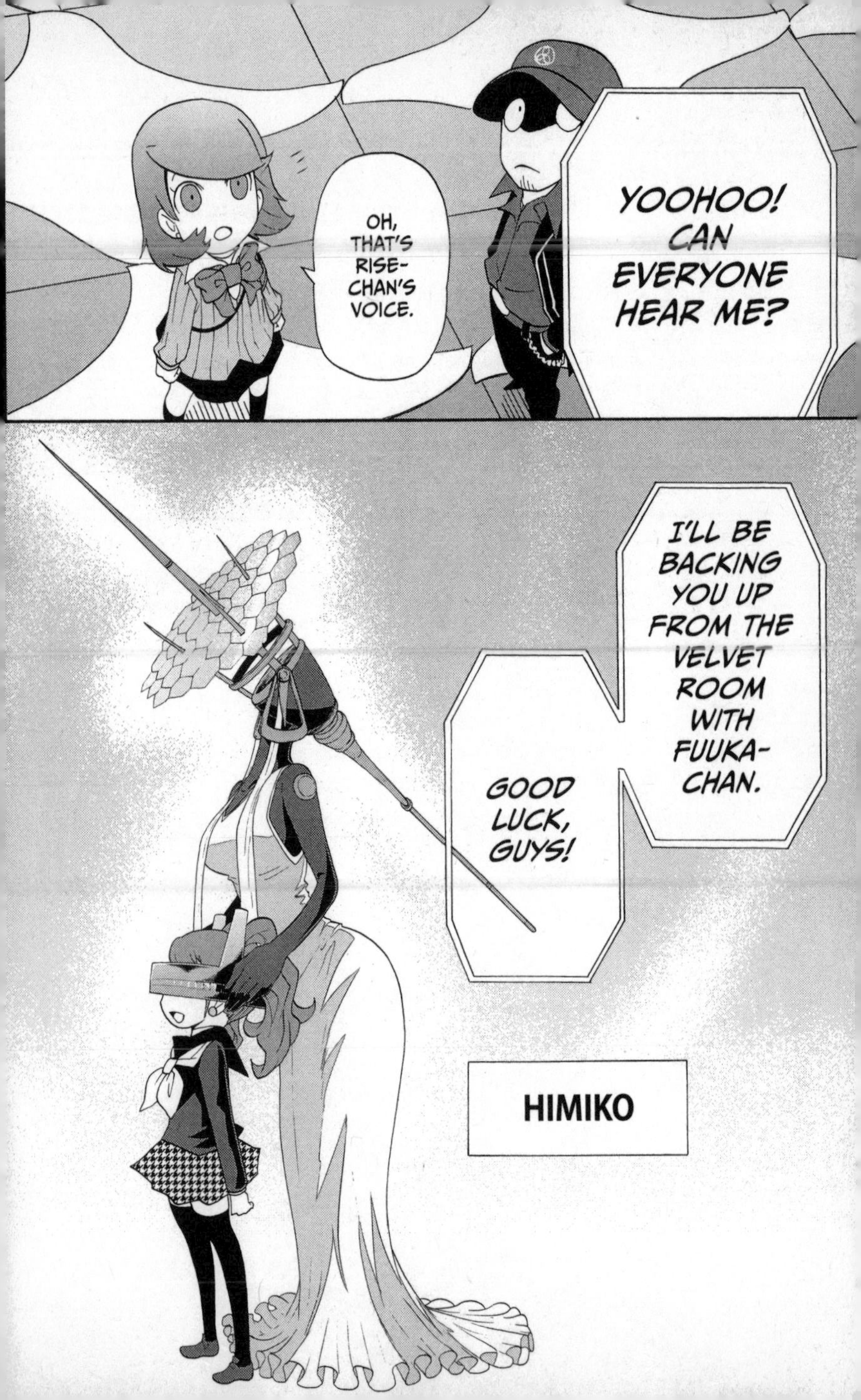
YOOHOO! CAN EVERYONE HEAR ME?
OH, THAT'S RISE-CHAN'S VOICE.
I'LL BE BACKING YOU UP FROM THE VELVET ROOM WITH FUUKA-CHAN.
GOOD LUCK, GUYS!
HIMIKO

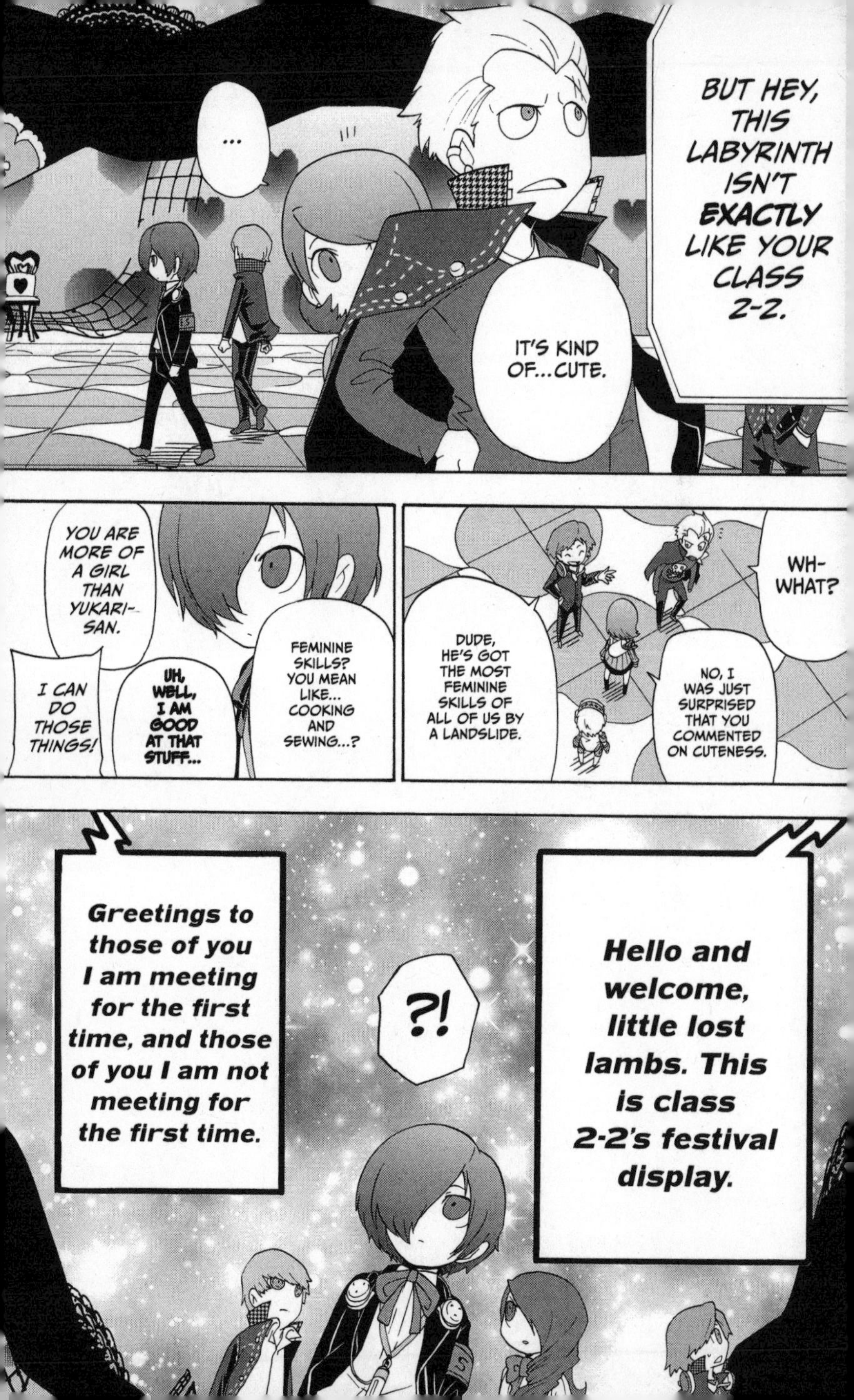
BUT HEY, THIS LABYRINTH ISN'T EXACTLY LIKE YOUR CLASS 2-2.
IT'S KIND OF...CUTE.
...
WH-WHAT?
NO, I WAS JUST SURPRISED THAT YOU COMMENTED ON CUTENESS.
DUDE, HE'S GOT THE MOST FEMININE SKILLS OF ALL OF US BY A LANDSLIDE.
FEMININE SKILLS? YOU MEAN LIKE... COOKING AND SEWING...?
UH, WELL, I AM GOOD AT THAT STUFF...
YOU ARE MORE OF A GIRL THAN YUKARI-SAN.
I CAN DO THOSE THINGS!
Hello and welcome, little lost lambs. This is class 2-2's festival display.
?!
Greetings to those of you I am meeting for the first time, and those of you I am not meeting for the first time.

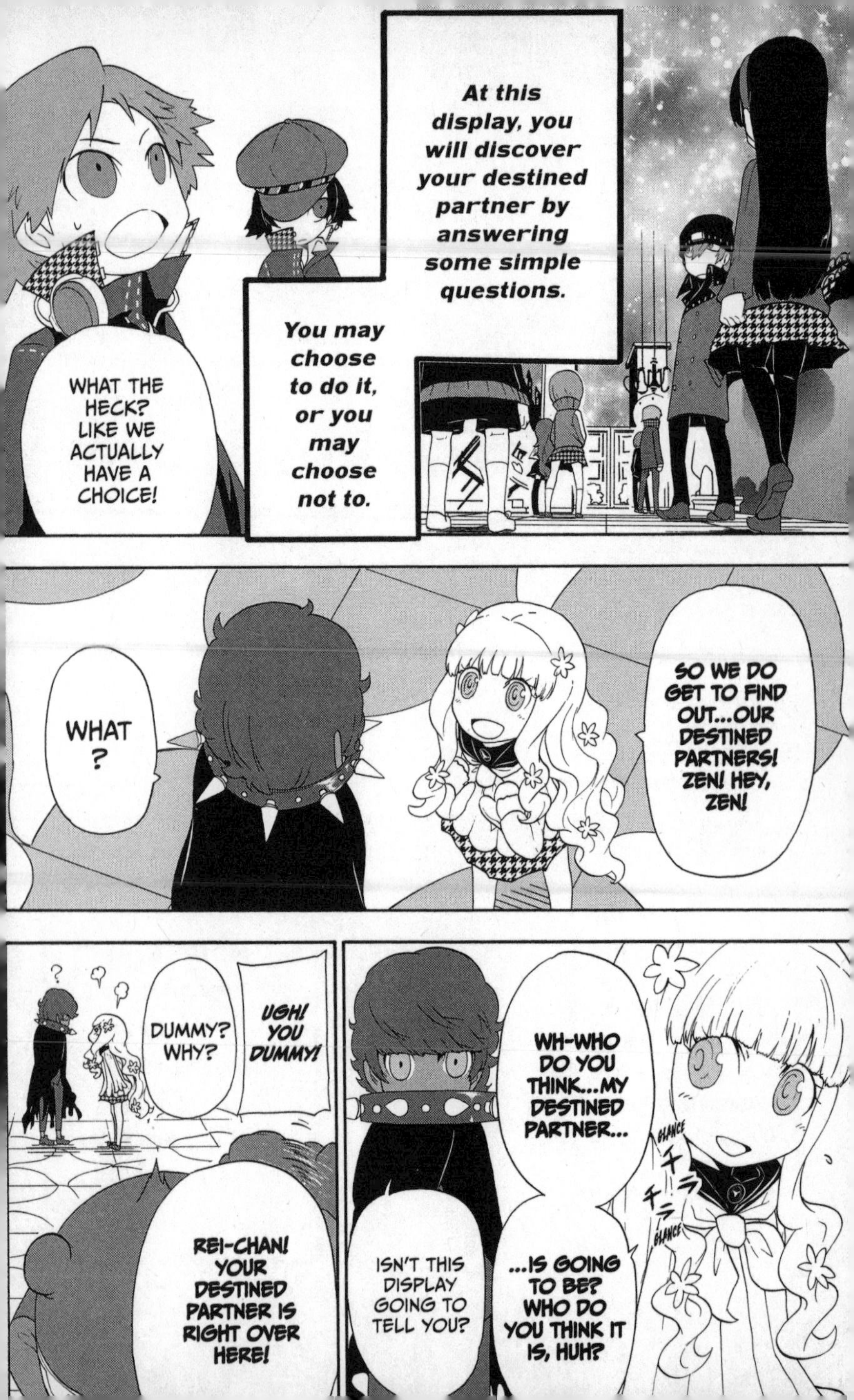
At this display, you will discover your destined partner by answering some simple questions.
You may choose to do it, or you may choose not to.
WHAT THE HECK? LIKE WE ACTUALLY HAVE A CHOICE!
SO WE DO GET TO FIND OUT...OUR DESTINED PARTNERS! ZEN! HEY, ZEN!
WHAT ?
WH-WHO DO YOU THINK...MY DESTINED PARTNER...
GLANCE
GLANCE
...IS GOING TO BE? WHO DO YOU THINK IT IS, HUH?
ISN'T THIS DISPLAY GOING TO TELL YOU?
UGH! YOU DUMMY!
DUMMY? WHY?
REI-CHAN! YOUR DESTINED PARTNER IS RIGHT OVER HERE!

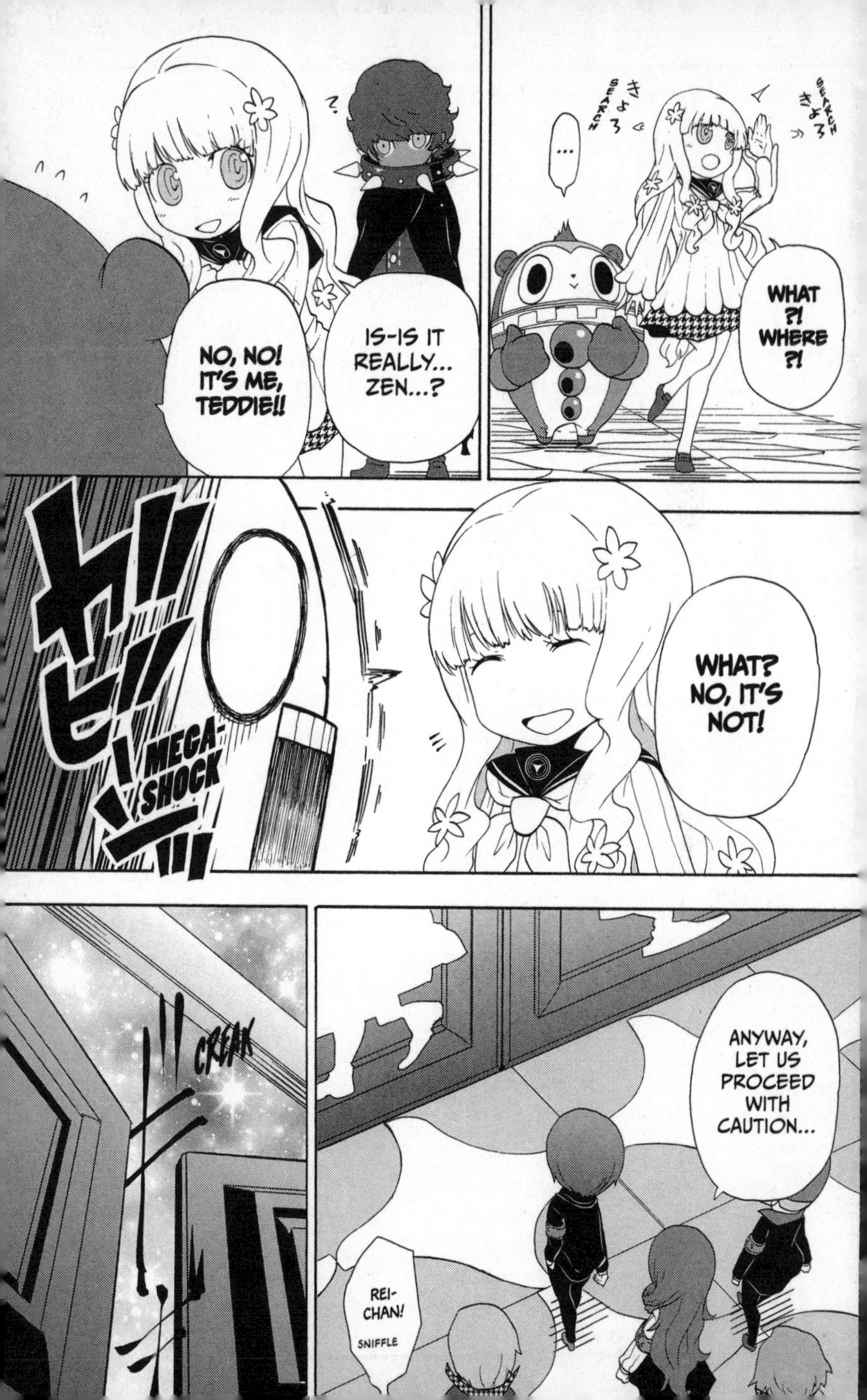

SEARCH
きょろ
SEARCH
きょろ
...
WHAT ?! WHERE ?!
?
IS-IS IT REALLY... ZEN...?
NO, NO! IT'S ME, TEDDIE!!
WHAT? NO, IT'S NOT!
MEGA-SHOCK
ANYWAY, LET US PROCEED WITH CAUTION...
REI-CHAN!
SNIFFLE
CREAK

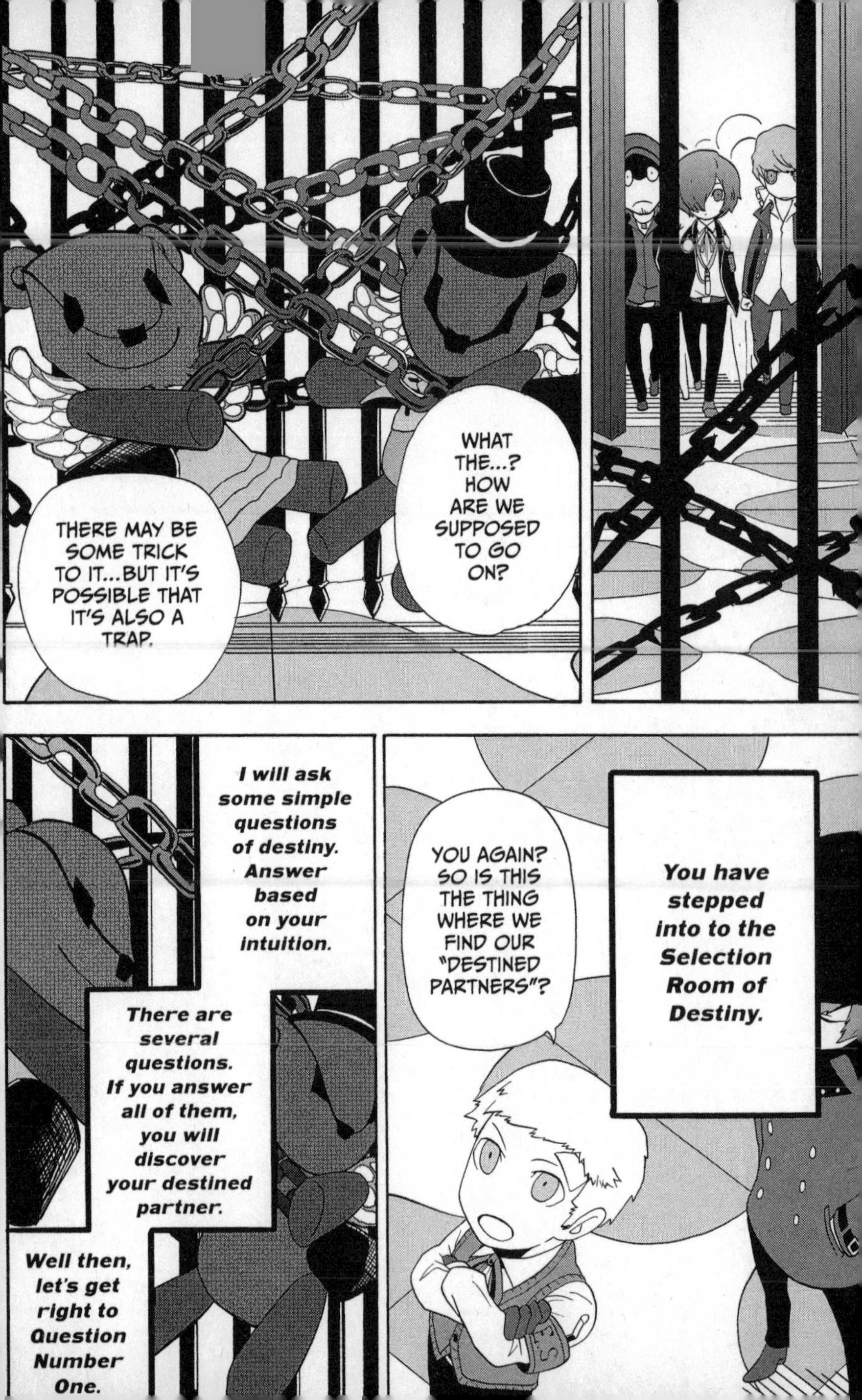
WHAT THE...? HOW ARE WE SUPPOSED TO GO ON?
THERE MAY BE SOME TRICK TO IT...BUT IT'S POSSIBLE THAT IT'S ALSO A TRAP.
You have stepped into to the Selection Room of Destiny.
YOU AGAIN? SO IS THIS THE THING WHERE WE FIND OUR "DESTINED PARTNERS"?
I will ask some simple questions of destiny. Answer based on your intuition.
There are several questions. If you answer all of them, you will discover your destined partner.
Well then, let's get right to Question Number One.

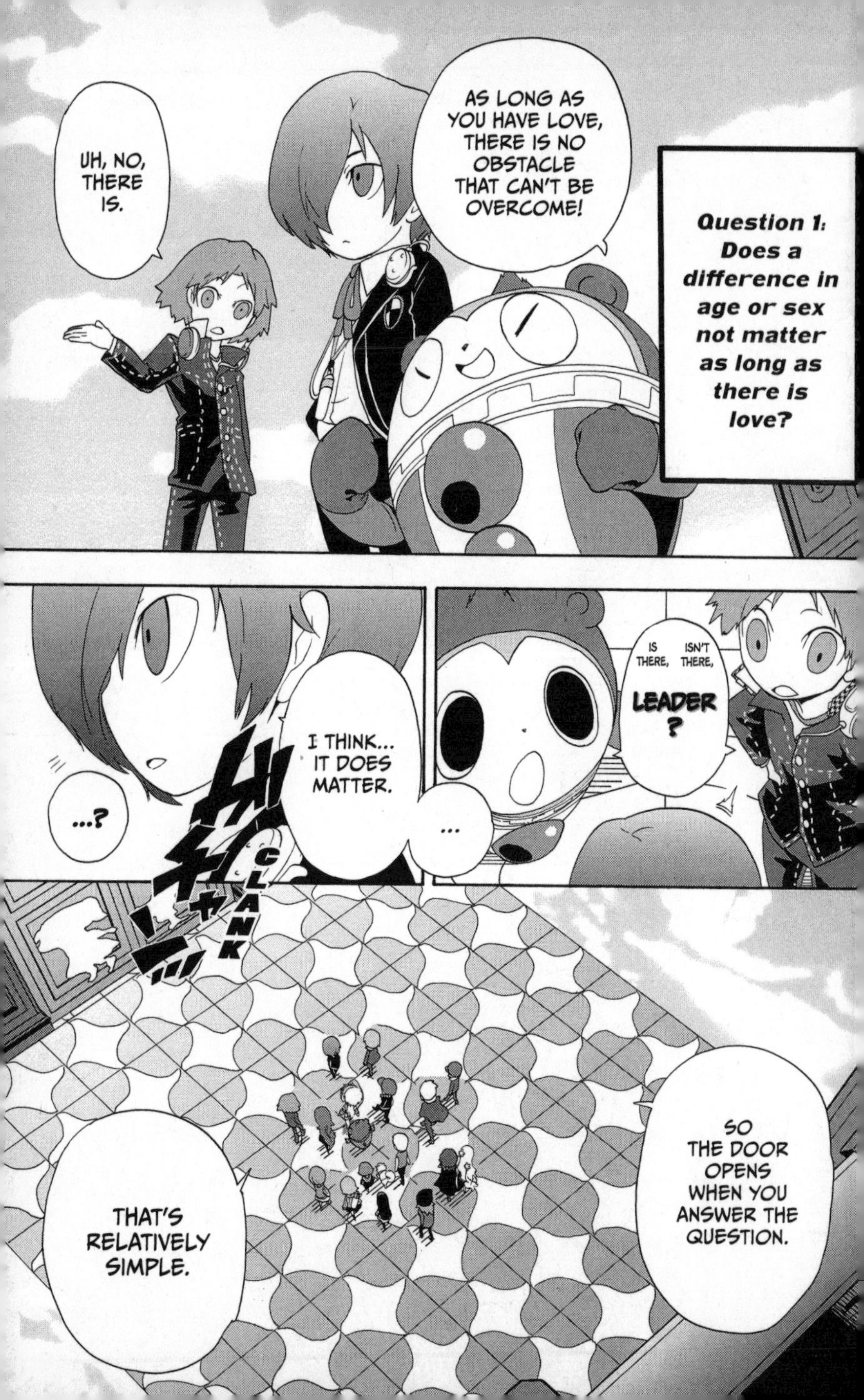

Question 1: Does a difference in age or sex not matter as long as there is love?
AS LONG AS YOU HAVE LOVE, THERE IS NO OBSTACLE THAT CAN'T BE OVERCOME!
UH, NO, THERE IS.
IS THERE, ISN'T THERE, LEADER?
...
I THINK... IT DOES MATTER.
...?
CLANK
SO THE DOOR OPENS WHEN YOU ANSWER THE QUESTION.
THAT'S RELATIVELY SIMPLE.

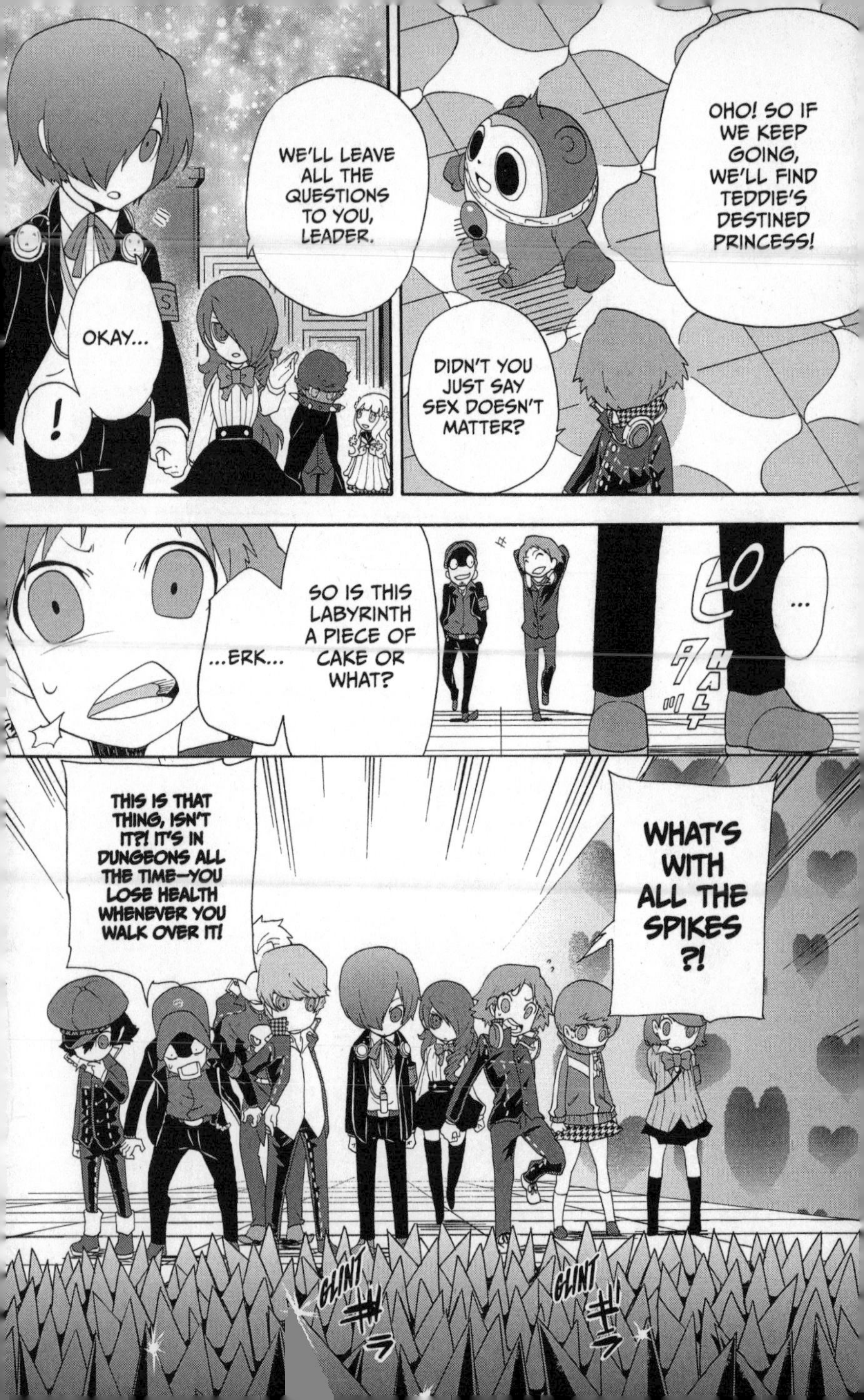
OHO! SO IF WE KEEP GOING, WE'LL FIND TEDDIE'S DESTINED PRINCESS!
DIDN'T YOU JUST SAY SEX DOESN'T MATTER?
WE'LL LEAVE ALL THE QUESTIONS TO YOU, LEADER.
OKAY...
!
...
HALT
SO IS THIS LABYRINTH A PIECE OF CAKE OR WHAT?
...ERK...
WHAT'S WITH ALL THE SPIKES?!
THIS IS THAT THING, ISN'T IT?! IT'S IN DUNGEONS ALL THE TIME—YOU LOSE HEALTH WHENEVER YOU WALK OVER IT!
GLINT
GLINT

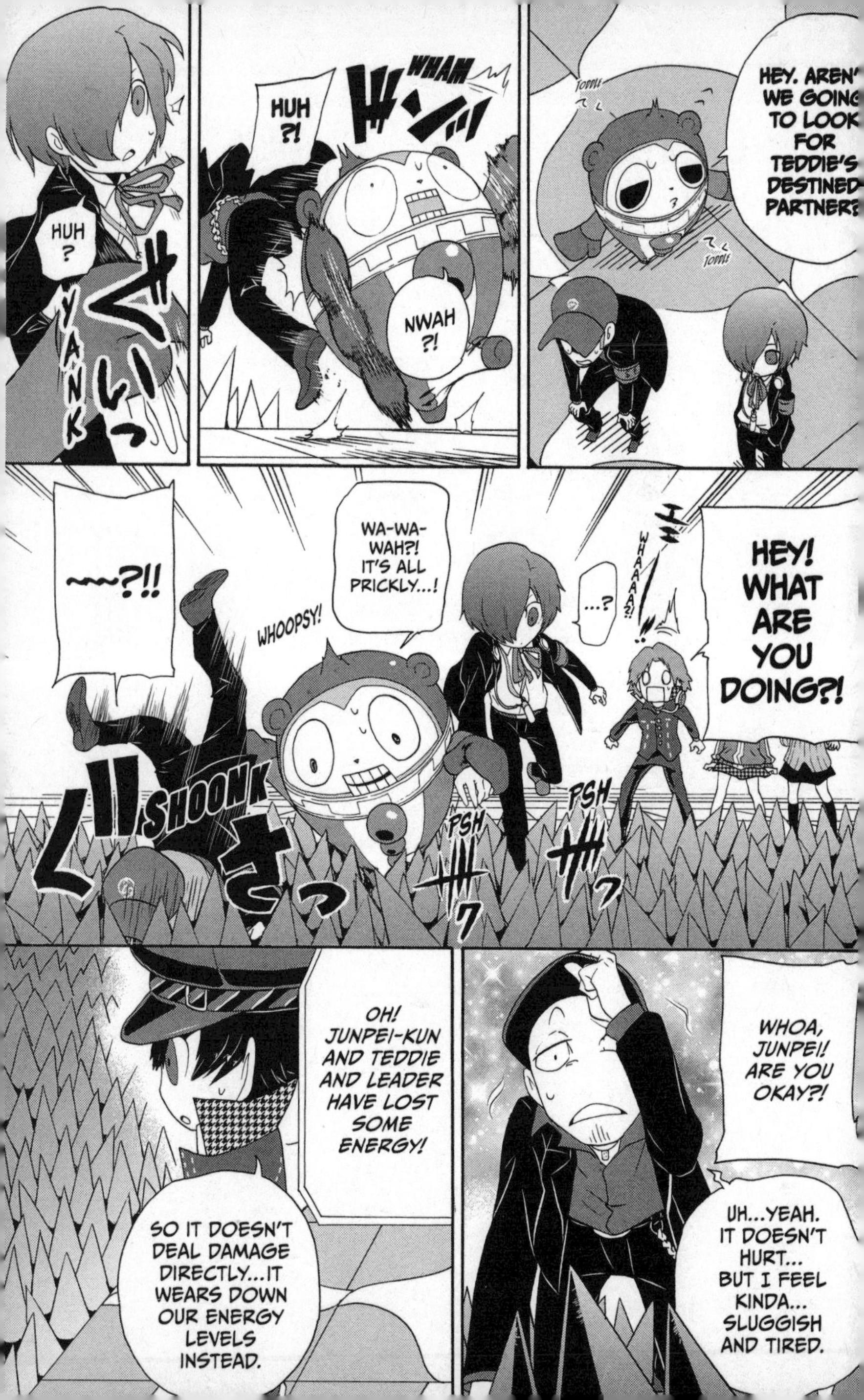
HEY. AREN'T WE GOING TO LOOK FOR TEDDIE'S DESTINED PARTNER?
TODDLE
TODDLE
WHAM
HUH ?!
NWAH ?!
HUH ?
YANK
HEY! WHAT ARE YOU DOING?!
WHAAAAA?!
...?
WA-WA-WAH?! IT'S ALL PRICKLY...!
WHOOPSY!
~~~?!!
SHOONK
PSH
PSH
WHOA, JUNPEI! ARE YOU OKAY?!
UH...YEAH. IT DOESN'T HURT... BUT I FEEL KINDA... SLUGGISH AND TIRED.
OH! JUNPEI-KUN AND TEDDIE AND LEADER HAVE LOST SOME ENERGY!
SO IT DOESN'T DEAL DAMAGE DIRECTLY...IT WEARS DOWN OUR ENERGY LEVELS INSTEAD.
~~~

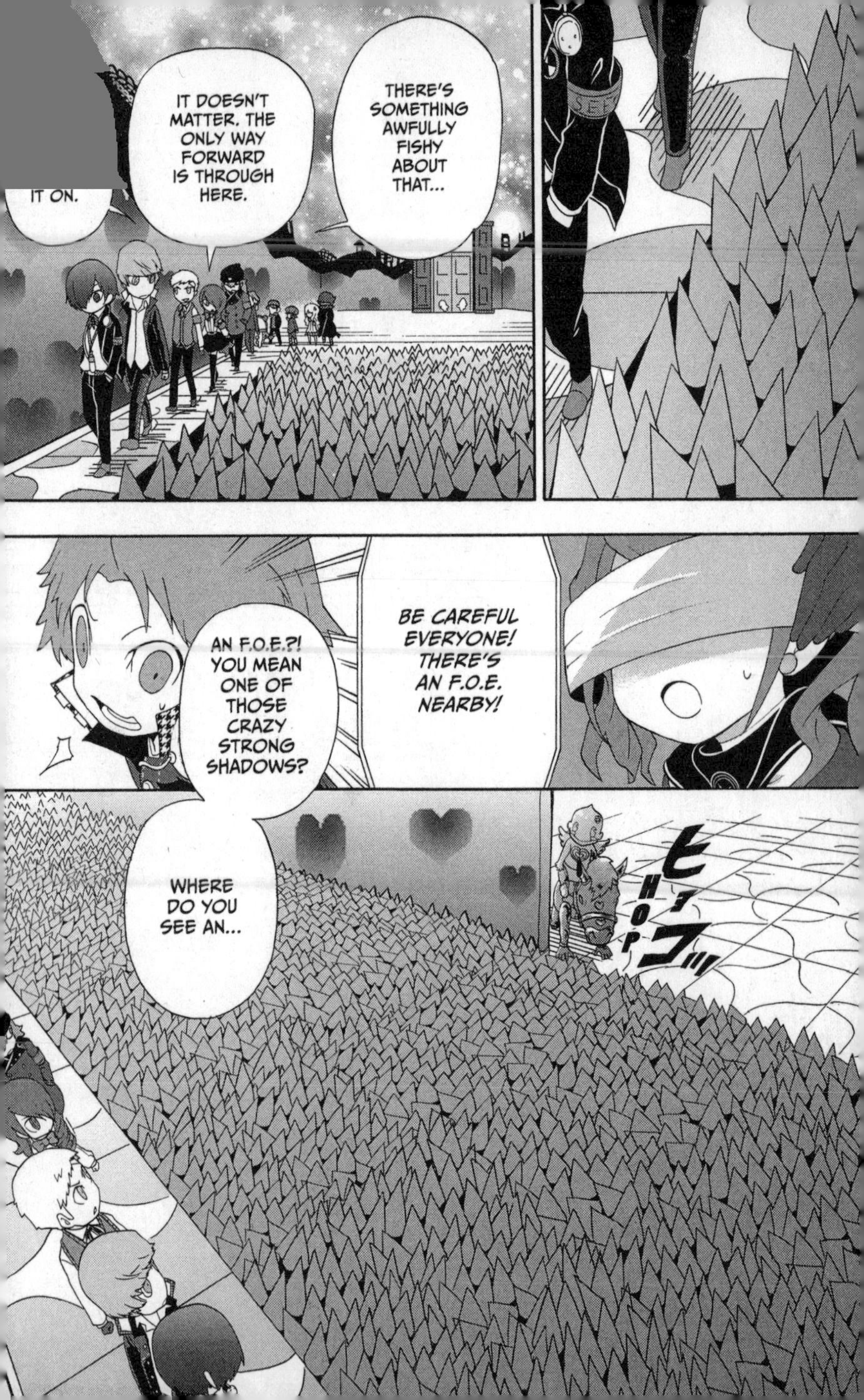
THERE'S SOMETHING AWFULLY FISHY ABOUT THAT...
IT DOESN'T MATTER. THE ONLY WAY FORWARD IS THROUGH HERE.
IT ON.
BE CAREFUL EVERYONE! THERE'S AN F.O.E. NEARBY!
AN F.O.E.?! YOU MEAN ONE OF THOSE CRAZY STRONG SHADOWS?
ヒョコッ
HOP
WHERE DO YOU SEE AN...

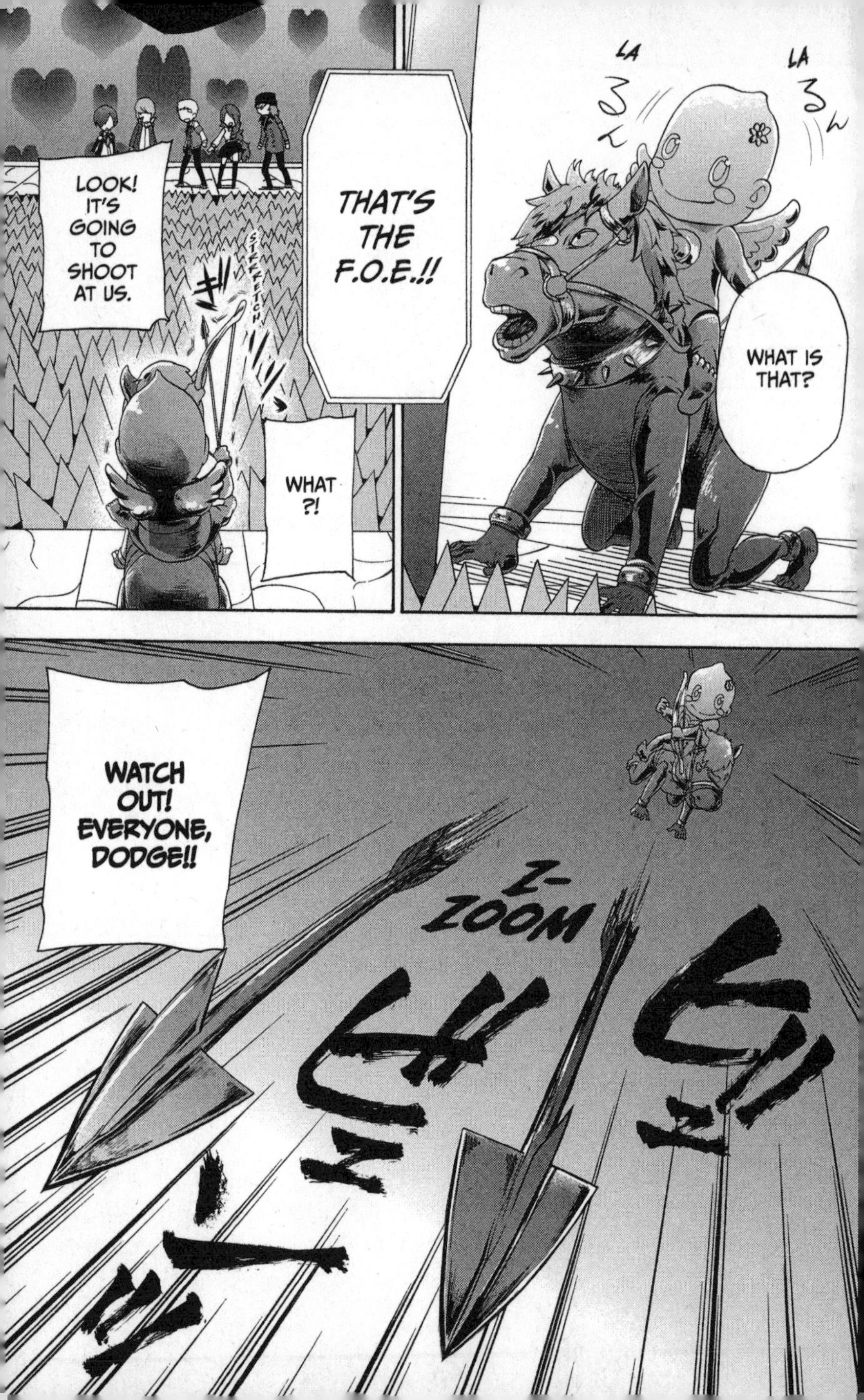
LA
るん
LA
るん
WHAT IS THAT?
THAT'S THE F.O.E.!!
WHAT ?!
LOOK! IT'S GOING TO SHOOT AT US.
STRRRETCH
WATCH OUT! EVERYONE, DODGE!!
Z-ZOOM

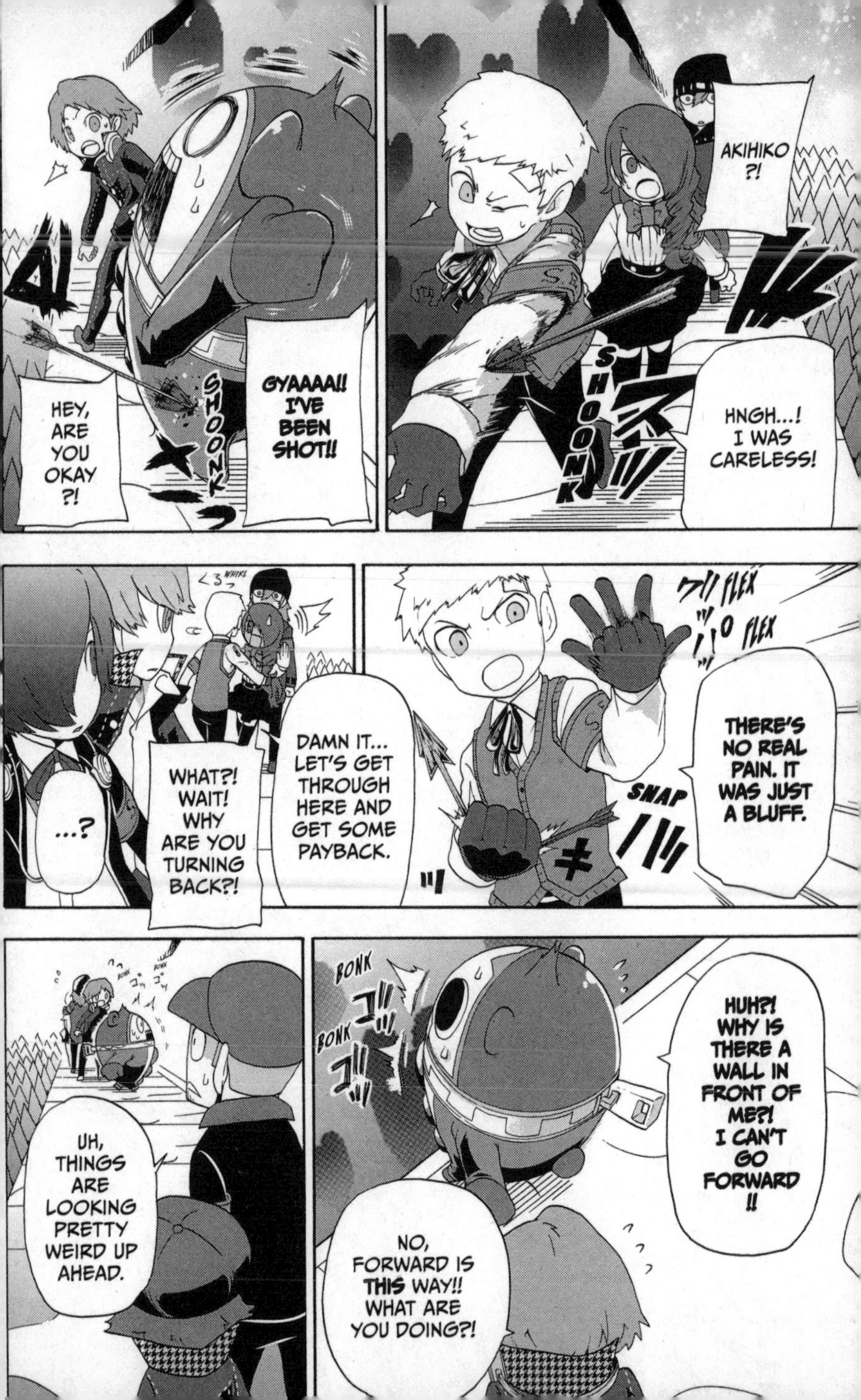
AKIHIKO ?!
HNGH...! I WAS CARELESS!
SHOONK
GYAAAA!! I'VE BEEN SHOT!!
SHOONK
HEY, ARE YOU OKAY ?!
FLEX
FLEX
THERE'S NO REAL PAIN. IT WAS JUST A BLUFF.
SNAP
WHIRL
DAMN IT... LET'S GET THROUGH HERE AND GET SOME PAYBACK.
WHAT?! WAIT! WHY ARE YOU TURNING BACK?!
...?
HUH?! WHY IS THERE A WALL IN FRONT OF ME?! I CAN'T GO FORWARD !!
BONK
BONK
NO, FORWARD IS **THIS** WAY!! WHAT ARE YOU DOING?!
BONK
BONK
UH, THINGS ARE LOOKING PRETTY WEIRD UP AHEAD.

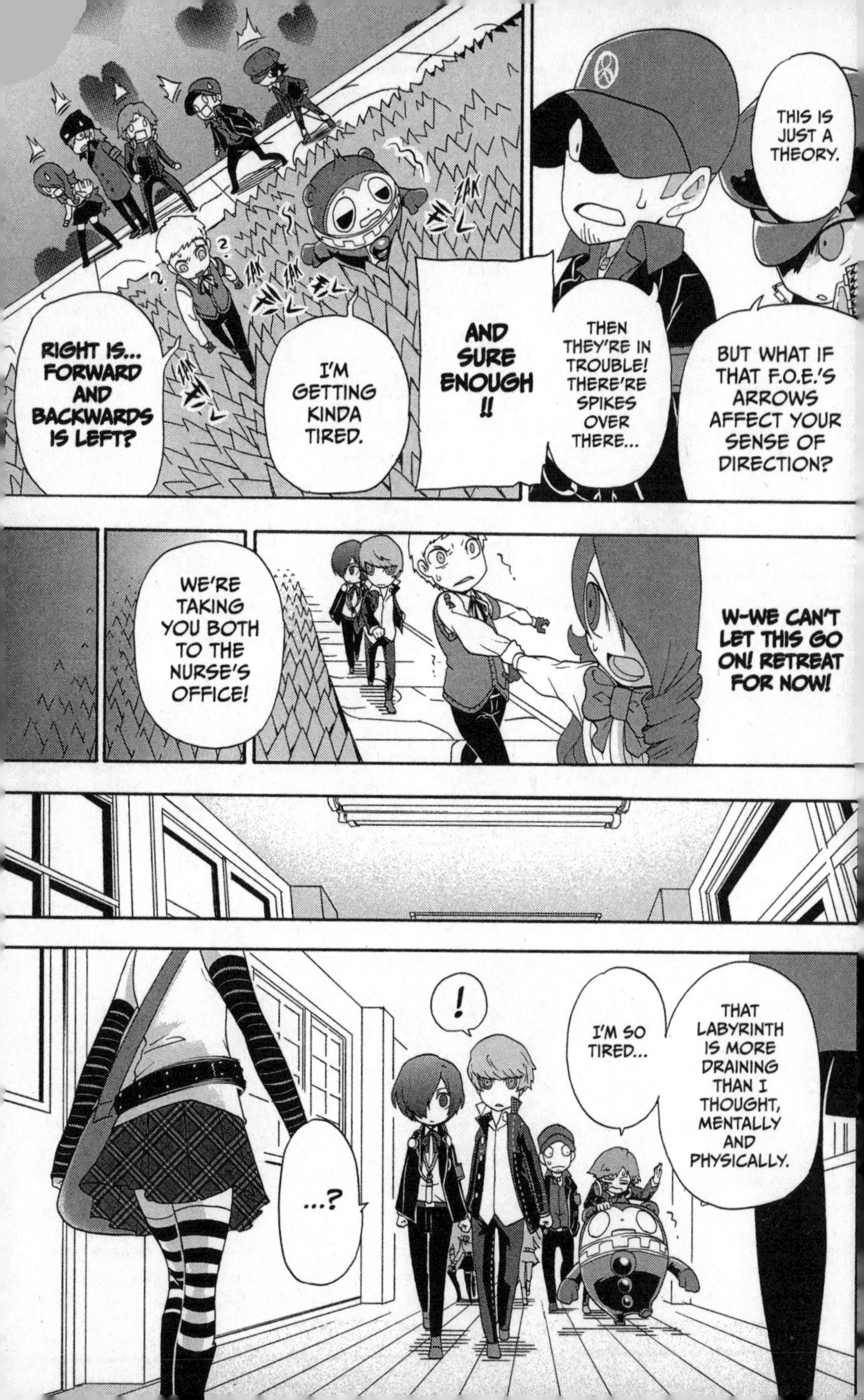
THIS IS JUST A THEORY.
BUT WHAT IF THAT F.O.E.'S ARROWS AFFECT YOUR SENSE OF DIRECTION?
THEN THEY'RE IN TROUBLE! THERE'RE SPIKES OVER THERE...
AND SURE ENOUGH!!
ZAK
ZAK
ZAK
I'M GETTING KINDA TIRED.
ZAK
RIGHT IS... FORWARD AND BACKWARDS IS LEFT?
W-WE CAN'T LET THIS GO ON! RETREAT FOR NOW!
WE'RE TAKING YOU BOTH TO THE NURSE'S OFFICE!
THAT LABYRINTH IS MORE DRAINING THAN I THOUGHT, MENTALLY AND PHYSICALLY.
I'M SO TIRED...
!
...?

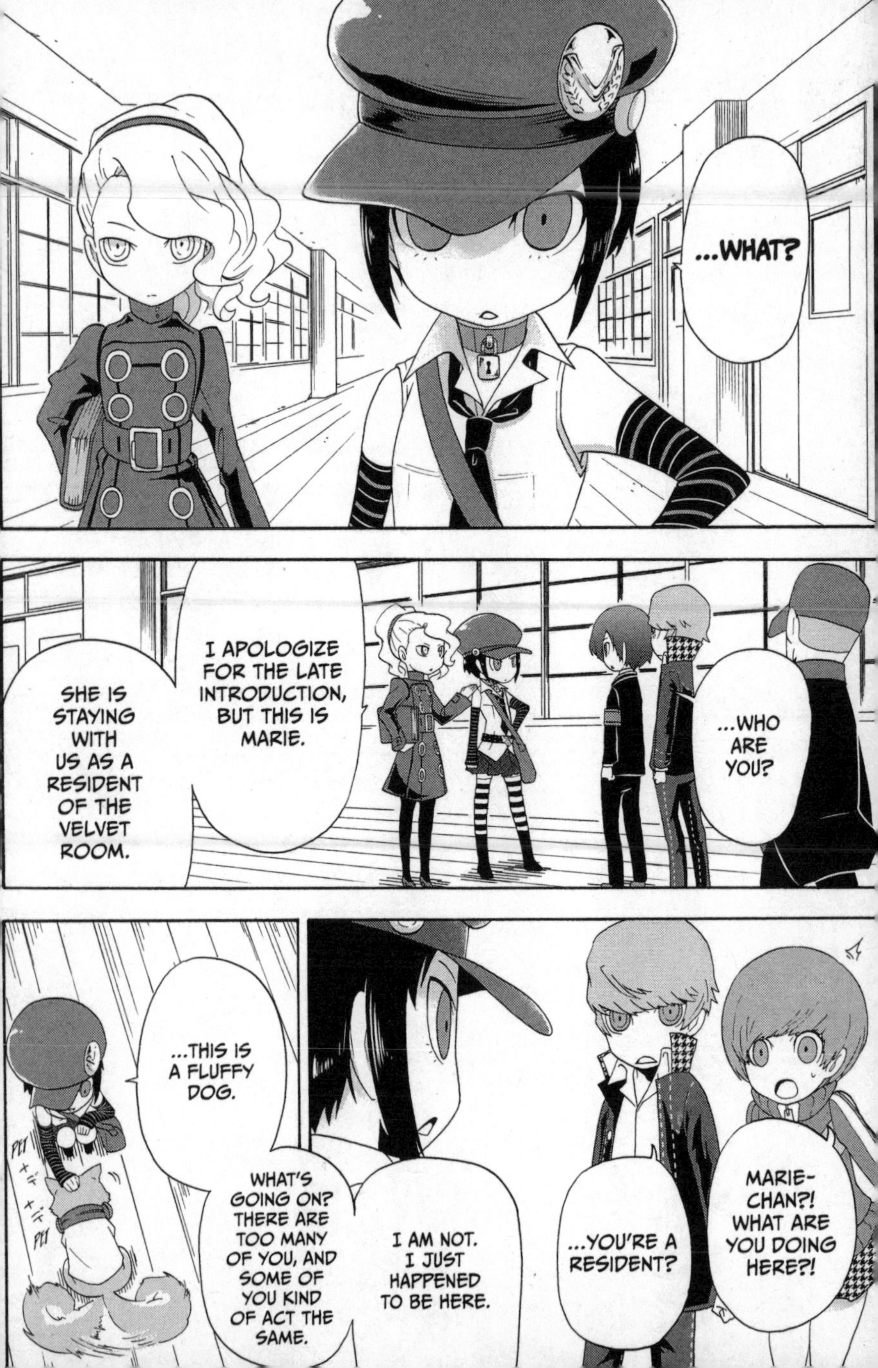
...WHAT?
...WHO ARE YOU?
I APOLOGIZE FOR THE LATE INTRODUCTION, BUT THIS IS MARIE.
SHE IS STAYING WITH US AS A RESIDENT OF THE VELVET ROOM.
MARIE-CHAN?! WHAT ARE YOU DOING HERE?!
...YOU'RE A RESIDENT?
I AM NOT. I JUST HAPPENED TO BE HERE.
WHAT'S GOING ON? THERE ARE TOO MANY OF YOU, AND SOME OF YOU KIND OF ACT THE SAME.
...THIS IS A FLUFFY DOG.

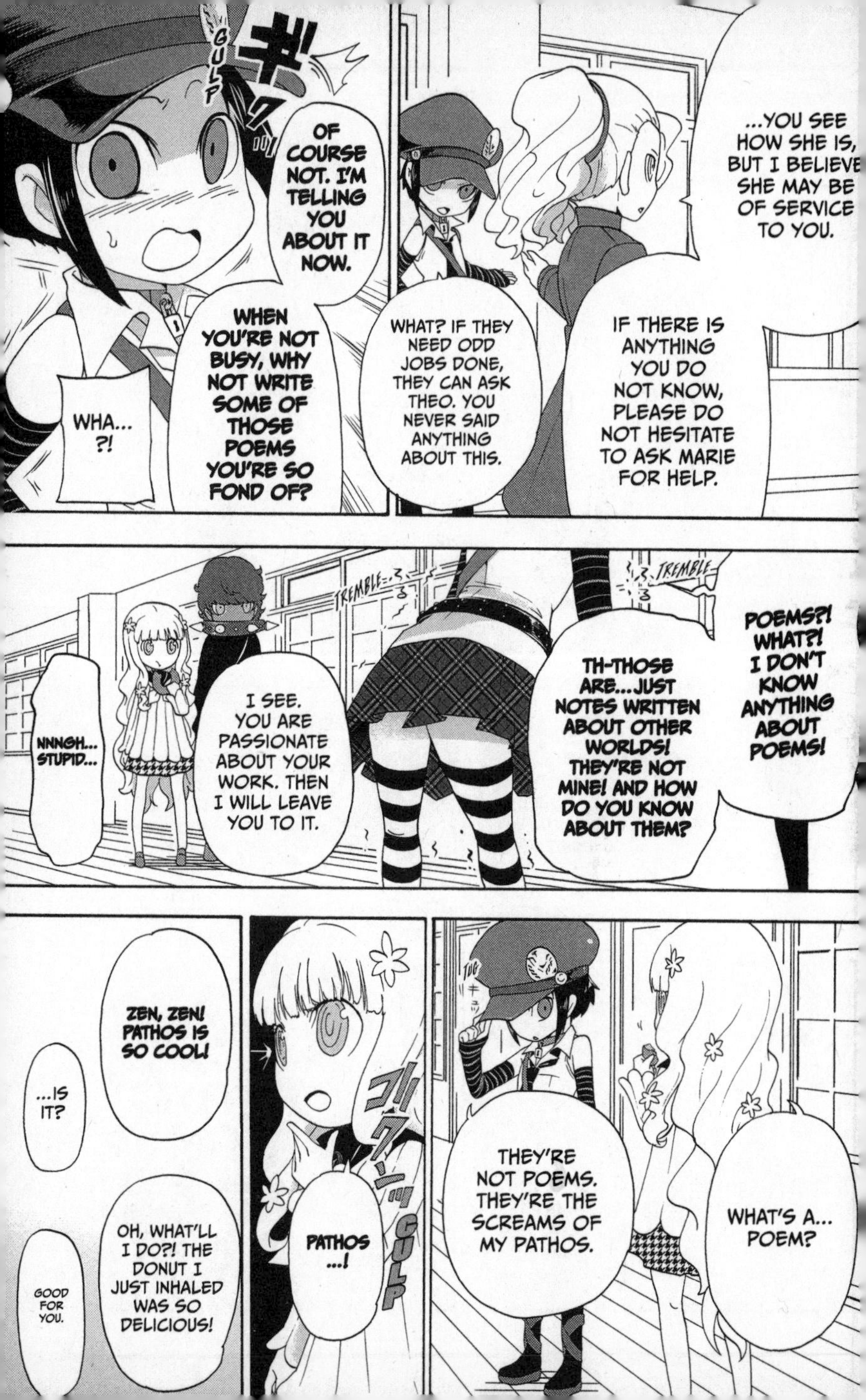
...YOU SEE HOW SHE IS, BUT I BELIEVE SHE MAY BE OF SERVICE TO YOU.
IF THERE IS ANYTHING YOU DO NOT KNOW, PLEASE DO NOT HESITATE TO ASK MARIE FOR HELP.
WHAT? IF THEY NEED ODD JOBS DONE, THEY CAN ASK THEO. YOU NEVER SAID ANYTHING ABOUT THIS.
GULP
OF COURSE NOT. I'M TELLING YOU ABOUT IT NOW.
WHEN YOU'RE NOT BUSY, WHY NOT WRITE SOME OF THOSE POEMS YOU'RE SO FOND OF?
WHA... ?!
TREMBLE
POEMS?! WHAT?! I DON'T KNOW ANYTHING ABOUT POEMS!
TH-THOSE ARE...JUST NOTES WRITTEN ABOUT OTHER WORLDS! THEY'RE NOT MINE! AND HOW DO YOU KNOW ABOUT THEM?
TREMBLE
I SEE. YOU ARE PASSIONATE ABOUT YOUR WORK. THEN I WILL LEAVE YOU TO IT.
NNNGH... STUPID...
WHAT'S A... POEM?
TUG
THEY'RE NOT POEMS. THEY'RE THE SCREAMS OF MY PATHOS.
PATHOS ...!
GULP
ZEN, ZEN! PATHOS IS SO COOL!
...IS IT?
OH, WHAT'LL I DO?! THE DONUT I JUST INHALED WAS SO DELICIOUS!
GOOD FOR YOU.

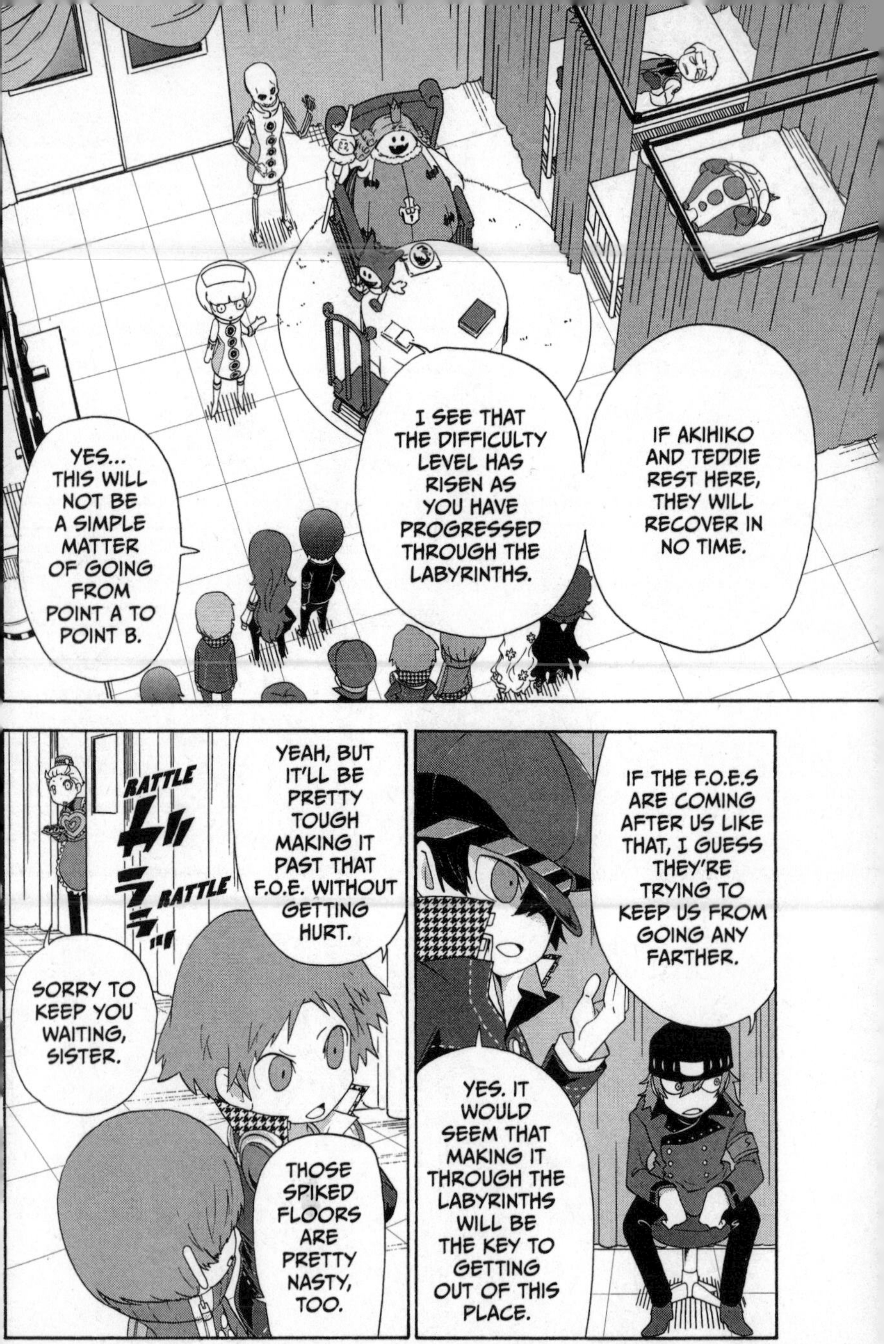
IF AKIHIKO AND TEDDIE REST HERE, THEY WILL RECOVER IN NO TIME.
I SEE THAT THE DIFFICULTY LEVEL HAS RISEN AS YOU HAVE PROGRESSED THROUGH THE LABYRINTHS.
YES... THIS WILL NOT BE A SIMPLE MATTER OF GOING FROM POINT A TO POINT B.
IF THE F.O.E.S ARE COMING AFTER US LIKE THAT, I GUESS THEY'RE TRYING TO KEEP US FROM GOING ANY FARTHER.
YES. IT WOULD SEEM THAT MAKING IT THROUGH THE LABYRINTHS WILL BE THE KEY TO GETTING OUT OF THIS PLACE.
YEAH, BUT IT'LL BE PRETTY TOUGH MAKING IT PAST THAT F.O.E. WITHOUT GETTING HURT.
RATTLE
RATTLE
SORRY TO KEEP YOU WAITING, SISTER.
THOSE SPIKED FLOORS ARE PRETTY NASTY, TOO.

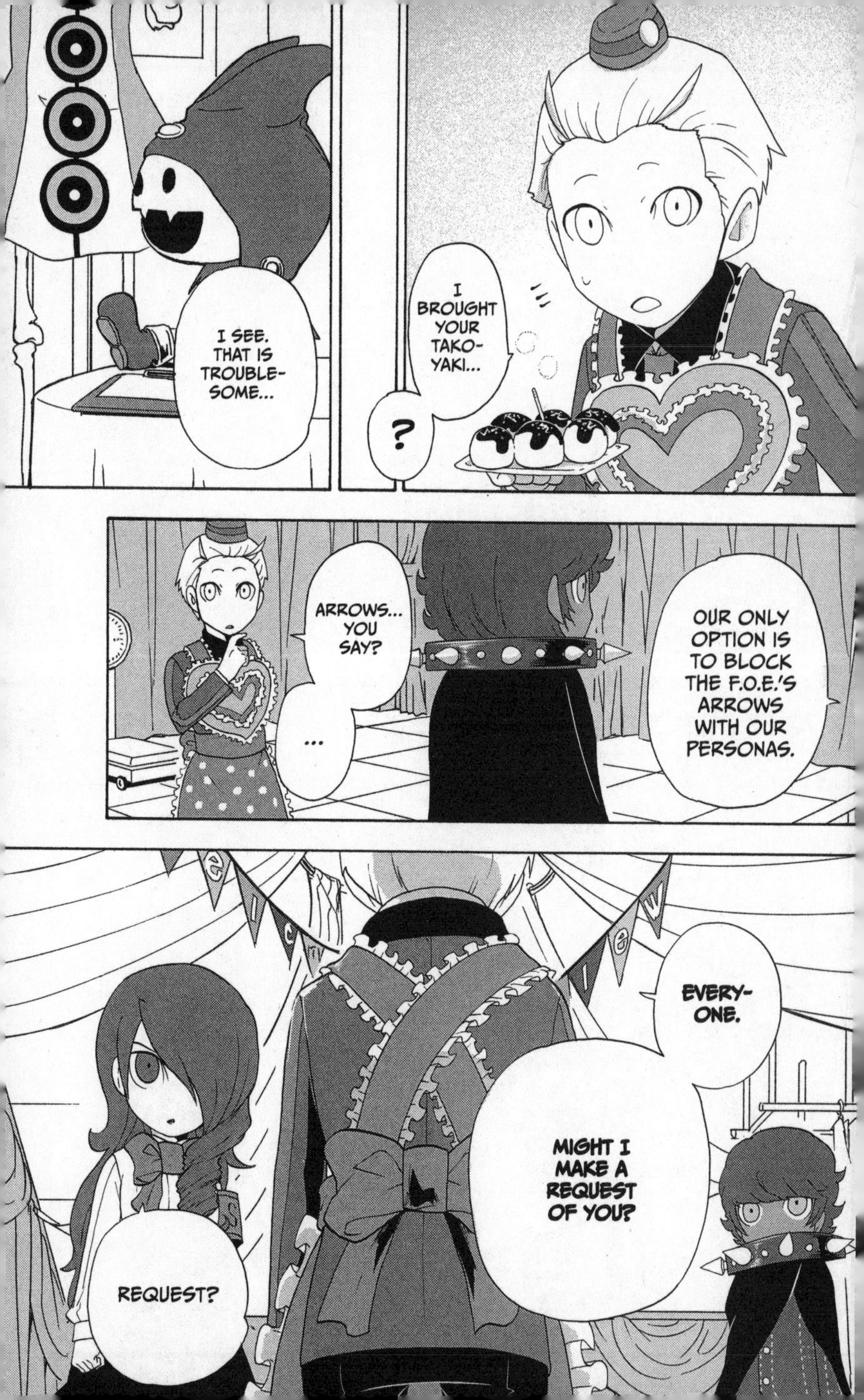
I BROUGHT YOUR TAKO-YAKI...
?
I SEE. THAT IS TROUBLE-SOME...
OUR ONLY OPTION IS TO BLOCK THE F.O.E.'S ARROWS WITH OUR PERSONAS.
ARROWS... YOU SAY?
...
EVERY-ONE.
MIGHT I MAKE A REQUEST OF YOU?
REQUEST?

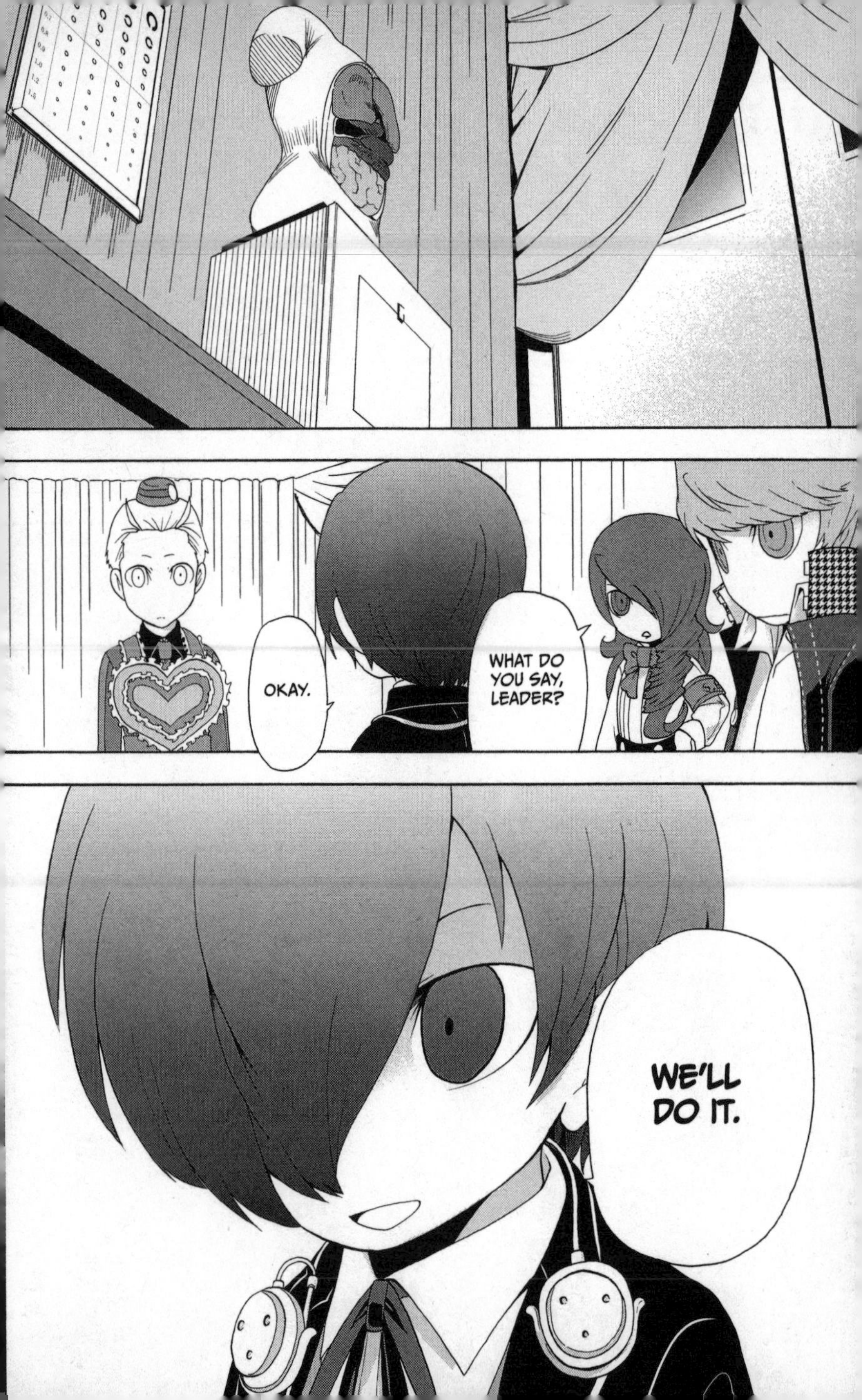
WHAT DO YOU SAY, LEADER?
OKAY.
WE'LL DO IT.

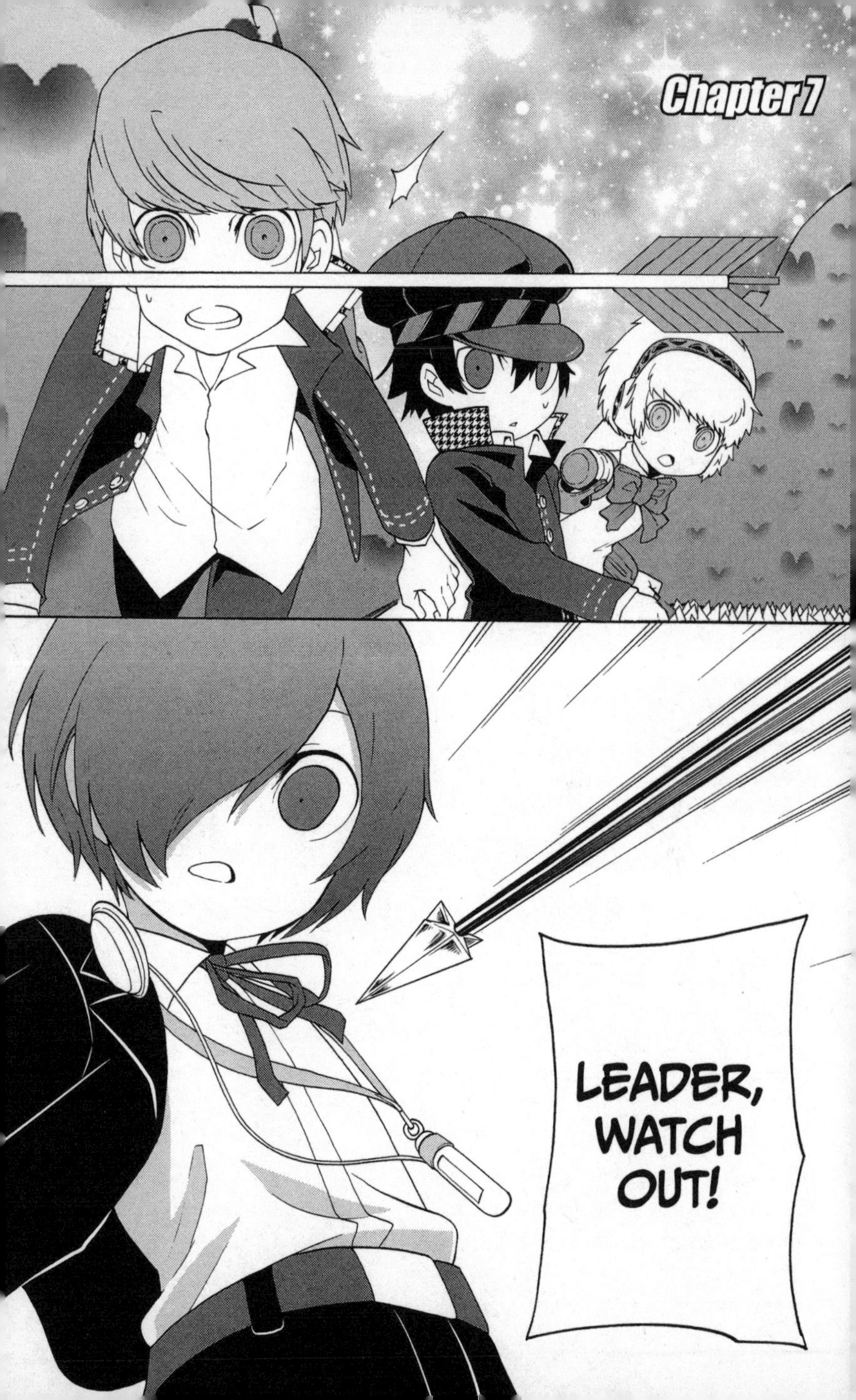
Chapter 7
LEADER, WATCH OUT!

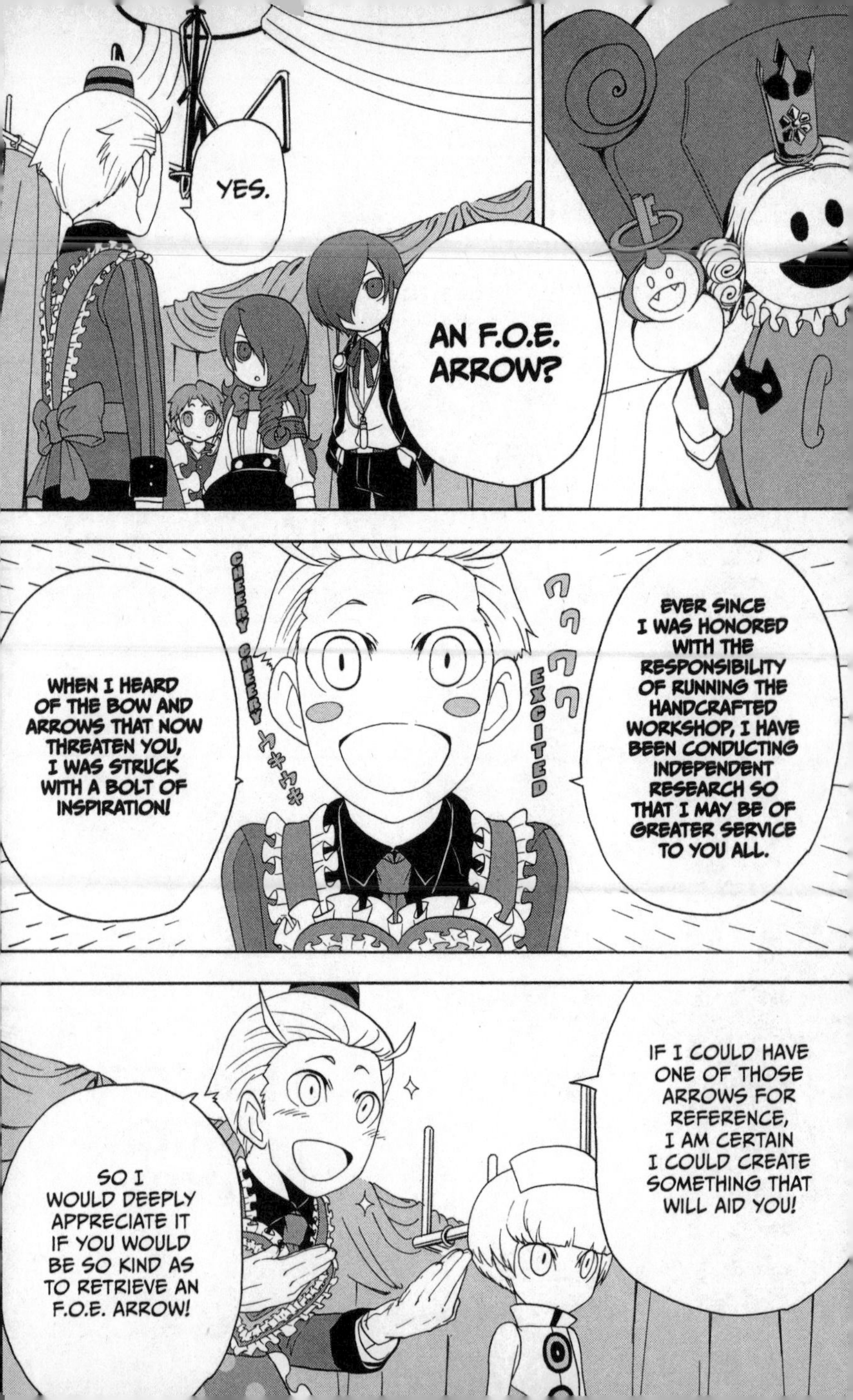
AN F.O.E. ARROW?
YES.
EVER SINCE I WAS HONORED WITH THE RESPONSIBILITY OF RUNNING THE HANDCRAFTED WORKSHOP, I HAVE BEEN CONDUCTING INDEPENDENT RESEARCH SO THAT I MAY BE OF GREATER SERVICE TO YOU ALL.
EXCITED
CHEERY CHEERY
WHEN I HEARD OF THE BOW AND ARROWS THAT NOW THREATEN YOU, I WAS STRUCK WITH A BOLT OF INSPIRATION!
IF I COULD HAVE ONE OF THOSE ARROWS FOR REFERENCE, I AM CERTAIN I COULD CREATE SOMETHING THAT WILL AID YOU!
SO I WOULD DEEPLY APPRECIATE IT IF YOU WOULD BE SO KIND AS TO RETRIEVE AN F.O.E. ARROW!

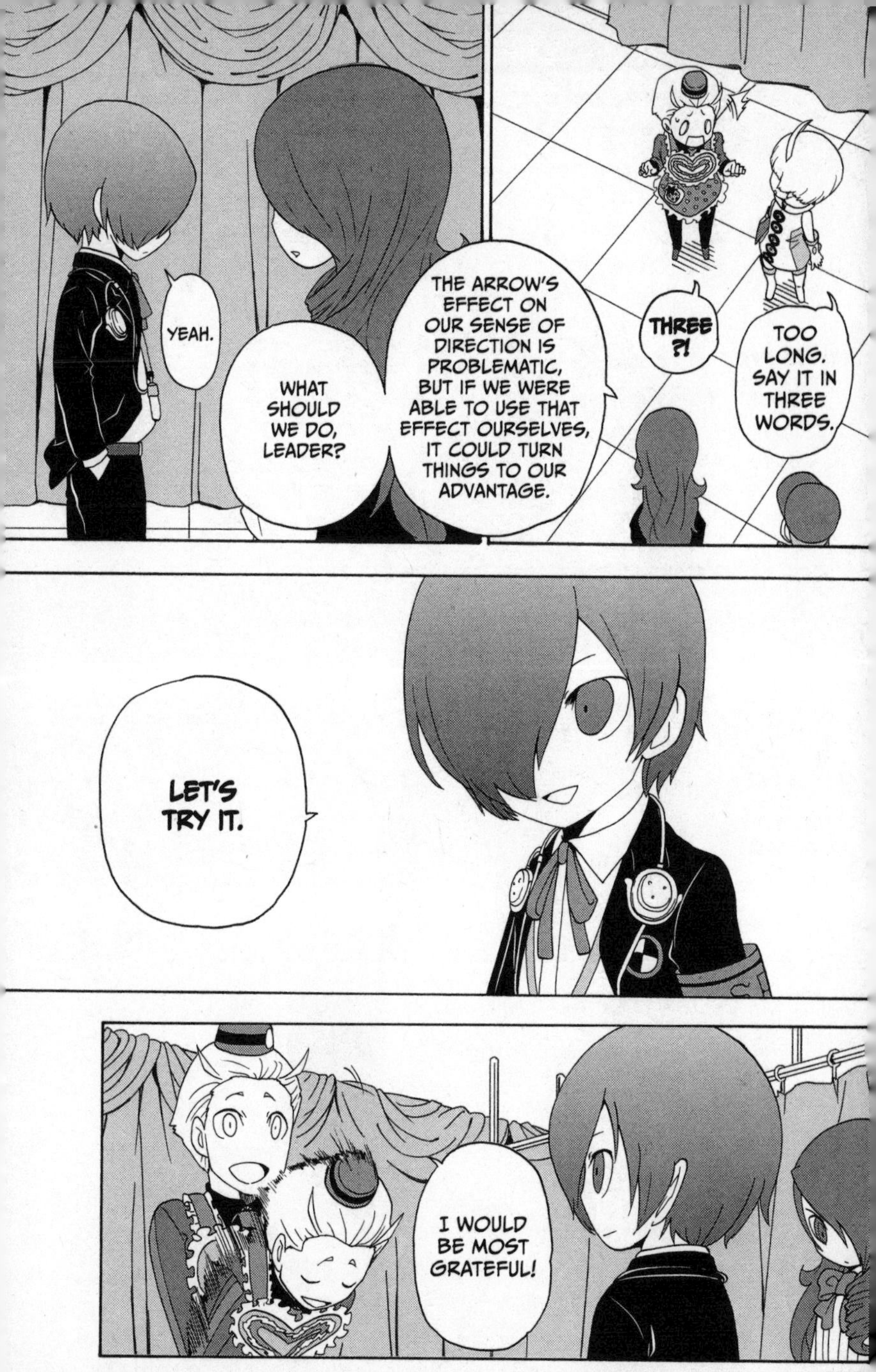
TOO LONG. SAY IT IN THREE WORDS.
THREE ?!
THE ARROW'S EFFECT ON OUR SENSE OF DIRECTION IS PROBLEMATIC, BUT IF WE WERE ABLE TO USE THAT EFFECT OURSELVES, IT COULD TURN THINGS TO OUR ADVANTAGE.
WHAT SHOULD WE DO, LEADER?
YEAH.
LET'S TRY IT.
I WOULD BE MOST GRATEFUL!

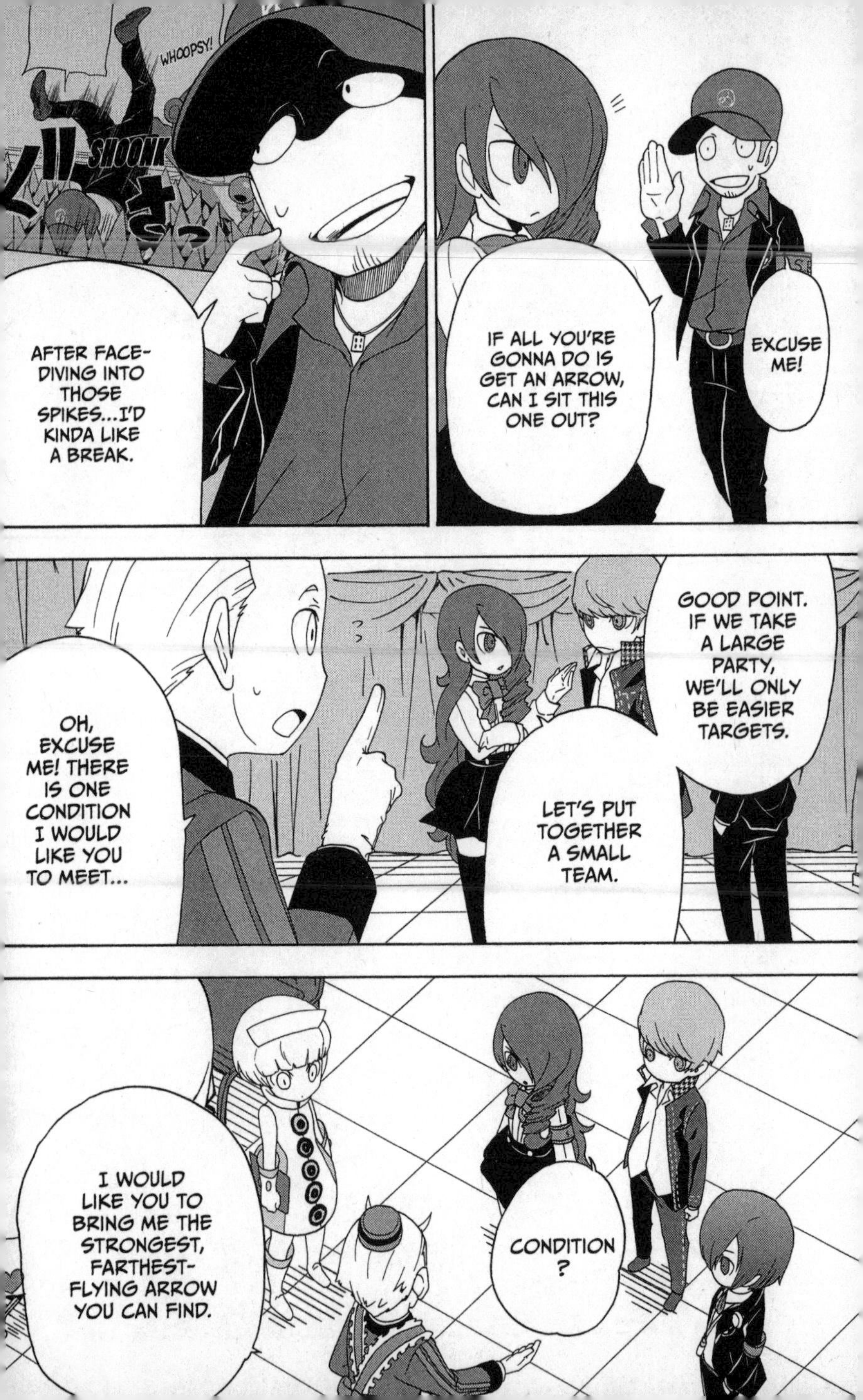
EXCUSE ME!
IF ALL YOU'RE GONNA DO IS GET AN ARROW, CAN I SIT THIS ONE OUT?
WHOOPSY!
SHOONK
AFTER FACE-DIVING INTO THOSE SPIKES...I'D KINDA LIKE A BREAK.
GOOD POINT. IF WE TAKE A LARGE PARTY, WE'LL ONLY BE EASIER TARGETS.
LET'S PUT TOGETHER A SMALL TEAM.
OH, EXCUSE ME! THERE IS ONE CONDITION I WOULD LIKE YOU TO MEET...
CONDITION?
I WOULD LIKE YOU TO BRING ME THE STRONGEST, FARTHEST-FLYING ARROW YOU CAN FIND.

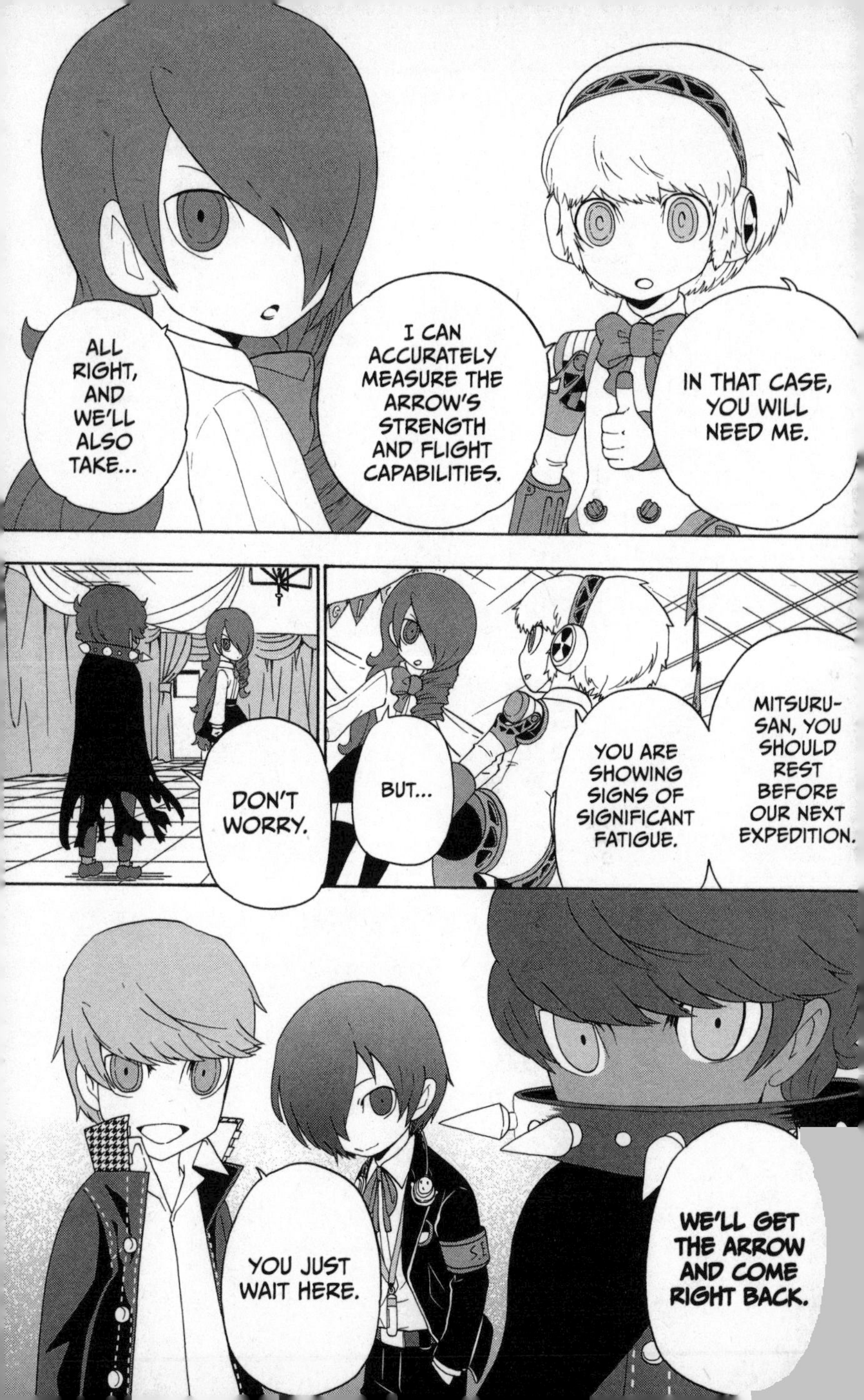
IN THAT CASE, YOU WILL NEED ME.
I CAN ACCURATELY MEASURE THE ARROW'S STRENGTH AND FLIGHT CAPABILITIES.
ALL RIGHT, AND WE'LL ALSO TAKE...
MITSURU-SAN, YOU SHOULD REST BEFORE OUR NEXT EXPEDITION.
YOU ARE SHOWING SIGNS OF SIGNIFICANT FATIGUE.
BUT...
DON'T WORRY.
WE'LL GET THE ARROW AND COME RIGHT BACK.
YOU JUST WAIT HERE.

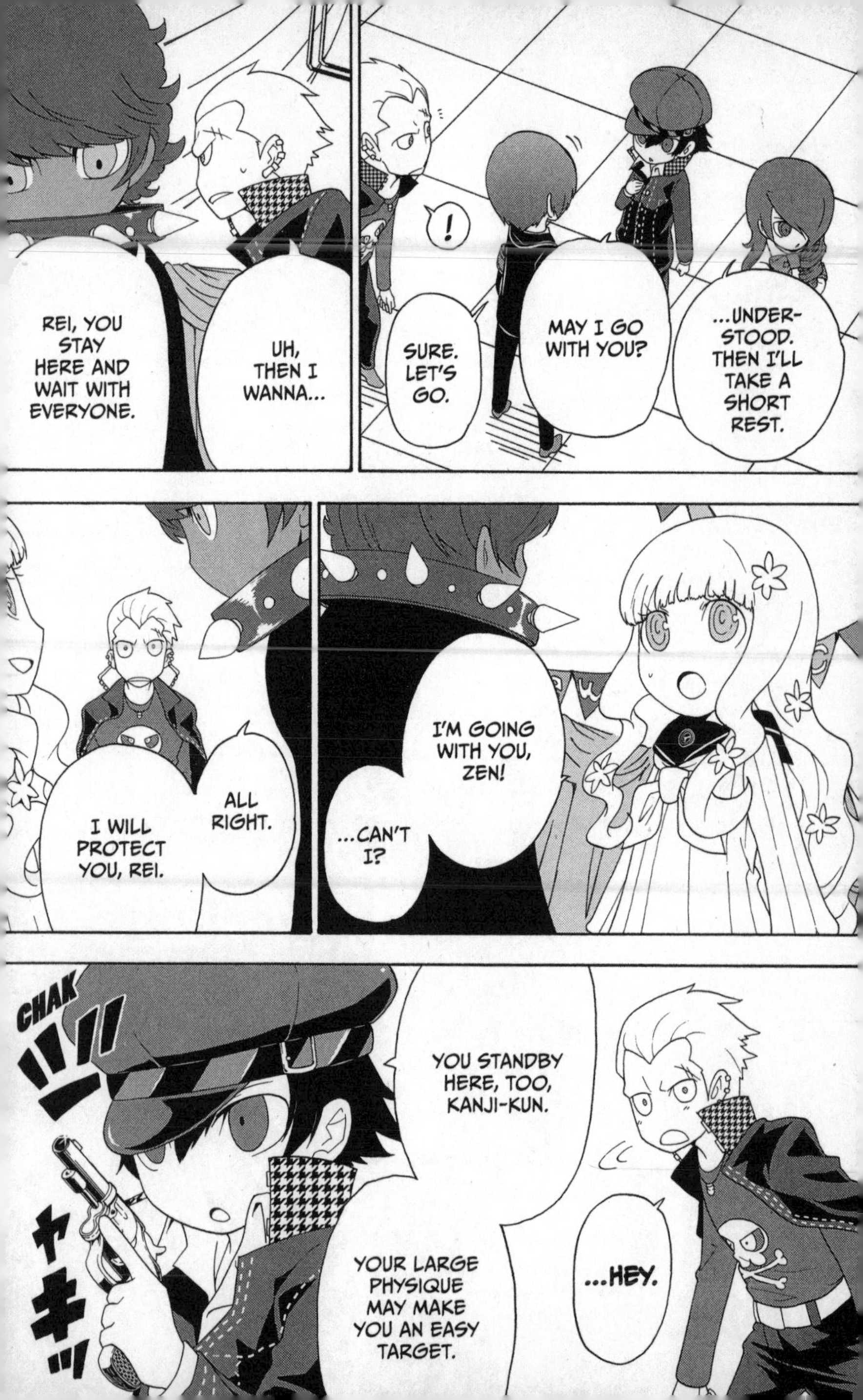
...UNDER-STOOD. THEN I'LL TAKE A SHORT REST.
MAY I GO WITH YOU?
!
SURE. LET'S GO.
UH, THEN I WANNA...
REI, YOU STAY HERE AND WAIT WITH EVERYONE.
I'M GOING WITH YOU, ZEN!
...CAN'T I?
ALL RIGHT.
I WILL PROTECT YOU, REI.
YOU STANDBY HERE, TOO, KANJI-KUN.
YOUR LARGE PHYSIQUE MAY MAKE YOU AN EASY TARGET.
...HEY.
CHAK

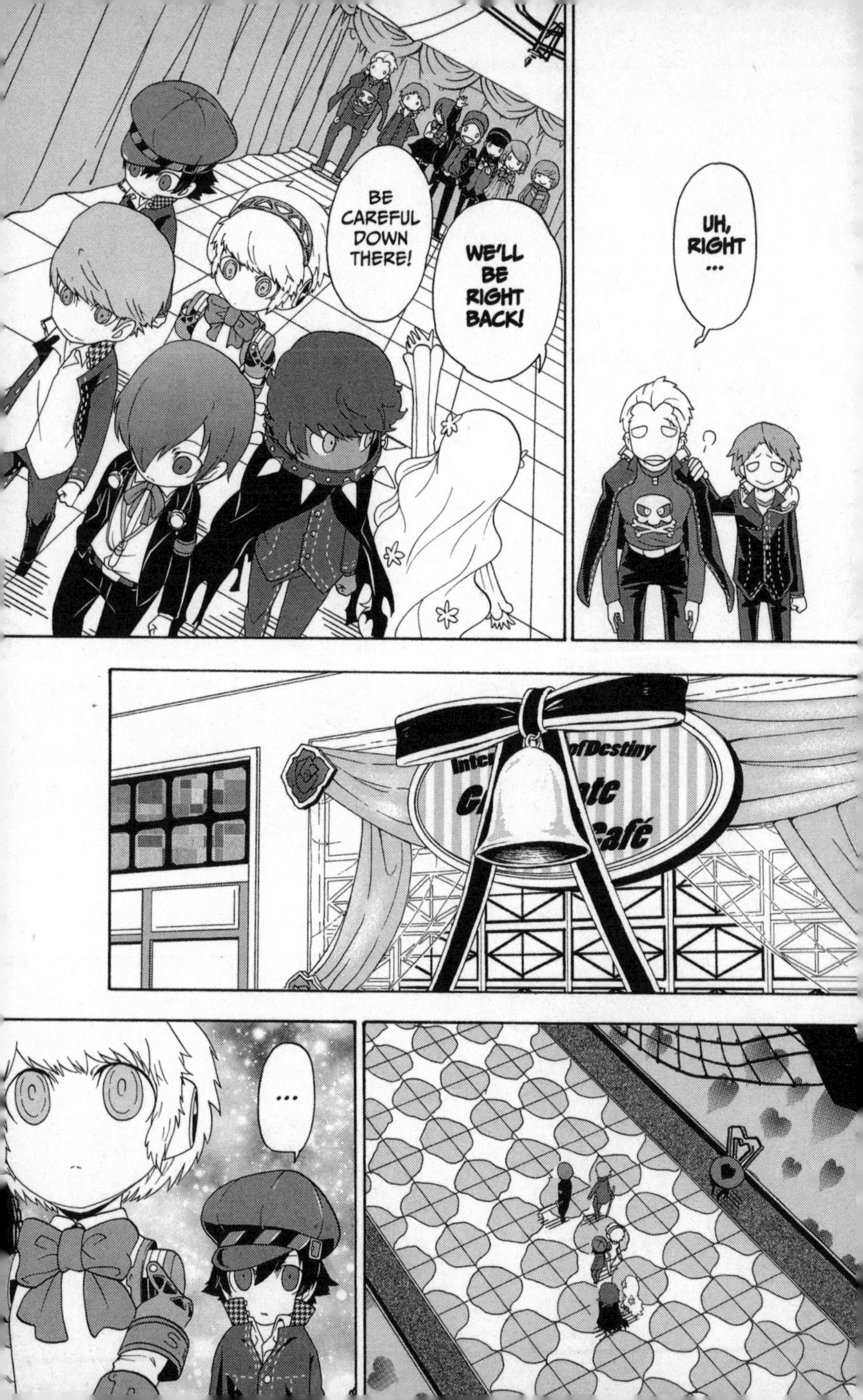
UH, RIGHT ...
BE CAREFUL DOWN THERE!
WE'LL BE RIGHT BACK!
...

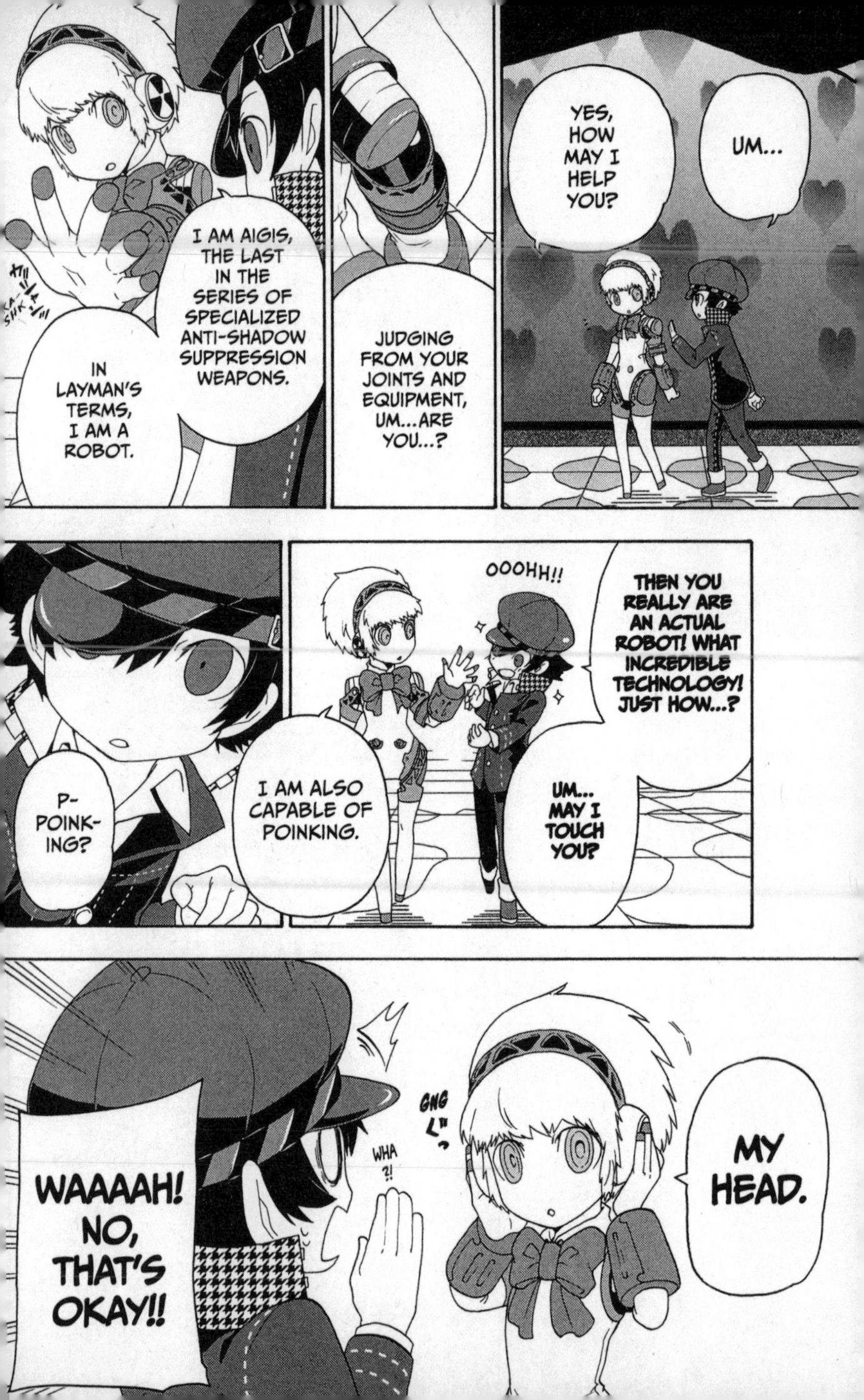
UM...
YES, HOW MAY I HELP YOU?
JUDGING FROM YOUR JOINTS AND EQUIPMENT, UM...ARE YOU...?
I AM AIGIS, THE LAST IN THE SERIES OF SPECIALIZED ANTI-SHADOW SUPPRESSION WEAPONS.
IN LAYMAN'S TERMS, I AM A ROBOT.
OOOHH!!
THEN YOU REALLY ARE AN ACTUAL ROBOT! WHAT INCREDIBLE TECHNOLOGY! JUST HOW...?
UM... MAY I TOUCH YOU?
I AM ALSO CAPABLE OF POINKING.
P-POINKING?
MY HEAD.
GNG
WHA ?!
WAAAAH! NO, THAT'S OKAY!!

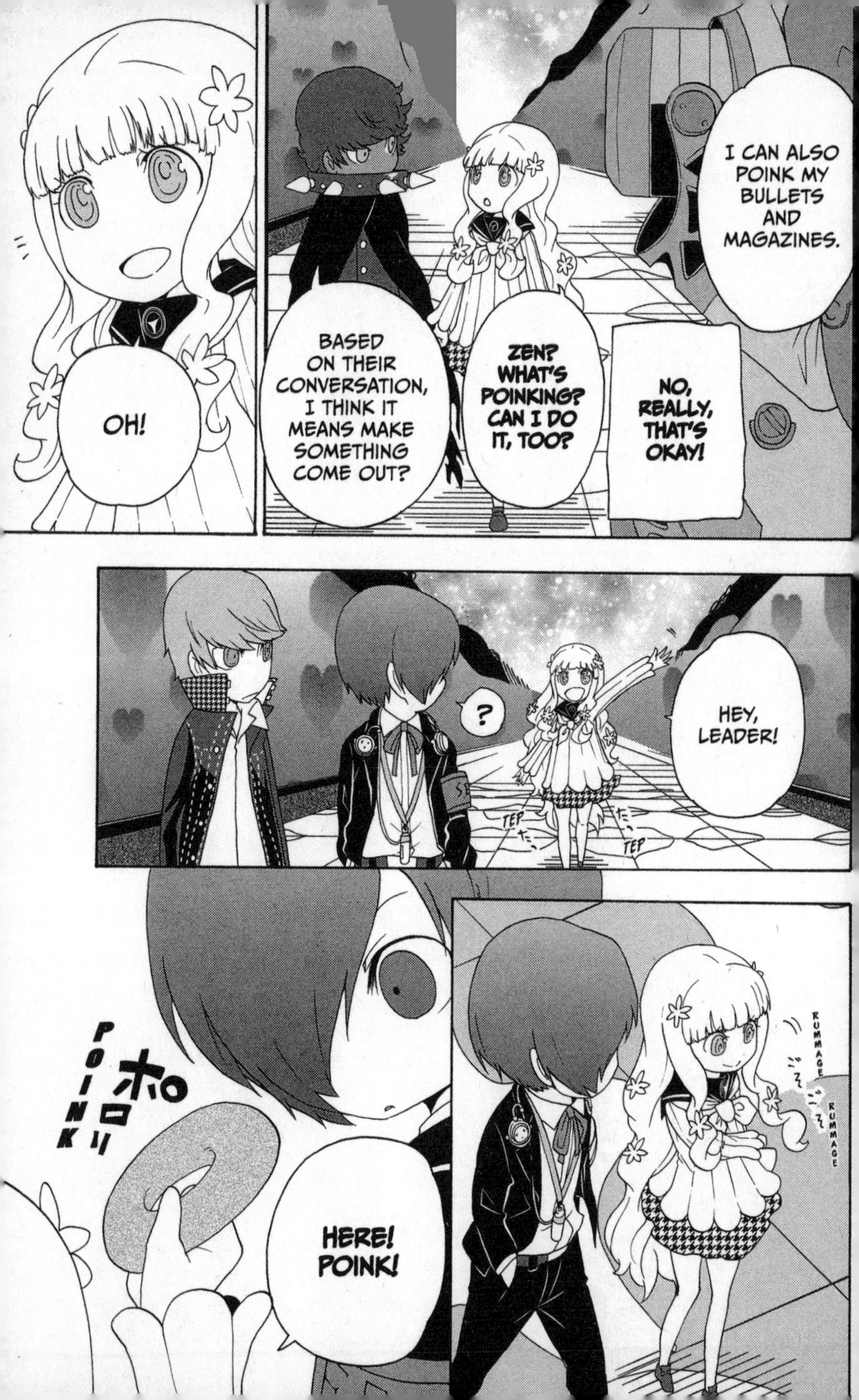
I CAN ALSO POINK MY BULLETS AND MAGAZINES.
NO, REALLY, THAT'S OKAY!
ZEN? WHAT'S POINKING? CAN I DO IT, TOO?
BASED ON THEIR CONVERSATION, I THINK IT MEANS MAKE SOMETHING COME OUT?
OH!
HEY, LEADER!
?
TEP TEP
RUMMAGE RUMMAGE
HERE! POINK!
POINK
ポロリ

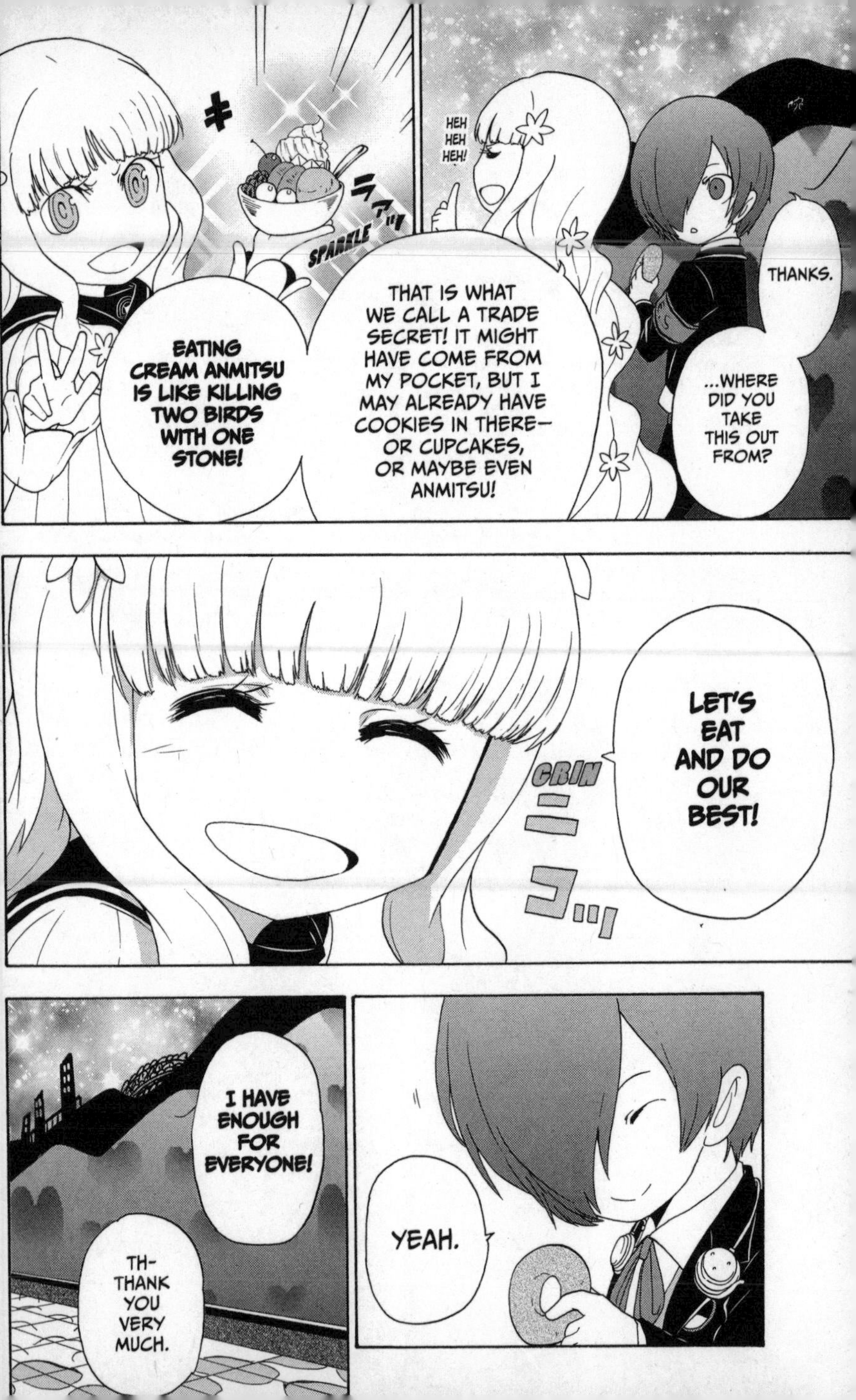
THANKS.
...WHERE DID YOU TAKE THIS OUT FROM?
HEH HEH HEH!
THAT IS WHAT WE CALL A TRADE SECRET! IT MIGHT HAVE COME FROM MY POCKET, BUT I MAY ALREADY HAVE COOKIES IN THERE— OR CUPCAKES, OR MAYBE EVEN ANMITSU!
SPARKLE
EATING CREAM ANMITSU IS LIKE KILLING TWO BIRDS WITH ONE STONE!
LET'S EAT AND DO OUR BEST!
GRIN
YEAH.
I HAVE ENOUGH FOR EVERYONE!
TH- THANK YOU VERY MUCH.

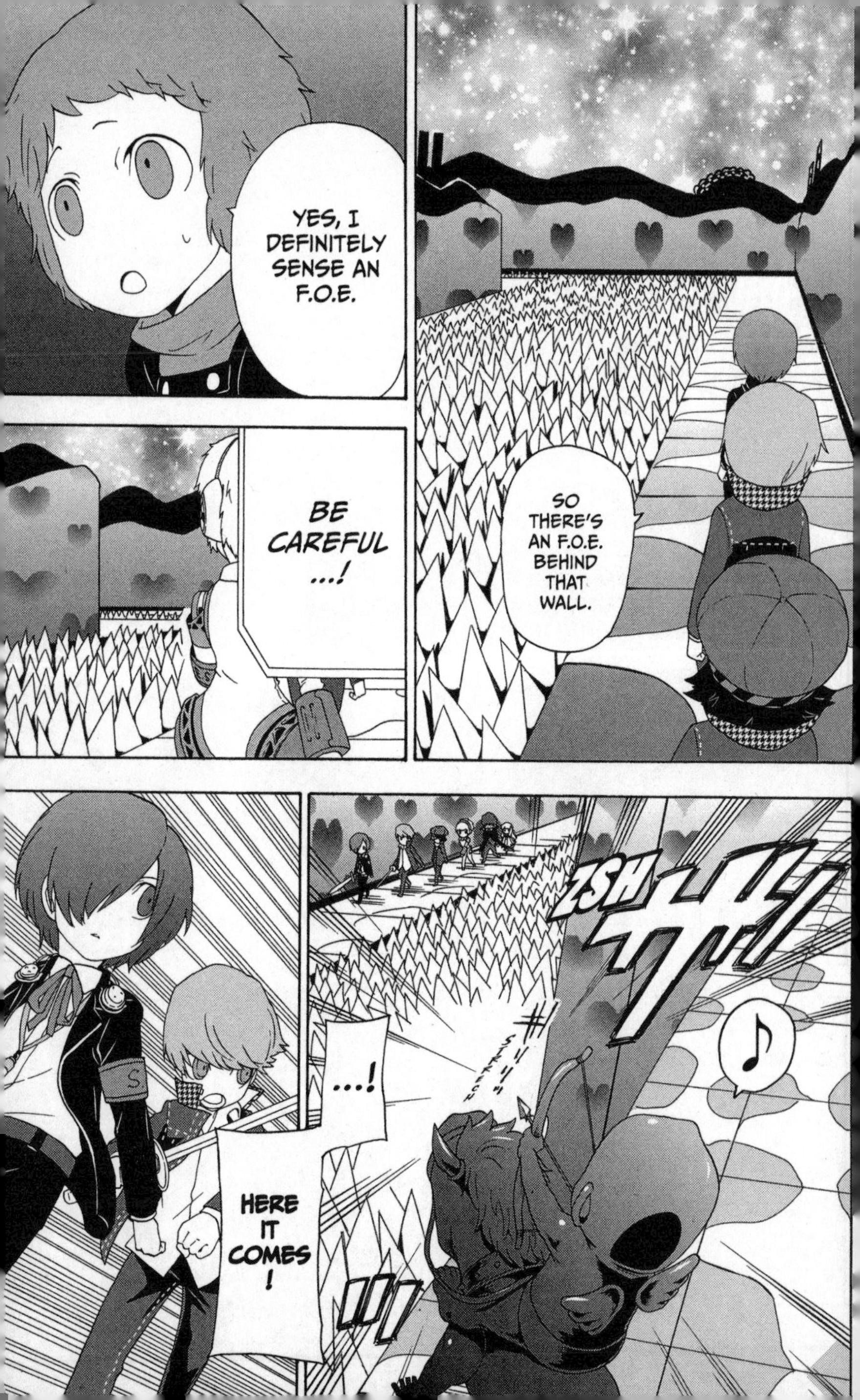
SO THERE'S AN F.O.E. BEHIND THAT WALL.
YES, I DEFINITELY SENSE AN F.O.E.
BE CAREFUL ...!
ZSH
STRETCH
♪
...!
HERE IT COMES!

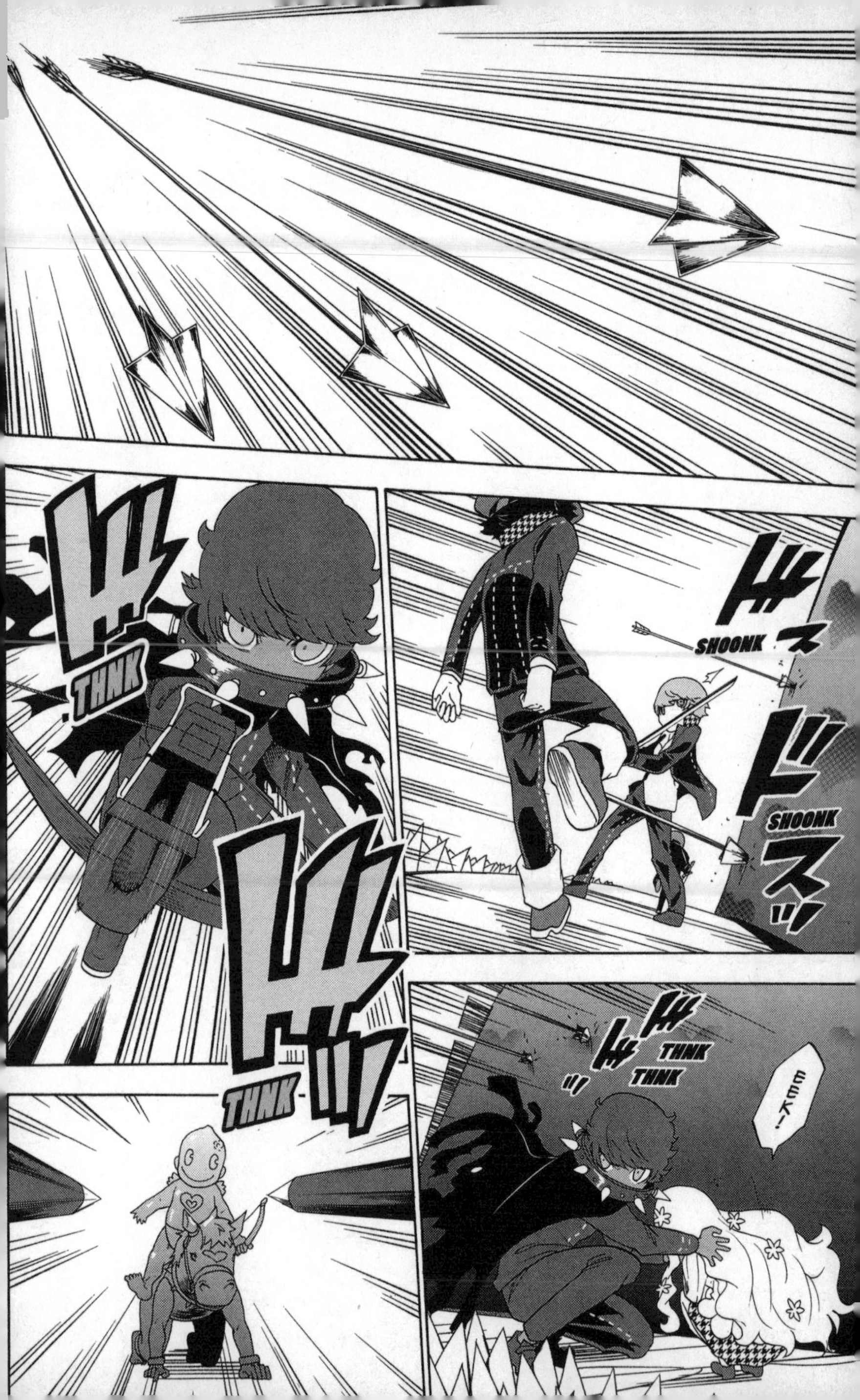
SHOONK
SHOONK
THNK
THNK
THNK
THNK
EEEK!

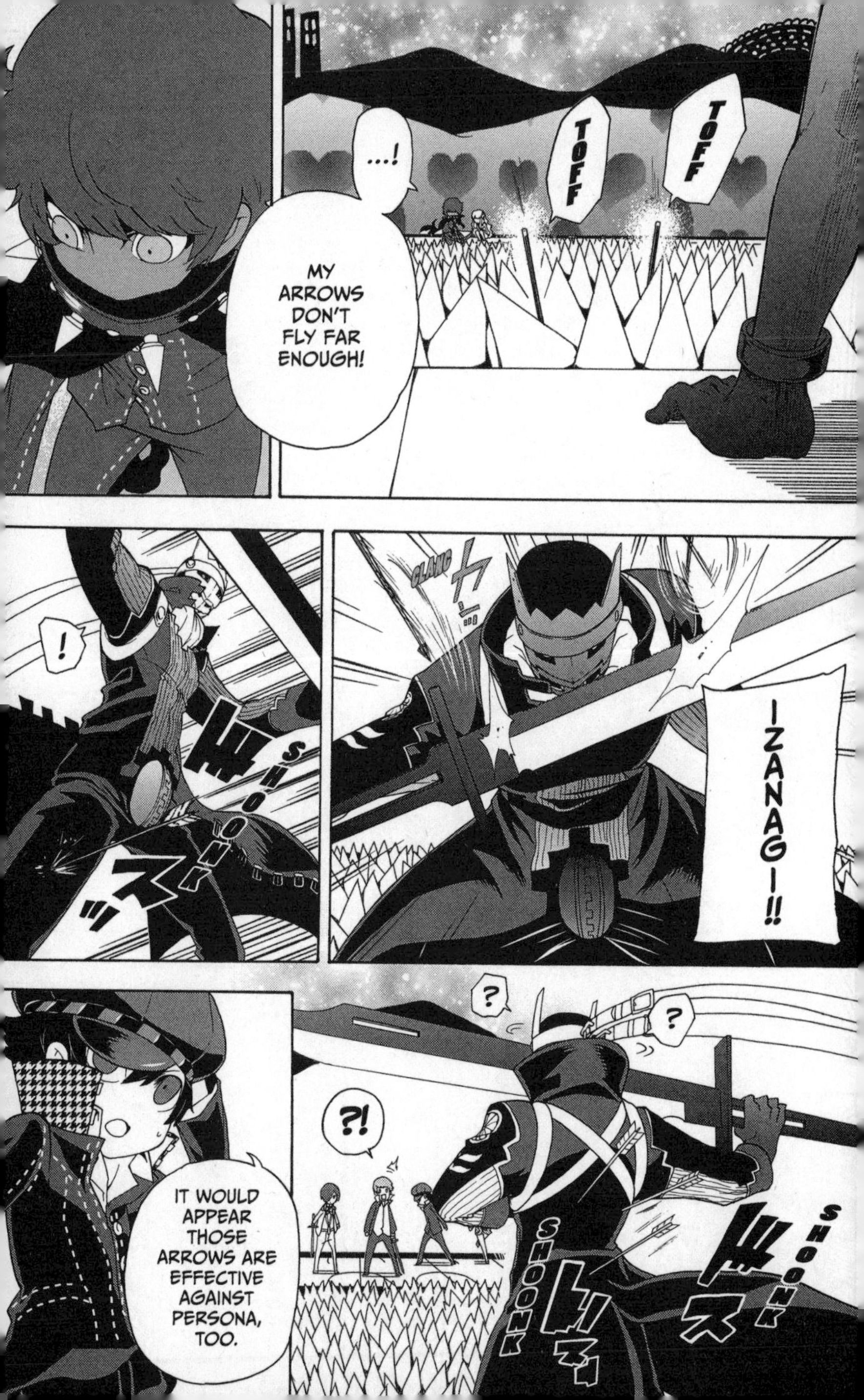

TOFF
TOFF
...!
MY ARROWS DON'T FLY FAR ENOUGH!
CLANG
IZANAGI!!
!
SHOONK
?
?
?!
IT WOULD APPEAR THOSE ARROWS ARE EFFECTIVE AGAINST PERSONA, TOO.
SHOONK
SHOONK

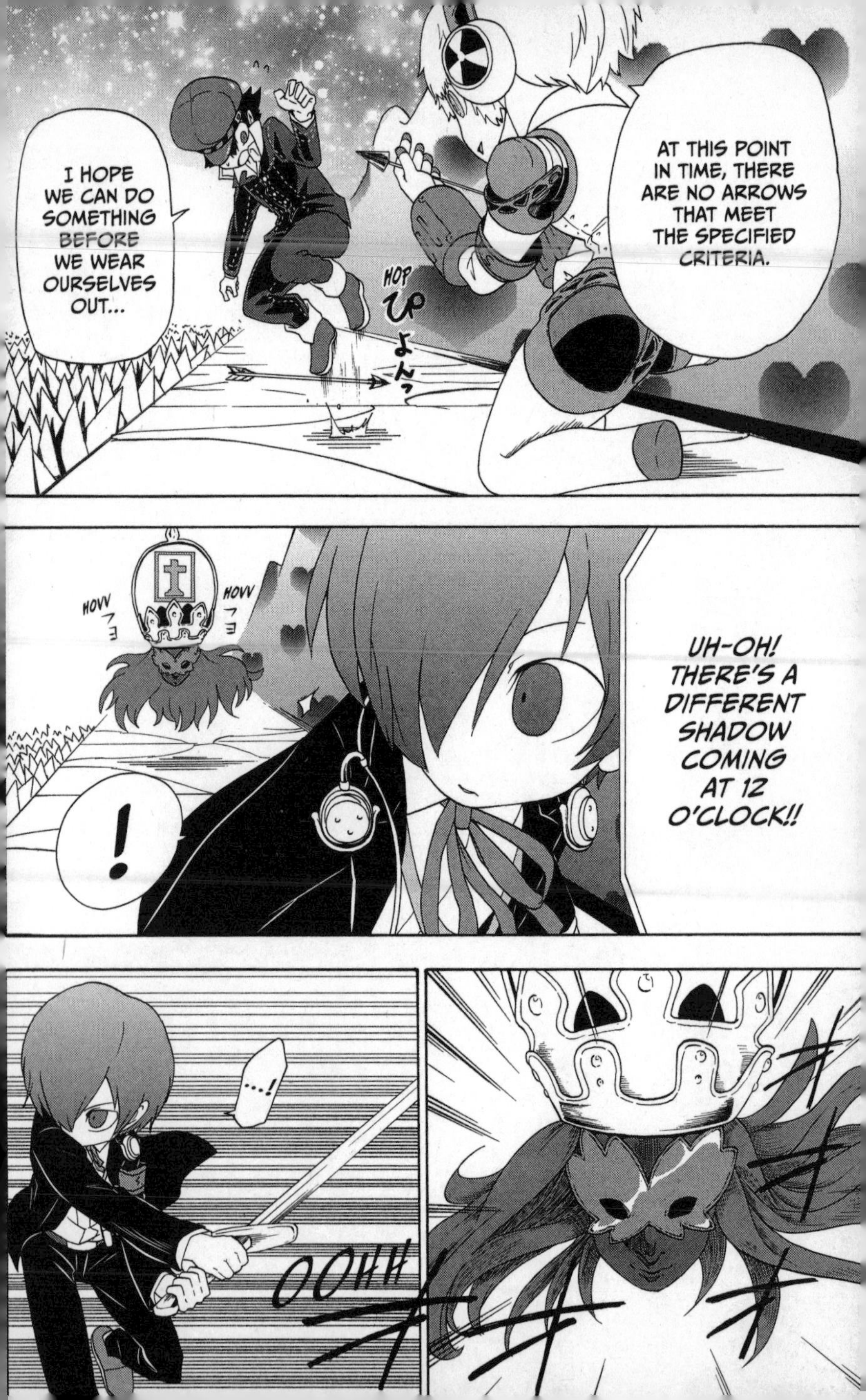
AT THIS POINT IN TIME, THERE ARE NO ARROWS THAT MEET THE SPECIFIED CRITERIA.
HOP
ぴょんっ
I HOPE WE CAN DO SOMETHING BEFORE WE WEAR OURSELVES OUT...
UH-OH! THERE'S A DIFFERENT SHADOW COMING AT 12 O'CLOCK!!
HOVV
HOVV
!
...!
OOHH

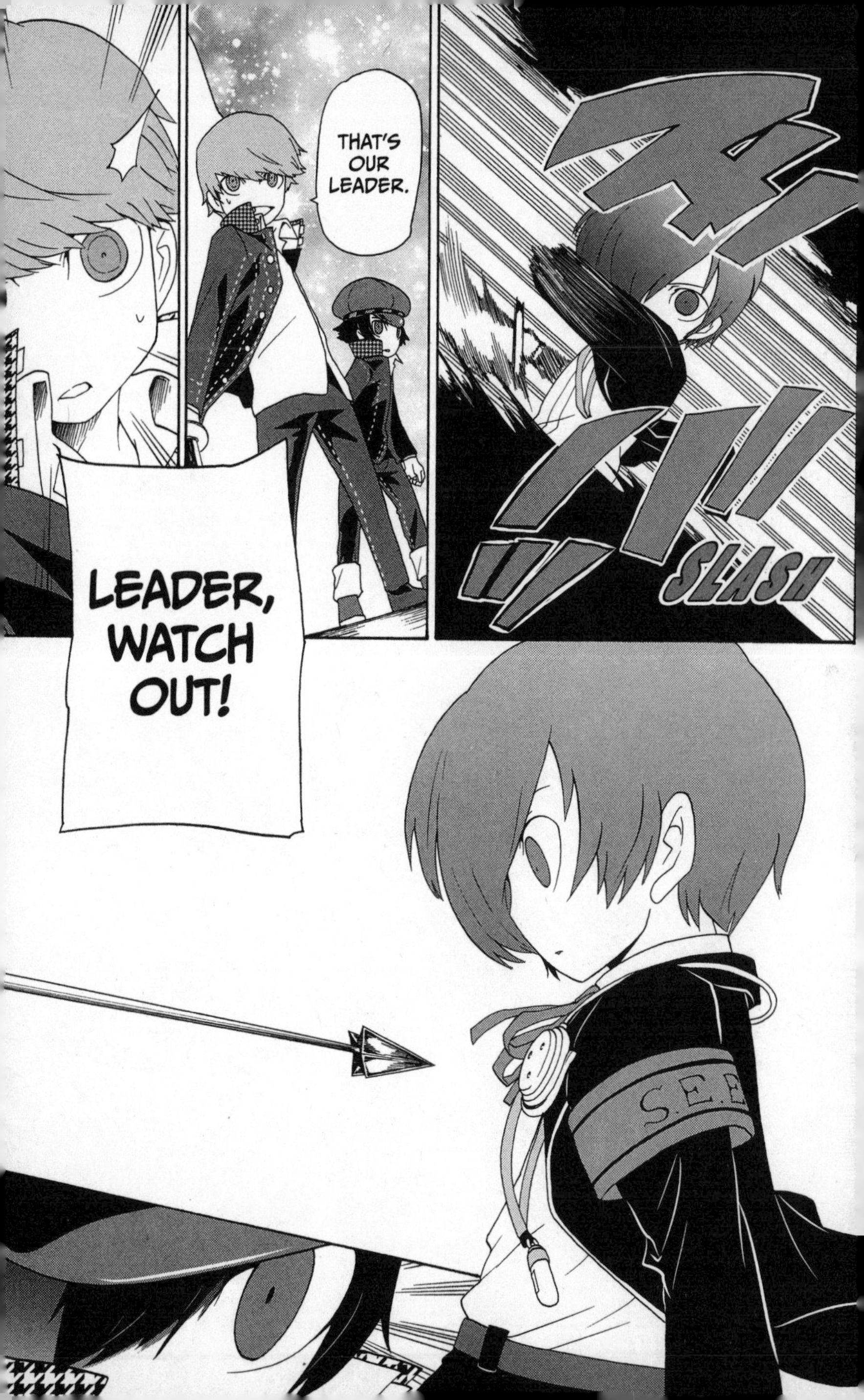
SLASH
THAT'S OUR LEADER.
LEADER, WATCH OUT!

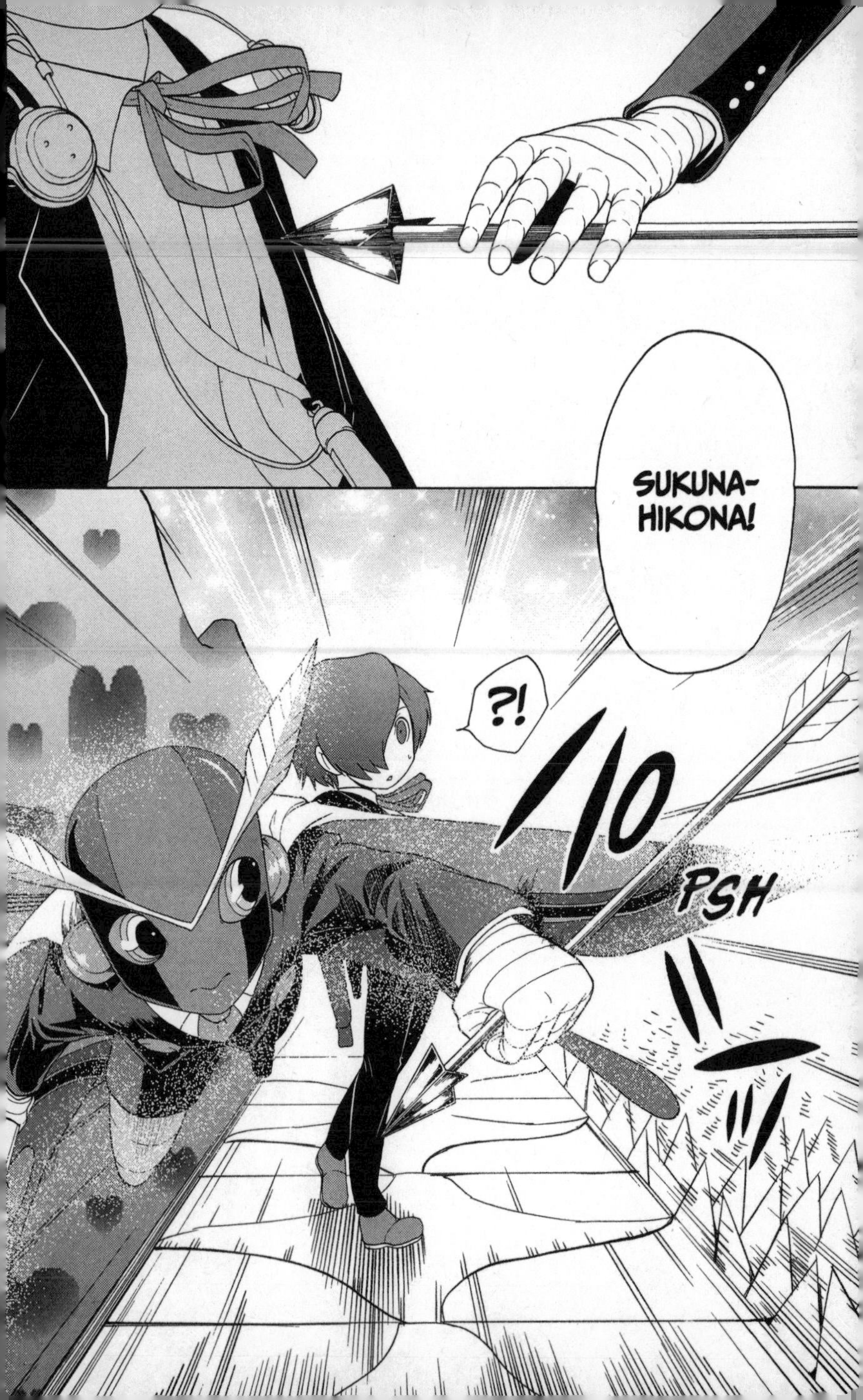
SUKUNA-HIKONA!
?!
PSH

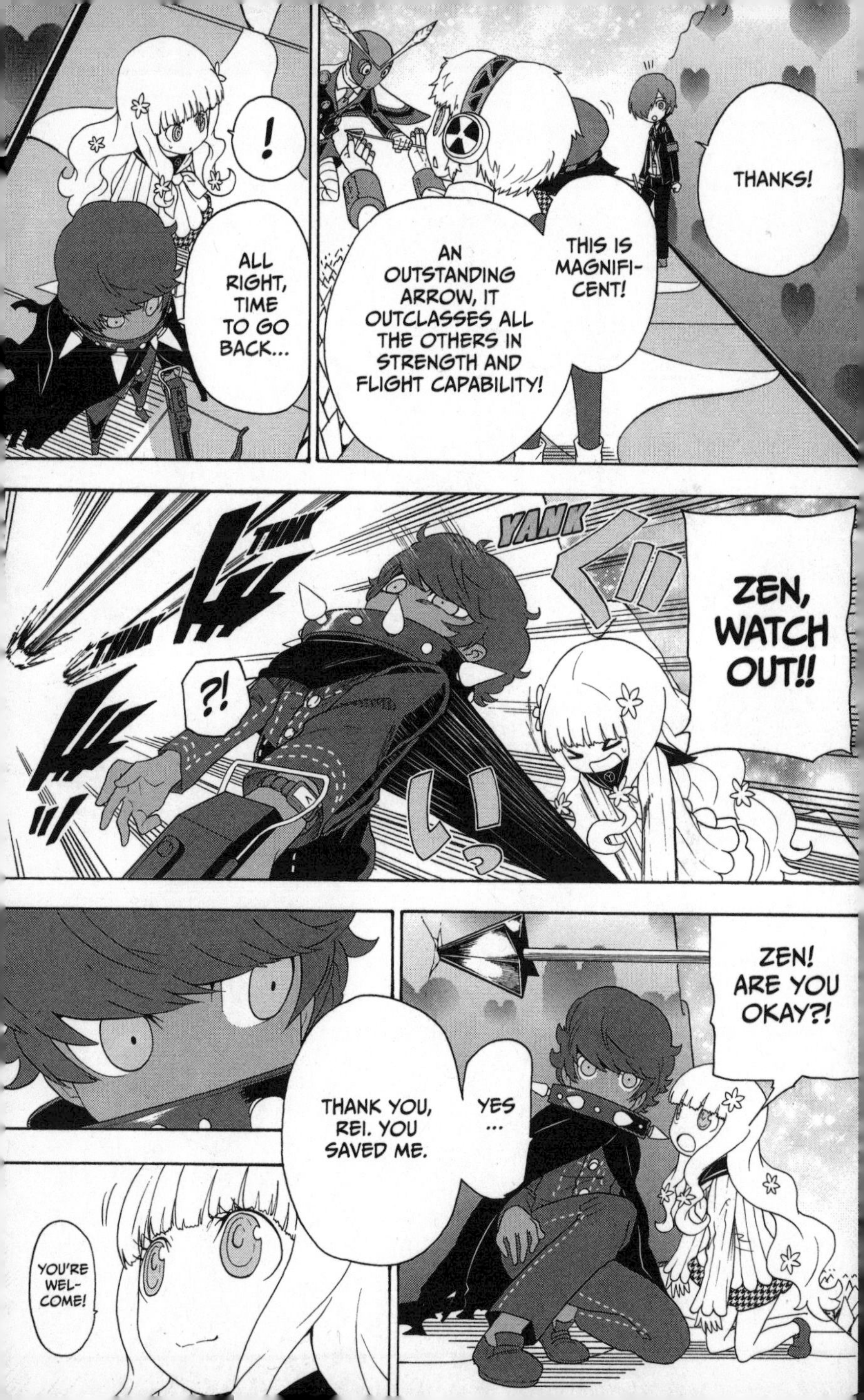
THANKS!
THIS IS MAGNIFI-CENT!
AN OUTSTANDING ARROW, IT OUTCLASSES ALL THE OTHERS IN STRENGTH AND FLIGHT CAPABILITY!
!
ALL RIGHT, TIME TO GO BACK...
ZEN, WATCH OUT!!
YANK
THNK
THNK
?!
ZEN! ARE YOU OKAY?!
YES...
THANK YOU, REI. YOU SAVED ME.
YOU'RE WEL-COME!

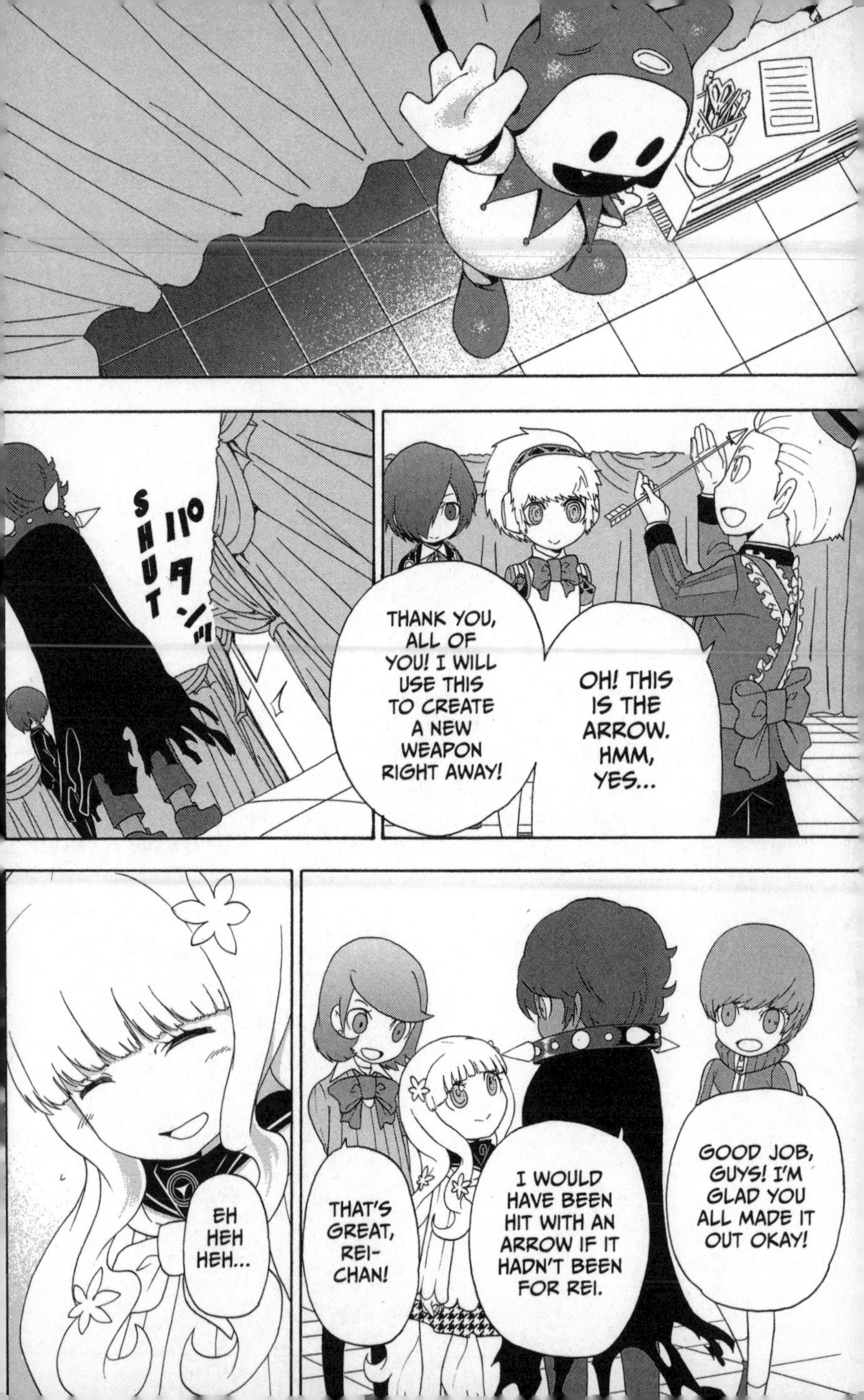
OH! THIS IS THE ARROW. HMM, YES...
THANK YOU, ALL OF YOU! I WILL USE THIS TO CREATE A NEW WEAPON RIGHT AWAY!
SHUT
GOOD JOB, GUYS! I'M GLAD YOU ALL MADE IT OUT OKAY!
I WOULD HAVE BEEN HIT WITH AN ARROW IF IT HADN'T BEEN FOR REI.
THAT'S GREAT, REI-CHAN!
EH HEH HEH...

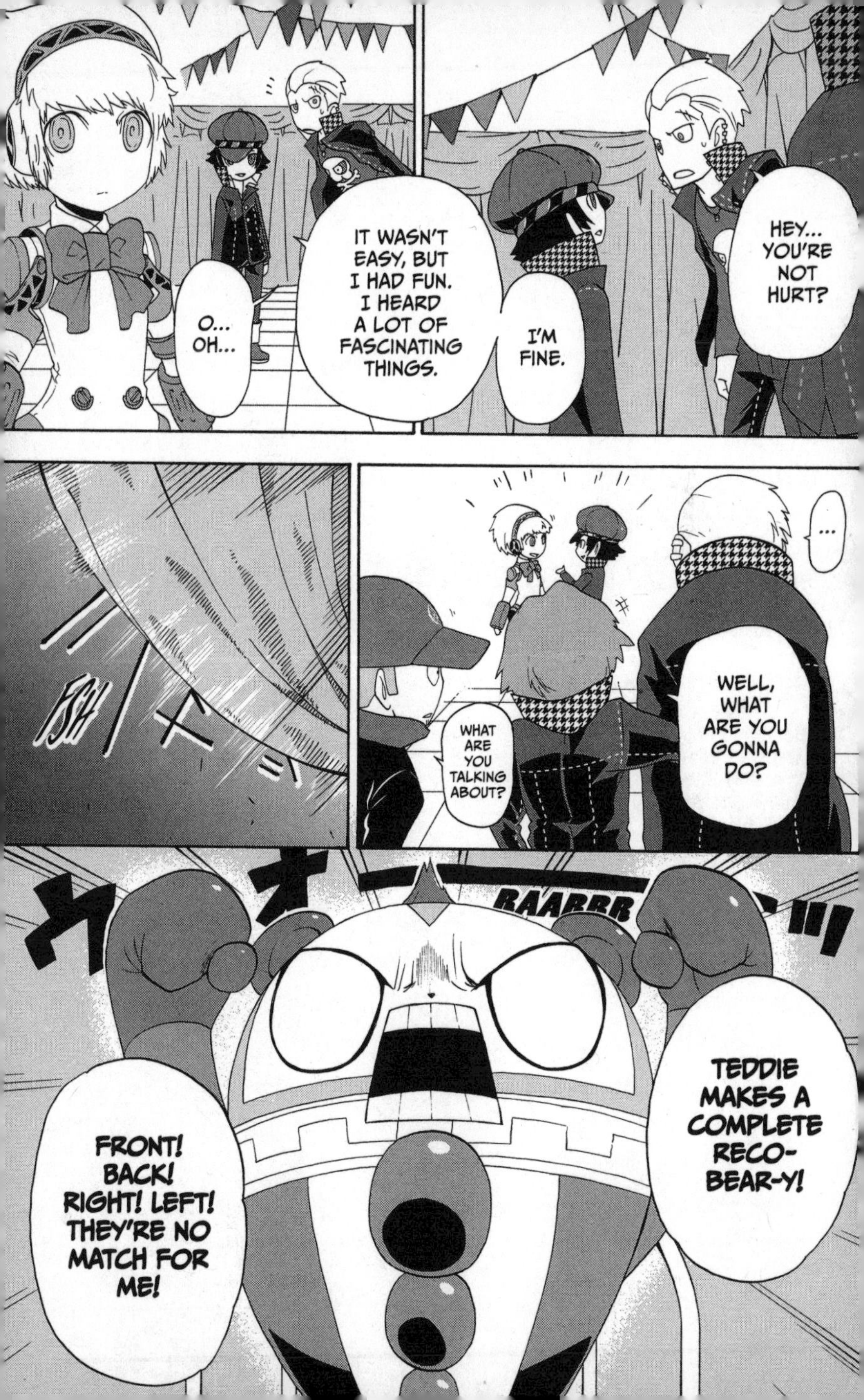
HEY... YOU'RE NOT HURT?
I'M FINE.
IT WASN'T EASY, BUT I HAD FUN. I HEARD A LOT OF FASCINATING THINGS.
O... OH...
...
WELL, WHAT ARE YOU GONNA DO?
WHAT ARE YOU TALKING ABOUT?
FSH
RAARRR
TEDDIE MAKES A COMPLETE RECO-BEAR-Y!
FRONT! BACK! RIGHT! LEFT! THEY'RE NO MATCH FOR ME!

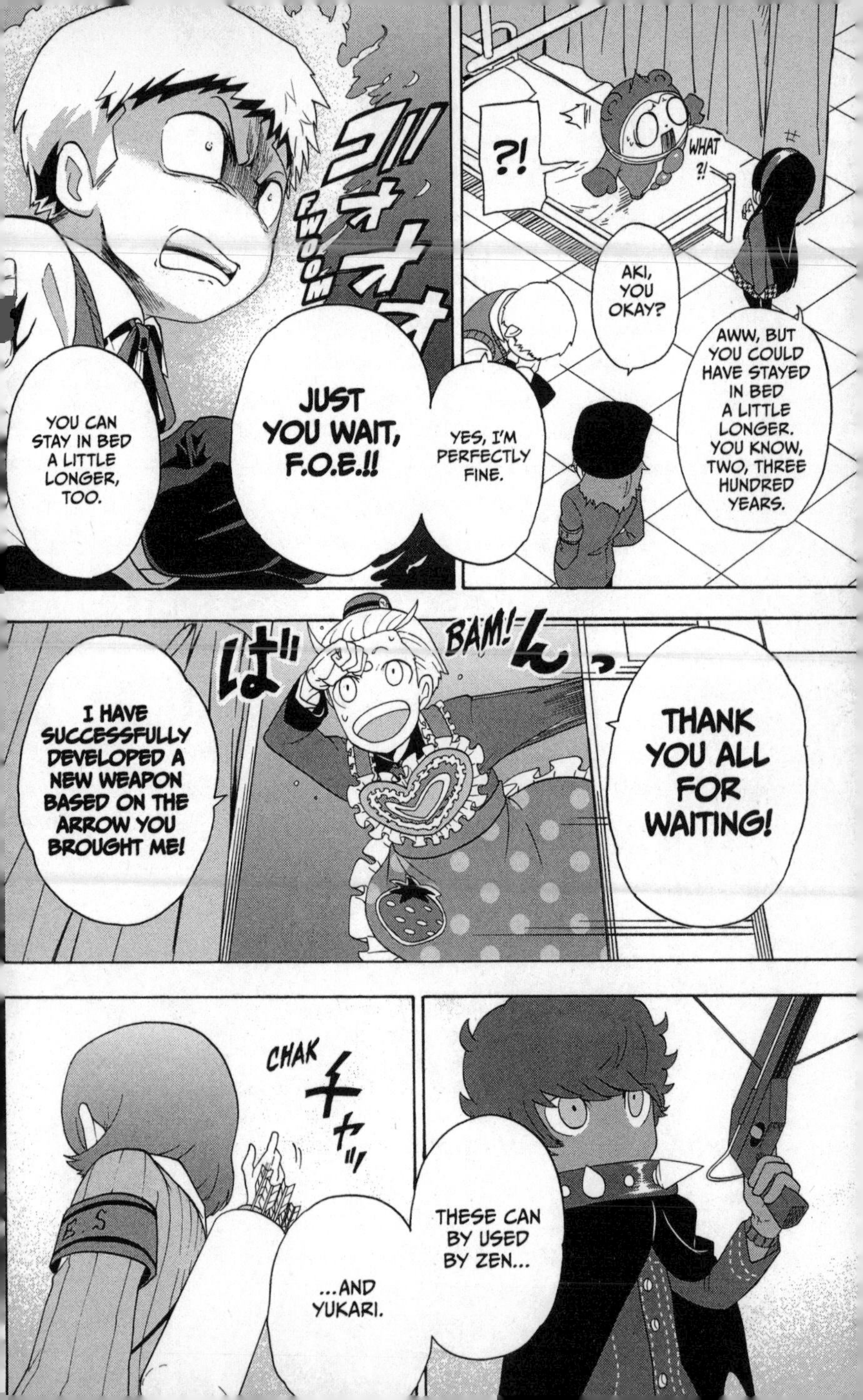
?!
WHAT ?!
AKI, YOU OKAY?
AWW, BUT YOU COULD HAVE STAYED IN BED A LITTLE LONGER. YOU KNOW, TWO, THREE HUNDRED YEARS.
YES, I'M PERFECTLY FINE.
FWOOM
JUST YOU WAIT, F.O.E.!!
YOU CAN STAY IN BED A LITTLE LONGER, TOO.
BAM!
THANK YOU ALL FOR WAITING!
I HAVE SUCCESSFULLY DEVELOPED A NEW WEAPON BASED ON THE ARROW YOU BROUGHT ME!
THESE CAN BY USED BY ZEN...
CHAK
...AND YUKARI.

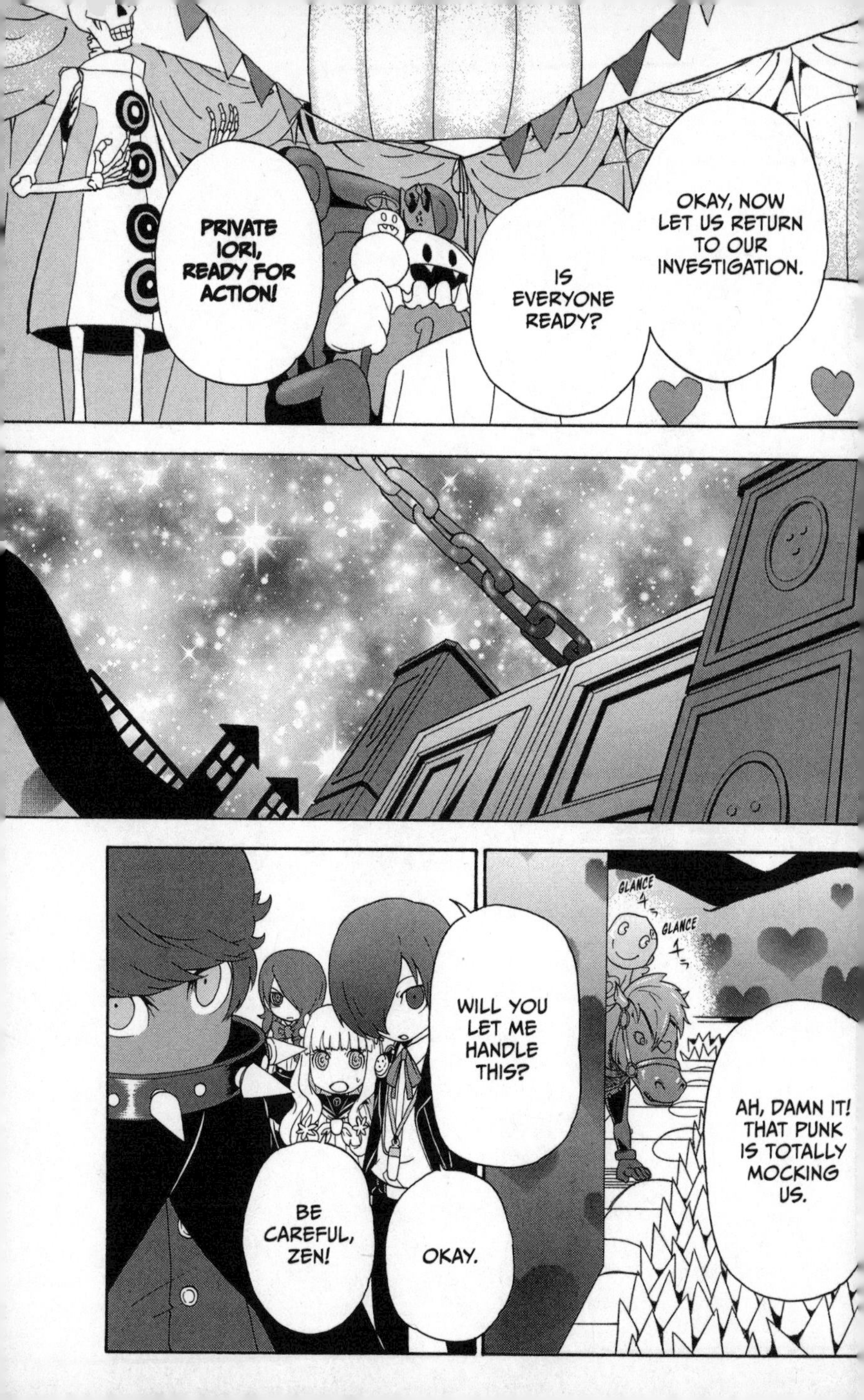
OKAY, NOW LET US RETURN TO OUR INVESTIGATION.
IS EVERYONE READY?
PRIVATE IORI, READY FOR ACTION!
GLANCE
GLANCE
AH, DAMN IT! THAT PUNK IS TOTALLY MOCKING US.
WILL YOU LET ME HANDLE THIS?
OKAY.
BE CAREFUL, ZEN!

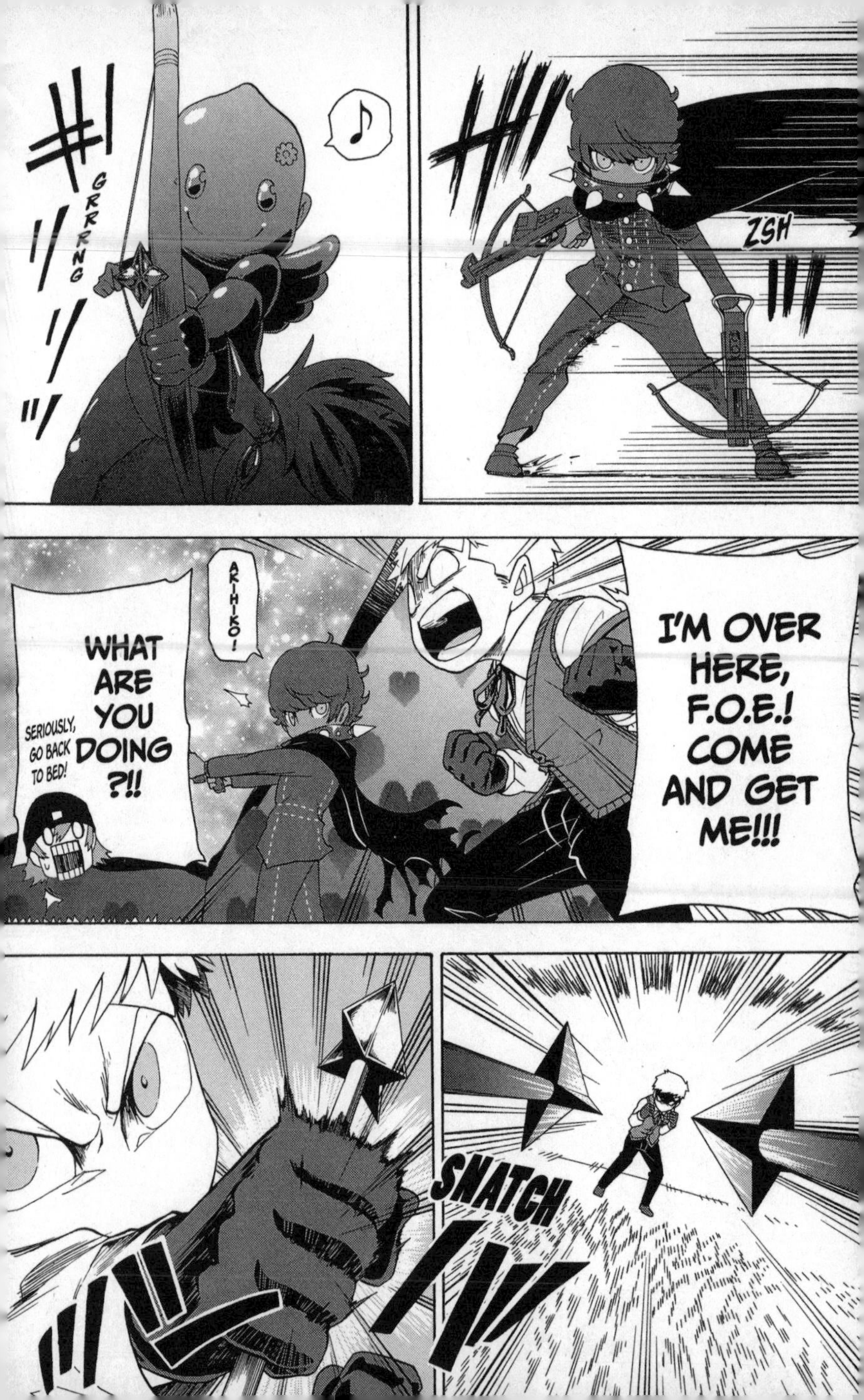
ZSH
♪
GRRRNG
I'M OVER HERE, F.O.E.! COME AND GET ME!!!
AKIHIKO!
WHAT ARE YOU DOING?!!
SERIOUSLY, GO BACK TO BED!
SNATCH

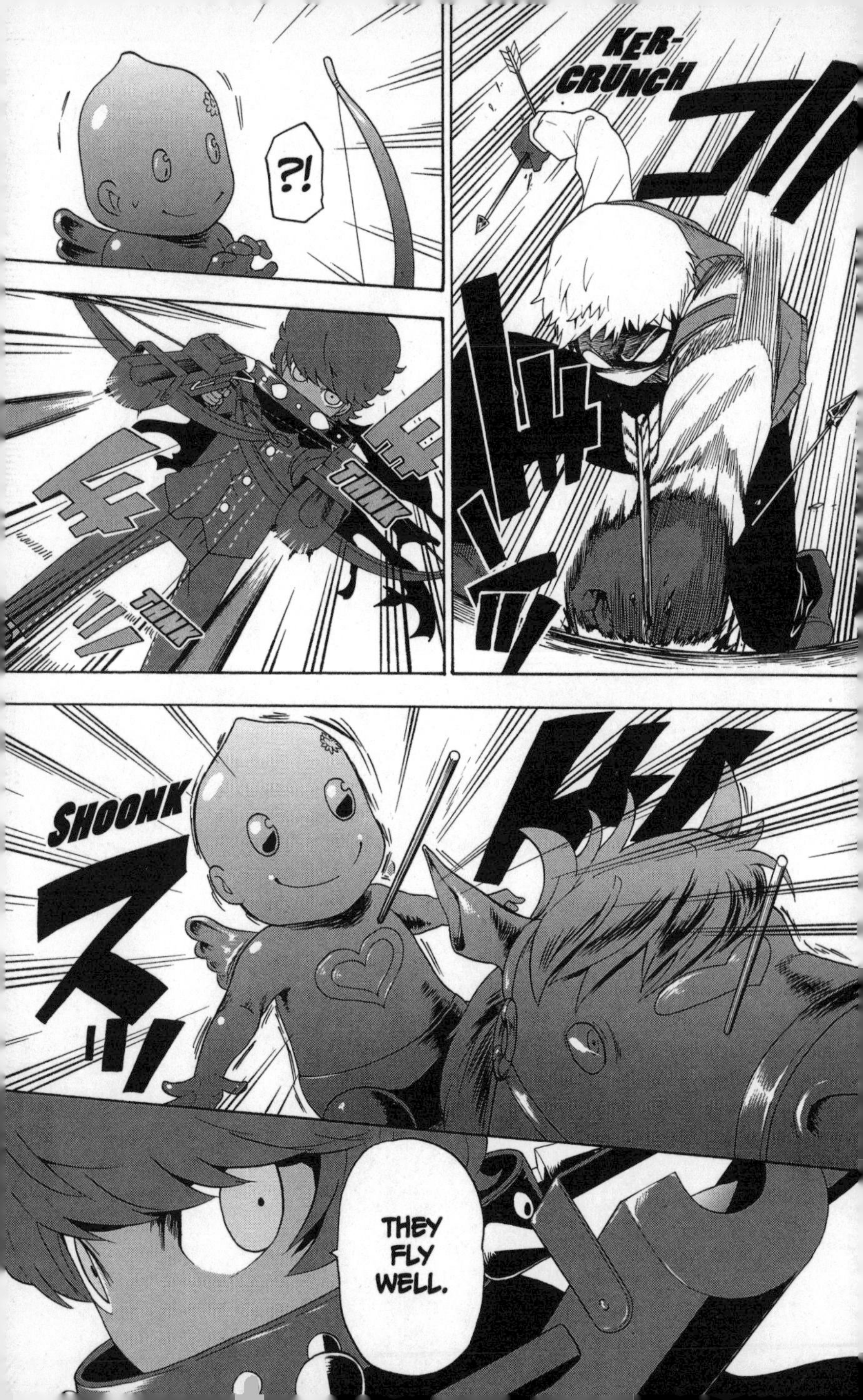
KER-CRUNCH
?!
THUNK
THUNK
SHOONK
THEY FLY WELL.

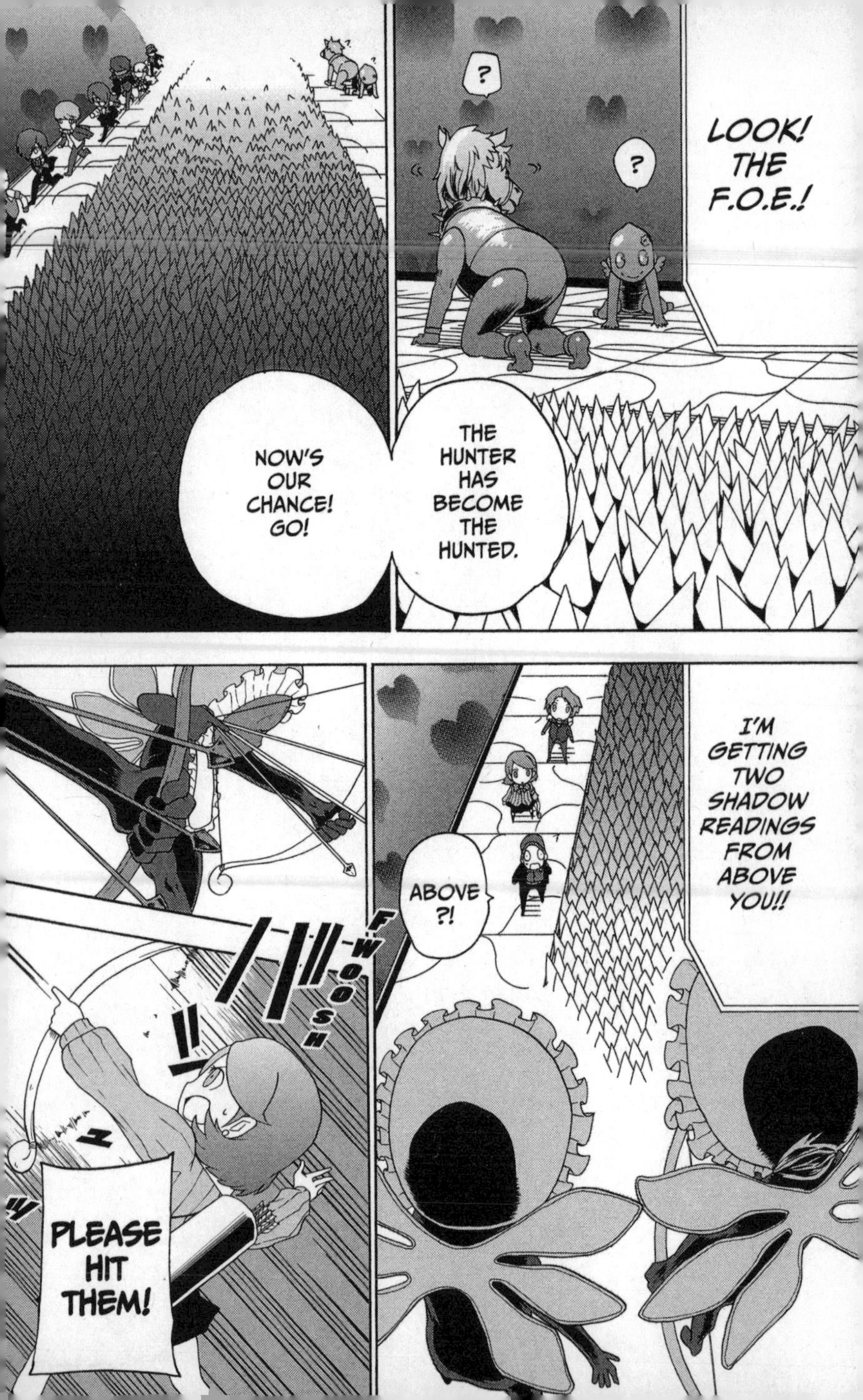
LOOK! THE F.O.E.!
?
?
THE HUNTER HAS BECOME THE HUNTED.
NOW'S OUR CHANCE! GO!
I'M GETTING TWO SHADOW READINGS FROM ABOVE YOU!!
ABOVE ?!
FWOOSH
PLEASE HIT THEM!

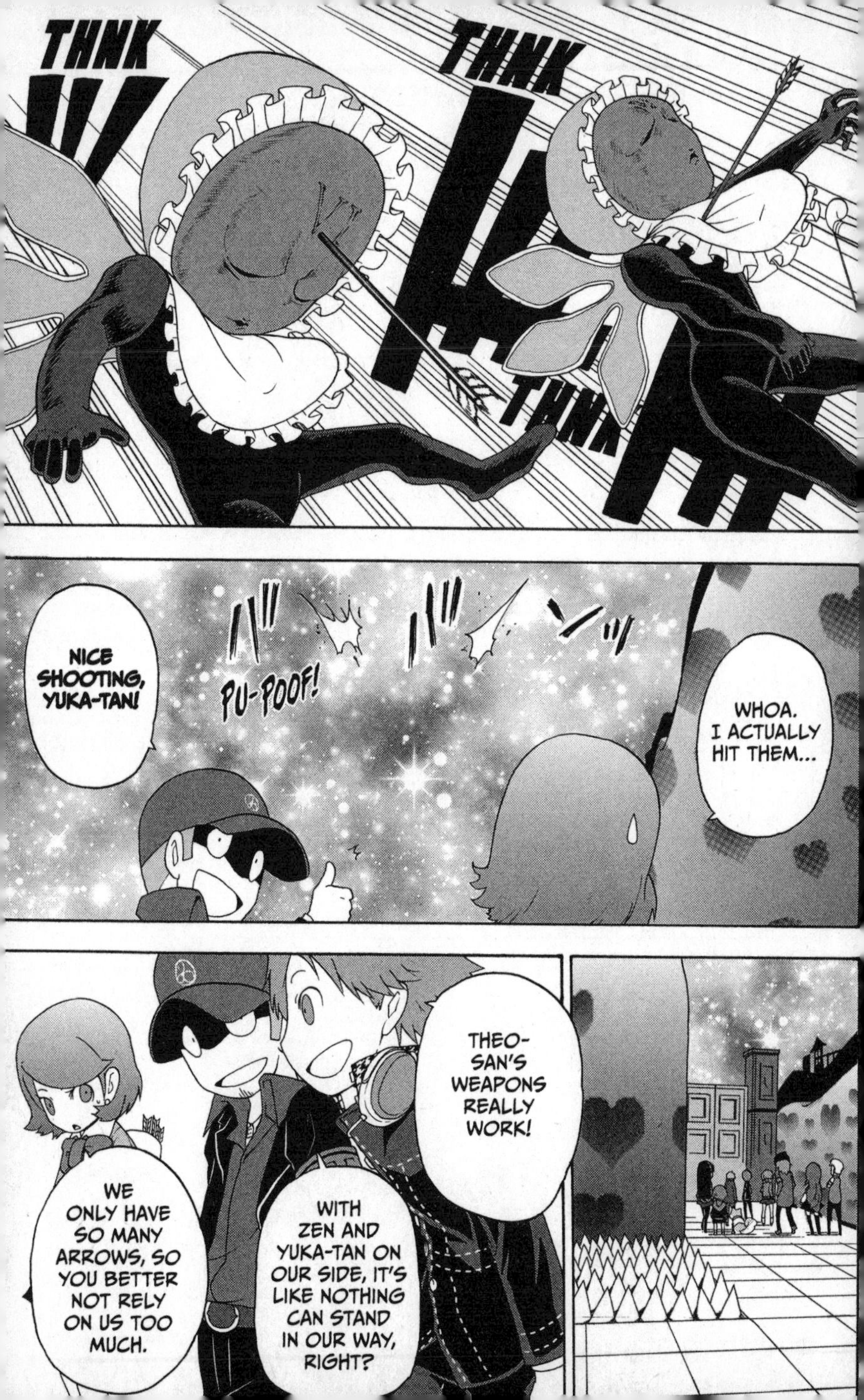
THNK
THNK
THNK
WHOA. I ACTUALLY HIT THEM...
PU-POOF!
NICE SHOOTING, YUKA-TAN!
THEO-SAN'S WEAPONS REALLY WORK!
WITH ZEN AND YUKA-TAN ON OUR SIDE, IT'S LIKE NOTHING CAN STAND IN OUR WAY, RIGHT?
WE ONLY HAVE SO MANY ARROWS, SO YOU BETTER NOT RELY ON US TOO MUCH.

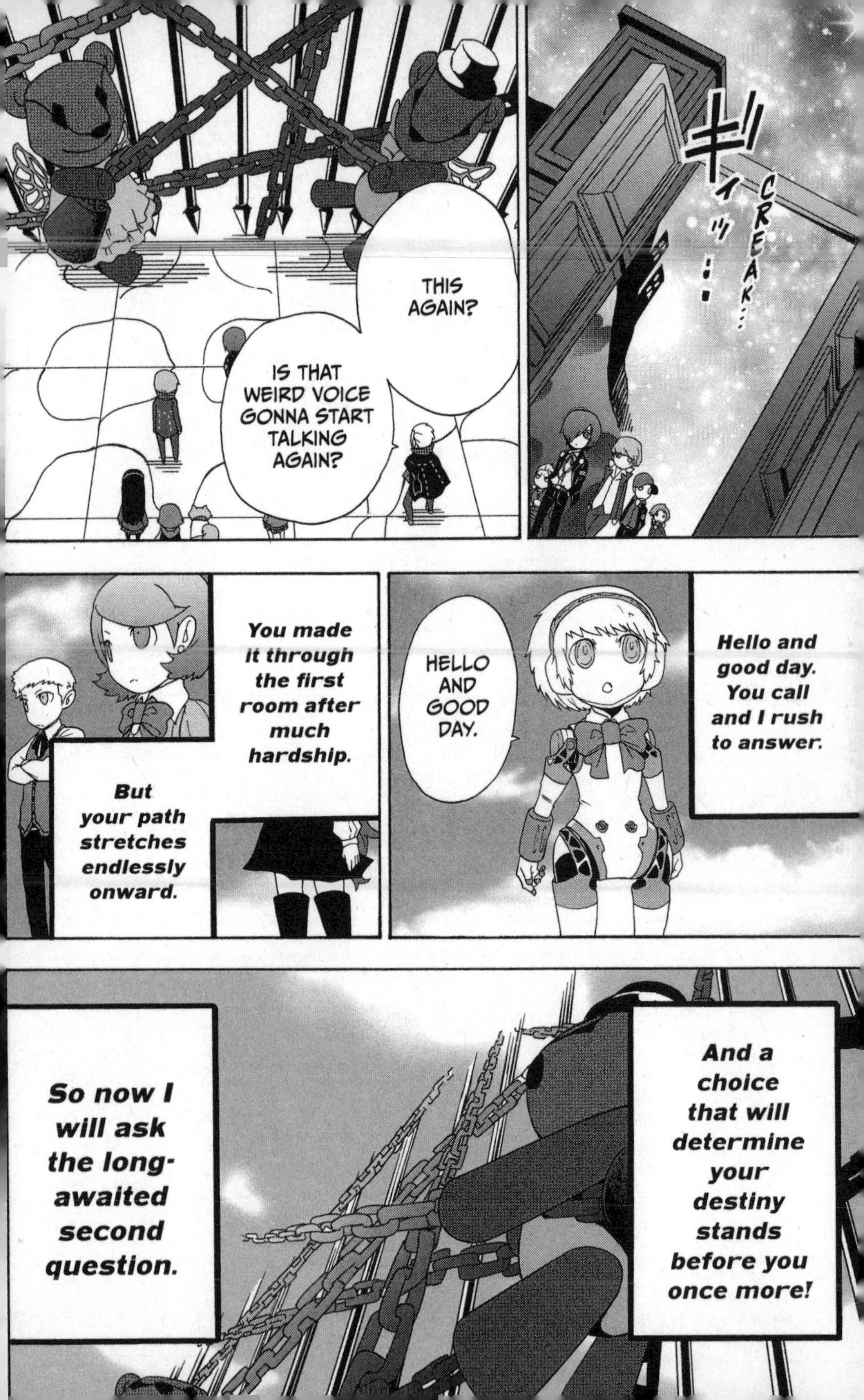
ギイッ…
CREAK…
THIS AGAIN?
IS THAT WEIRD VOICE GONNA START TALKING AGAIN?
Hello and good day. You call and I rush to answer.
HELLO AND GOOD DAY.
You made it through the first room after much hardship.
But your path stretches endlessly onward.
And a choice that will determine your destiny stands before you once more!
So now I will ask the long-awaited second question.

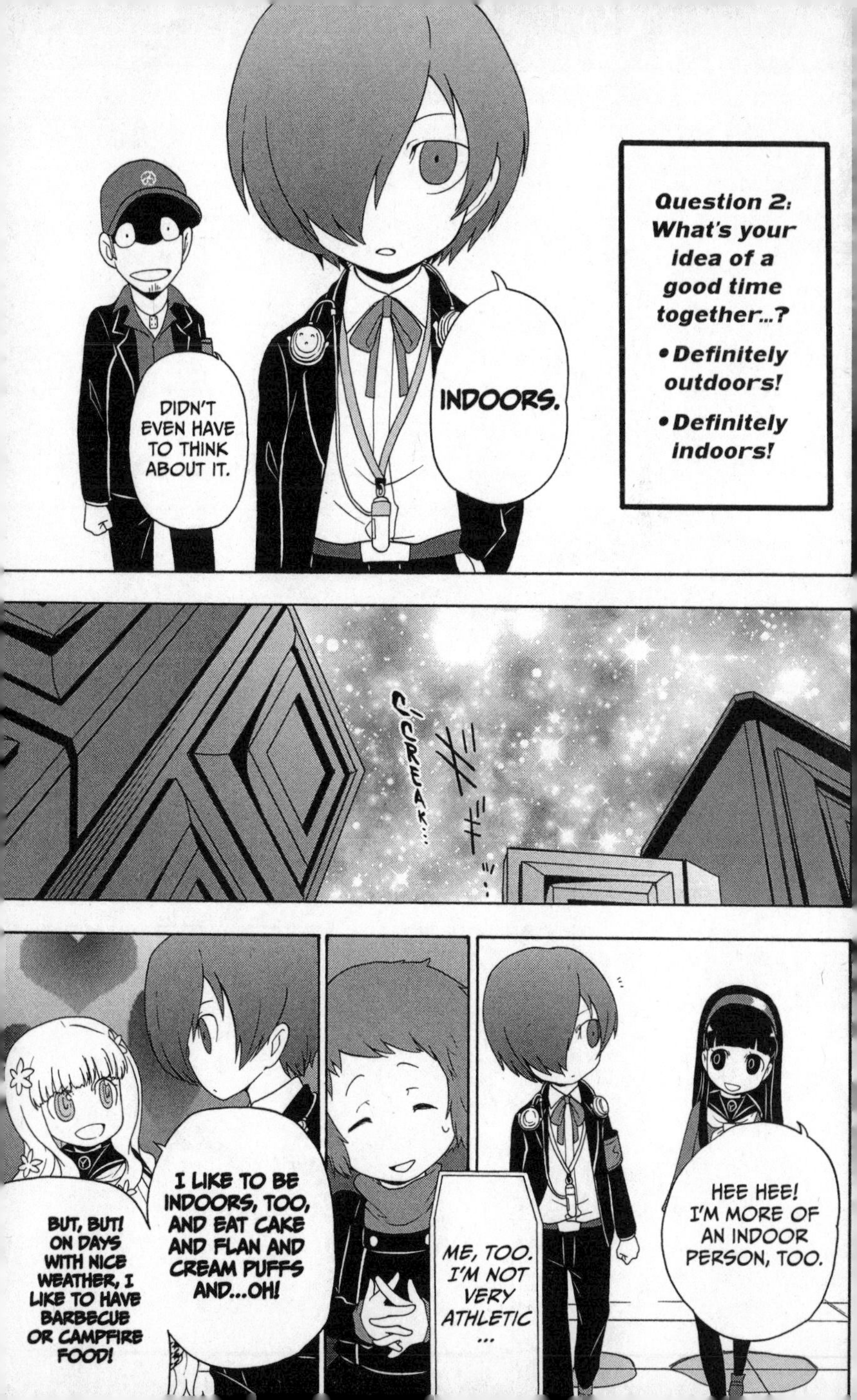
Question 2: What's your idea of a good time together...?
• Definitely outdoors!
• Definitely indoors!
INDOORS.
DIDN'T EVEN HAVE TO THINK ABOUT IT.
CREAK...
HEE HEE! I'M MORE OF AN INDOOR PERSON, TOO.
ME, TOO. I'M NOT VERY ATHLETIC ...
I LIKE TO BE INDOORS, TOO, AND EAT CAKE AND FLAN AND CREAM PUFFS AND...OH!
BUT, BUT! ON DAYS WITH NICE WEATHER, I LIKE TO HAVE BARBECUE OR CAMPFIRE FOOD!

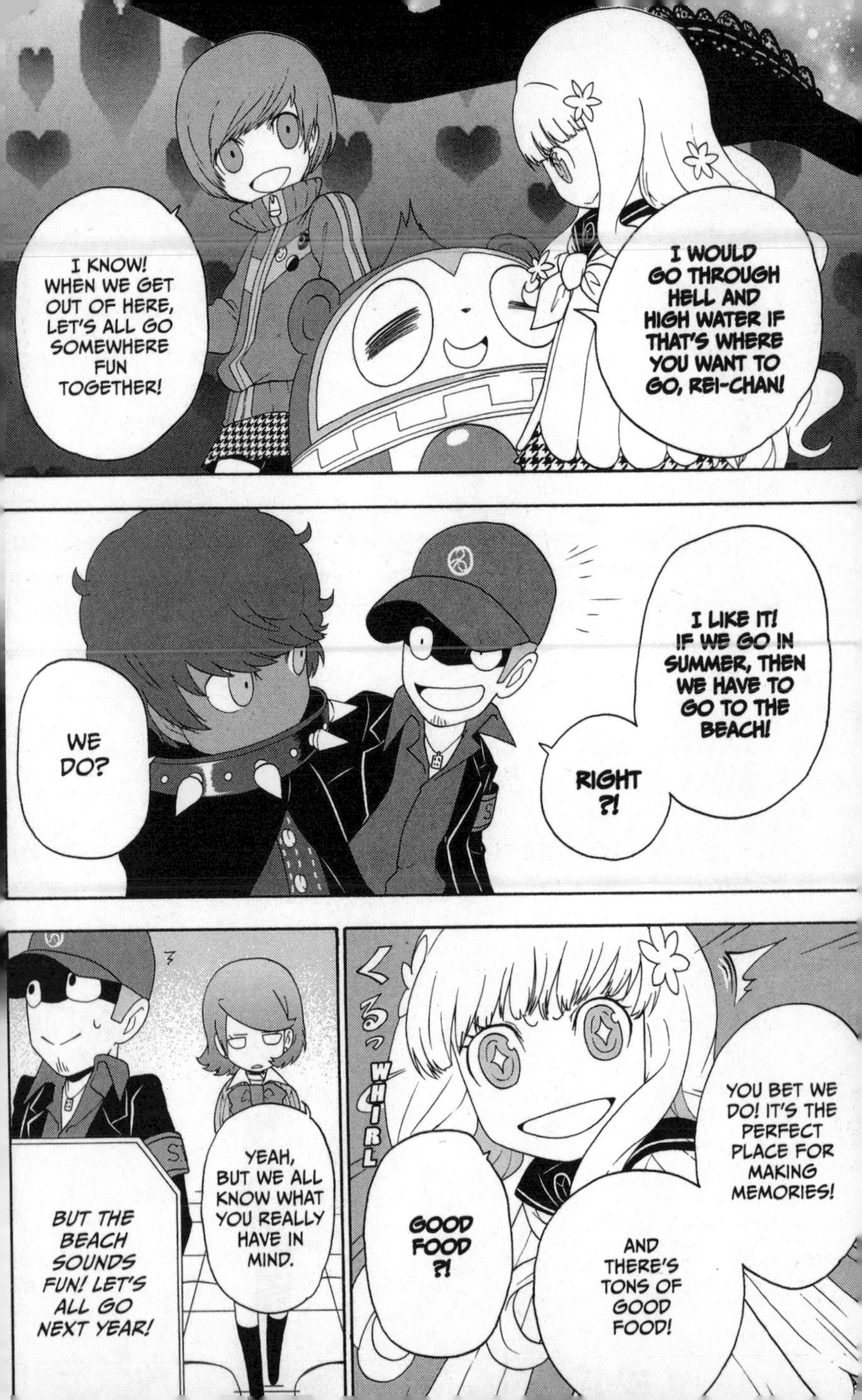
I WOULD GO THROUGH HELL AND HIGH WATER IF THAT'S WHERE YOU WANT TO GO, REI-CHAN!
I KNOW! WHEN WE GET OUT OF HERE, LET'S ALL GO SOMEWHERE FUN TOGETHER!
I LIKE IT! IF WE GO IN SUMMER, THEN WE HAVE TO GO TO THE BEACH!
RIGHT?!
WE DO?
YOU BET WE DO! IT'S THE PERFECT PLACE FOR MAKING MEMORIES!
AND THERE'S TONS OF GOOD FOOD!
くるっ WHIRL
GOOD FOOD?!
YEAH, BUT WE ALL KNOW WHAT YOU REALLY HAVE IN MIND.
BUT THE BEACH SOUNDS FUN! LET'S ALL GO NEXT YEAR!

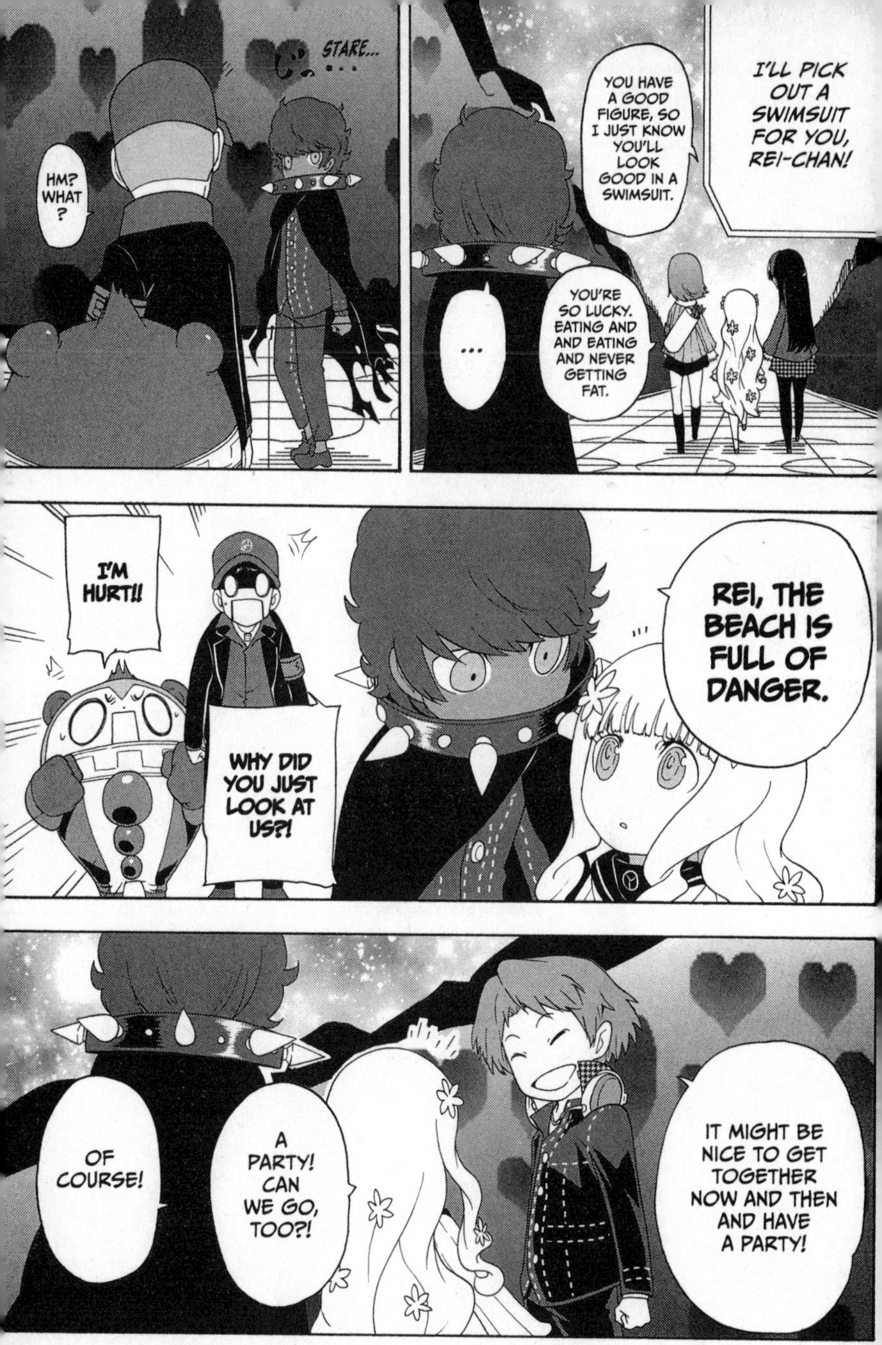
I'LL PICK OUT A SWIMSUIT FOR YOU, REI-CHAN!
YOU HAVE A GOOD FIGURE, SO I JUST KNOW YOU'LL LOOK GOOD IN A SWIMSUIT.
YOU'RE SO LUCKY. EATING AND AND EATING AND NEVER GETTING FAT.
...
STARE...
HM? WHAT?
REI, THE BEACH IS FULL OF DANGER.
WHY DID YOU JUST LOOK AT US?!
I'M HURT!!
IT MIGHT BE NICE TO GET TOGETHER NOW AND THEN AND HAVE A PARTY!
A PARTY! CAN WE GO, TOO?!
OF COURSE!

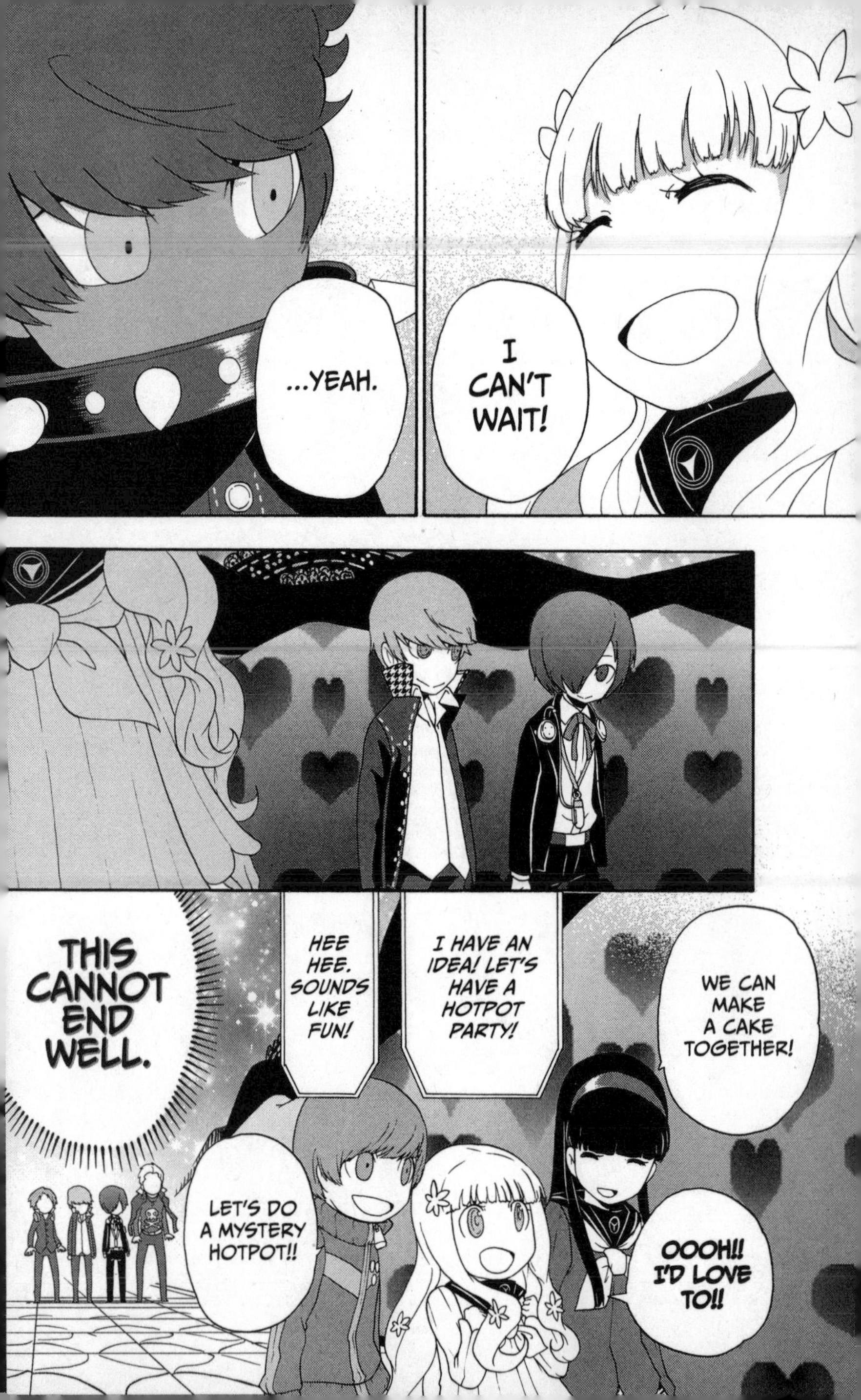
I CAN'T WAIT!
...YEAH.
WE CAN MAKE A CAKE TOGETHER!
OOOH!! I'D LOVE TO!!
I HAVE AN IDEA! LET'S HAVE A HOTPOT PARTY!
HEE HEE. SOUNDS LIKE FUN!
LET'S DO A MYSTERY HOTPOT!!
THIS CANNOT END WELL.

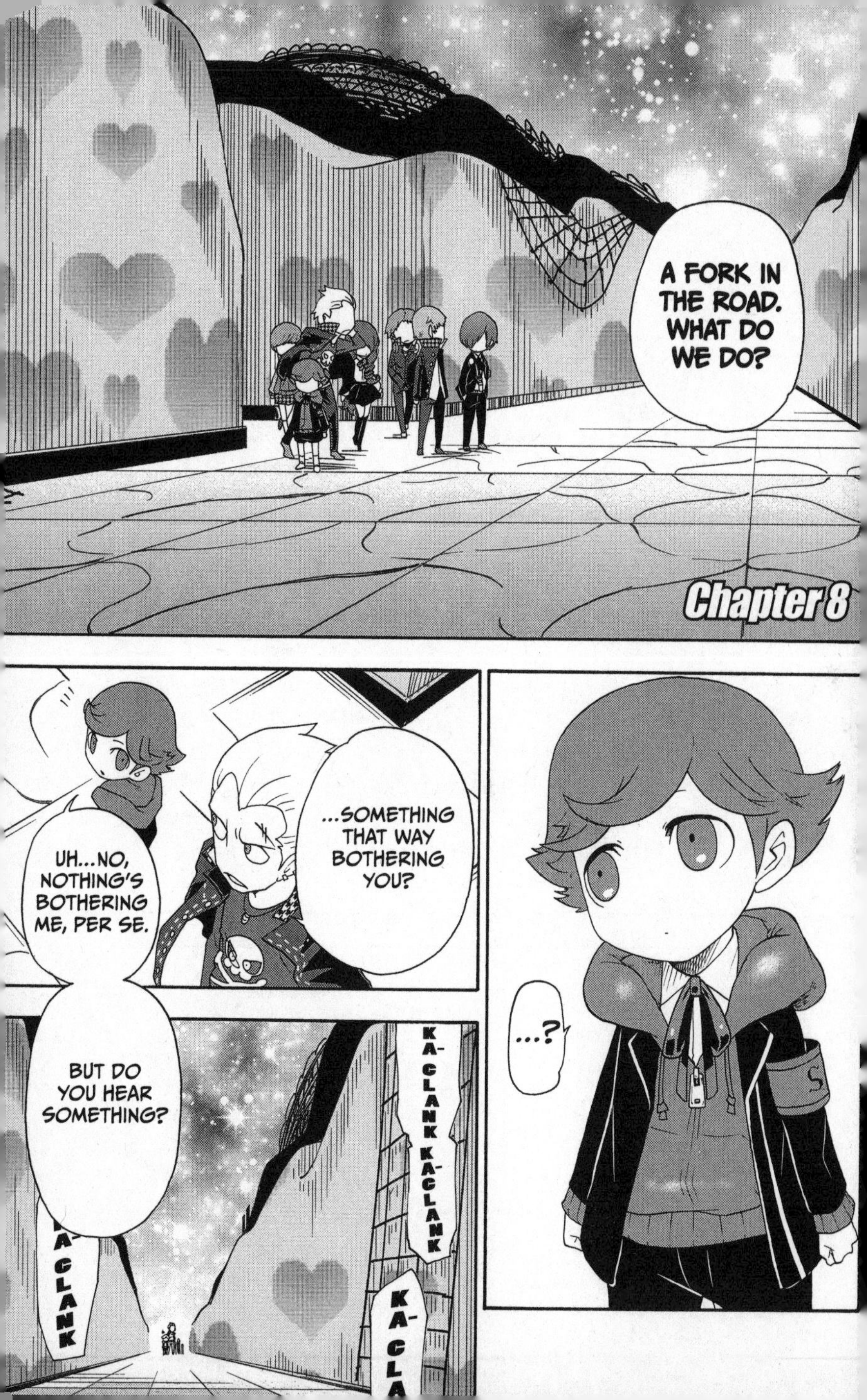
A FORK IN THE ROAD. WHAT DO WE DO?
Chapter 8
...?
...SOMETHING THAT WAY BOTHERING YOU?
UH...NO, NOTHING'S BOTHERING ME, PER SE.
BUT DO YOU HEAR SOMETHING?
KA-CLANK KA-CLANK
KA-CLA
KA-CLANK

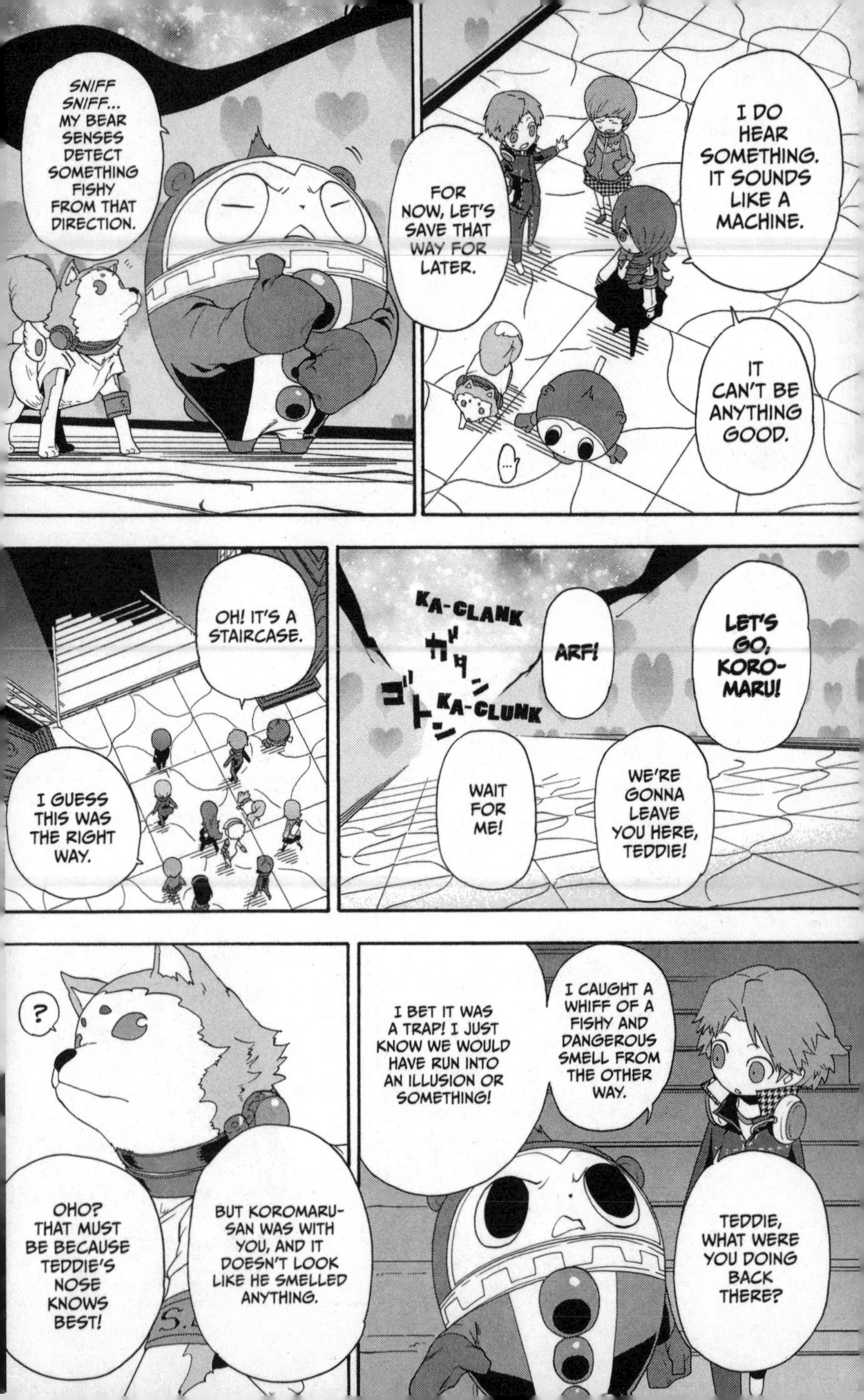
I DO HEAR SOMETHING. IT SOUNDS LIKE A MACHINE.
FOR NOW, LET'S SAVE THAT WAY FOR LATER.
IT CAN'T BE ANYTHING GOOD.
...
SNIFF SNIFF... MY BEAR SENSES DETECT SOMETHING FISHY FROM THAT DIRECTION.
LET'S GO, KORO-MARU!
ARF!
KA-CLANK
ガタン
KA-CLUNK
ゴトン
WE'RE GONNA LEAVE YOU HERE, TEDDIE!
WAIT FOR ME!
OH! IT'S A STAIRCASE.
I GUESS THIS WAS THE RIGHT WAY.
TEDDIE, WHAT WERE YOU DOING BACK THERE?
I CAUGHT A WHIFF OF A FISHY AND DANGEROUS SMELL FROM THE OTHER WAY.
I BET IT WAS A TRAP! I JUST KNOW WE WOULD HAVE RUN INTO AN ILLUSION OR SOMETHING!
BUT KOROMARU-SAN WAS WITH YOU, AND IT DOESN'T LOOK LIKE HE SMELLED ANYTHING.
OHO? THAT MUST BE BECAUSE TEDDIE'S NOSE KNOWS BEST!
?

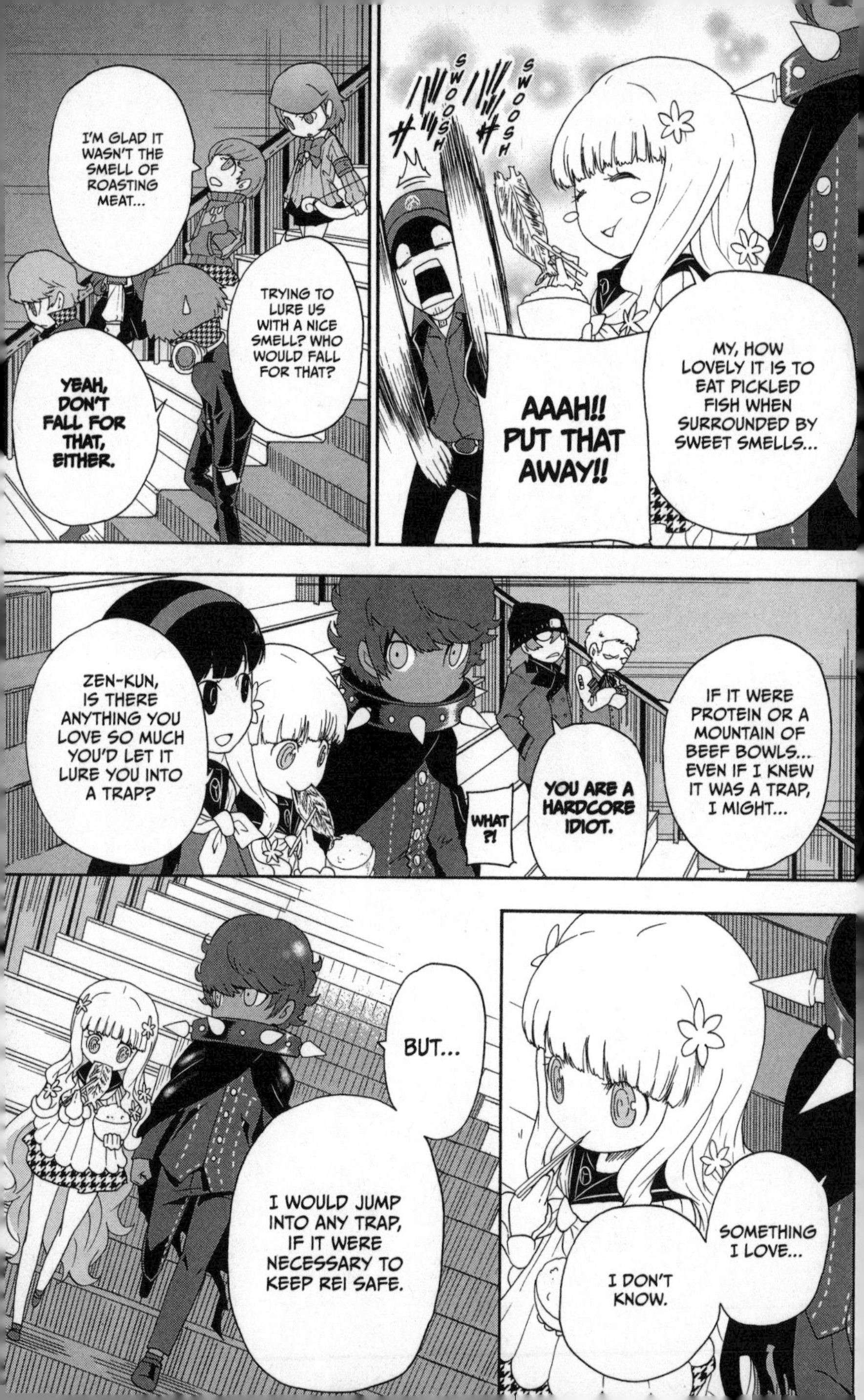
SWOOSH
SWOOSH
MY, HOW LOVELY IT IS TO EAT PICKLED FISH WHEN SURROUNDED BY SWEET SMELLS...
AAAH!! PUT THAT AWAY!!
TRYING TO LURE US WITH A NICE SMELL? WHO WOULD FALL FOR THAT?
I'M GLAD IT WASN'T THE SMELL OF ROASTING MEAT...
YEAH, DON'T FALL FOR THAT, EITHER.
IF IT WERE PROTEIN OR A MOUNTAIN OF BEEF BOWLS... EVEN IF I KNEW IT WAS A TRAP, I MIGHT...
YOU ARE A HARDCORE IDIOT.
WHAT ?!
ZEN-KUN, IS THERE ANYTHING YOU LOVE SO MUCH YOU'D LET IT LURE YOU INTO A TRAP?
SOMETHING I LOVE...
I DON'T KNOW.
BUT...
I WOULD JUMP INTO ANY TRAP, IF IT WERE NECESSARY TO KEEP REI SAFE.

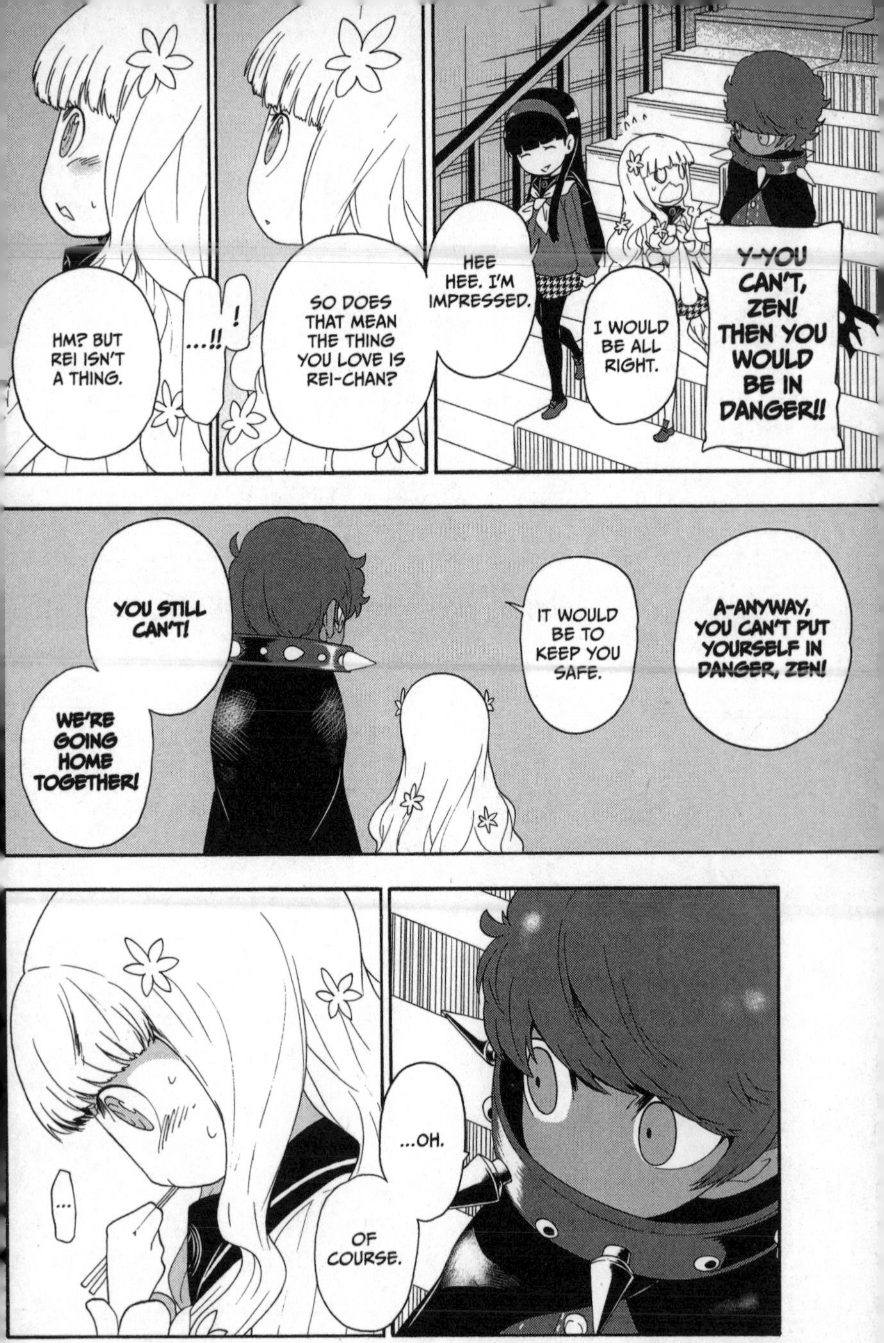
Y-YOU CAN'T, ZEN! THEN YOU WOULD BE IN DANGER!!
I WOULD BE ALL RIGHT.
HEE HEE. I'M IMPRESSED.
SO DOES THAT MEAN THE THING YOU LOVE IS REI-CHAN?
...!!
!
HM? BUT REI ISN'T A THING.
A-ANYWAY, YOU CAN'T PUT YOURSELF IN DANGER, ZEN!
IT WOULD BE TO KEEP YOU SAFE.
YOU STILL CAN'T!
WE'RE GOING HOME TOGETHER!
...OH.
OF COURSE.
...

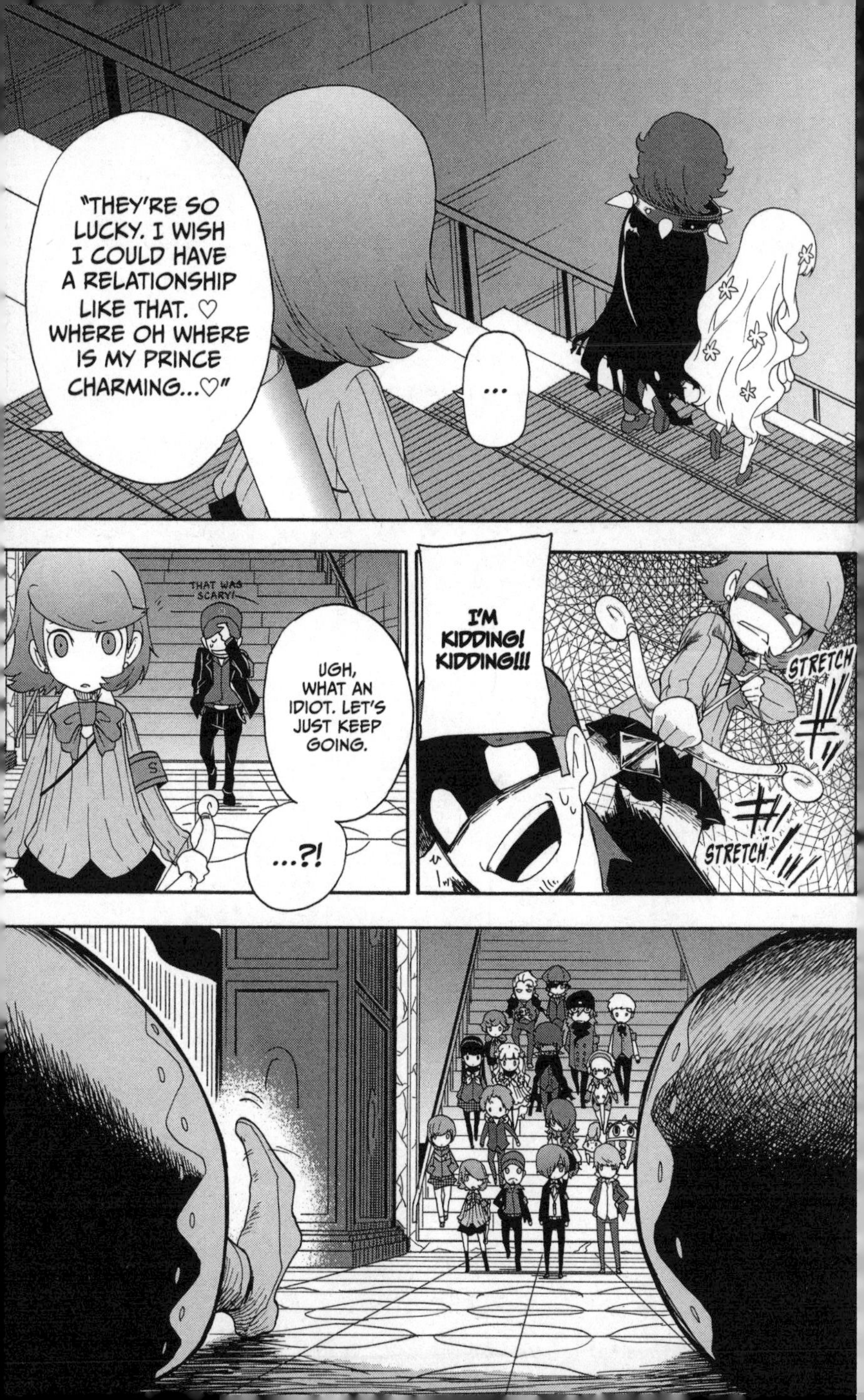
"THEY'RE SO LUCKY. I WISH I COULD HAVE A RELATIONSHIP LIKE THAT. ♡ WHERE OH WHERE IS MY PRINCE CHARMING...♡"
...
I'M KIDDING! KIDDING!!!
STRETCH
STRETCH
THAT WAS SCARY!
UGH, WHAT AN IDIOT. LET'S JUST KEEP GOING.
...?!

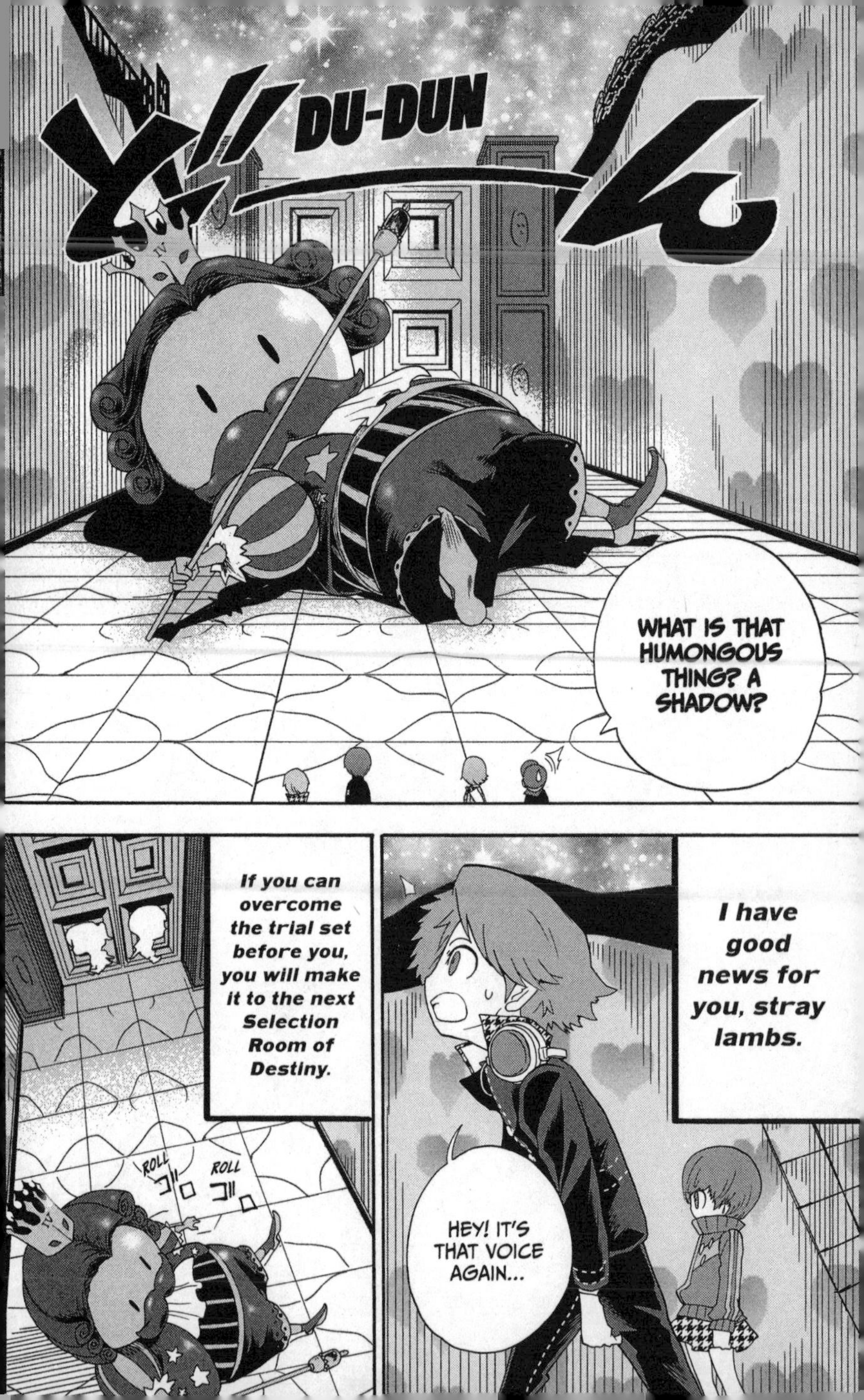
DU-DUN
WHAT IS THAT HUMONGOUS THING? A SHADOW?
I have good news for you, stray lambs.
HEY! IT'S THAT VOICE AGAIN...
If you can overcome the trial set before you, you will make it to the next Selection Room of Destiny.
ROLL
ROLL

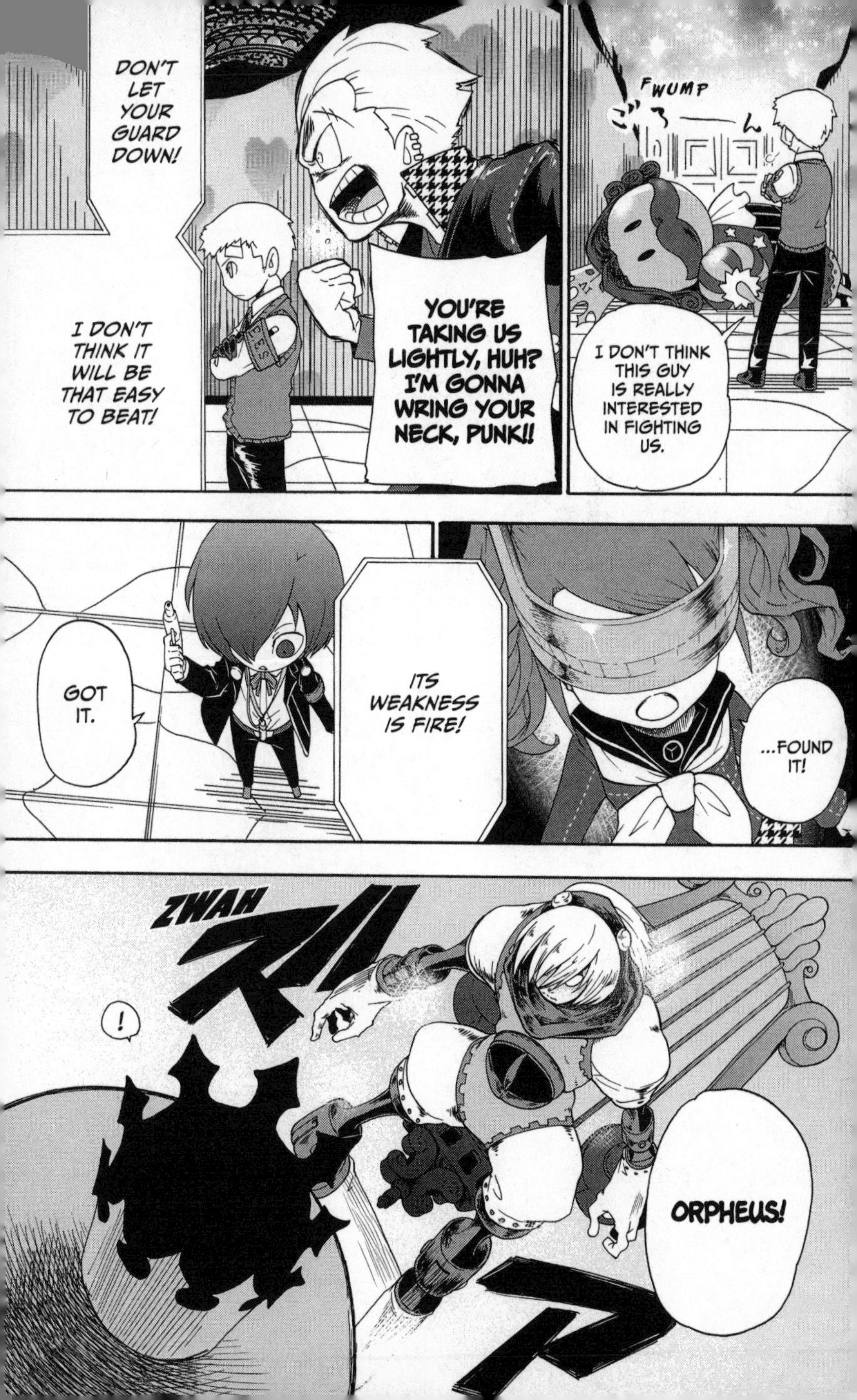
FWUMP
I DON'T THINK THIS GUY IS REALLY INTERESTED IN FIGHTING US.
YOU'RE TAKING US LIGHTLY, HUH? I'M GONNA WRING YOUR NECK, PUNK!!
DON'T LET YOUR GUARD DOWN!
I DON'T THINK IT WILL BE THAT EASY TO BEAT!
...FOUND IT!
ITS WEAKNESS IS FIRE!
GOT IT.
ORPHEUS!
ZWAH
!

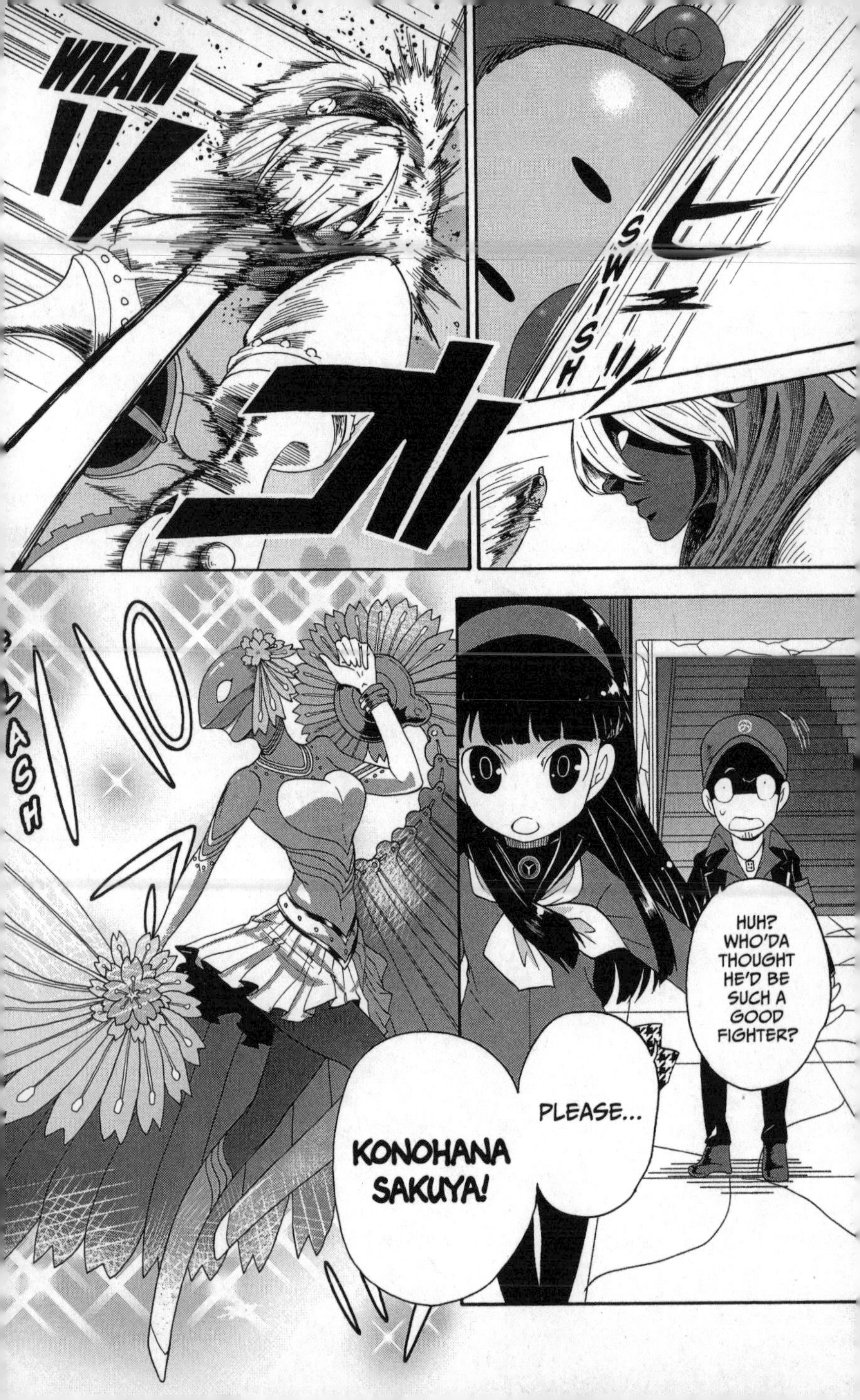
SWISH!!
WHAM!!
HUH? WHO'DA THOUGHT HE'D BE SUCH A GOOD FIGHTER?
PLEASE... KONOHANA SAKUYA!

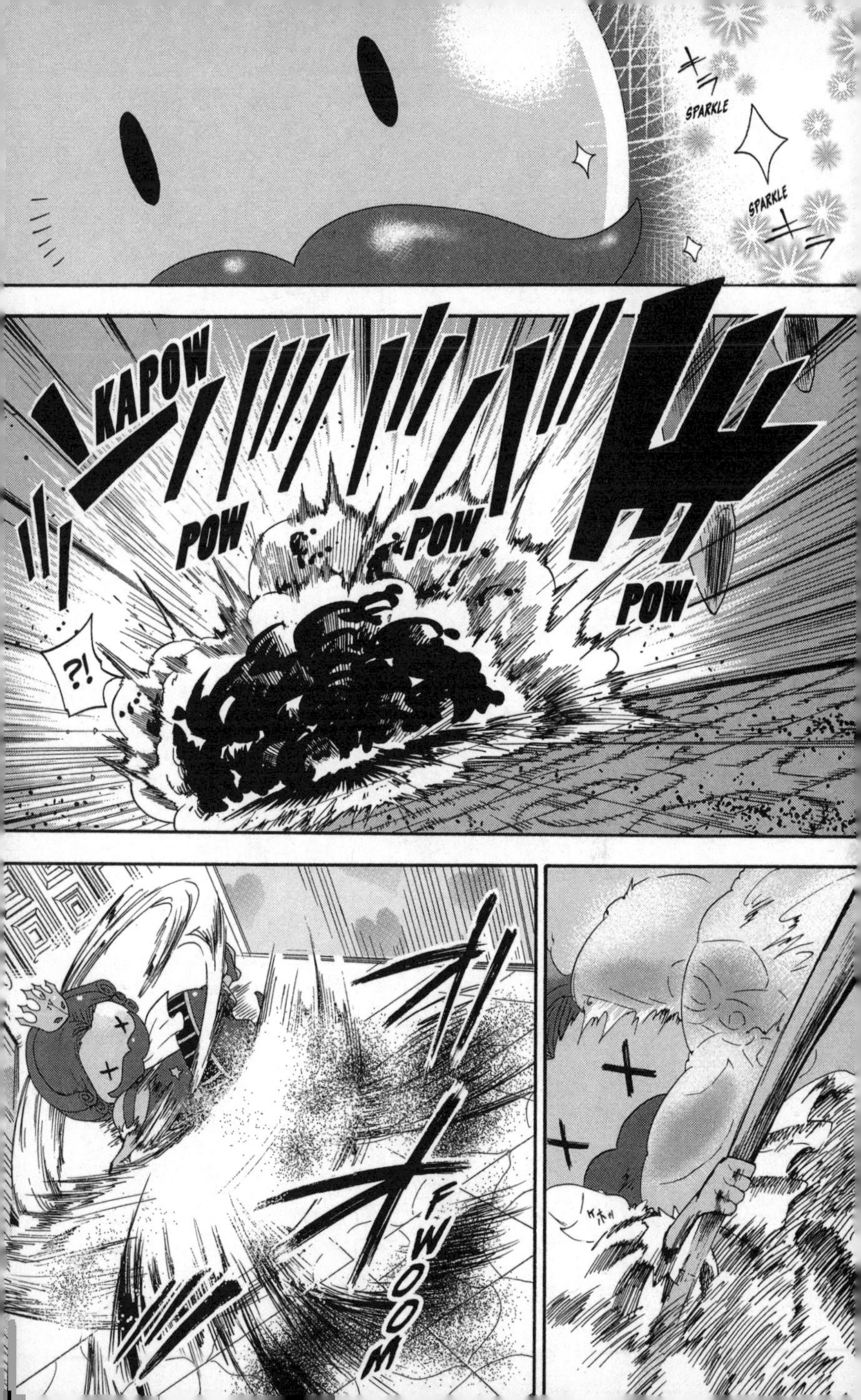
キラ
SPARKLE
SPARKLE
キラ
KAPOW
POW
POW
POW
?!
FWOOOM

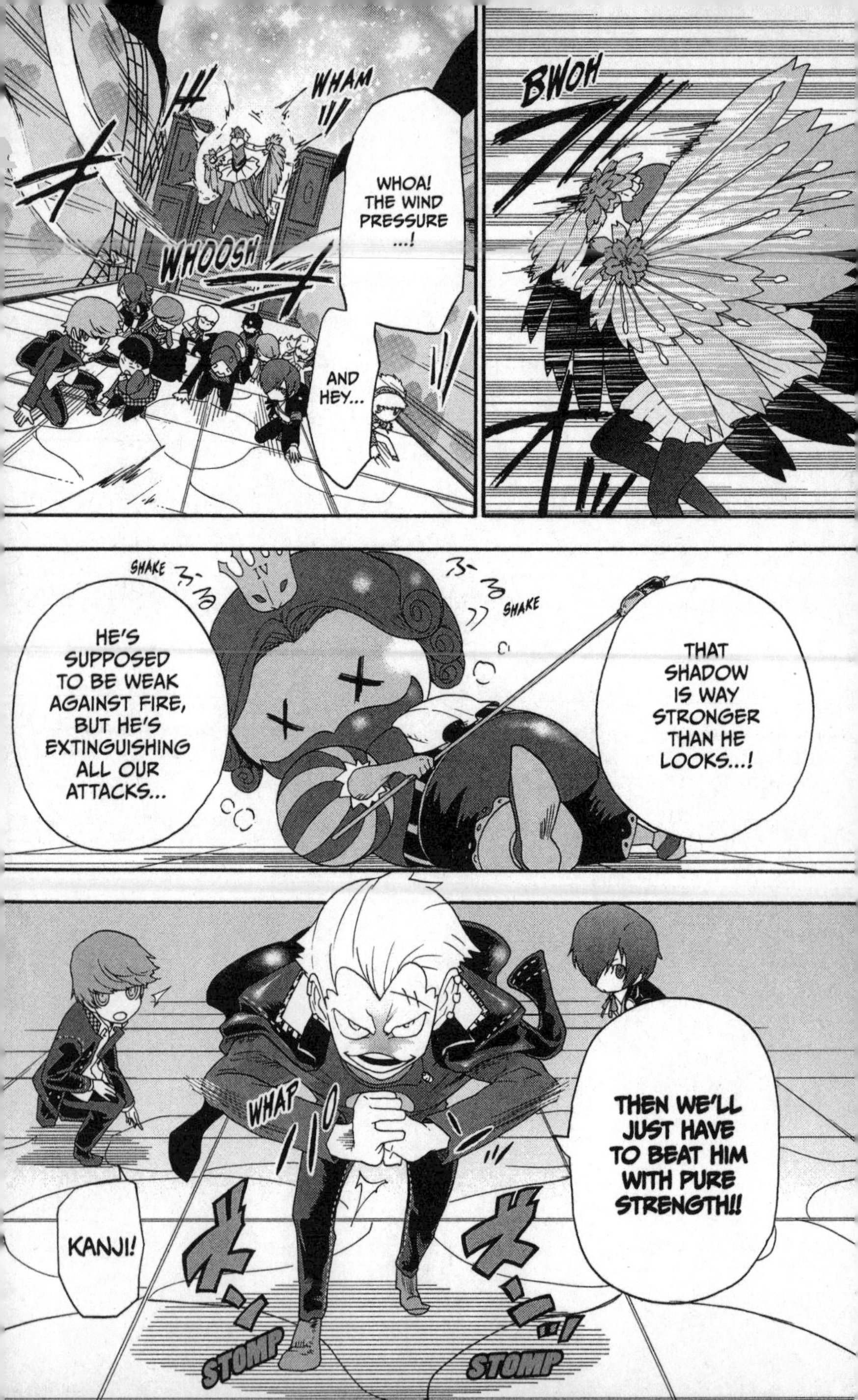
BWOH
WHAM
WHOA! THE WIND PRESSURE ...!
WHOOSH
AND HEY...
ふる SHAKE
THAT SHADOW IS WAY STRONGER THAN HE LOOKS...!
SHAKE ふる
HE'S SUPPOSED TO BE WEAK AGAINST FIRE, BUT HE'S EXTINGUISHING ALL OUR ATTACKS...
THEN WE'LL JUST HAVE TO BEAT HIM WITH PURE STRENGTH!!
WHAP
STOMP
STOMP
KANJI!

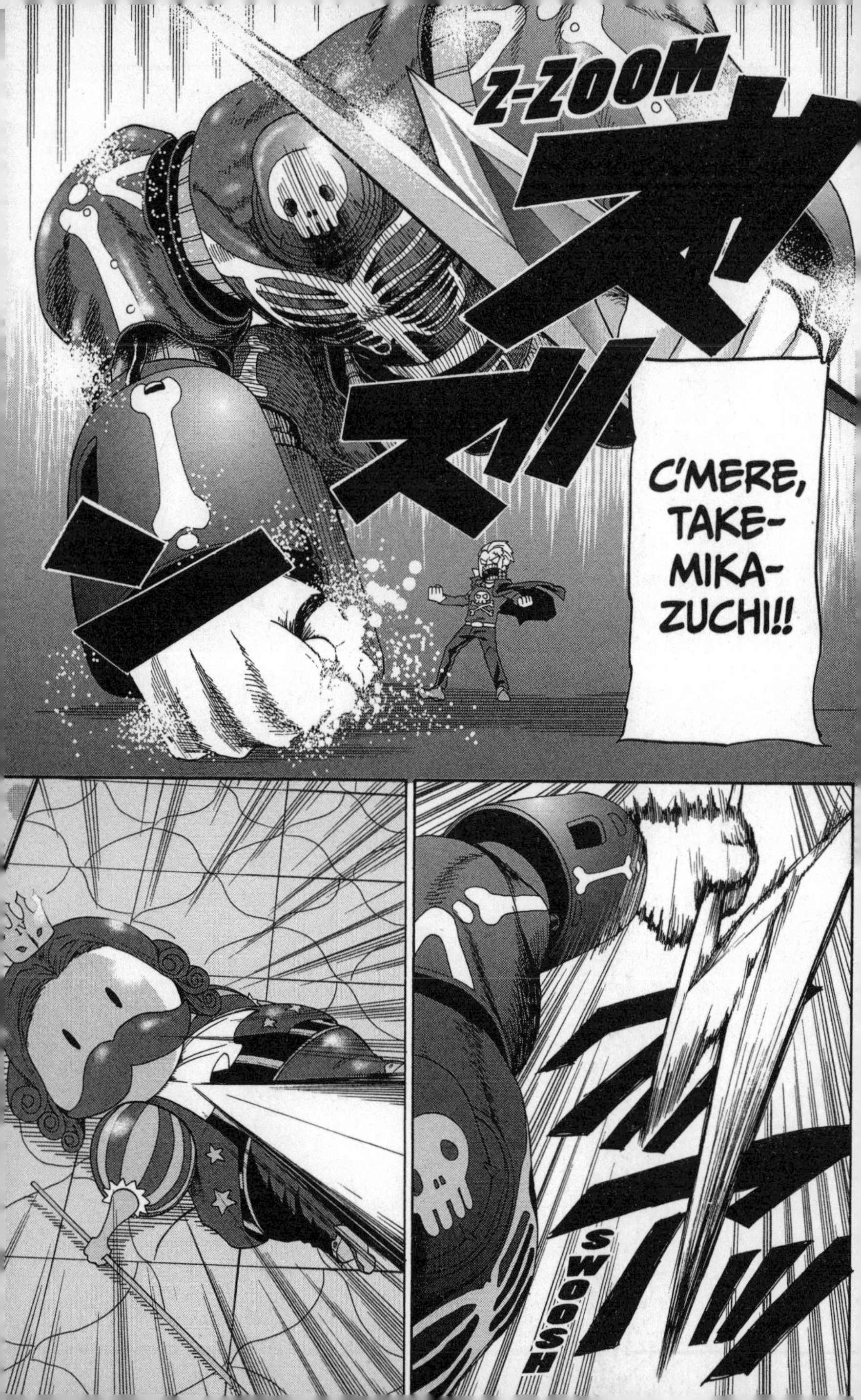
Z-ZOOM
C'MERE, TAKE-MIKA-ZUCHI!!
SWOOSH

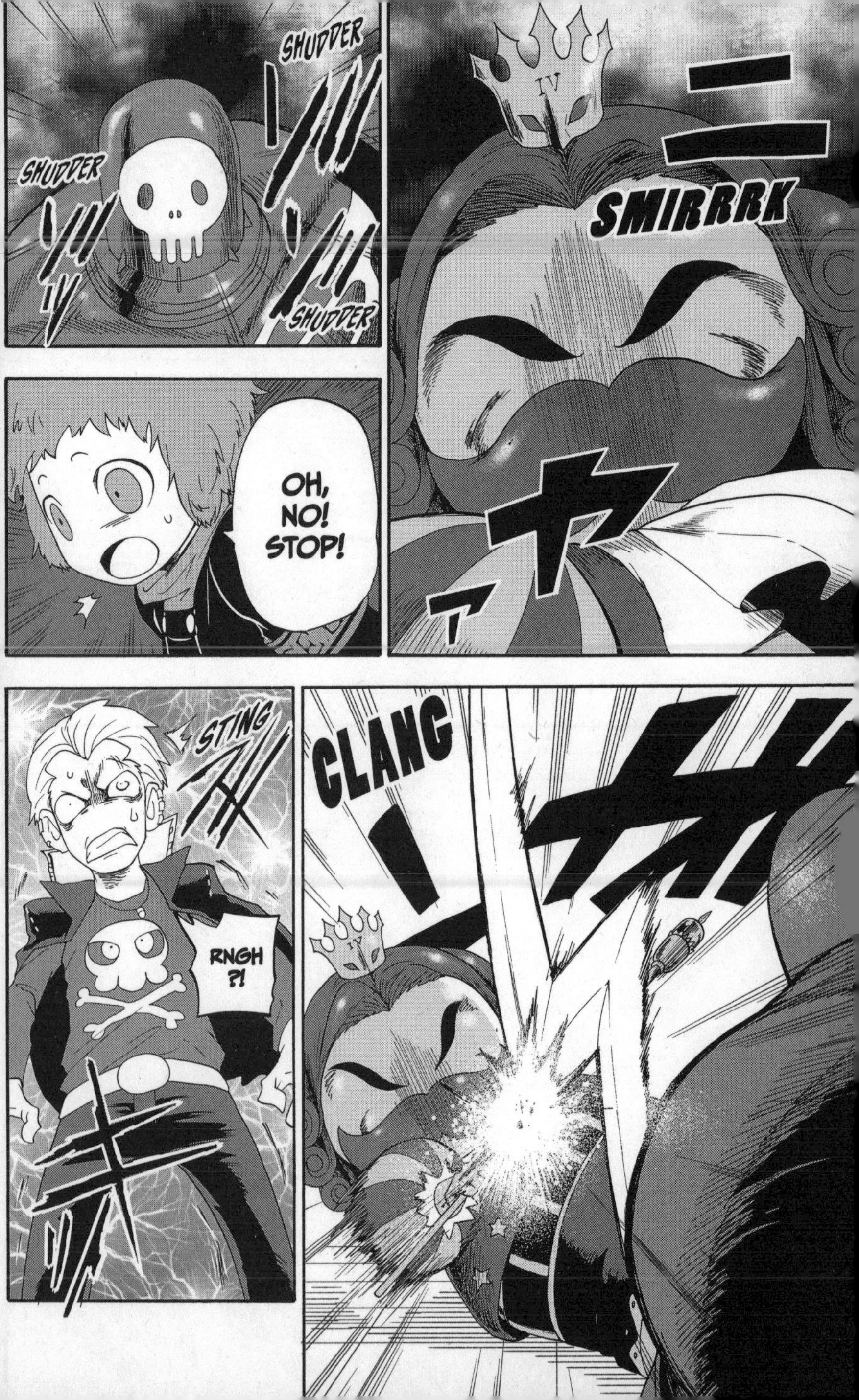
SMIRRRK
SHUDDER
SHUDDER
SHUDDER
OH, NO! STOP!
CLANG
STING
RNGH ?!

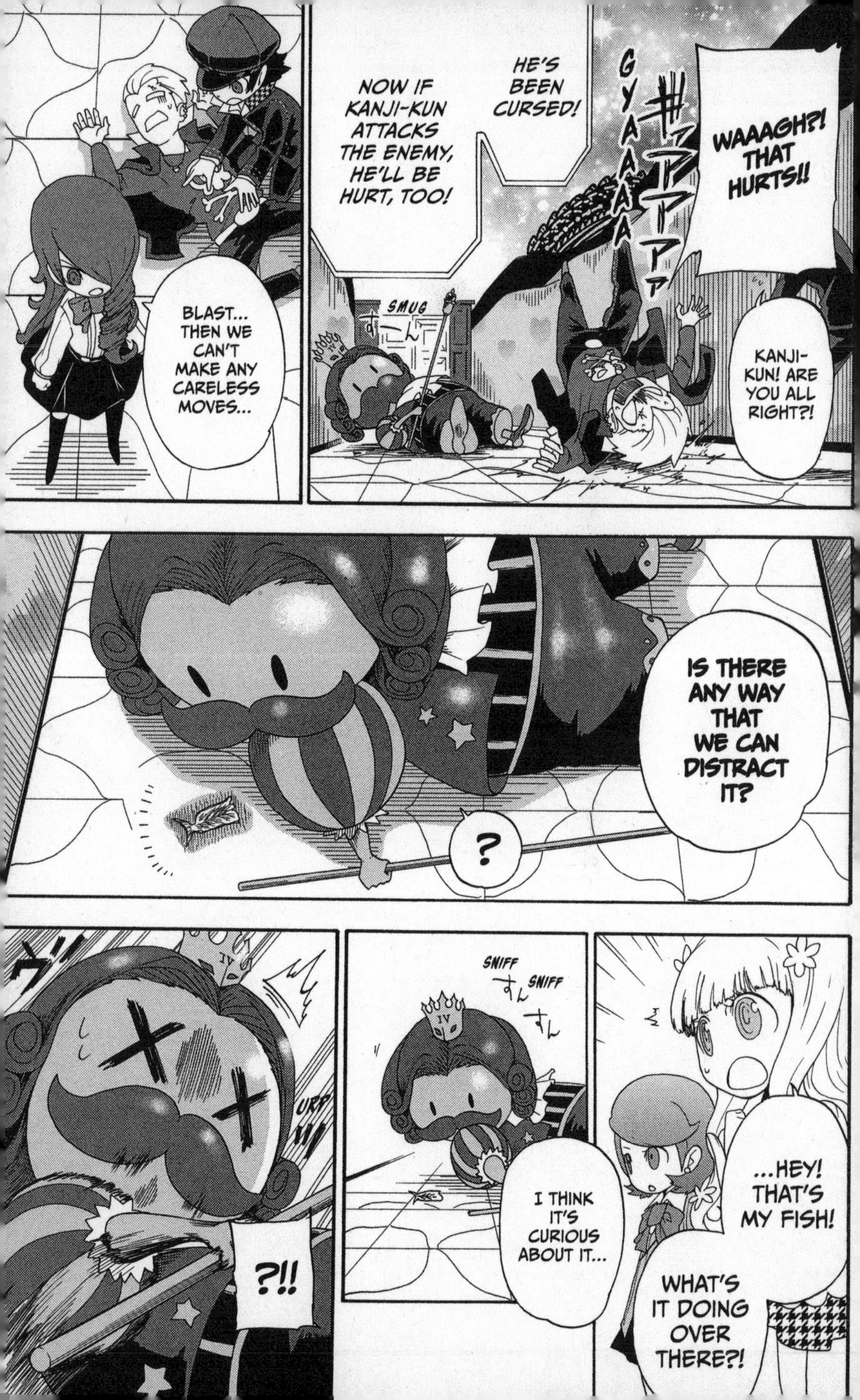
WAAAGH?! THAT HURTS!!
GYAAAAA
HE'S BEEN CURSED!
NOW IF KANJI-KUN ATTACKS THE ENEMY, HE'LL BE HURT, TOO!
KANJI-KUN! ARE YOU ALL RIGHT?!
SMUG
BLAST... THEN WE CAN'T MAKE ANY CARELESS MOVES...
IS THERE ANY WAY THAT WE CAN DISTRACT IT?
?
...HEY! THAT'S MY FISH!
WHAT'S IT DOING OVER THERE?!
SNIFF
SNIFF
I THINK IT'S CURIOUS ABOUT IT...
URP
?!!

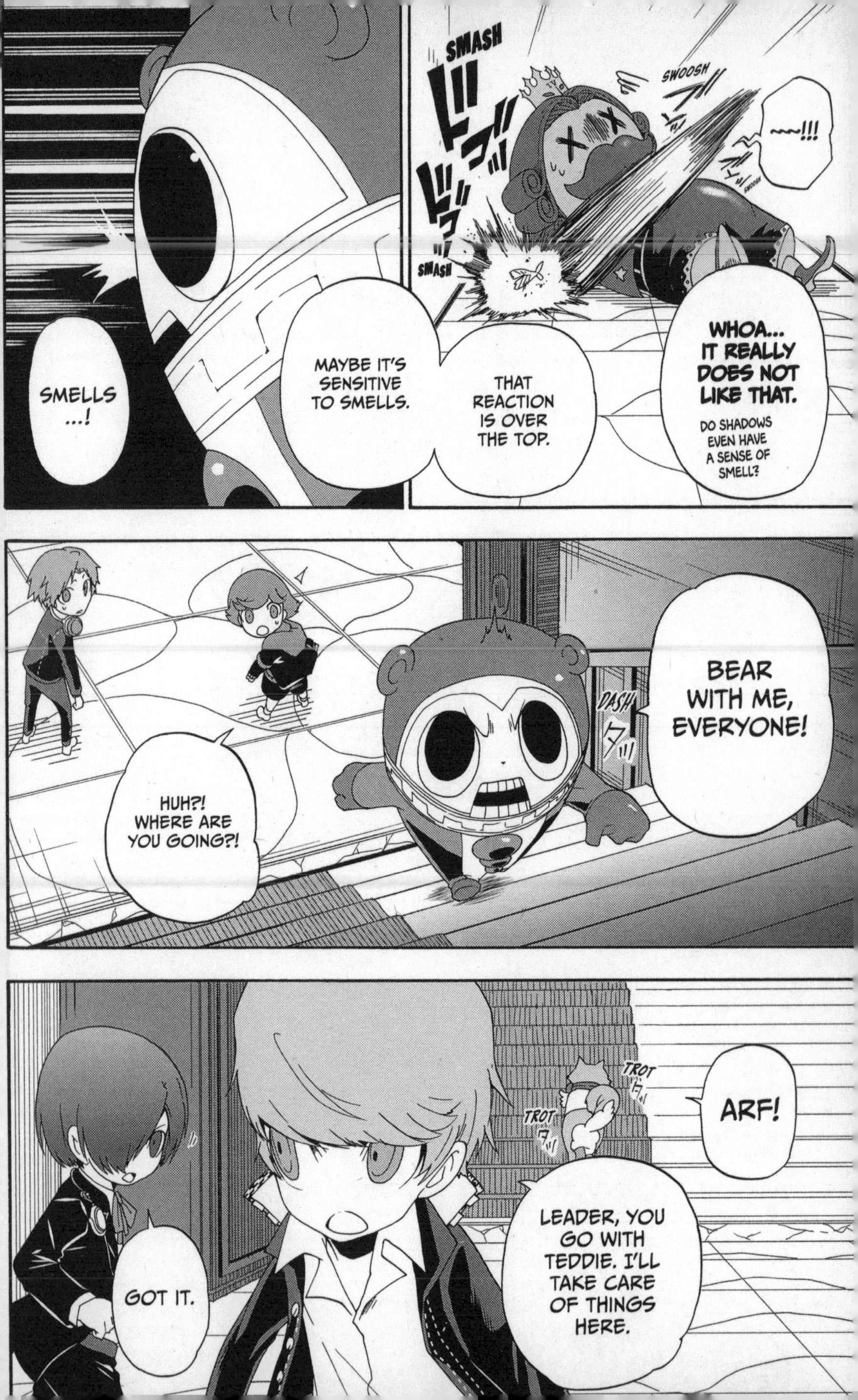

SMASH
SMASH
SWOOSH
SWOOSH
~~~!!!
WHOA... IT REALLY DOES NOT LIKE THAT.
DO SHADOWS EVEN HAVE A SENSE OF SMELL?
THAT REACTION IS OVER THE TOP.
MAYBE IT'S SENSITIVE TO SMELLS.
SMELLS ...!
BEAR WITH ME, EVERYONE!
DASH
HUH?! WHERE ARE YOU GOING?!
ARF!
TROT
TROT
LEADER, YOU GO WITH TEDDIE. I'LL TAKE CARE OF THINGS HERE.
GOT IT.
~~~

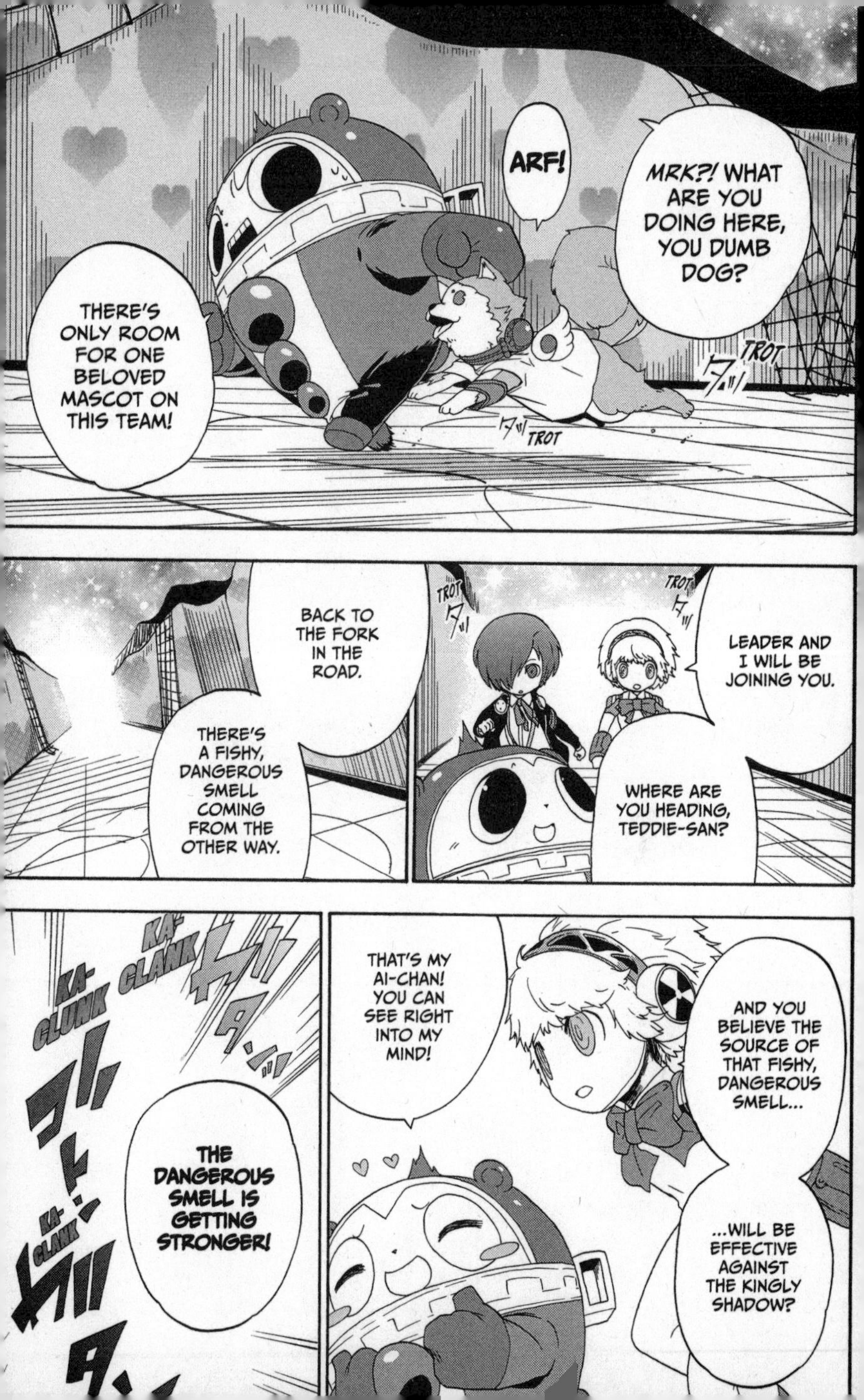
MRK?! WHAT ARE YOU DOING HERE, YOU DUMB DOG?
ARF!
TROT
TROT
THERE'S ONLY ROOM FOR ONE BELOVED MASCOT ON THIS TEAM!
TROT
LEADER AND I WILL BE JOINING YOU.
TROT
WHERE ARE YOU HEADING, TEDDIE-SAN?
BACK TO THE FORK IN THE ROAD.
THERE'S A FISHY, DANGEROUS SMELL COMING FROM THE OTHER WAY.
AND YOU BELIEVE THE SOURCE OF THAT FISHY, DANGEROUS SMELL...
...WILL BE EFFECTIVE AGAINST THE KINGLY SHADOW?
THAT'S MY AI-CHAN! YOU CAN SEE RIGHT INTO MY MIND!
KA-CLANK
KA-CLUNK
THE DANGEROUS SMELL IS GETTING STRONGER!
KA-CLANK

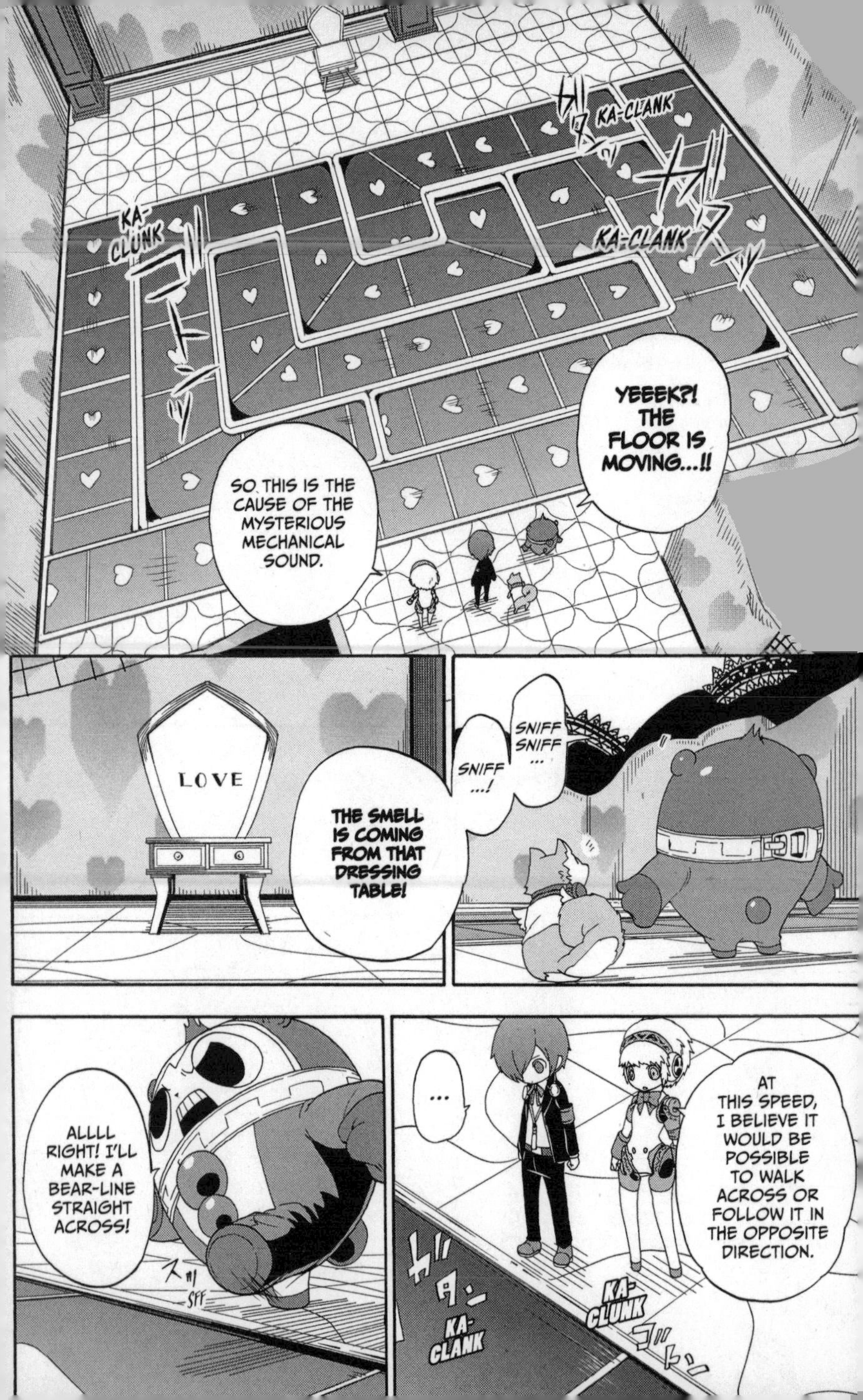
KA-CLANK
KA-CLANK
YEEEK?! THE FLOOR IS MOVING...!!
KA-CLUNK
SO, THIS IS THE CAUSE OF THE MYSTERIOUS MECHANICAL SOUND.
SNIFF SNIFF ...
SNIFF ...!
THE SMELL IS COMING FROM THAT DRESSING TABLE!
LOVE
...
AT THIS SPEED, I BELIEVE IT WOULD BE POSSIBLE TO WALK ACROSS OR FOLLOW IT IN THE OPPOSITE DIRECTION.
KA-CLUNK
KA-CLANK
ALLLL RIGHT! I'LL MAKE A BEAR-LINE STRAIGHT ACROSS!
SFF

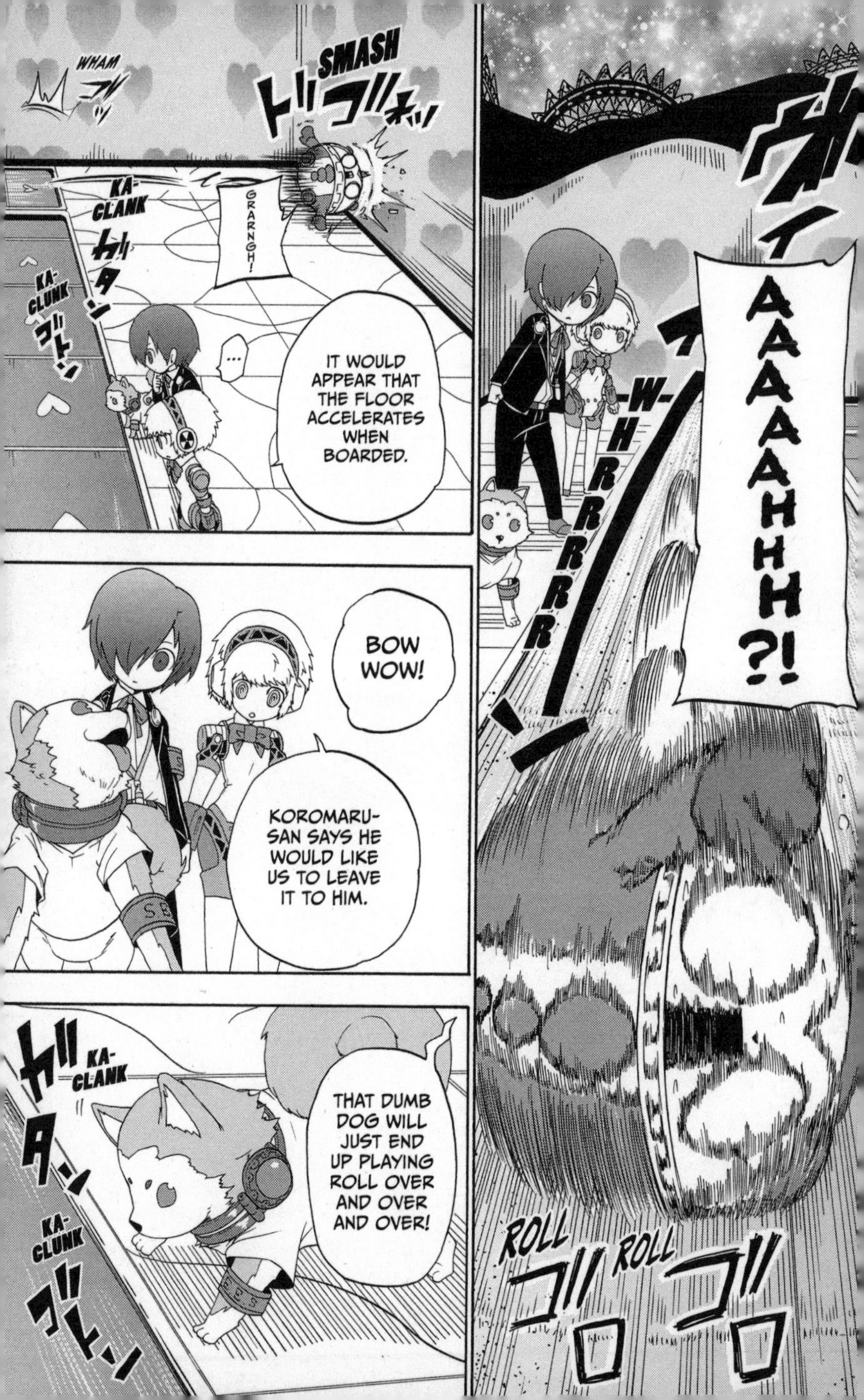
AAAAAHHH?!
W-WHRRRRRR
ROLL
ROLL
SMASH
WHAM
GRARNGH!
KA-CLANK
IT WOULD APPEAR THAT THE FLOOR ACCELERATES WHEN BOARDED.
...
KA-CLUNK
BOW WOW!
KOROMARU-SAN SAYS HE WOULD LIKE US TO LEAVE IT TO HIM.
THAT DUMB DOG WILL JUST END UP PLAYING ROLL OVER AND OVER AND OVER!
KA-CLANK
KA-CLUNK

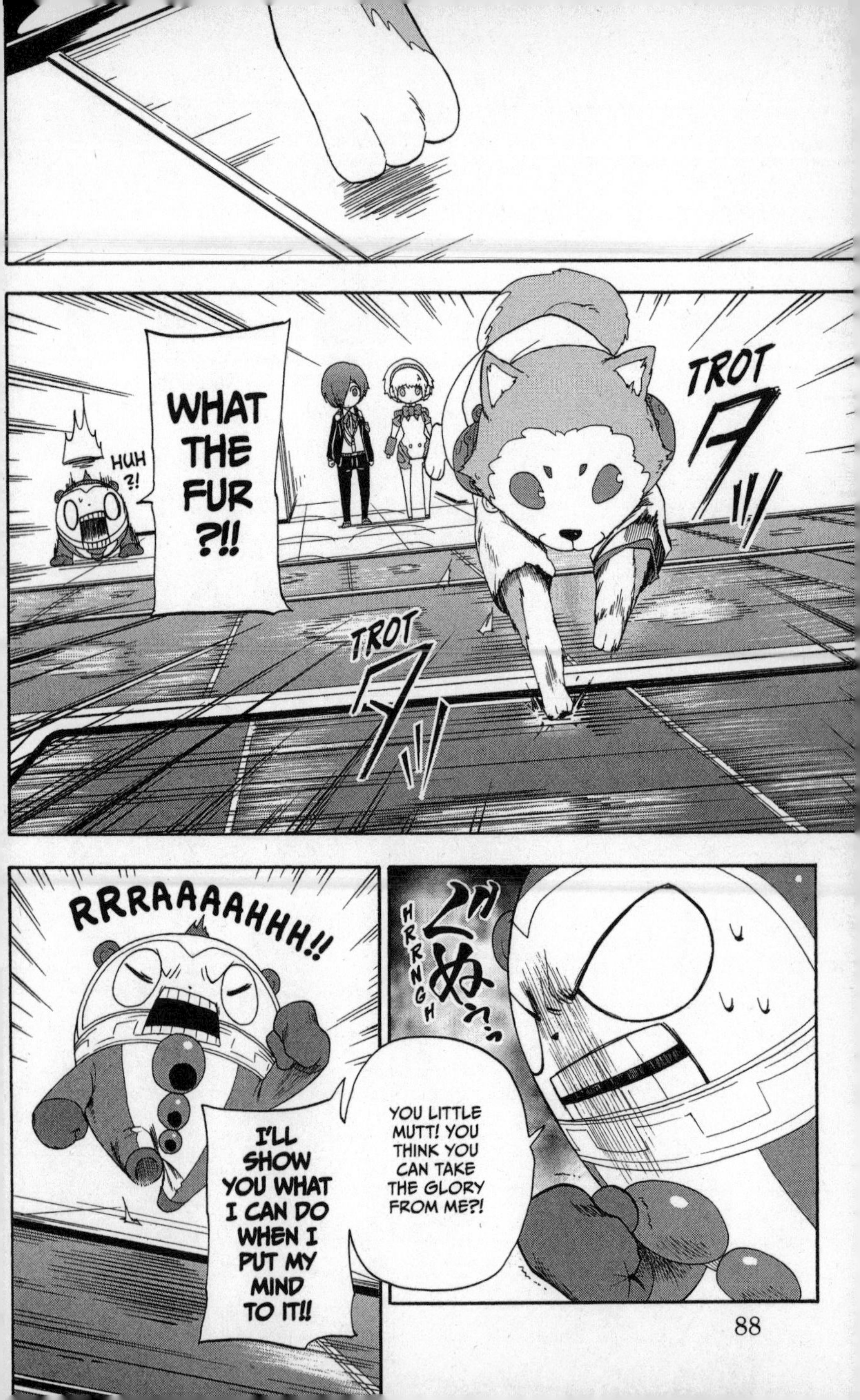
TROT
TROT
WHAT THE FUR ?!!
HUH ?!
HRRNGH
YOU LITTLE MUTT! YOU THINK YOU CAN TAKE THE GLORY FROM ME?!
RRRAAAAHHHH!!
I'LL SHOW YOU WHAT I CAN DO WHEN I PUT MY MIND TO IT!!

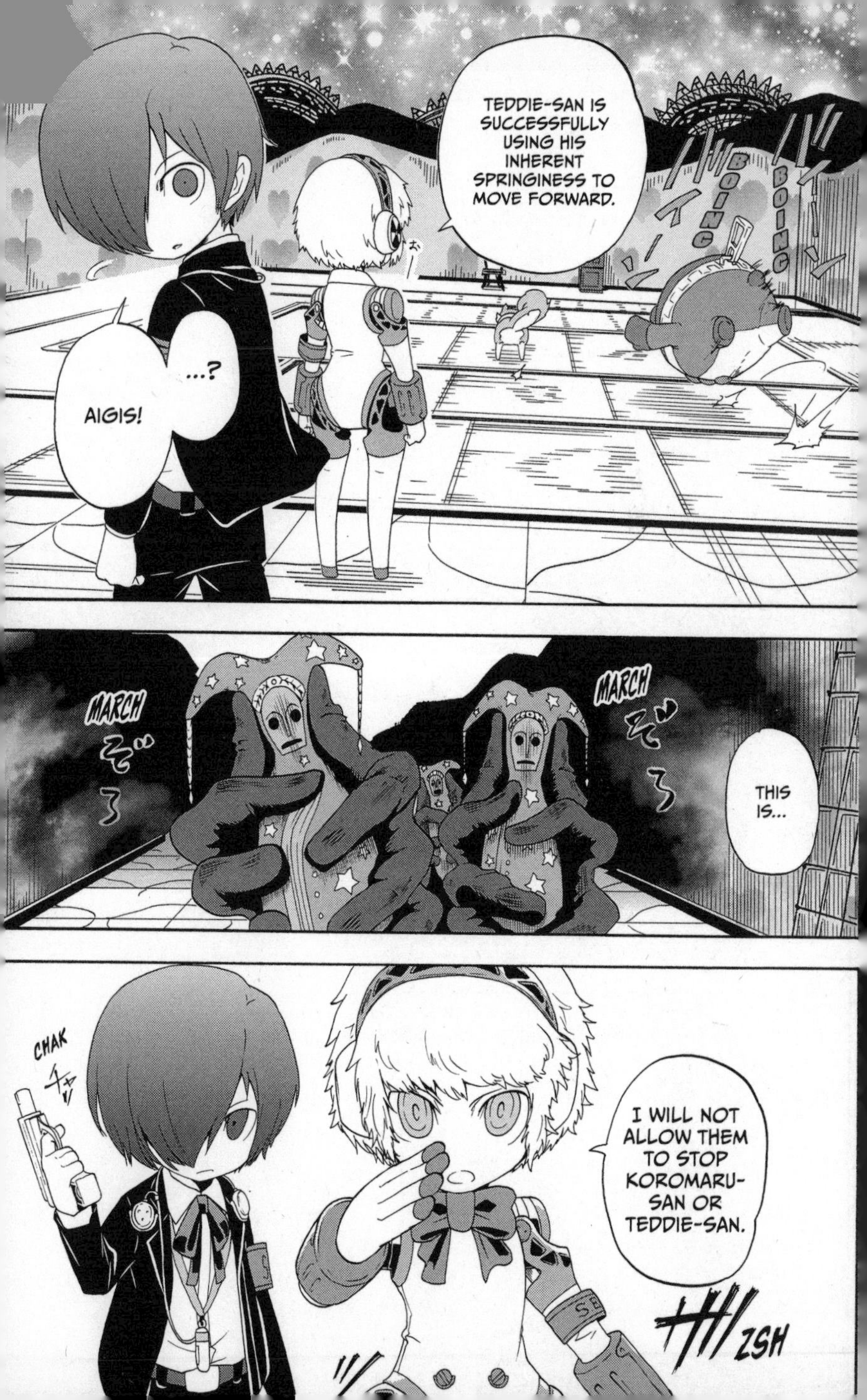
TEDDIE-SAN IS SUCCESSFULLY USING HIS INHERENT SPRINGINESS TO MOVE FORWARD.
BOING
BOING
...?
AIGIS!
THIS IS...
MARCH
MARCH
I WILL NOT ALLOW THEM TO STOP KOROMARU-SAN OR TEDDIE-SAN.
ZSH
CHAK

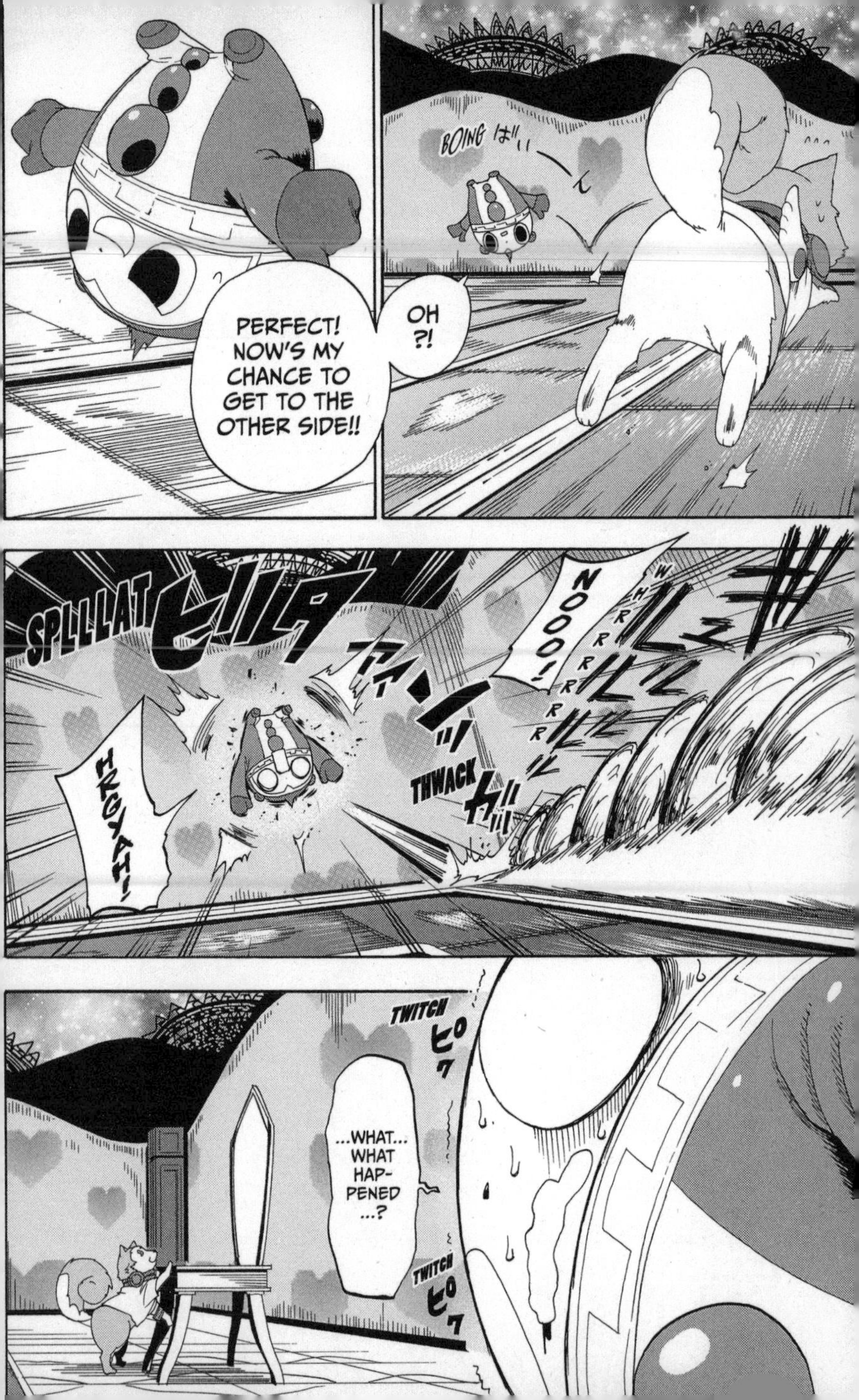
BOING
OH ?!
PERFECT! NOW'S MY CHANCE TO GET TO THE OTHER SIDE!!
WHRRRRRRRR
NOOOO!
THWACK
SPLLLAT
HRGYAH!
TWITCH
...WHAT... WHAT HAP-PENED ...?
TWITCH

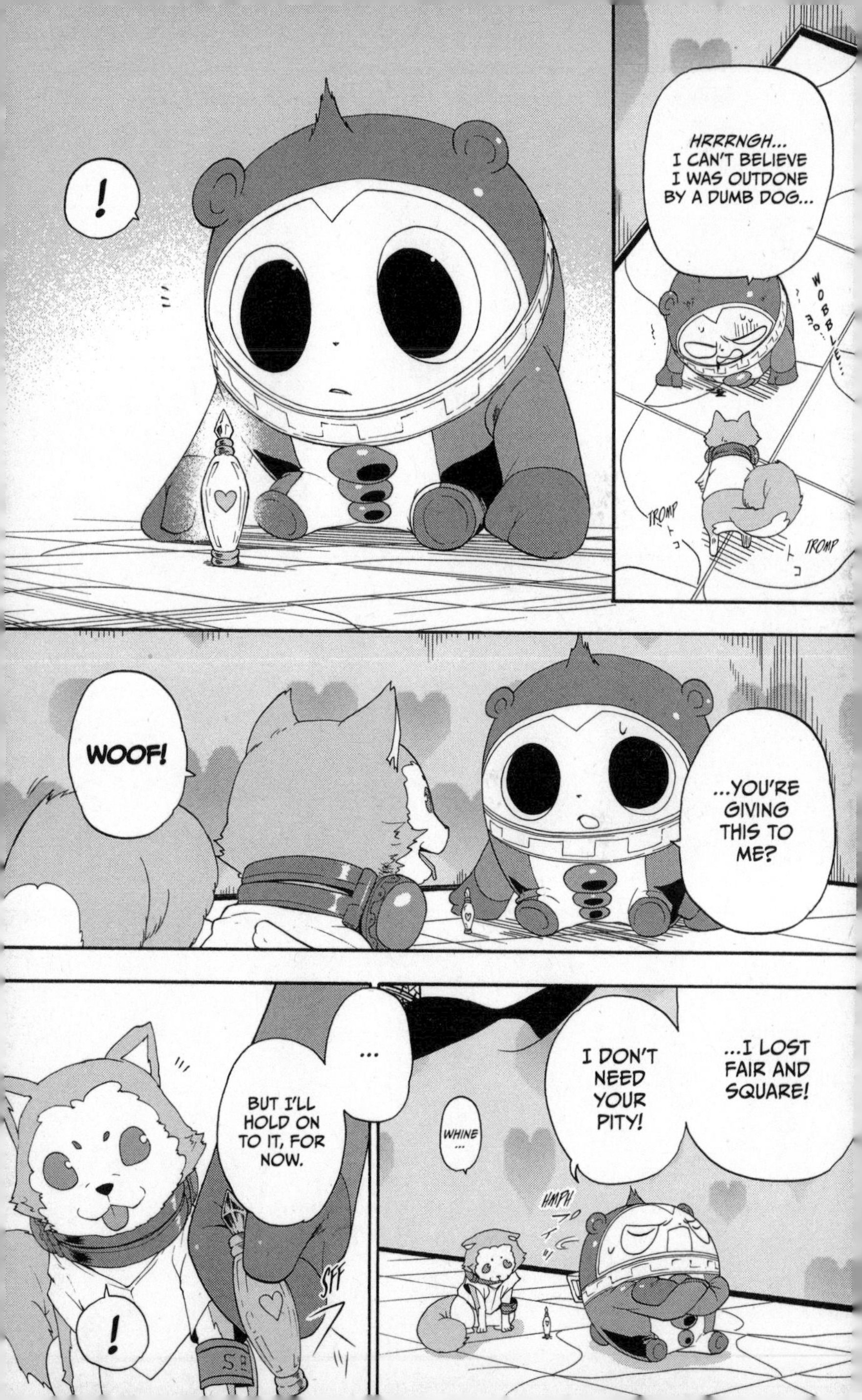
HRRRNGH... I CAN'T BELIEVE I WAS OUTDONE BY A DUMB DOG...
WOBBLE...
TROMP
TROMP
!
...YOU'RE GIVING THIS TO ME?
WOOF!
...I LOST FAIR AND SQUARE!
I DON'T NEED YOUR PITY!
WHINE...
HMPH
...
BUT I'LL HOLD ON TO IT, FOR NOW.
SFF
!

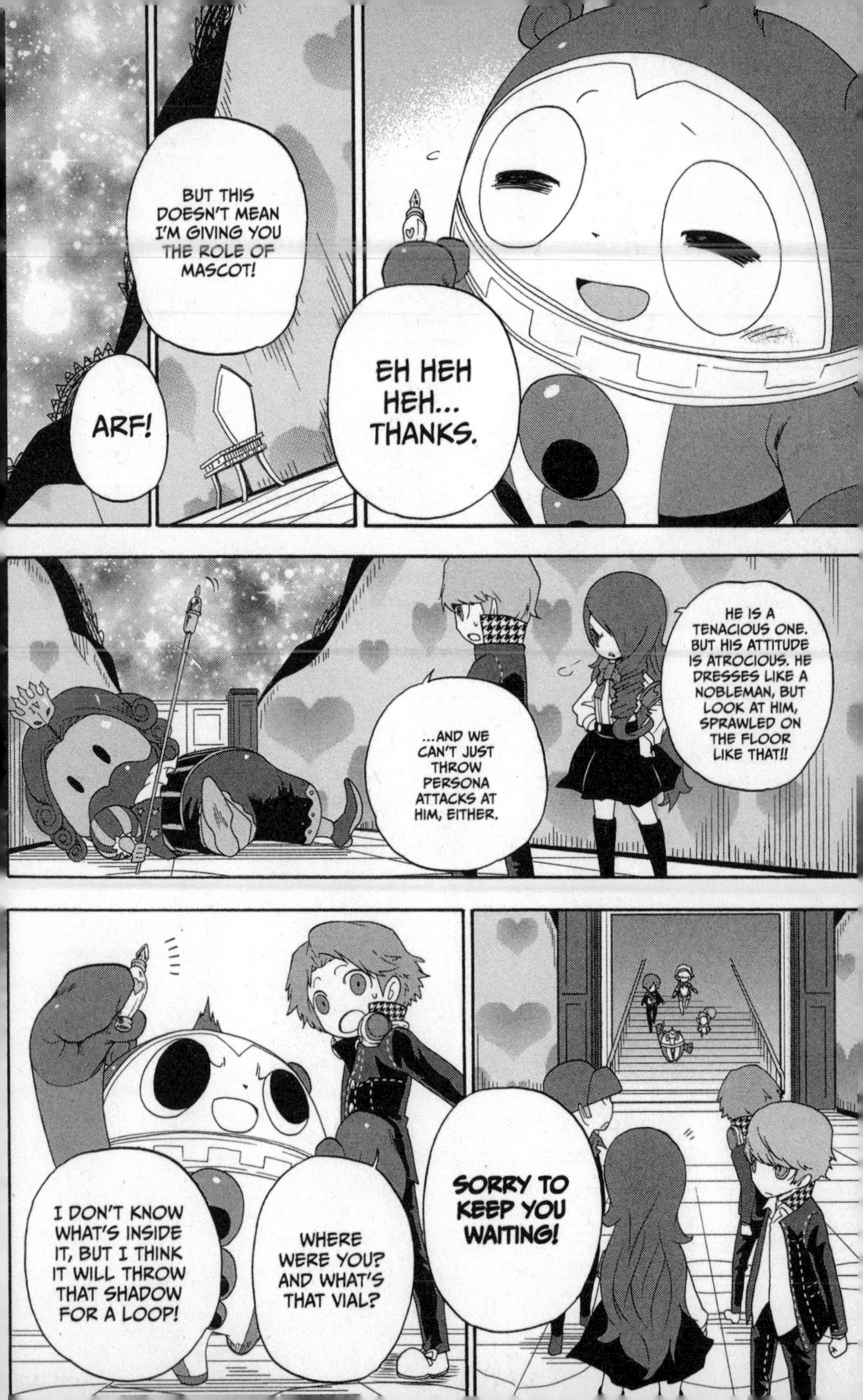
EH HEH HEH... THANKS.
BUT THIS DOESN'T MEAN I'M GIVING YOU THE ROLE OF MASCOT!
ARF!
HE IS A TENACIOUS ONE. BUT HIS ATTITUDE IS ATROCIOUS. HE DRESSES LIKE A NOBLEMAN, BUT LOOK AT HIM, SPRAWLED ON THE FLOOR LIKE THAT!!
...AND WE CAN'T JUST THROW PERSONA ATTACKS AT HIM, EITHER.
SORRY TO KEEP YOU WAITING!
WHERE WERE YOU? AND WHAT'S THAT VIAL?
I DON'T KNOW WHAT'S INSIDE IT, BUT I THINK IT WILL THROW THAT SHADOW FOR A LOOP!

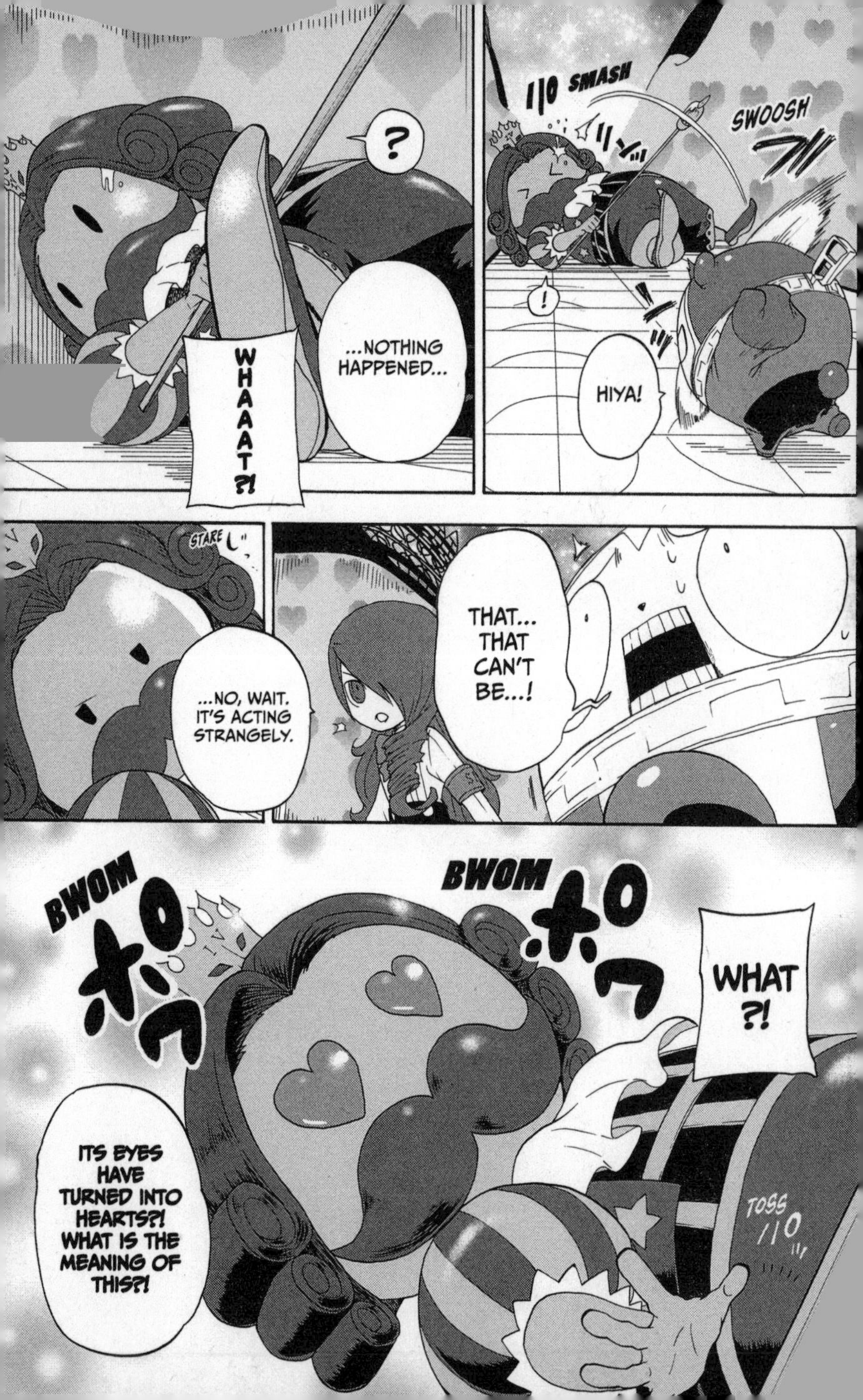
SMASH
SWOOSH
!
HIYA!
?
...NOTHING HAPPENED...
WHAAAT?!
THAT... THAT CAN'T BE...!
STARE
...NO, WAIT. IT'S ACTING STRANGELY.
BWOM
WHAT?!
BWOM
ITS EYES HAVE TURNED INTO HEARTS?! WHAT IS THE MEANING OF THIS?!
TOSS

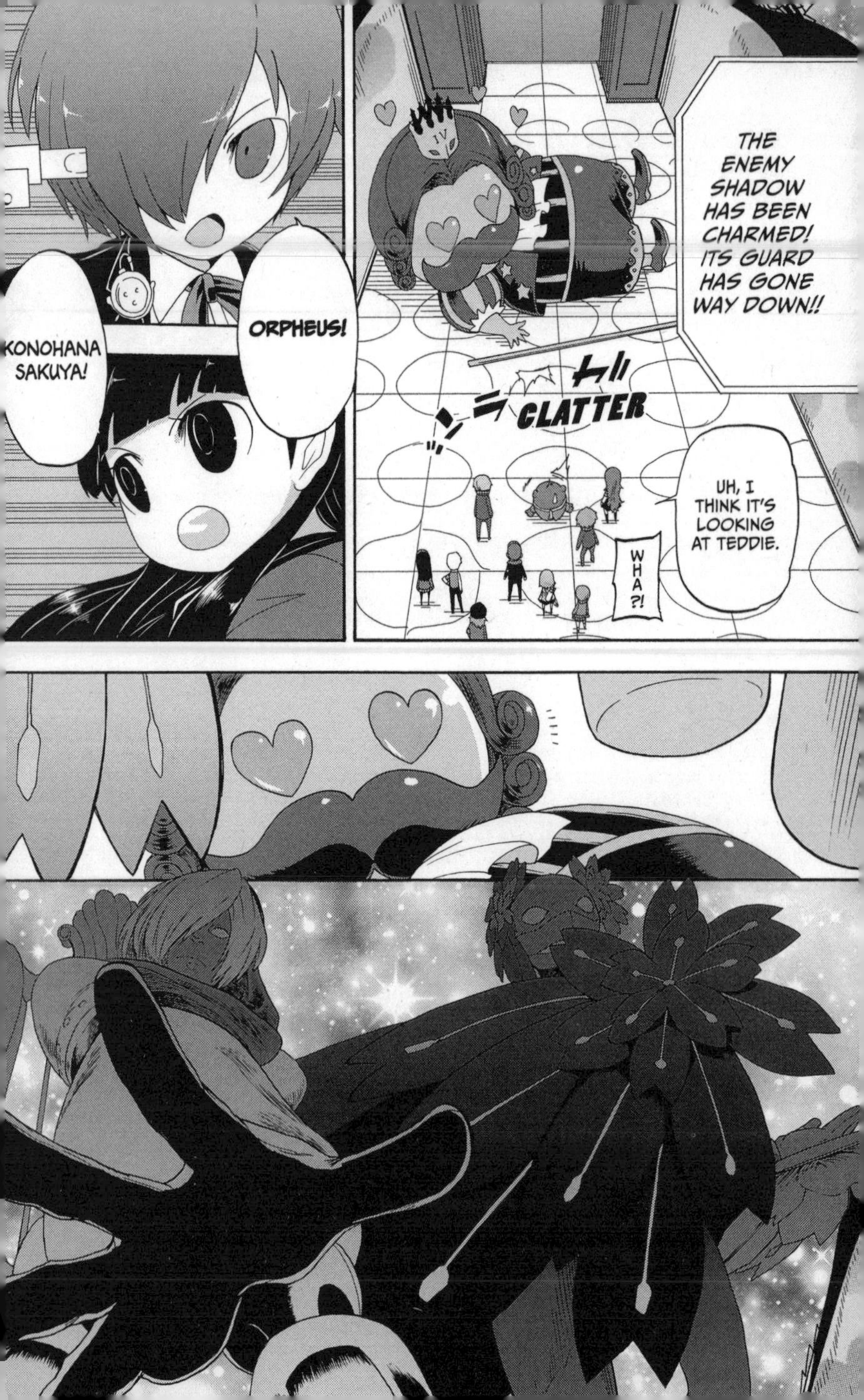
THE ENEMY SHADOW HAS BEEN CHARMED! ITS GUARD HAS GONE WAY DOWN!!
CLATTER
UH, I THINK IT'S LOOKING AT TEDDIE.
WHA?!
ORPHEUS!
KONOHANA SAKUYA!

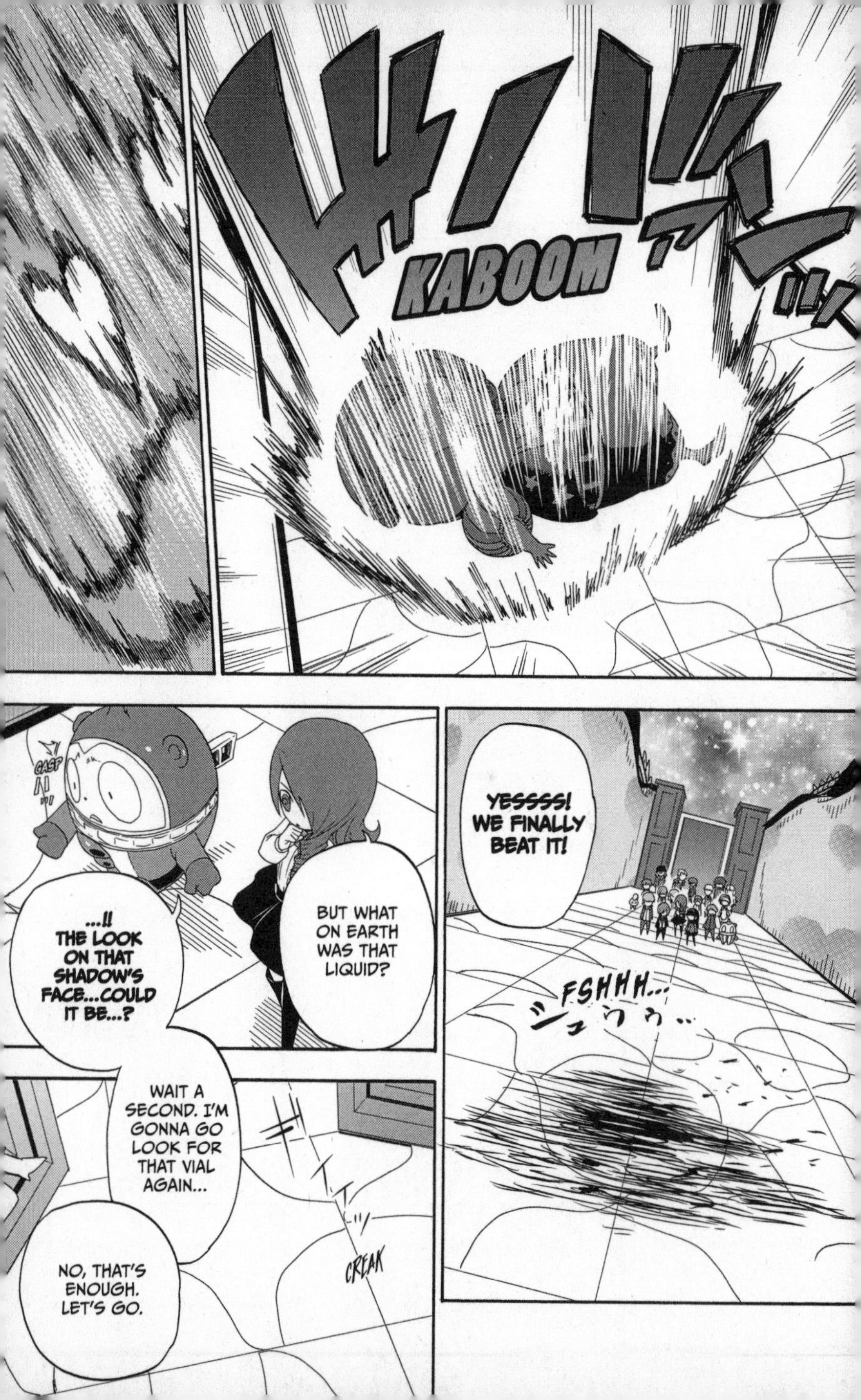
KABOOM
YESSSSS! WE FINALLY BEAT IT!
FSHHH...
GASP
BUT WHAT ON EARTH WAS THAT LIQUID?
...!! THE LOOK ON THAT SHADOW'S FACE...COULD IT BE...?
WAIT A SECOND. I'M GONNA GO LOOK FOR THAT VIAL AGAIN...
CREAK
NO, THAT'S ENOUGH. LET'S GO.

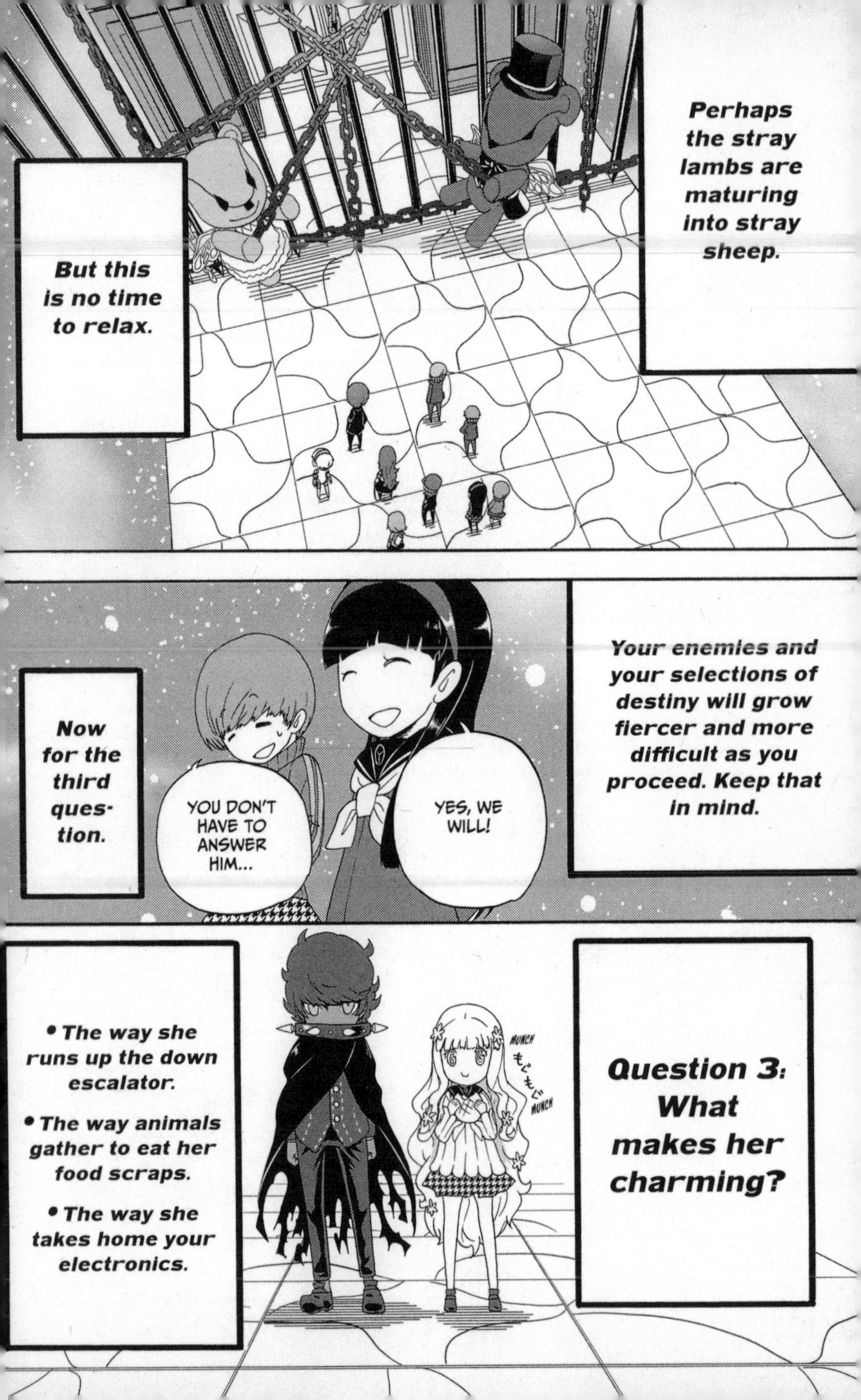
Perhaps the stray lambs are maturing into stray sheep.
But this is no time to relax.
Your enemies and your selections of destiny will grow fiercer and more difficult as you proceed. Keep that in mind.
YES, WE WILL!
YOU DON'T HAVE TO ANSWER HIM...
Now for the third ques-tion.
Question 3: What makes her charming?
MUNCH
もぐもぐ
MUNCH
• The way she runs up the down escalator.
• The way animals gather to eat her food scraps.
• The way she takes home your electronics.

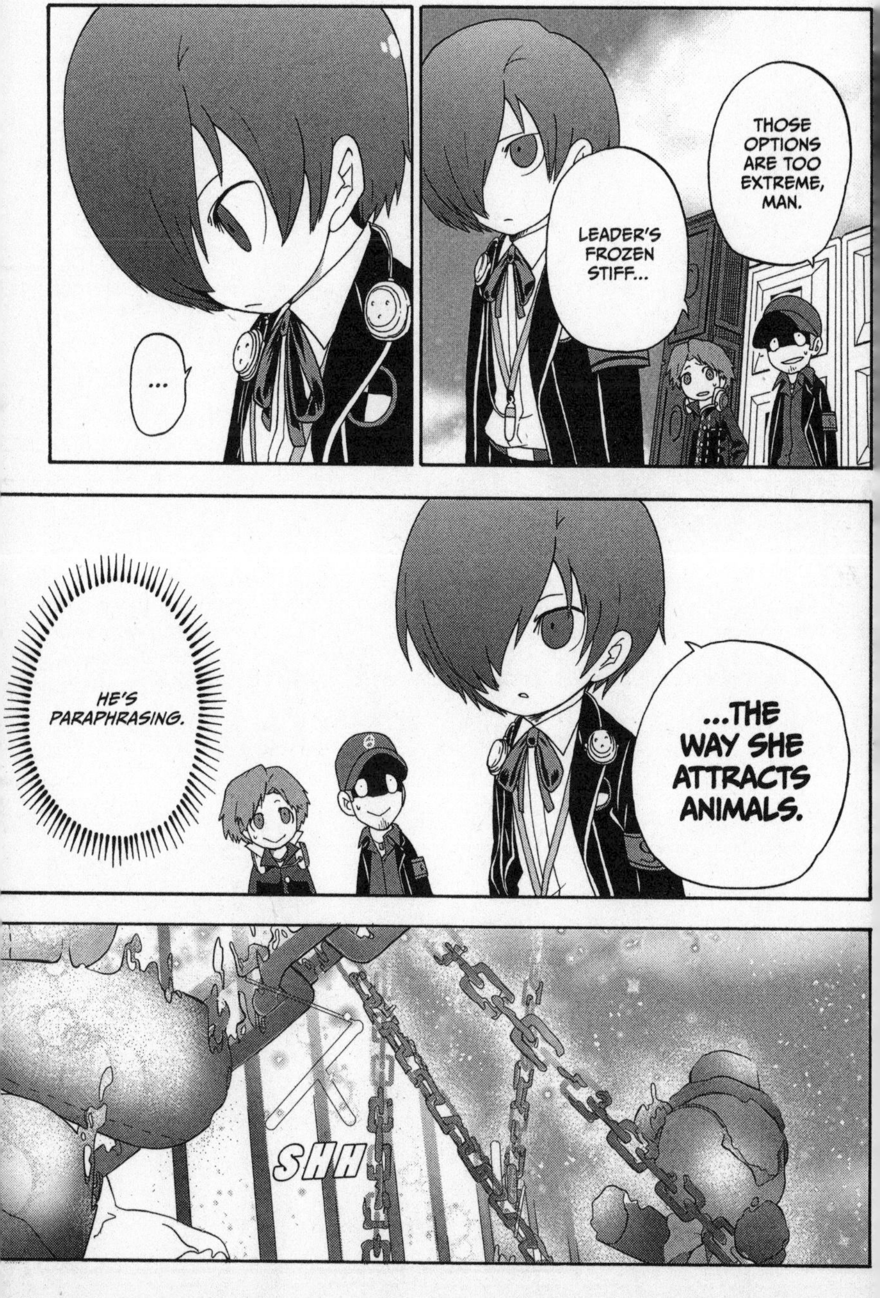
THOSE OPTIONS ARE TOO EXTREME, MAN.
LEADER'S FROZEN STIFF...
...
...THE WAY SHE ATTRACTS ANIMALS.
HE'S PARAPHRASING.
SHH

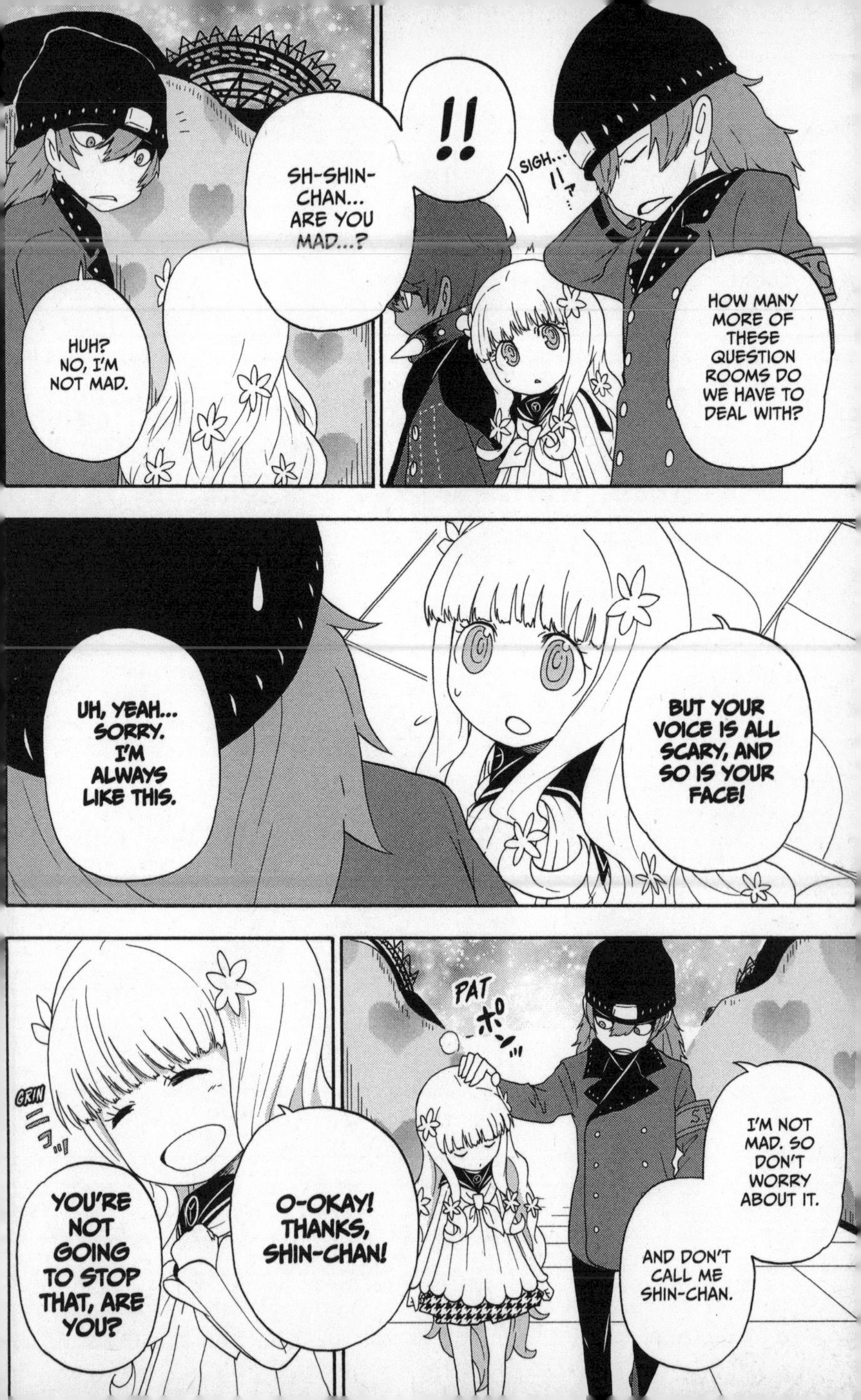
SIGH...
HOW MANY MORE OF THESE QUESTION ROOMS DO WE HAVE TO DEAL WITH?
!!
SH-SHIN-CHAN... ARE YOU MAD...?
HUH? NO, I'M NOT MAD.
BUT YOUR VOICE IS ALL SCARY, AND SO IS YOUR FACE!
UH, YEAH... SORRY. I'M ALWAYS LIKE THIS.
PAT
I'M NOT MAD. SO DON'T WORRY ABOUT IT.
AND DON'T CALL ME SHIN-CHAN.
GRIN
O-OKAY! THANKS, SHIN-CHAN!
YOU'RE NOT GOING TO STOP THAT, ARE YOU?

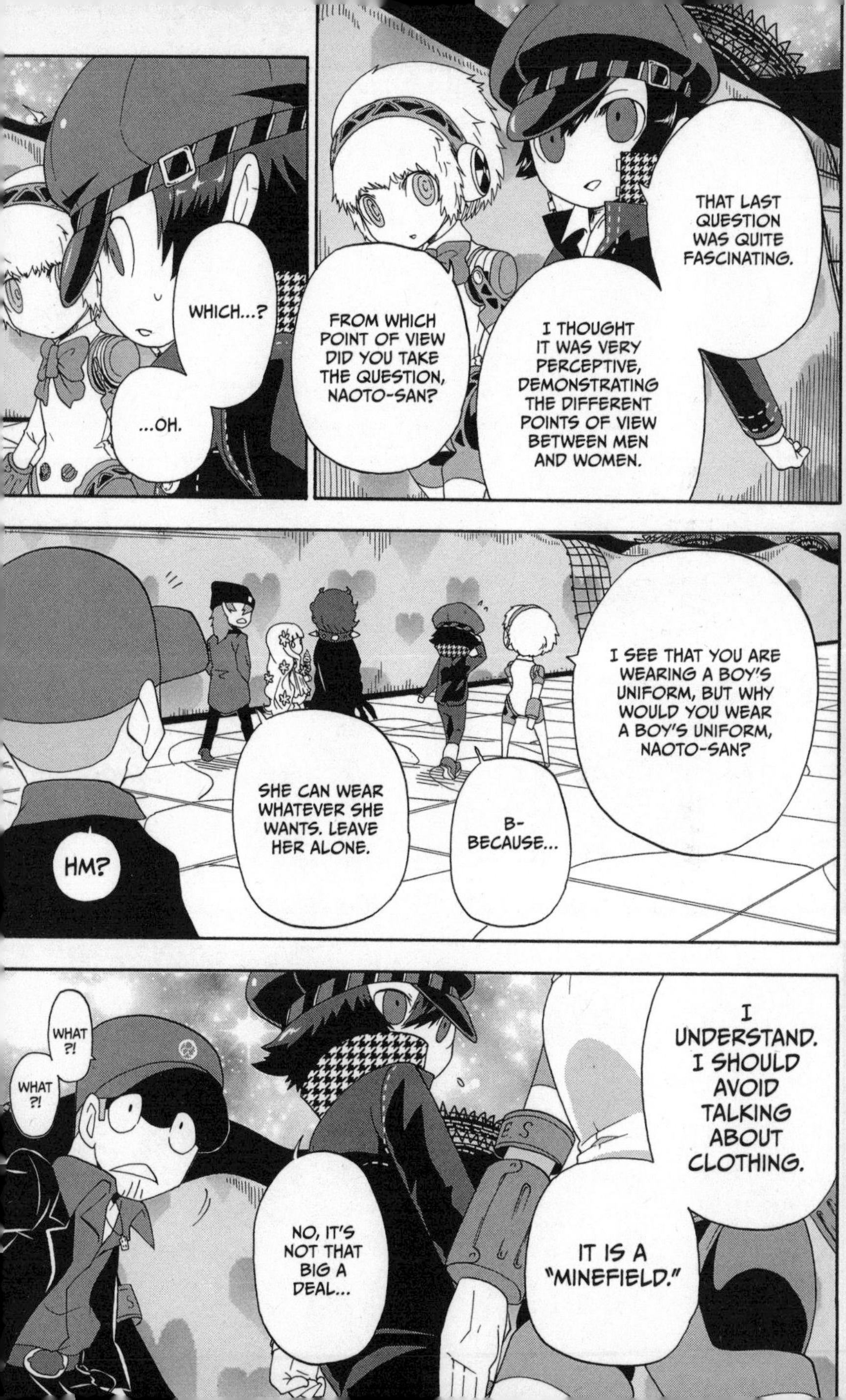
THAT LAST QUESTION WAS QUITE FASCINATING.
I THOUGHT IT WAS VERY PERCEPTIVE, DEMONSTRATING THE DIFFERENT POINTS OF VIEW BETWEEN MEN AND WOMEN.
FROM WHICH POINT OF VIEW DID YOU TAKE THE QUESTION, NAOTO-SAN?
WHICH...?
...OH.
I SEE THAT YOU ARE WEARING A BOY'S UNIFORM, BUT WHY WOULD YOU WEAR A BOY'S UNIFORM, NAOTO-SAN?
B-BECAUSE...
SHE CAN WEAR WHATEVER SHE WANTS. LEAVE HER ALONE.
HM?
I UNDERSTAND. I SHOULD AVOID TALKING ABOUT CLOTHING.
IT IS A "MINEFIELD."
NO, IT'S NOT THAT BIG A DEAL...
WHAT?!
WHAT?!

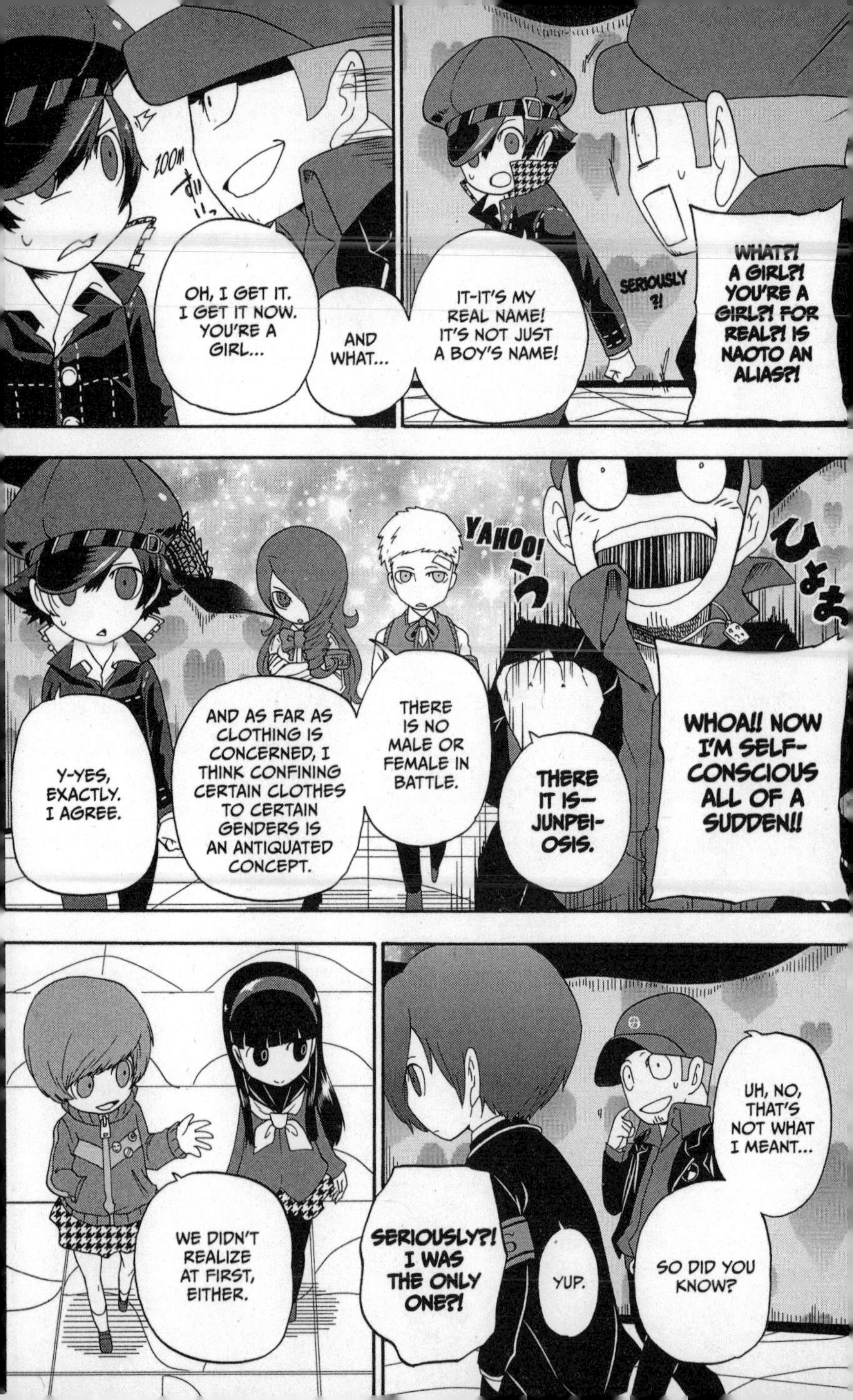
WHAT?! A GIRL?! YOU'RE A GIRL?! FOR REAL?! IS NAOTO AN ALIAS?!
SERIOUSLY ?!
IT-IT'S MY REAL NAME! IT'S NOT JUST A BOY'S NAME!
AND WHAT...
ZOOM
OH, I GET IT. I GET IT NOW. YOU'RE A GIRL...
WHOA!! NOW I'M SELF-CONSCIOUS ALL OF A SUDDEN!!
YAHOO!
THERE IT IS— JUNPEI-OSIS.
THERE IS NO MALE OR FEMALE IN BATTLE.
AND AS FAR AS CLOTHING IS CONCERNED, I THINK CONFINING CERTAIN CLOTHES TO CERTAIN GENDERS IS AN ANTIQUATED CONCEPT.
Y-YES, EXACTLY. I AGREE.
UH, NO, THAT'S NOT WHAT I MEANT...
SO DID YOU KNOW?
YUP.
SERIOUSLY?! I WAS THE ONLY ONE?!
WE DIDN'T REALIZE AT FIRST, EITHER.

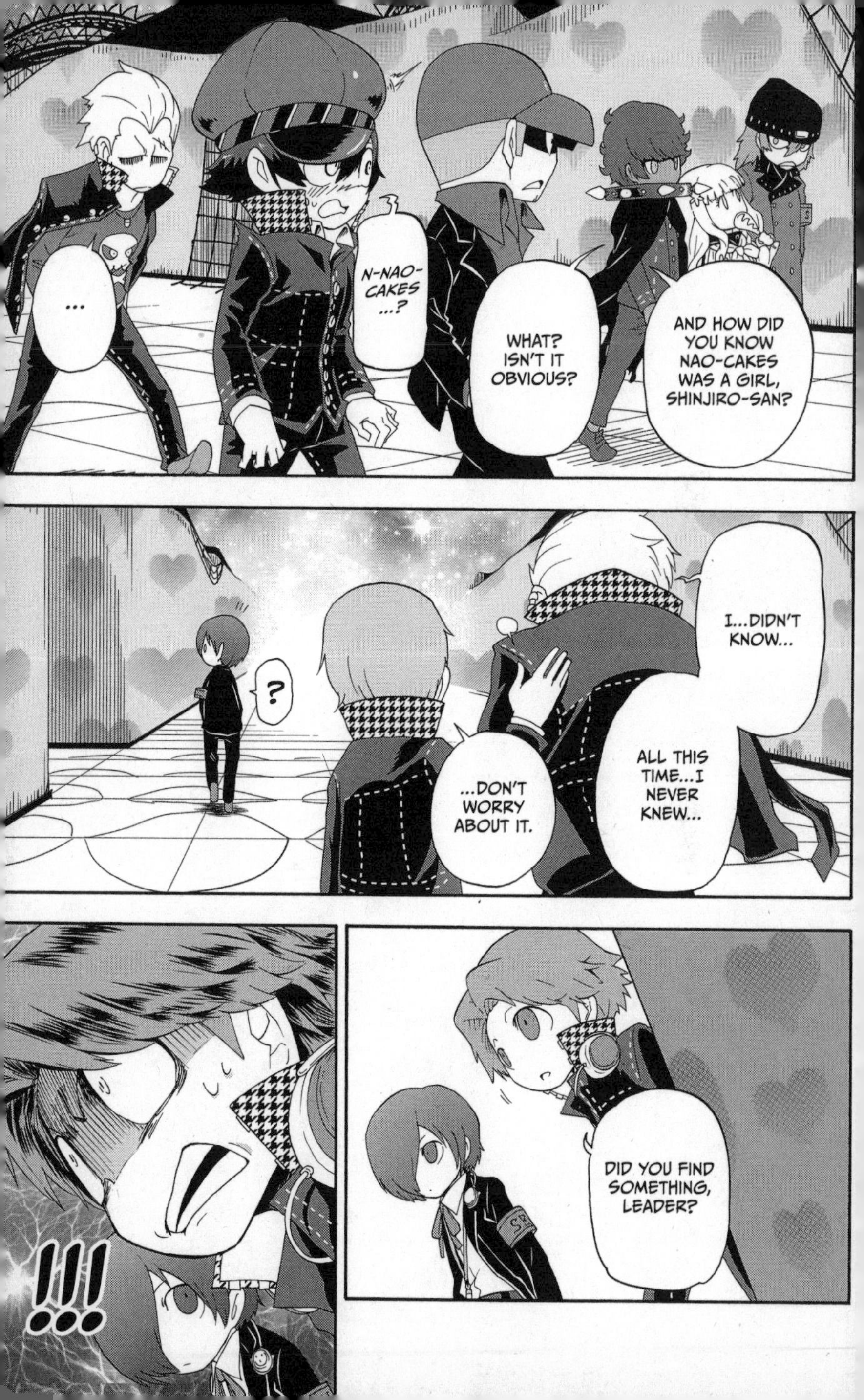
AND HOW DID YOU KNOW NAO-CAKES WAS A GIRL, SHINJIRO-SAN?
WHAT? ISN'T IT OBVIOUS?
N-NAO-CAKES ...?
...
I...DIDN'T KNOW...
ALL THIS TIME...I NEVER KNEW...
...DON'T WORRY ABOUT IT.
?
DID YOU FIND SOMETHING, LEADER?
!!!

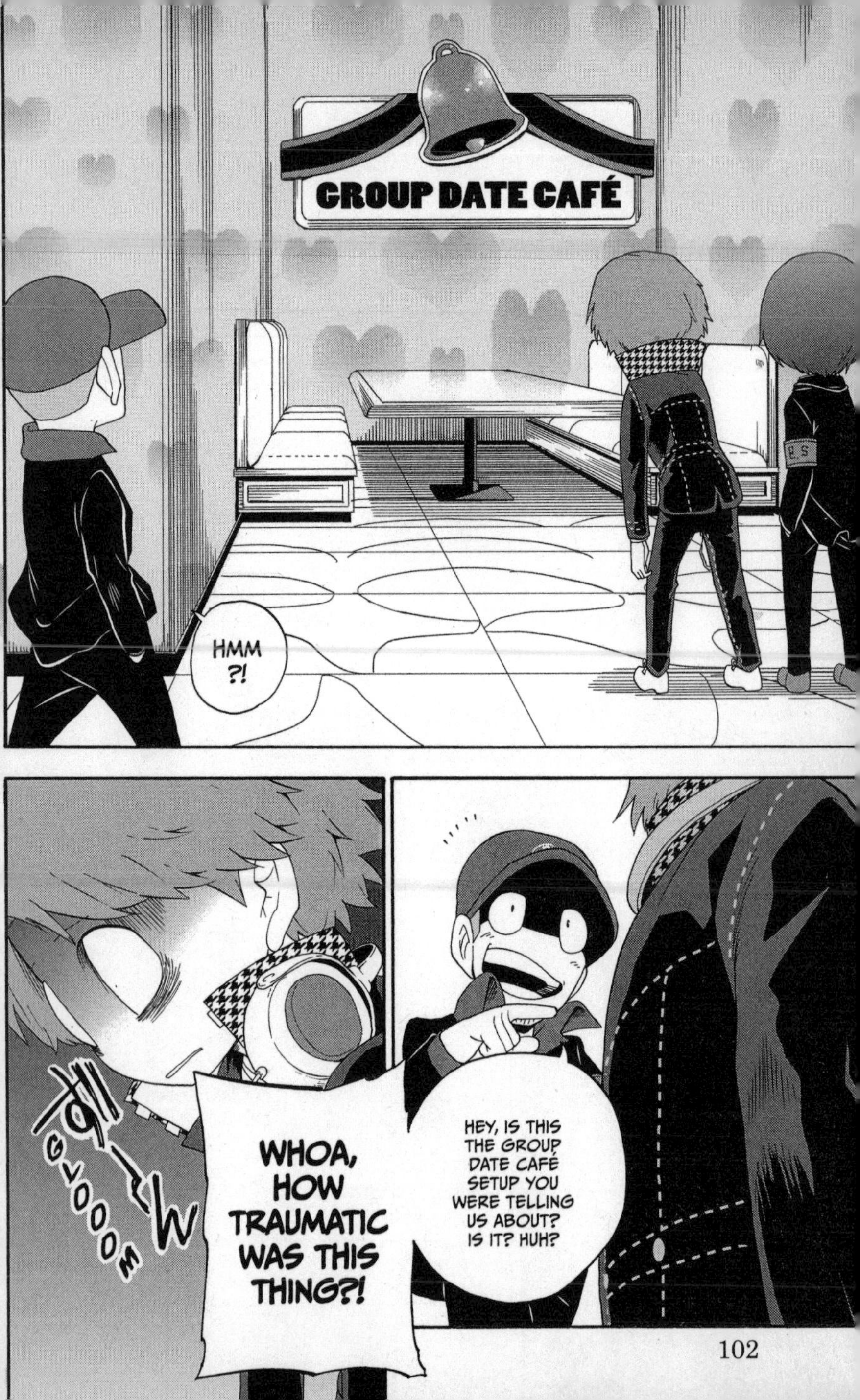
GROUP DATE CAFÉ
HMM ?!
HEY, IS THIS THE GROUP DATE CAFÉ SETUP YOU WERE TELLING US ABOUT? IS IT? HUH?
WHOA, HOW TRAUMATIC WAS THIS THING?!
GVOOOM

Chapter 9

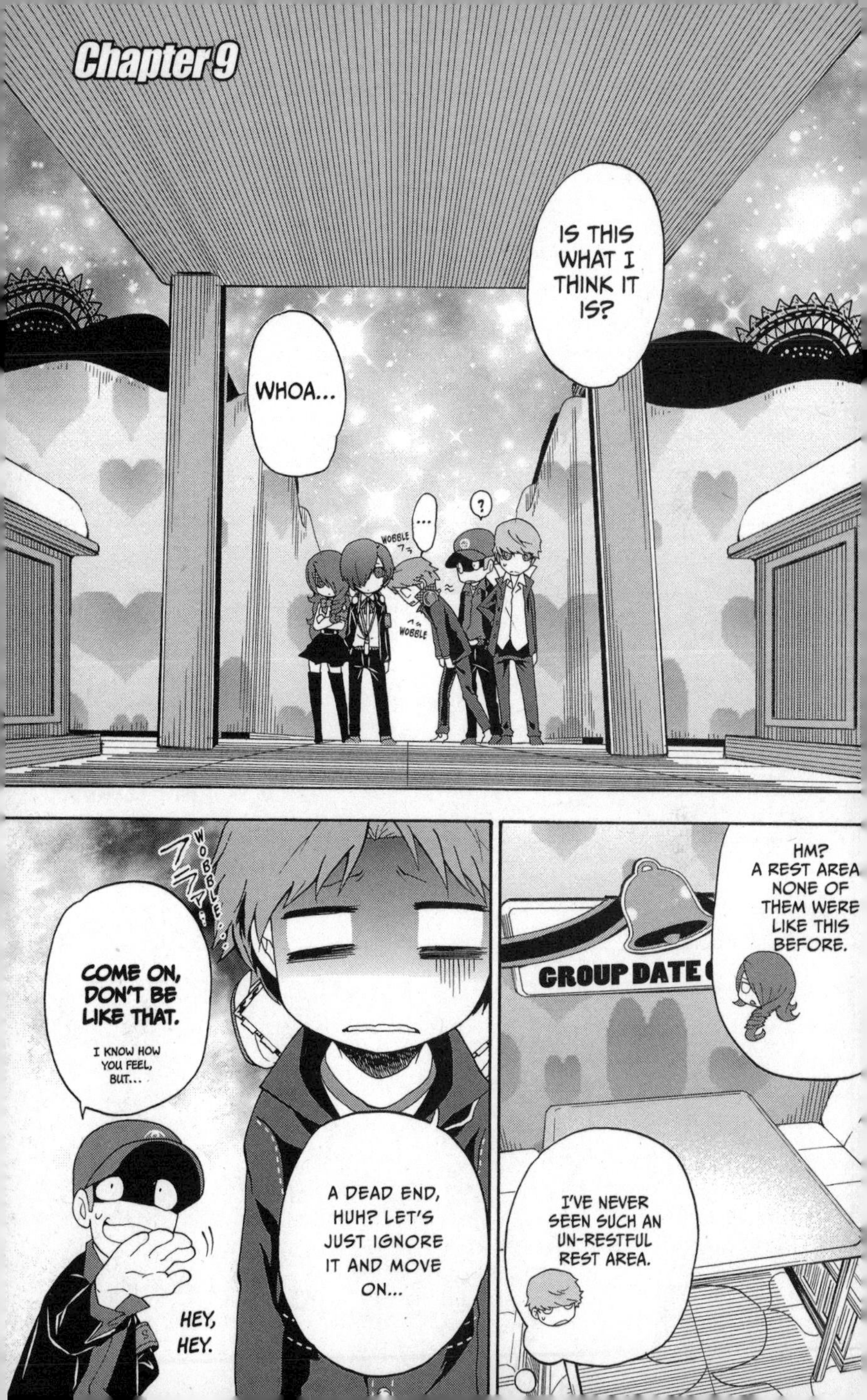
IS THIS WHAT I THINK IT IS?
WHOA...
...
?
WOBBLE
WOBBLE
HM? A REST AREA NONE OF THEM WERE LIKE THIS BEFORE.
GROUP DATE
I'VE NEVER SEEN SUCH AN UN-RESTFUL REST AREA.
WOBBLE...
A DEAD END, HUH? LET'S JUST IGNORE IT AND MOVE ON...
COME ON, DON'T BE LIKE THAT.
I KNOW HOW YOU FEEL, BUT...
HEY, HEY.

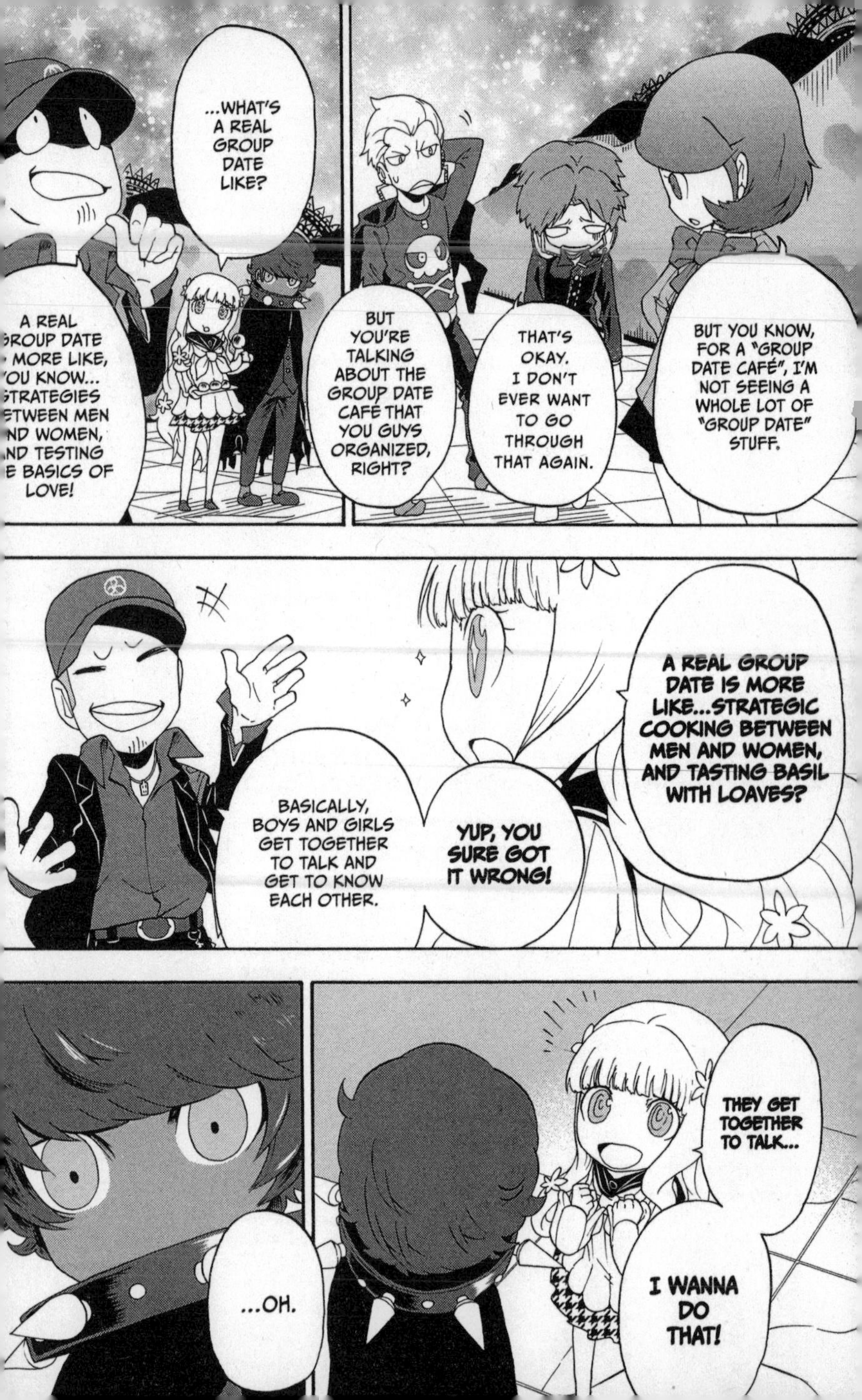
BUT YOU KNOW, FOR A "GROUP DATE CAFÉ", I'M NOT SEEING A WHOLE LOT OF "GROUP DATE" STUFF.
THAT'S OKAY. I DON'T EVER WANT TO GO THROUGH THAT AGAIN.
BUT YOU'RE TALKING ABOUT THE GROUP DATE CAFÉ THAT YOU GUYS ORGANIZED, RIGHT?
...WHAT'S A REAL GROUP DATE LIKE?
A REAL ROUP DATE MORE LIKE, OU KNOW... TRATEGIES ETWEEN MEN ND WOMEN, ND TESTING E BASICS OF LOVE!
A REAL GROUP DATE IS MORE LIKE...STRATEGIC COOKING BETWEEN MEN AND WOMEN, AND TASTING BASIL WITH LOAVES?
YUP, YOU SURE GOT IT WRONG!
BASICALLY, BOYS AND GIRLS GET TOGETHER TO TALK AND GET TO KNOW EACH OTHER.
THEY GET TOGETHER TO TALK...
I WANNA DO THAT!
...OH.

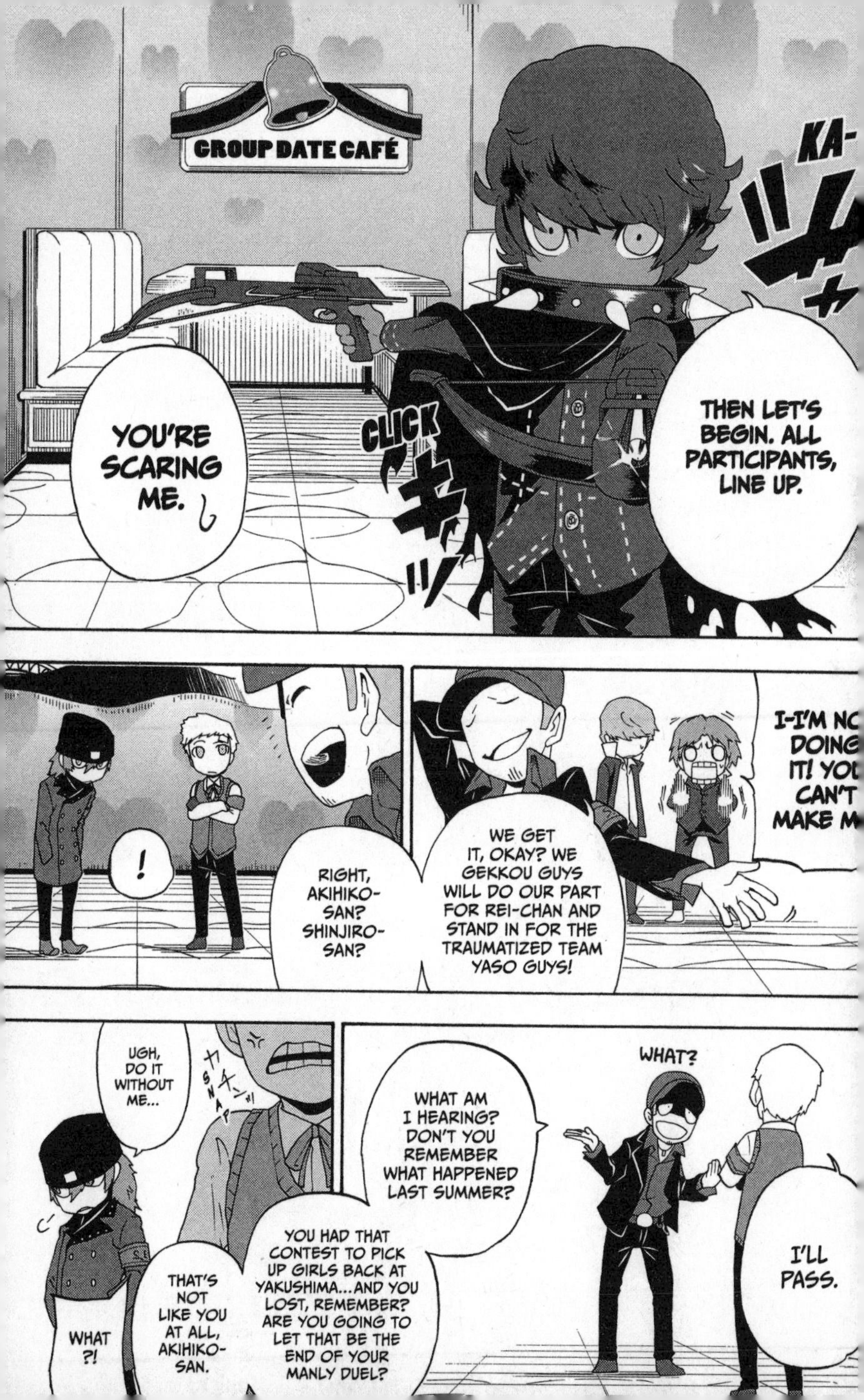
GROUP DATE CAFÉ
KA-
THEN LET'S BEGIN. ALL PARTICIPANTS, LINE UP.
CLICK
YOU'RE SCARING ME.
I-I'M NO DOING IT! YOU CAN'T MAKE M
WE GET IT, OKAY? WE GEKKOU GUYS WILL DO OUR PART FOR REI-CHAN AND STAND IN FOR THE TRAUMATIZED TEAM YASO GUYS!
RIGHT, AKIHIKO-SAN? SHINJIRO-SAN?
!
WHAT?
I'LL PASS.
WHAT AM I HEARING? DON'T YOU REMEMBER WHAT HAPPENED LAST SUMMER?
UGH, DO IT WITHOUT ME...
SNAP
YOU HAD THAT CONTEST TO PICK UP GIRLS BACK AT YAKUSHIMA...AND YOU LOST, REMEMBER? ARE YOU GOING TO LET THAT BE THE END OF YOUR MANLY DUEL?
THAT'S NOT LIKE YOU AT ALL, AKIHIKO-SAN.
WHAT ?!

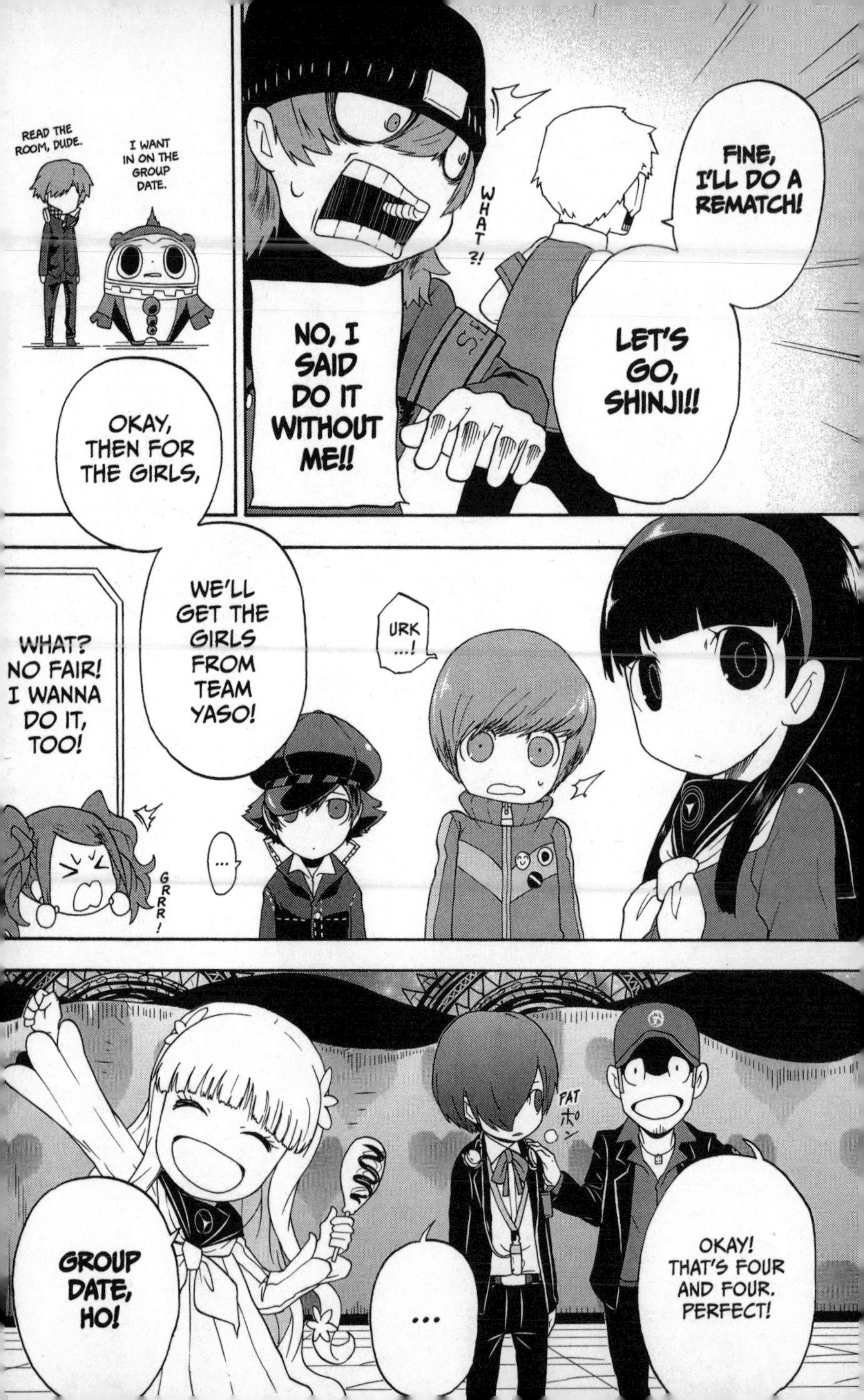

FINE, I'LL DO A REMATCH!
WHAT?!
LET'S GO, SHINJI!!
NO, I SAID DO IT WITHOUT ME!!
I WANT IN ON THE GROUP DATE.
READ THE ROOM, DUDE.
OKAY, THEN FOR THE GIRLS,
WE'LL GET THE GIRLS FROM TEAM YASO!
URK...!
...
WHAT? NO FAIR! I WANNA DO IT, TOO!
GRRR!
OKAY! THAT'S FOUR AND FOUR. PERFECT!
PAT
...
GROUP DATE, HO!

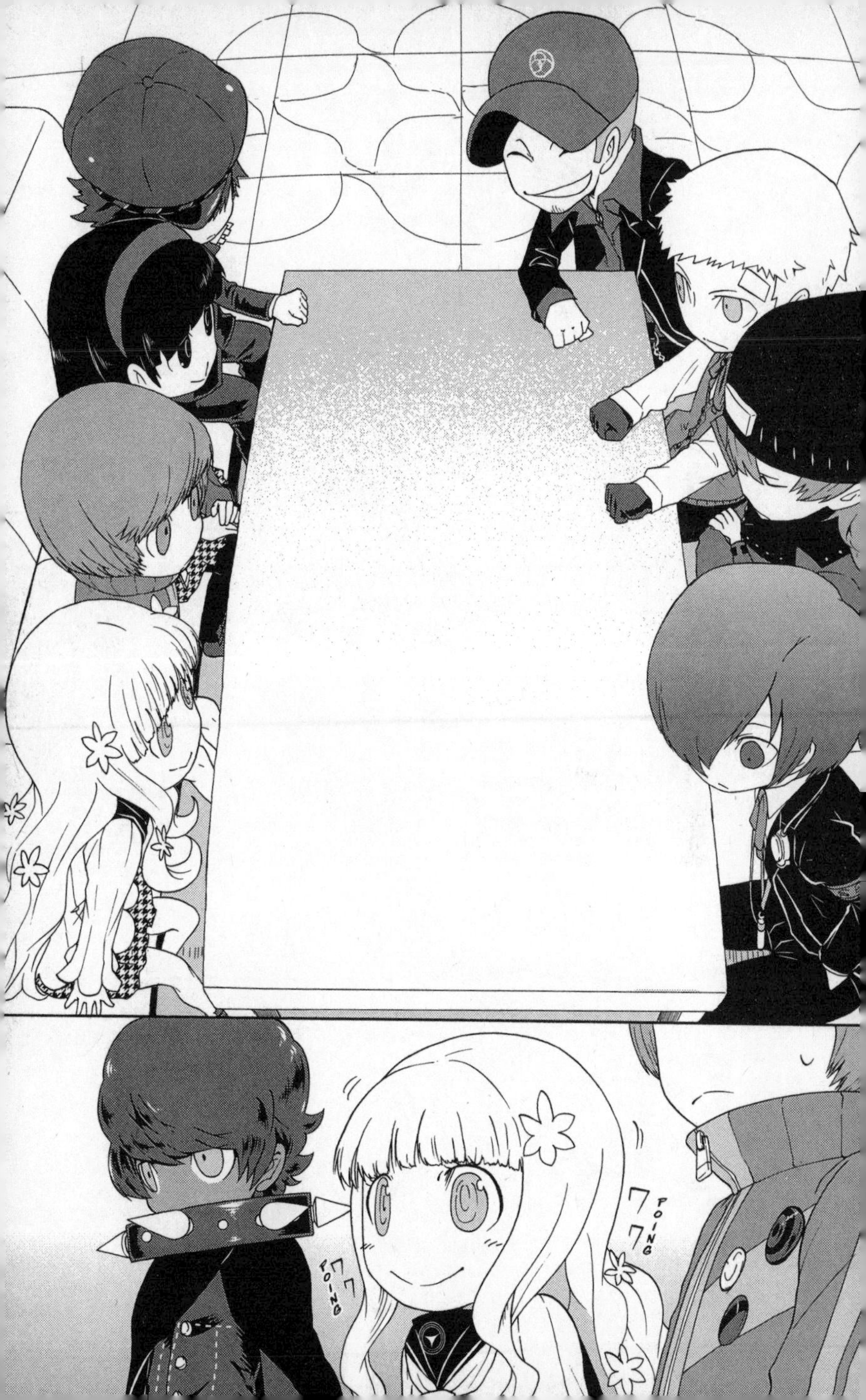
FOING
FOING

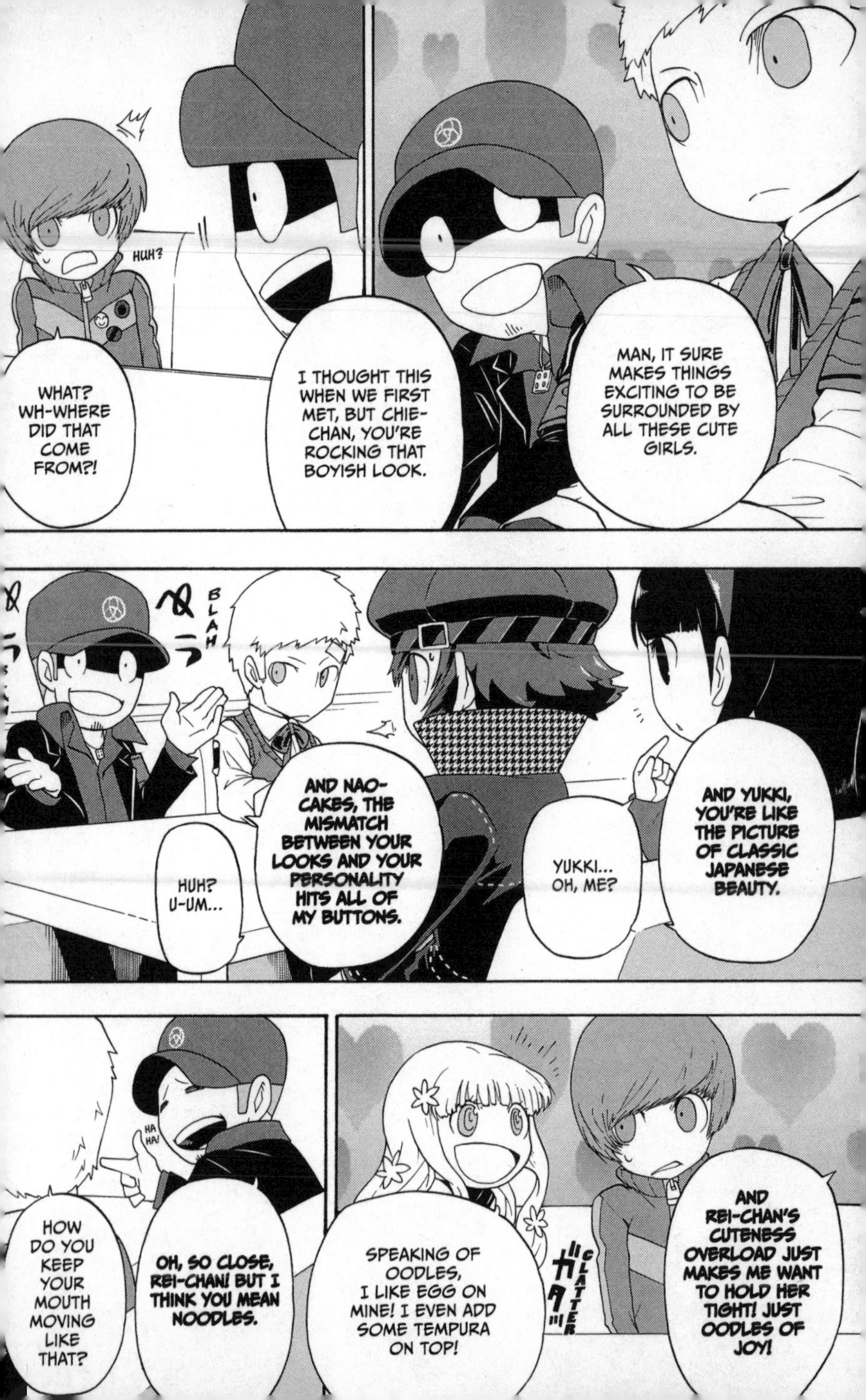
MAN, IT SURE MAKES THINGS EXCITING TO BE SURROUNDED BY ALL THESE CUTE GIRLS.
I THOUGHT THIS WHEN WE FIRST MET, BUT CHIE-CHAN, YOU'RE ROCKING THAT BOYISH LOOK.
HUH?
WHAT? WH-WHERE DID THAT COME FROM?!
AND YUKKI, YOU'RE LIKE THE PICTURE OF CLASSIC JAPANESE BEAUTY.
YUKKI... OH, ME?
AND NAO-CAKES, THE MISMATCH BETWEEN YOUR LOOKS AND YOUR PERSONALITY HITS ALL OF MY BUTTONS.
HUH? U-UM...
BLAH
AND REI-CHAN'S CUTENESS OVERLOAD JUST MAKES ME WANT TO HOLD HER TIGHT! JUST OODLES OF JOY!
CLATTER
SPEAKING OF OODLES, I LIKE EGG ON MINE! I EVEN ADD SOME TEMPURA ON TOP!
HA HA!
OH, SO CLOSE, REI-CHAN! BUT I THINK YOU MEAN NOODLES.
HOW DO YOU KEEP YOUR MOUTH MOVING LIKE THAT?

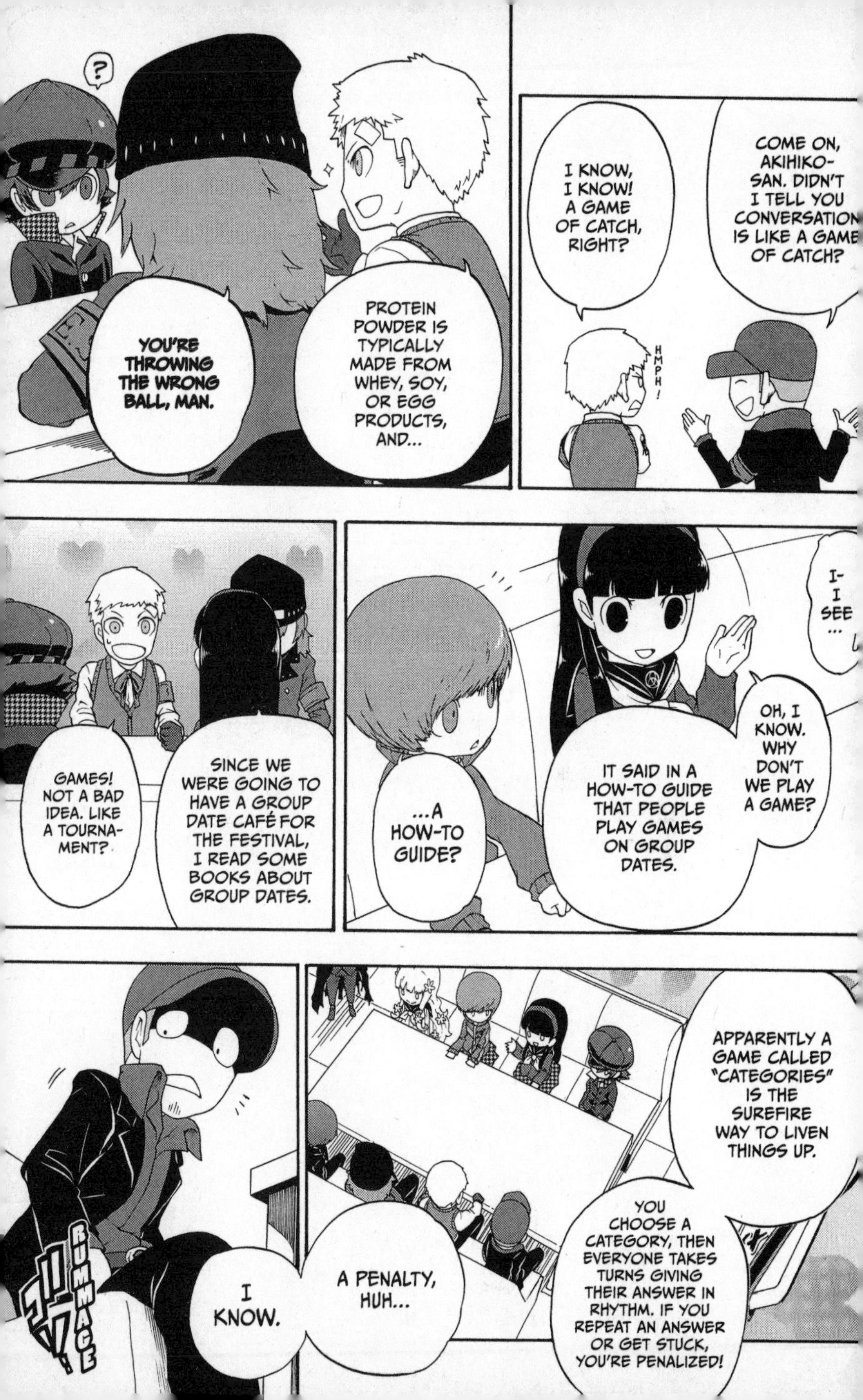
COME ON, AKIHIKO-SAN. DIDN'T I TELL YOU CONVERSATION IS LIKE A GAME OF CATCH?
I KNOW, I KNOW! A GAME OF CATCH, RIGHT?
HMPH!
?
PROTEIN POWDER IS TYPICALLY MADE FROM WHEY, SOY, OR EGG PRODUCTS, AND...
YOU'RE THROWING THE WRONG BALL, MAN.
I- I SEE...
OH, I KNOW. WHY DON'T WE PLAY A GAME?
IT SAID IN A HOW-TO GUIDE THAT PEOPLE PLAY GAMES ON GROUP DATES.
...A HOW-TO GUIDE?
SINCE WE WERE GOING TO HAVE A GROUP DATE CAFÉ FOR THE FESTIVAL, I READ SOME BOOKS ABOUT GROUP DATES.
GAMES! NOT A BAD IDEA. LIKE A TOURNAMENT?
APPARENTLY A GAME CALLED "CATEGORIES" IS THE SUREFIRE WAY TO LIVEN THINGS UP.
YOU CHOOSE A CATEGORY, THEN EVERYONE TAKES TURNS GIVING THEIR ANSWER IN RHYTHM. IF YOU REPEAT AN ANSWER OR GET STUCK, YOU'RE PENALIZED!
A PENALTY, HUH...
I KNOW.
RUMMAGE

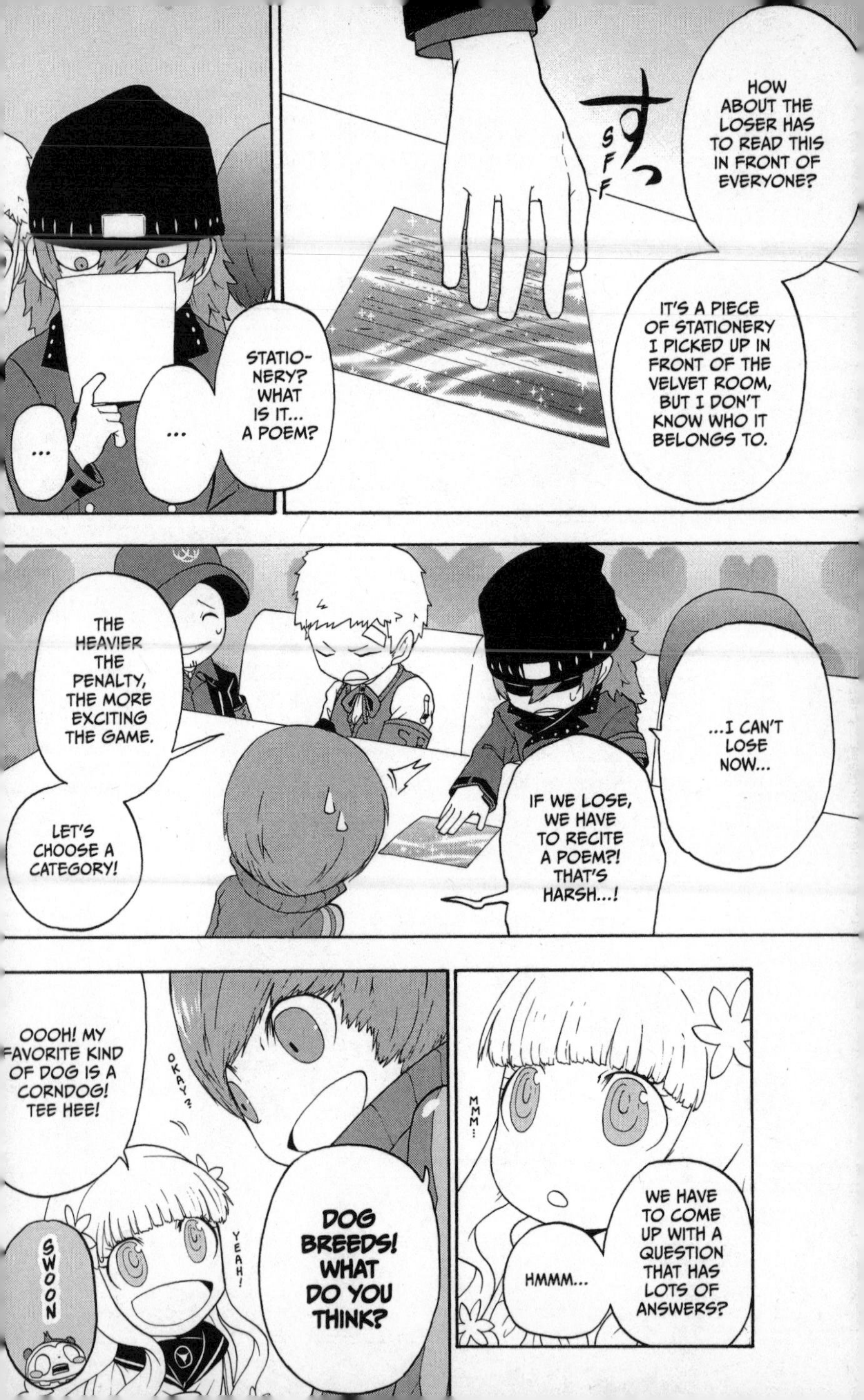
HOW ABOUT THE LOSER HAS TO READ THIS IN FRONT OF EVERYONE?
SFF
IT'S A PIECE OF STATIONERY I PICKED UP IN FRONT OF THE VELVET ROOM, BUT I DON'T KNOW WHO IT BELONGS TO.
STATIO-NERY? WHAT IS IT... A POEM?
...
...
...I CAN'T LOSE NOW...
IF WE LOSE, WE HAVE TO RECITE A POEM?! THAT'S HARSH...!
THE HEAVIER THE PENALTY, THE MORE EXCITING THE GAME.
LET'S CHOOSE A CATEGORY!
MMM...
WE HAVE TO COME UP WITH A QUESTION THAT HAS LOTS OF ANSWERS?
HMMM...
DOG BREEDS! WHAT DO YOU THINK?
OKAY?
OOOH! MY FAVORITE KIND OF DOG IS A CORNDOG! TEE HEE!
YEAH!
SWOON

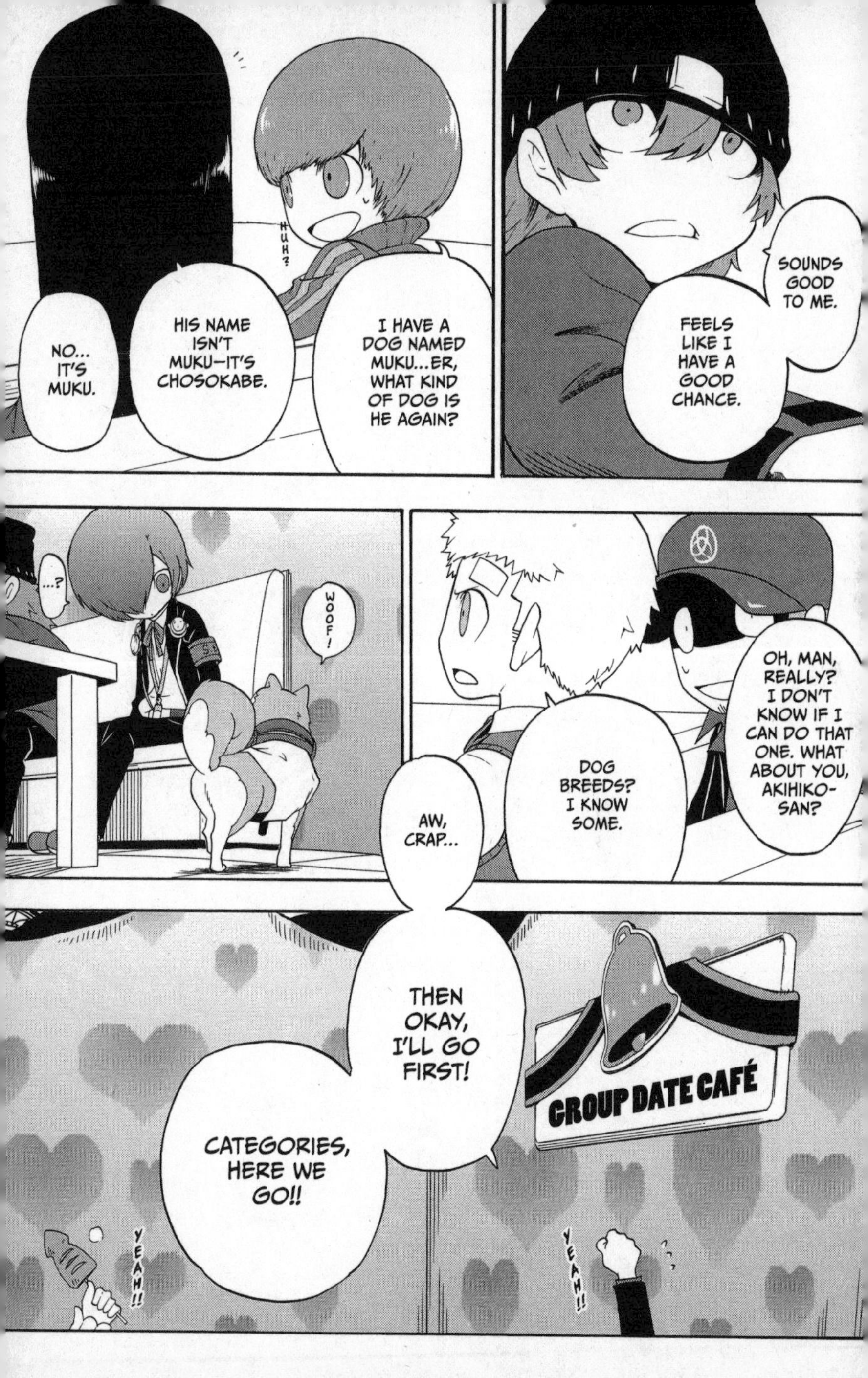
SOUNDS GOOD TO ME.
FEELS LIKE I HAVE A GOOD CHANCE.
HUH?
I HAVE A DOG NAMED MUKU...ER, WHAT KIND OF DOG IS HE AGAIN?
HIS NAME ISN'T MUKU—IT'S CHOSOKABE.
NO... IT'S MUKU.
OH, MAN, REALLY? I DON'T KNOW IF I CAN DO THAT ONE. WHAT ABOUT YOU, AKIHIKO-SAN?
DOG BREEDS? I KNOW SOME.
AW, CRAP...
WOOF!
...?
GROUP DATE CAFÉ
THEN OKAY, I'LL GO FIRST!
CATEGORIES, HERE WE GO!!
YEAH!!
YEAH!!

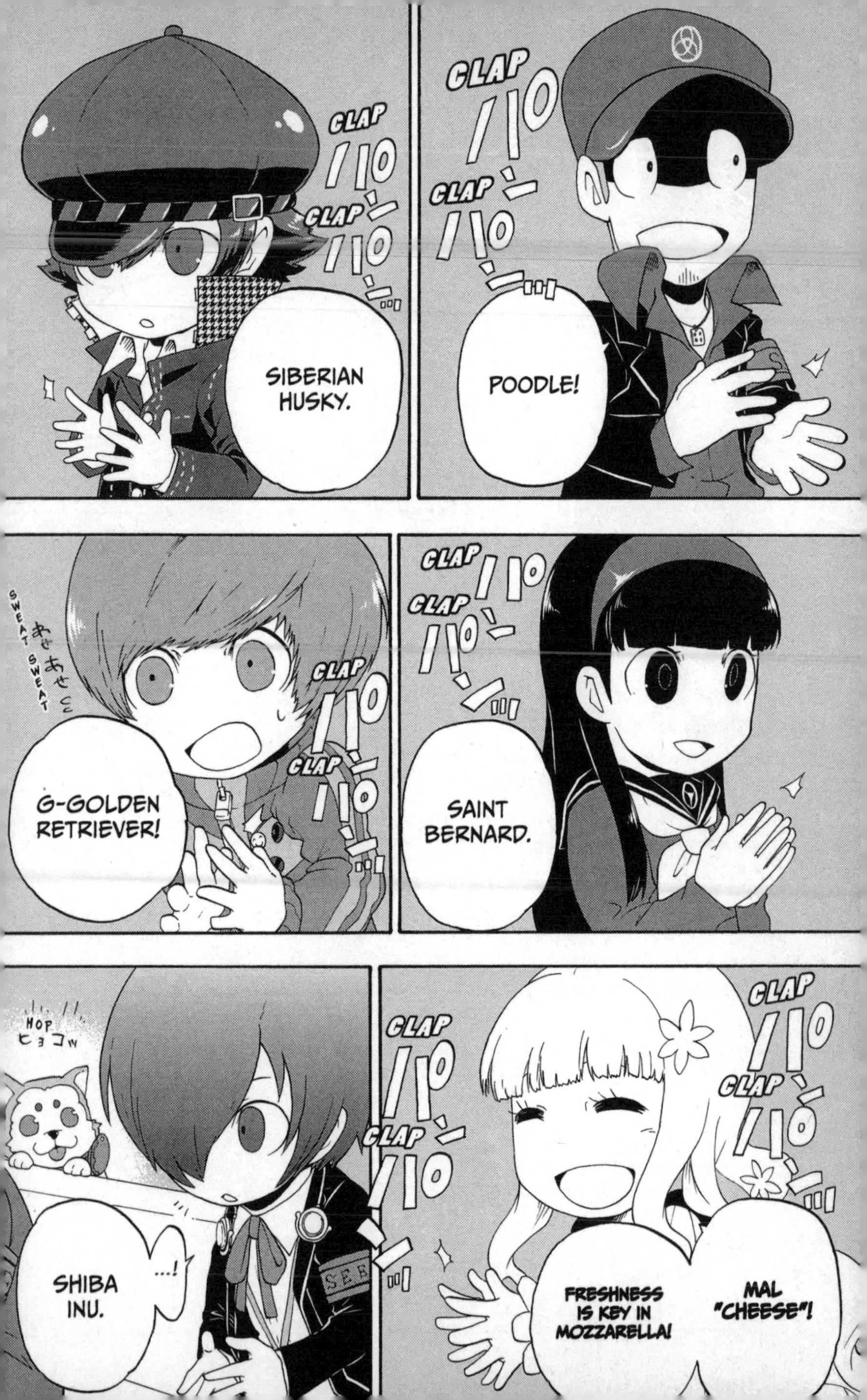
CLAP
CLAP
POODLE!
CLAP
CLAP
SIBERIAN HUSKY.
CLAP
CLAP
SAINT BERNARD.
SWEAT SWEAT
あせあせ
CLAP
CLAP
G-GOLDEN RETRIEVER!
CLAP
CLAP
MAL "CHEESE"!
CLAP
CLAP
FRESHNESS IS KEY IN MOZZARELLA!
CLAP
CLAP
HOP
ヒョコッ
...!
SHIBA INU.

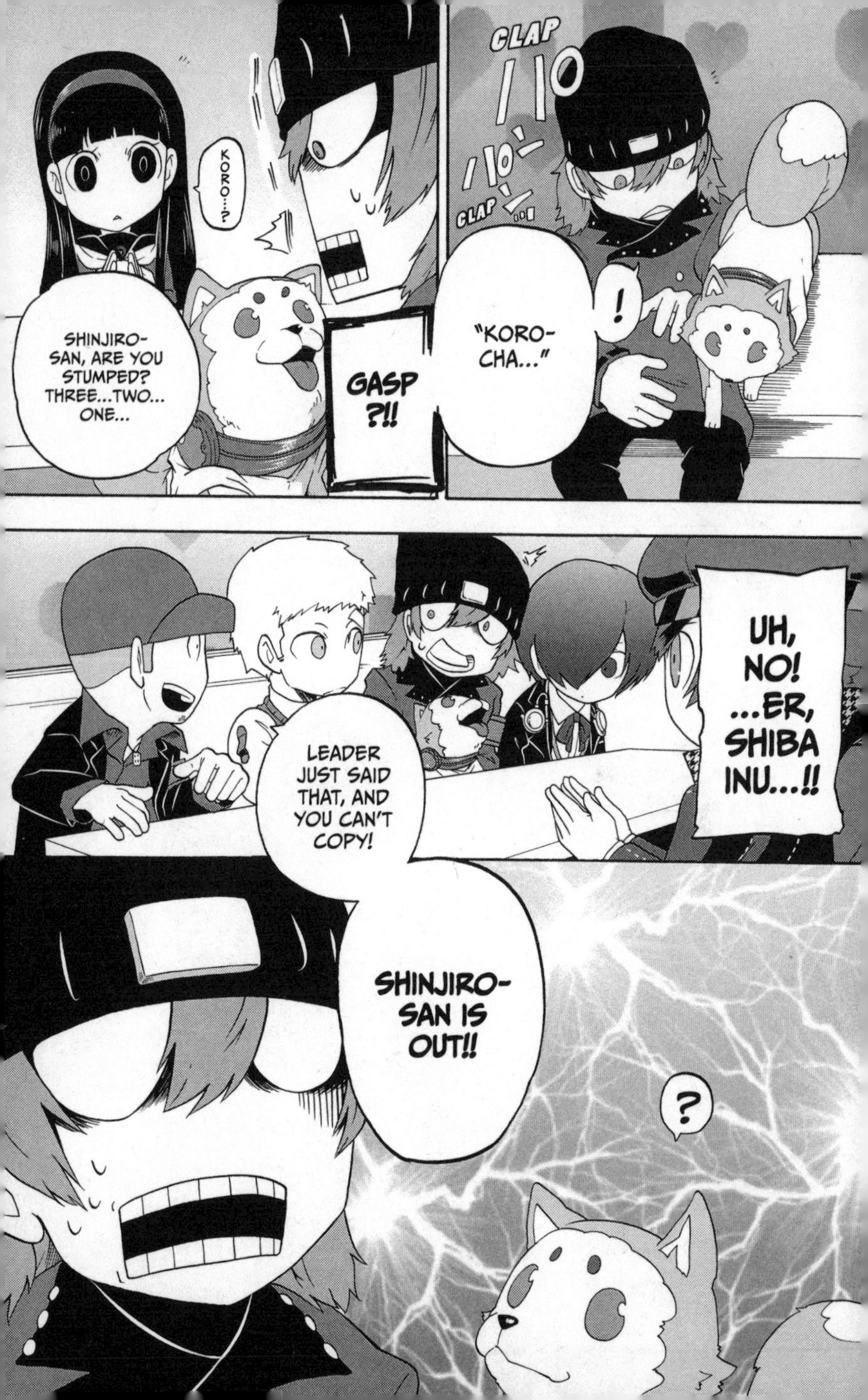
CLAP
CLAP
"KORO-CHA..."
!
KORO...?
GASP ?!!
SHINJIRO-SAN, ARE YOU STUMPED? THREE...TWO... ONE...
UH, NO! ...ER, SHIBA INU...!!
LEADER JUST SAID THAT, AND YOU CAN'T COPY!
SHINJIRO-SAN IS OUT!!
?

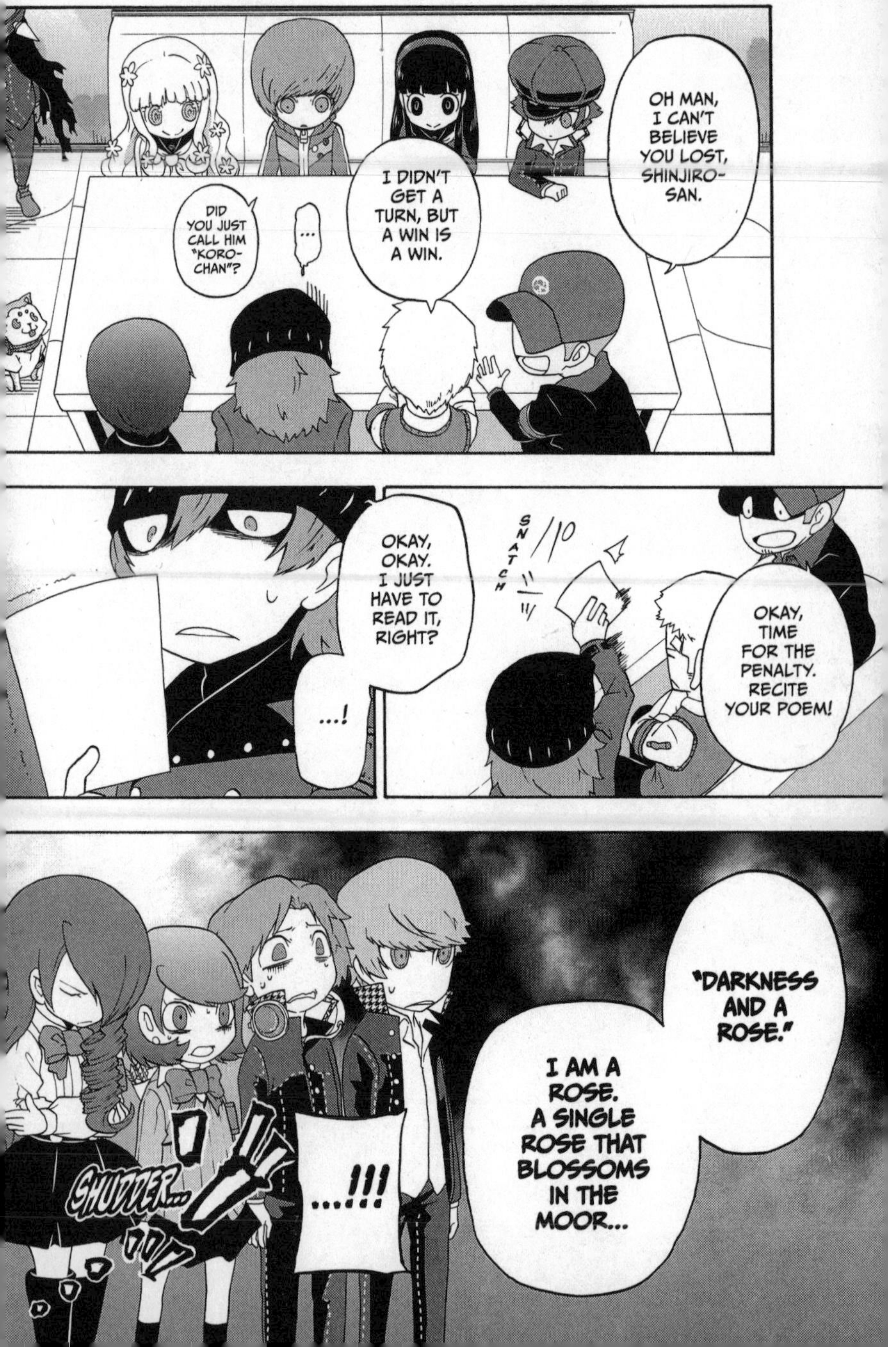
OH MAN, I CAN'T BELIEVE YOU LOST, SHINJIRO-SAN.
I DIDN'T GET A TURN, BUT A WIN IS A WIN.
...
DID YOU JUST CALL HIM "KORO-CHAN"?
OKAY, TIME FOR THE PENALTY. RECITE YOUR POEM!
SNATCH
OKAY, OKAY. I JUST HAVE TO READ IT, RIGHT?
...!
"DARKNESS AND A ROSE."
I AM A ROSE. A SINGLE ROSE THAT BLOSSOMS IN THE MOOR...
...!!!
SHUDDER...

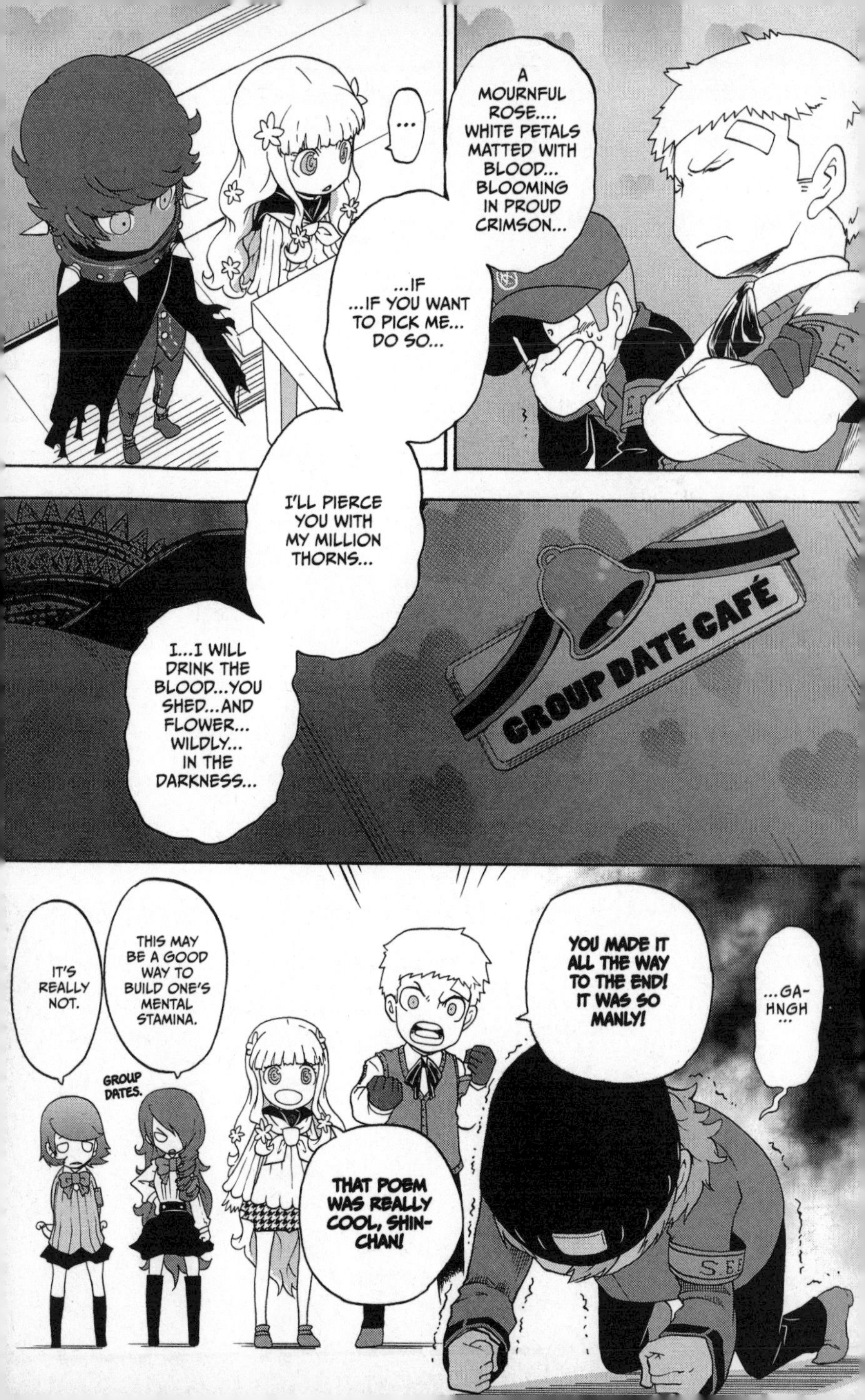
A MOURNFUL ROSE.... WHITE PETALS MATTED WITH BLOOD... BLOOMING IN PROUD CRIMSON...
...IF ...IF YOU WANT TO PICK ME... DO SO...
...
I'LL PIERCE YOU WITH MY MILLION THORNS...
GROUP DATE CAFÉ
I...I WILL DRINK THE BLOOD...YOU SHED...AND FLOWER... WILDLY... IN THE DARKNESS...
...GA-HNGH...
YOU MADE IT ALL THE WAY TO THE END! IT WAS SO MANLY!
THAT POEM WAS REALLY COOL, SHIN-CHAN!
THIS MAY BE A GOOD WAY TO BUILD ONE'S MENTAL STAMINA.
GROUP DATES.
IT'S REALLY NOT.

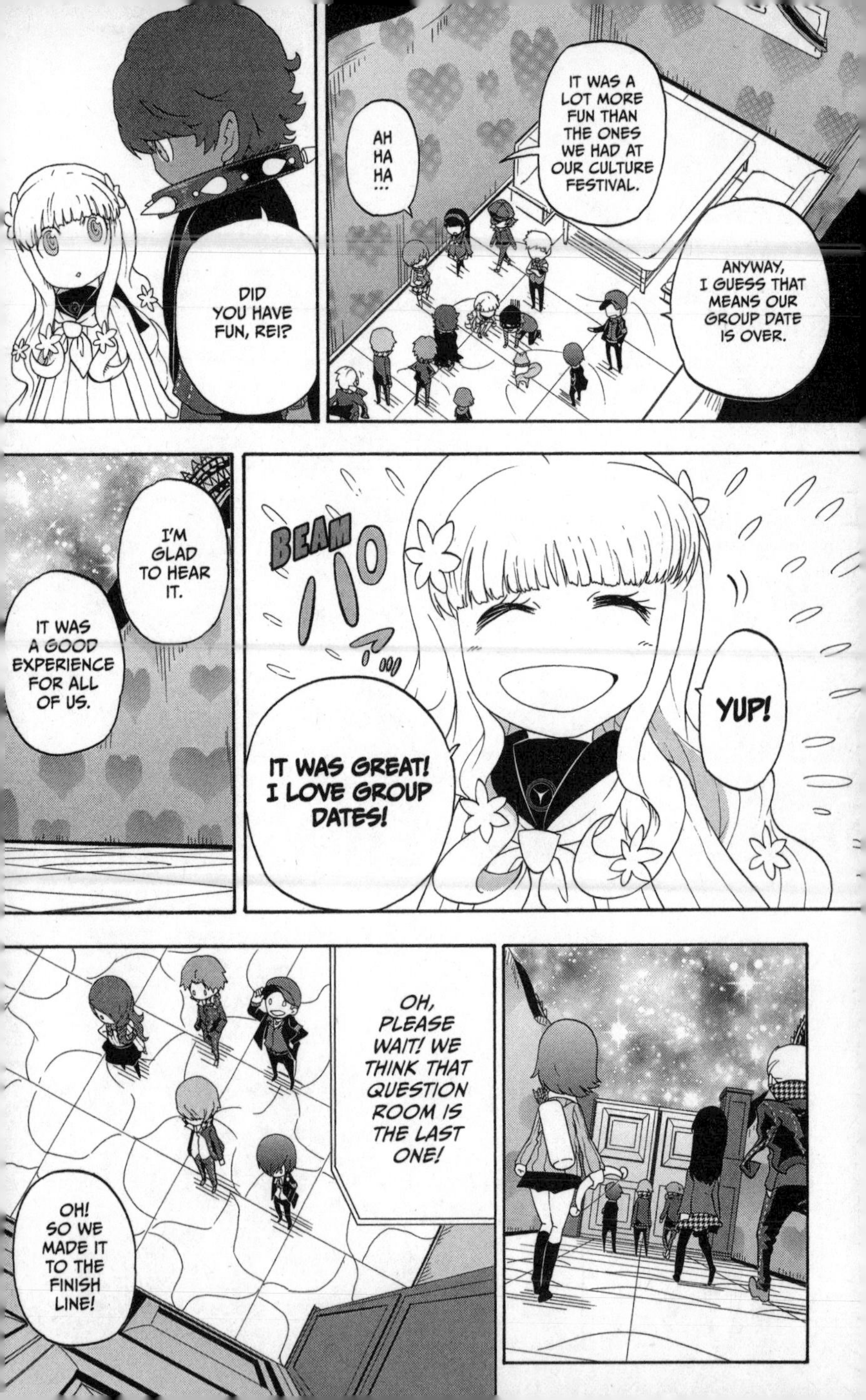
IT WAS A LOT MORE FUN THAN THE ONES WE HAD AT OUR CULTURE FESTIVAL.
AH HA HA...
ANYWAY, I GUESS THAT MEANS OUR GROUP DATE IS OVER.
DID YOU HAVE FUN, REI?
YUP!
BEAM
IT WAS GREAT! I LOVE GROUP DATES!
I'M GLAD TO HEAR IT.
IT WAS A GOOD EXPERIENCE FOR ALL OF US.
OH, PLEASE WAIT! WE THINK THAT QUESTION ROOM IS THE LAST ONE!
OH! SO WE MADE IT TO THE FINISH LINE!

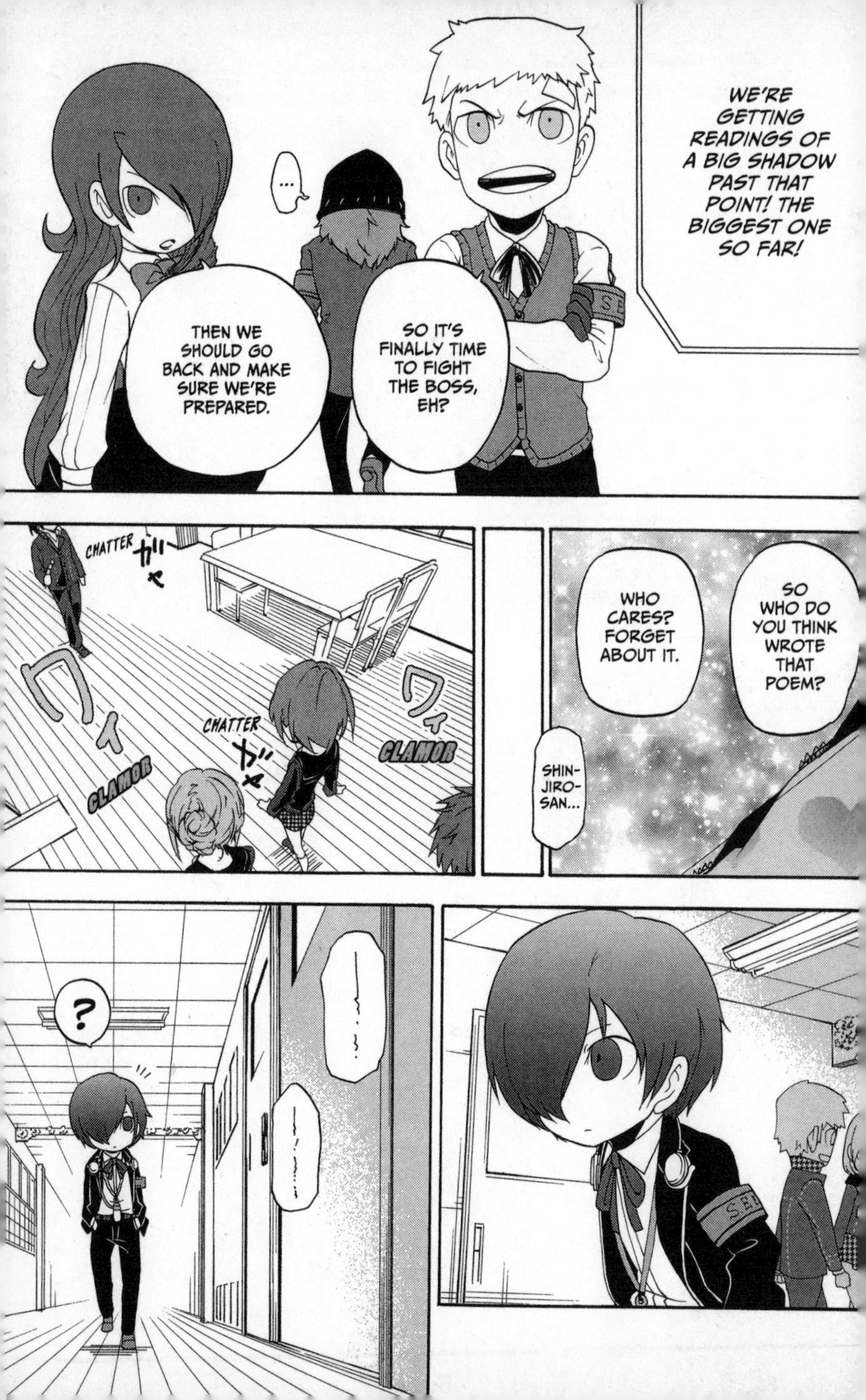
WE'RE GETTING READINGS OF A BIG SHADOW PAST THAT POINT! THE BIGGEST ONE SO FAR!
SO IT'S FINALLY TIME TO FIGHT THE BOSS, EH?
...
THEN WE SHOULD GO BACK AND MAKE SURE WE'RE PREPARED.
SO WHO DO YOU THINK WROTE THAT POEM?
WHO CARES? FORGET ABOUT IT.
SHIN-JIRO-SAN...
ワイ CLAMOR
CHATTER ガヤ
CHATTER ガヤ
ワイ CLAMOR
?

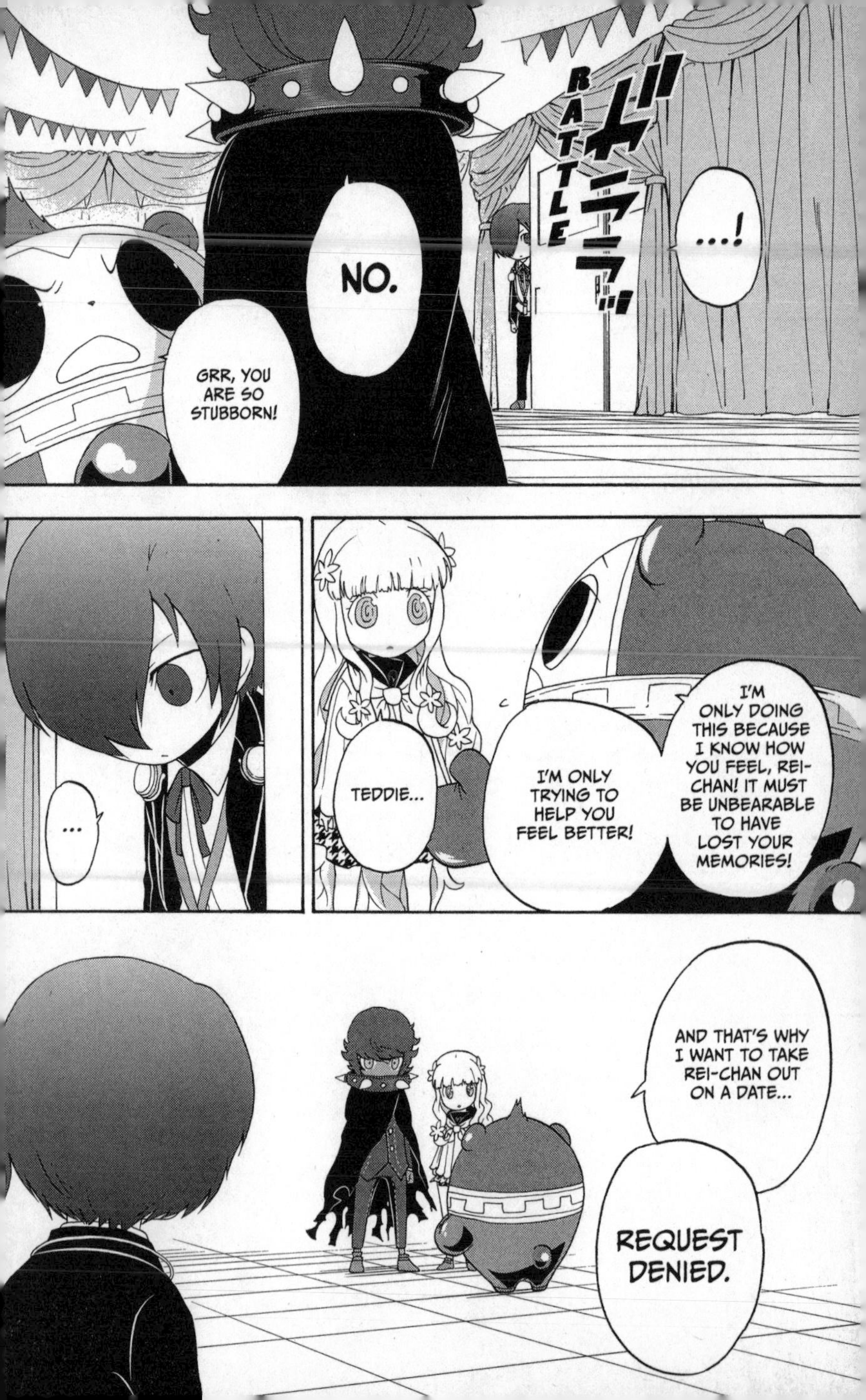
RATTLE
...!
NO.
GRR, YOU ARE SO STUBBORN!
I'M ONLY DOING THIS BECAUSE I KNOW HOW YOU FEEL, REI-CHAN! IT MUST BE UNBEARABLE TO HAVE LOST YOUR MEMORIES!
I'M ONLY TRYING TO HELP YOU FEEL BETTER!
TEDDIE...
...
AND THAT'S WHY I WANT TO TAKE REI-CHAN OUT ON A DATE...
REQUEST DENIED.

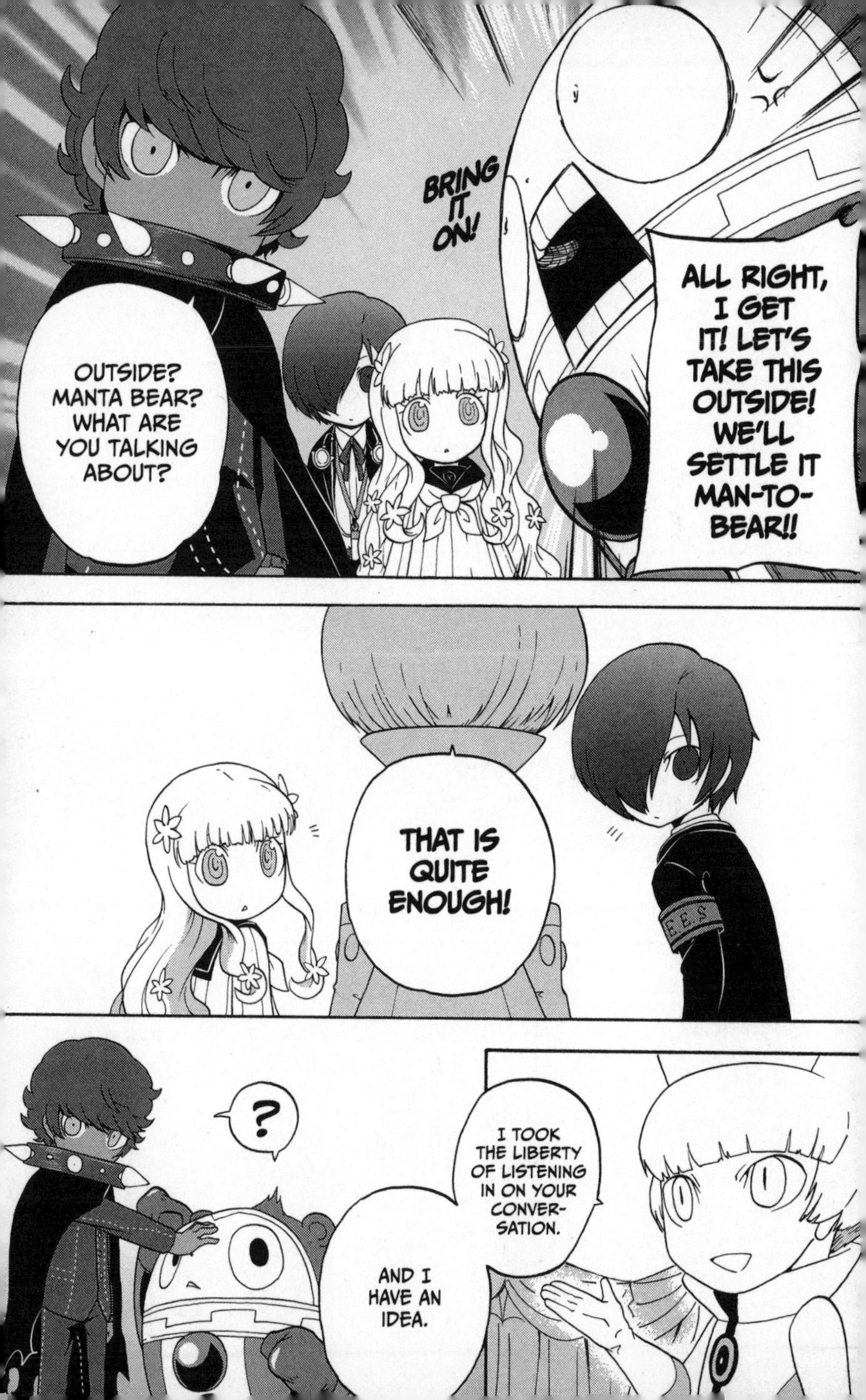
ALL RIGHT, I GET IT! LET'S TAKE THIS OUTSIDE! WE'LL SETTLE IT MAN-TO-BEAR!!
BRING IT ON!
OUTSIDE? MANTA BEAR? WHAT ARE YOU TALKING ABOUT?
THAT IS QUITE ENOUGH!
I TOOK THE LIBERTY OF LISTENING IN ON YOUR CONVER-SATION.
AND I HAVE AN IDEA.
?

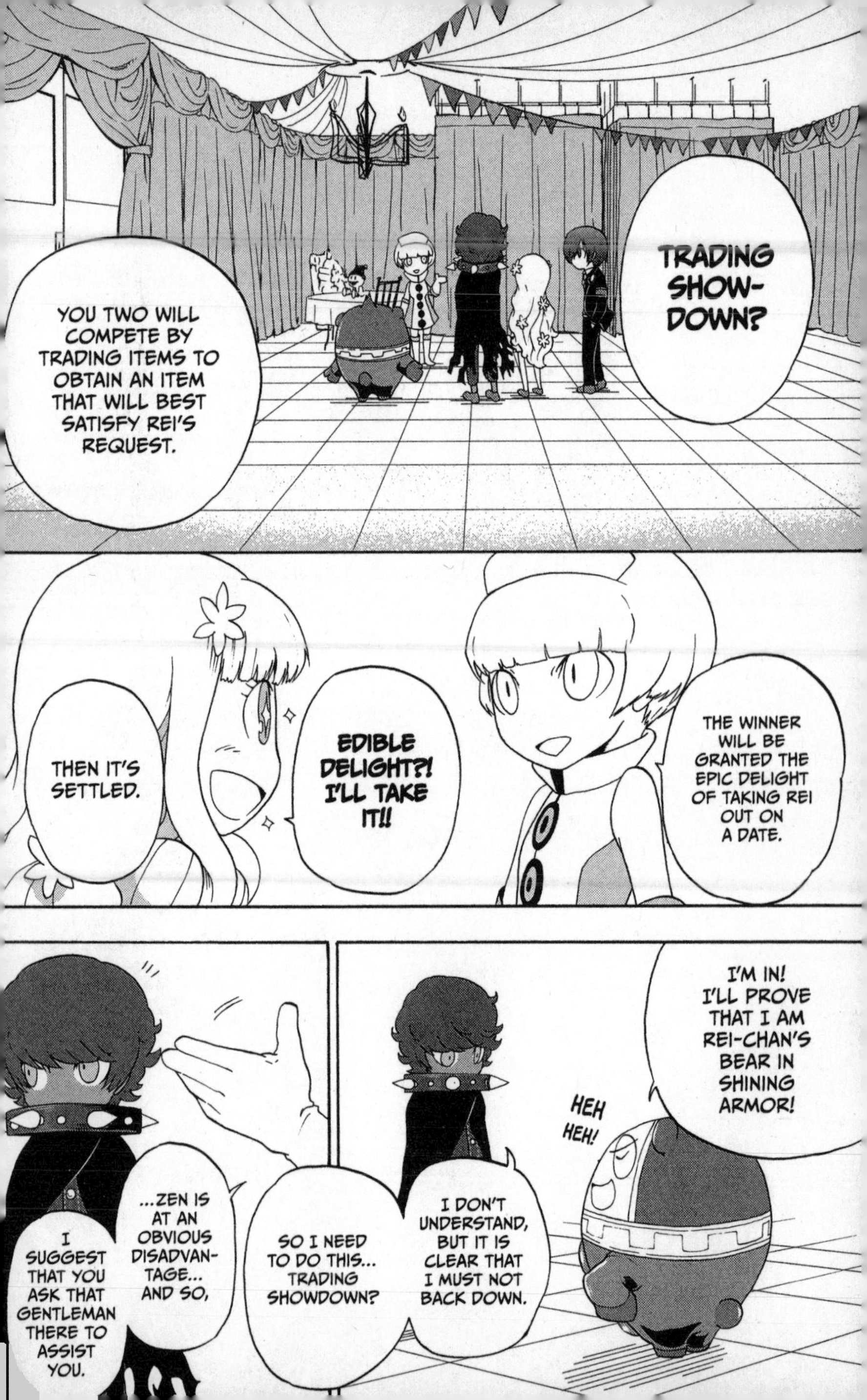
TRADING SHOW-DOWN?
YOU TWO WILL COMPETE BY TRADING ITEMS TO OBTAIN AN ITEM THAT WILL BEST SATISFY REI'S REQUEST.
THE WINNER WILL BE GRANTED THE EPIC DELIGHT OF TAKING REI OUT ON A DATE.
EDIBLE DELIGHT?! I'LL TAKE IT!!
THEN IT'S SETTLED.
I'M IN! I'LL PROVE THAT I AM REI-CHAN'S BEAR IN SHINING ARMOR!
HEH HEH!
I DON'T UNDERSTAND, BUT IT IS CLEAR THAT I MUST NOT BACK DOWN.
SO I NEED TO DO THIS... TRADING SHOWDOWN?
...ZEN IS AT AN OBVIOUS DISADVAN-TAGE... AND SO,
I SUGGEST THAT YOU ASK THAT GENTLEMAN THERE TO ASSIST YOU.

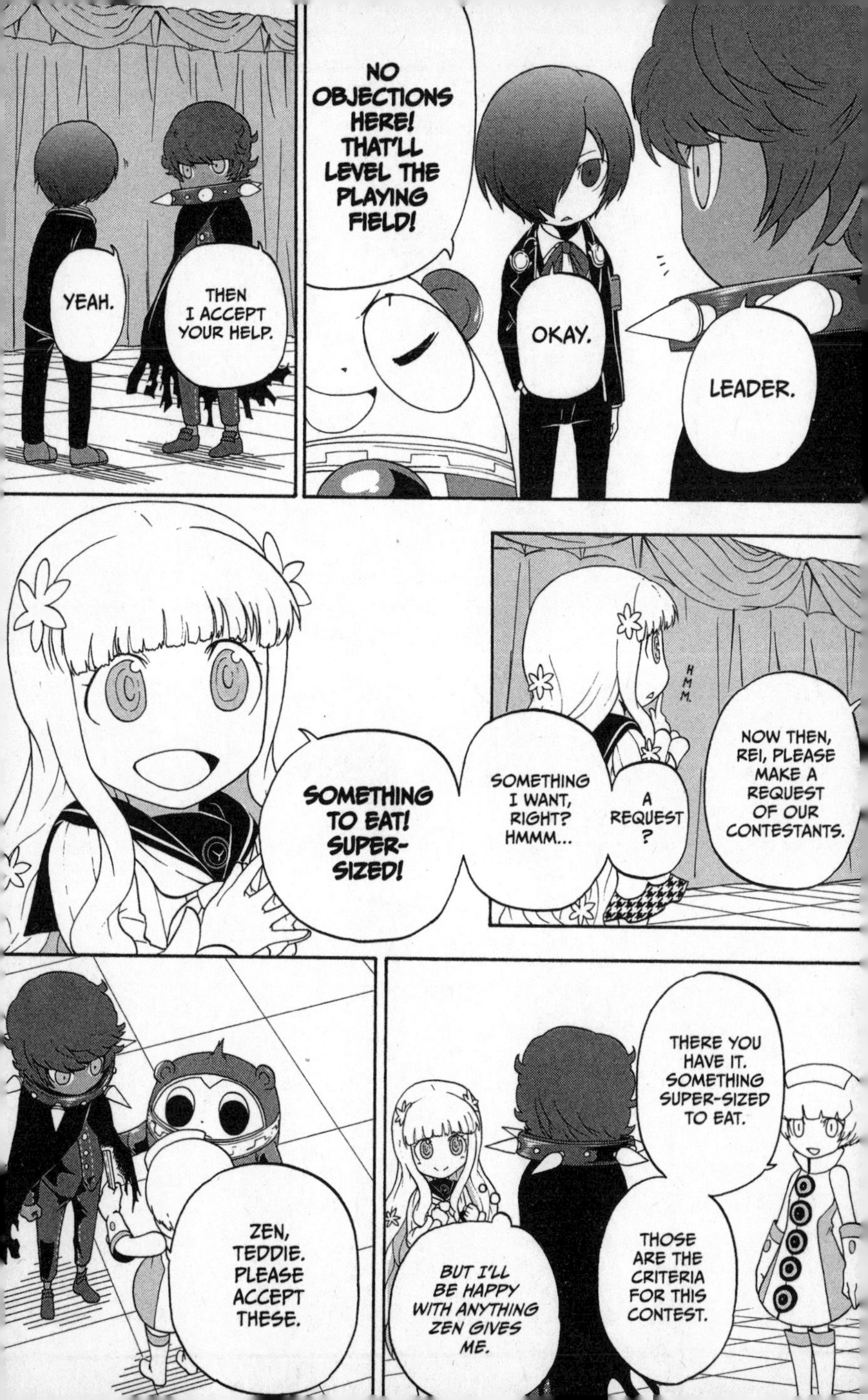
LEADER.
OKAY.
NO OBJECTIONS HERE! THAT'LL LEVEL THE PLAYING FIELD!
THEN I ACCEPT YOUR HELP.
YEAH.
NOW THEN, REI, PLEASE MAKE A REQUEST OF OUR CONTESTANTS.
HMM.
A REQUEST?
SOMETHING I WANT, RIGHT? HMMM...
SOMETHING TO EAT! SUPER-SIZED!
THERE YOU HAVE IT. SOMETHING SUPER-SIZED TO EAT.
THOSE ARE THE CRITERIA FOR THIS CONTEST.
BUT I'LL BE HAPPY WITH ANYTHING ZEN GIVES ME.
ZEN, TEDDIE. PLEASE ACCEPT THESE.

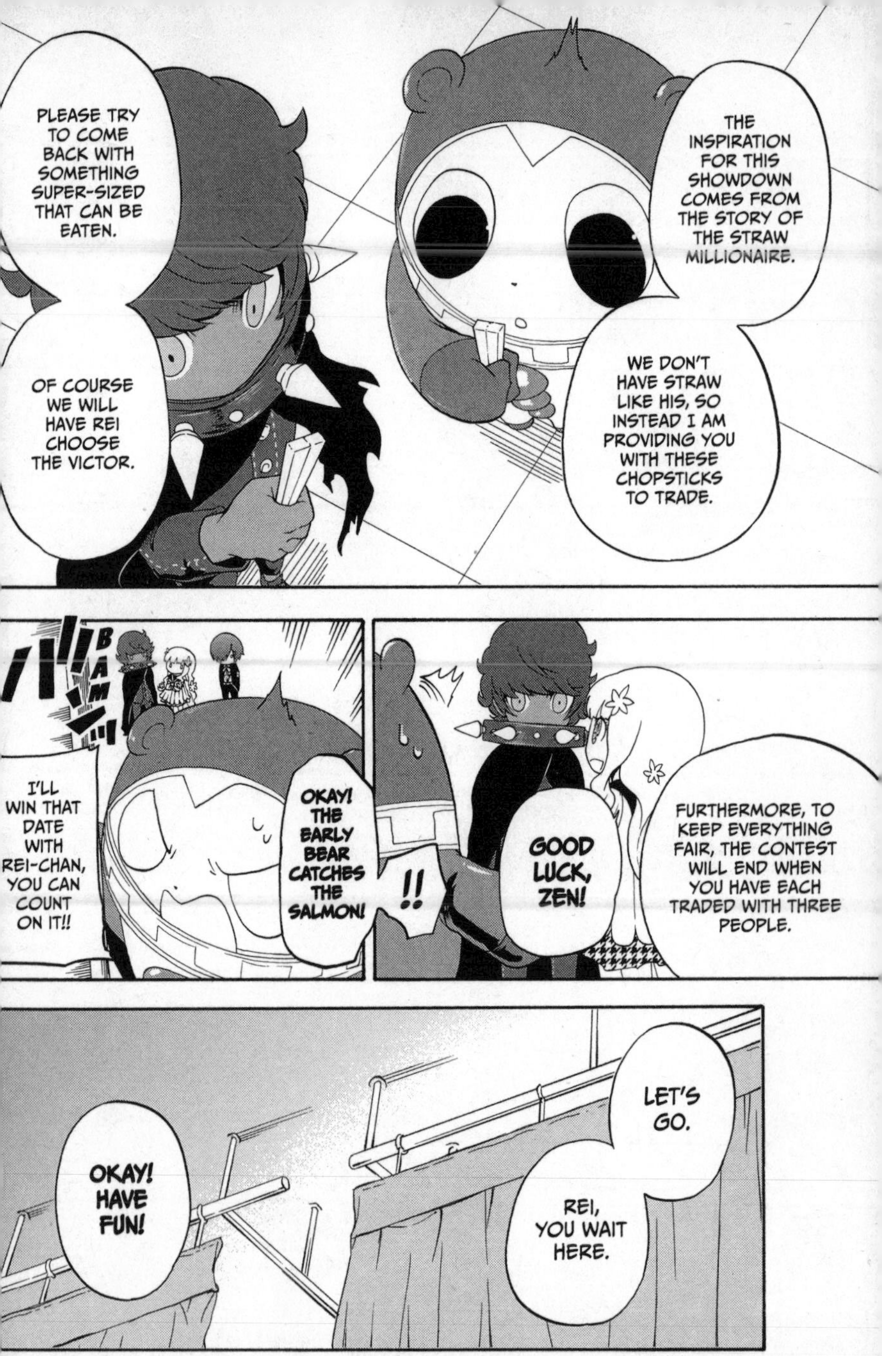
THE INSPIRATION FOR THIS SHOWDOWN COMES FROM THE STORY OF THE STRAW MILLIONAIRE.
WE DON'T HAVE STRAW LIKE HIS, SO INSTEAD I AM PROVIDING YOU WITH THESE CHOPSTICKS TO TRADE.
PLEASE TRY TO COME BACK WITH SOMETHING SUPER-SIZED THAT CAN BE EATEN.
OF COURSE WE WILL HAVE REI CHOOSE THE VICTOR.
FURTHERMORE, TO KEEP EVERYTHING FAIR, THE CONTEST WILL END WHEN YOU HAVE EACH TRADED WITH THREE PEOPLE.
GOOD LUCK, ZEN!
!!
BAM
OKAY! THE EARLY BEAR CATCHES THE SALMON!
I'LL WIN THAT DATE WITH REI-CHAN, YOU CAN COUNT ON IT!!
LET'S GO.
REI, YOU WAIT HERE.
OKAY! HAVE FUN!

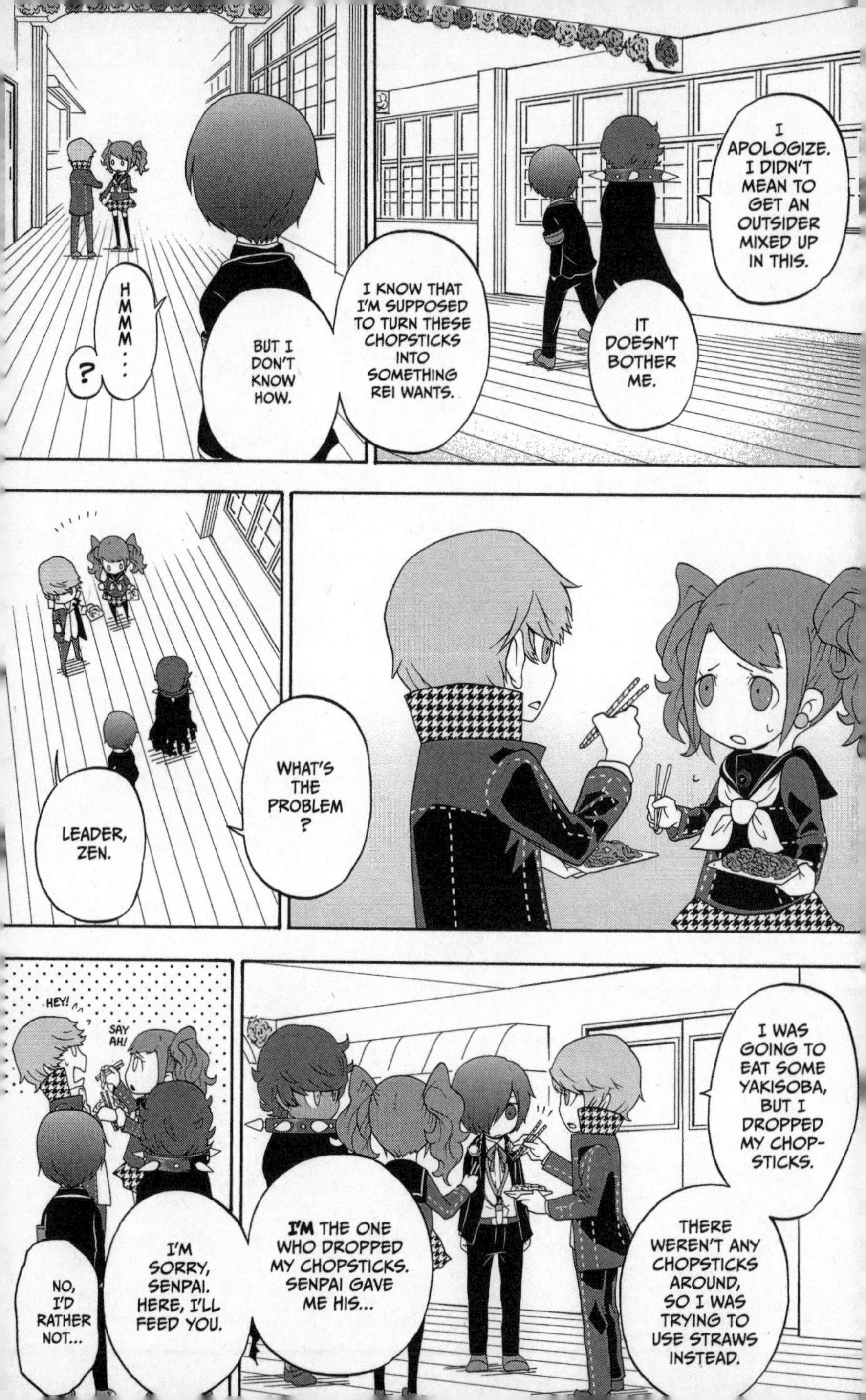
I APOLOGIZE. I DIDN'T MEAN TO GET AN OUTSIDER MIXED UP IN THIS.
IT DOESN'T BOTHER ME.
I KNOW THAT I'M SUPPOSED TO TURN THESE CHOPSTICKS INTO SOMETHING REI WANTS.
BUT I DON'T KNOW HOW.
HMMM...
?
WHAT'S THE PROBLEM?
LEADER, ZEN.
I WAS GOING TO EAT SOME YAKISOBA, BUT I DROPPED MY CHOP-STICKS.
THERE WEREN'T ANY CHOPSTICKS AROUND, SO I WAS TRYING TO USE STRAWS INSTEAD.
I'M THE ONE WHO DROPPED MY CHOPSTICKS. SENPAI GAVE ME HIS...
SAY AH!
HEY!
I'M SORRY, SENPAI. HERE, I'LL FEED YOU.
NO, I'D RATHER NOT...

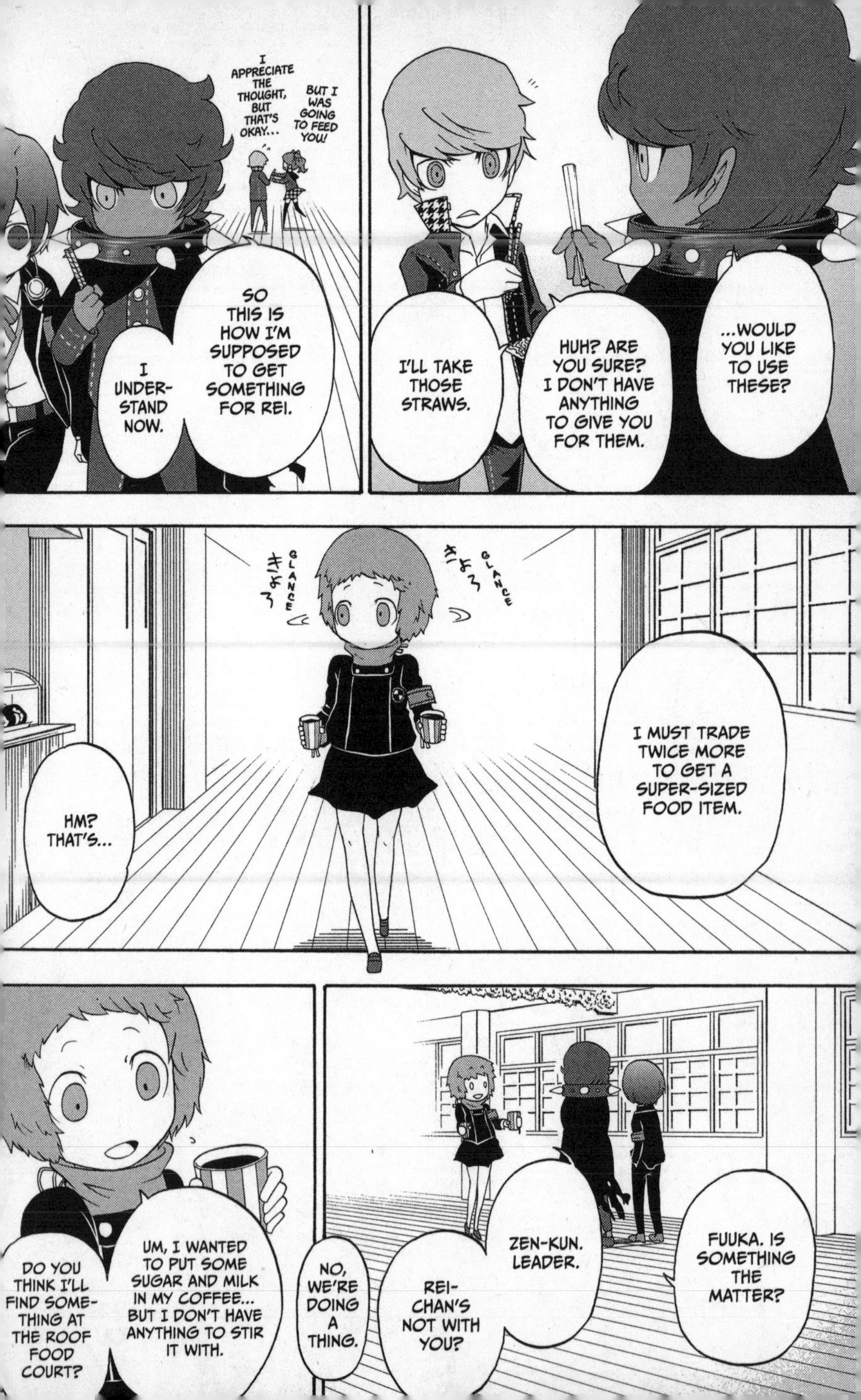
...WOULD YOU LIKE TO USE THESE?
HUH? ARE YOU SURE? I DON'T HAVE ANYTHING TO GIVE YOU FOR THEM.
I'LL TAKE THOSE STRAWS.
I APPRECIATE THE THOUGHT, BUT THAT'S OKAY...
BUT I WAS GOING TO FEED YOU!
SO THIS IS HOW I'M SUPPOSED TO GET SOMETHING FOR REI.
I UNDERSTAND NOW.
きょろ GLANCE
きょろ GLANCE
I MUST TRADE TWICE MORE TO GET A SUPER-SIZED FOOD ITEM.
HM? THAT'S...
FUUKA. IS SOMETHING THE MATTER?
ZEN-KUN. LEADER.
REI-CHAN'S NOT WITH YOU?
NO, WE'RE DOING A THING.
UM, I WANTED TO PUT SOME SUGAR AND MILK IN MY COFFEE... BUT I DON'T HAVE ANYTHING TO STIR IT WITH.
DO YOU THINK I'LL FIND SOME-THING AT THE ROOF FOOD COURT?

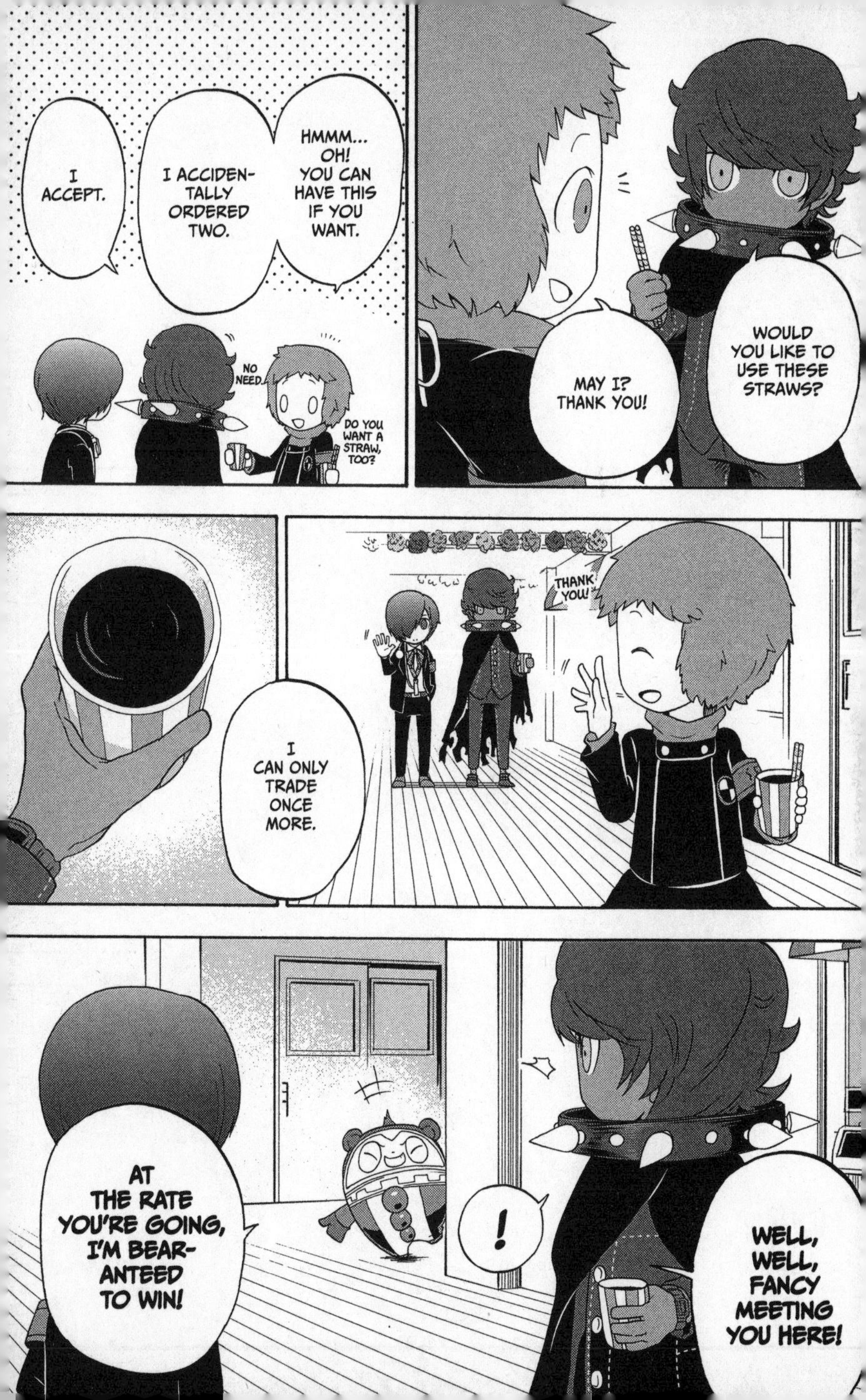
WOULD YOU LIKE TO USE THESE STRAWS?
MAY I? THANK YOU!
HMMM... OH! YOU CAN HAVE THIS IF YOU WANT.
I ACCIDENTALLY ORDERED TWO.
I ACCEPT.
DO YOU WANT A STRAW, TOO?
NO NEED.
THANK YOU!
I CAN ONLY TRADE ONCE MORE.
WELL, WELL, FANCY MEETING YOU HERE!
!
AT THE RATE YOU'RE GOING, I'M BEAR-ANTEED TO WIN!

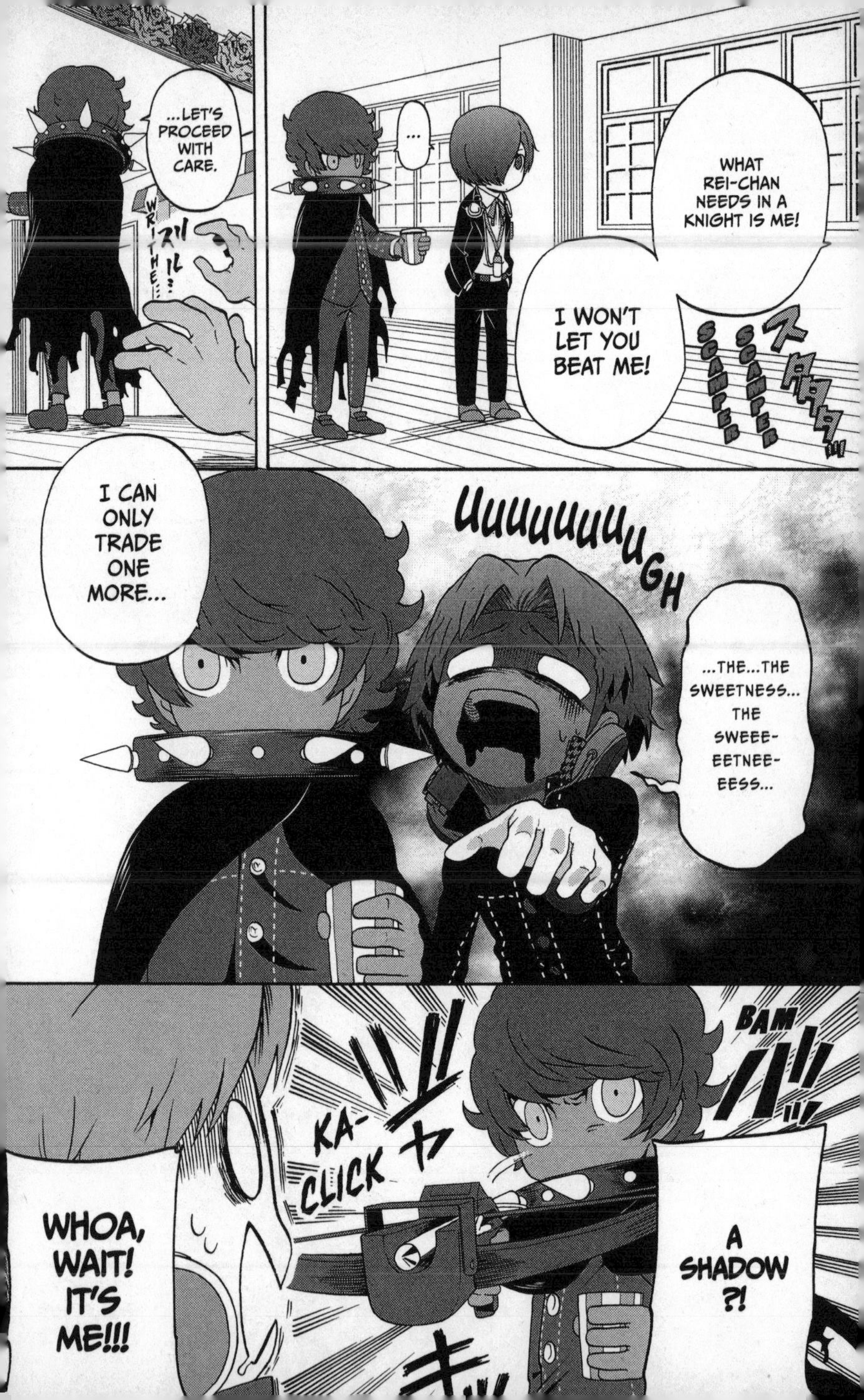
WHAT REI-CHAN NEEDS IN A KNIGHT IS ME!
I WON'T LET YOU BEAT ME!
SCAMPER SCAMPER
...
...LET'S PROCEED WITH CARE.
WRITHE...
UUUUUUUUUUGH
...THE...THE SWEETNESS... THE SWEEE-EETNEE-EESS...
I CAN ONLY TRADE ONE MORE...
BAM
A SHADOW?!
KA-CLICK
WHOA, WAIT! IT'S ME!!!

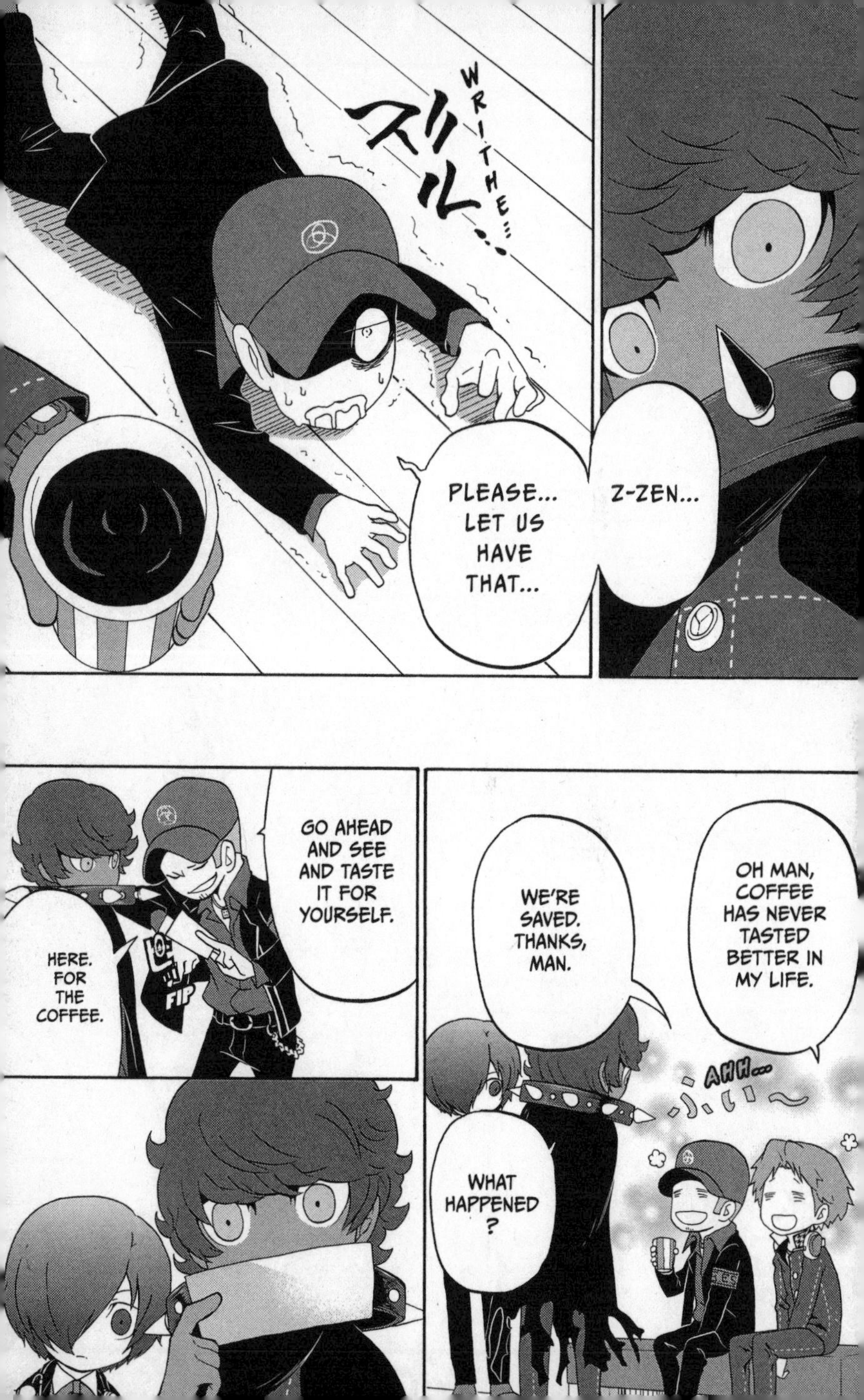
Z-ZEN...
WRITHE...
PLEASE... LET US HAVE THAT...
OH MAN, COFFEE HAS NEVER TASTED BETTER IN MY LIFE.
WE'RE SAVED. THANKS, MAN.
AHH...
WHAT HAPPENED?
GO AHEAD AND SEE AND TASTE IT FOR YOURSELF.
HERE. FOR THE COFFEE.

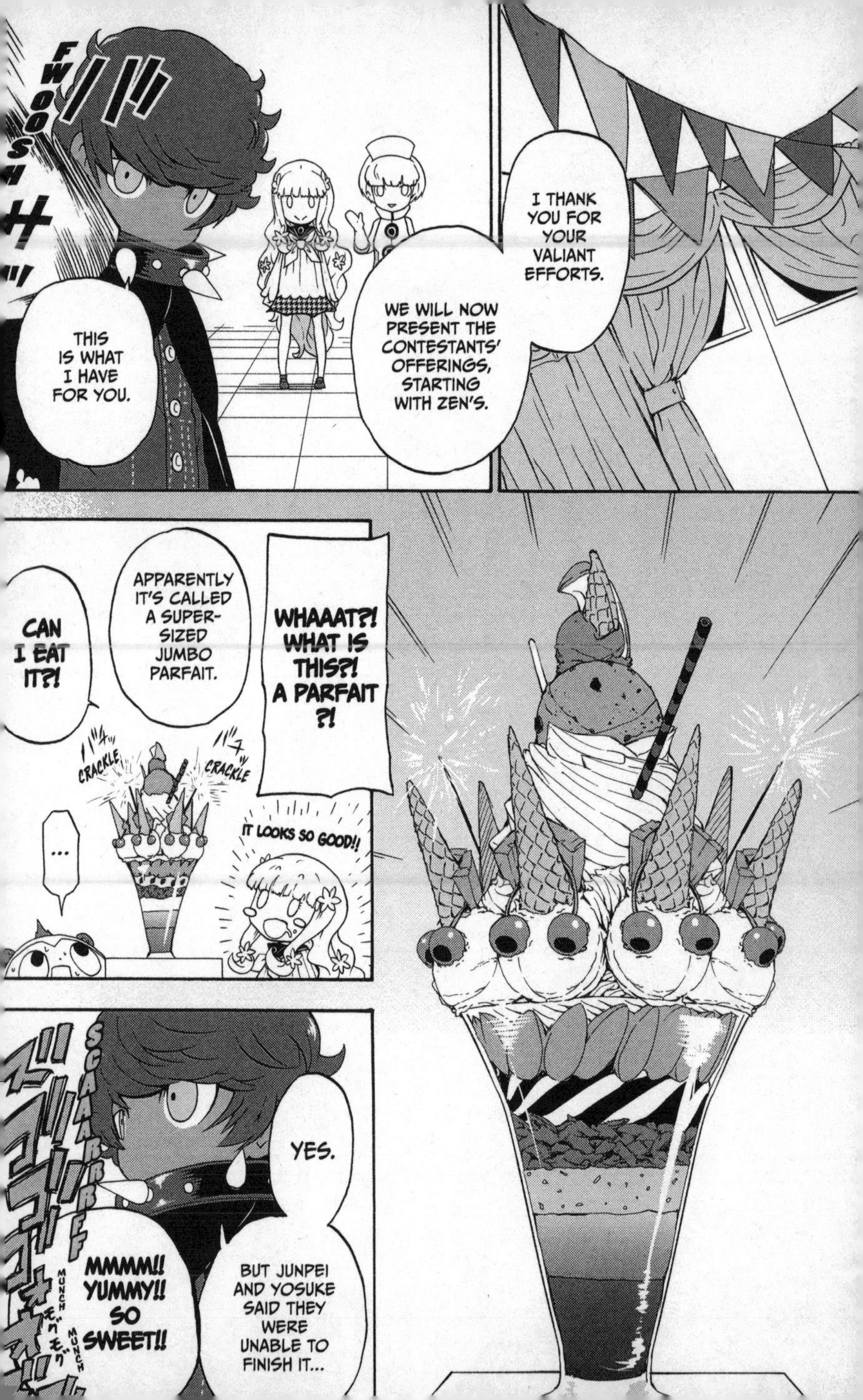
I THANK YOU FOR YOUR VALIANT EFFORTS.
WE WILL NOW PRESENT THE CONTESTANTS' OFFERINGS, STARTING WITH ZEN'S.
FWOOSH
THIS IS WHAT I HAVE FOR YOU.
WHAAAT?! WHAT IS THIS?! A PARFAIT?!
APPARENTLY IT'S CALLED A SUPER-SIZED JUMBO PARFAIT.
CAN I EAT IT?!
CRACKLE
CRACKLE
IT LOOKS SO GOOD!!
...
YES.
BUT JUNPEI AND YOSUKE SAID THEY WERE UNABLE TO FINISH IT...
SCAAARRRF
MMMM!! YUMMY!! SO SWEET!!
MUNCH
MUNCH

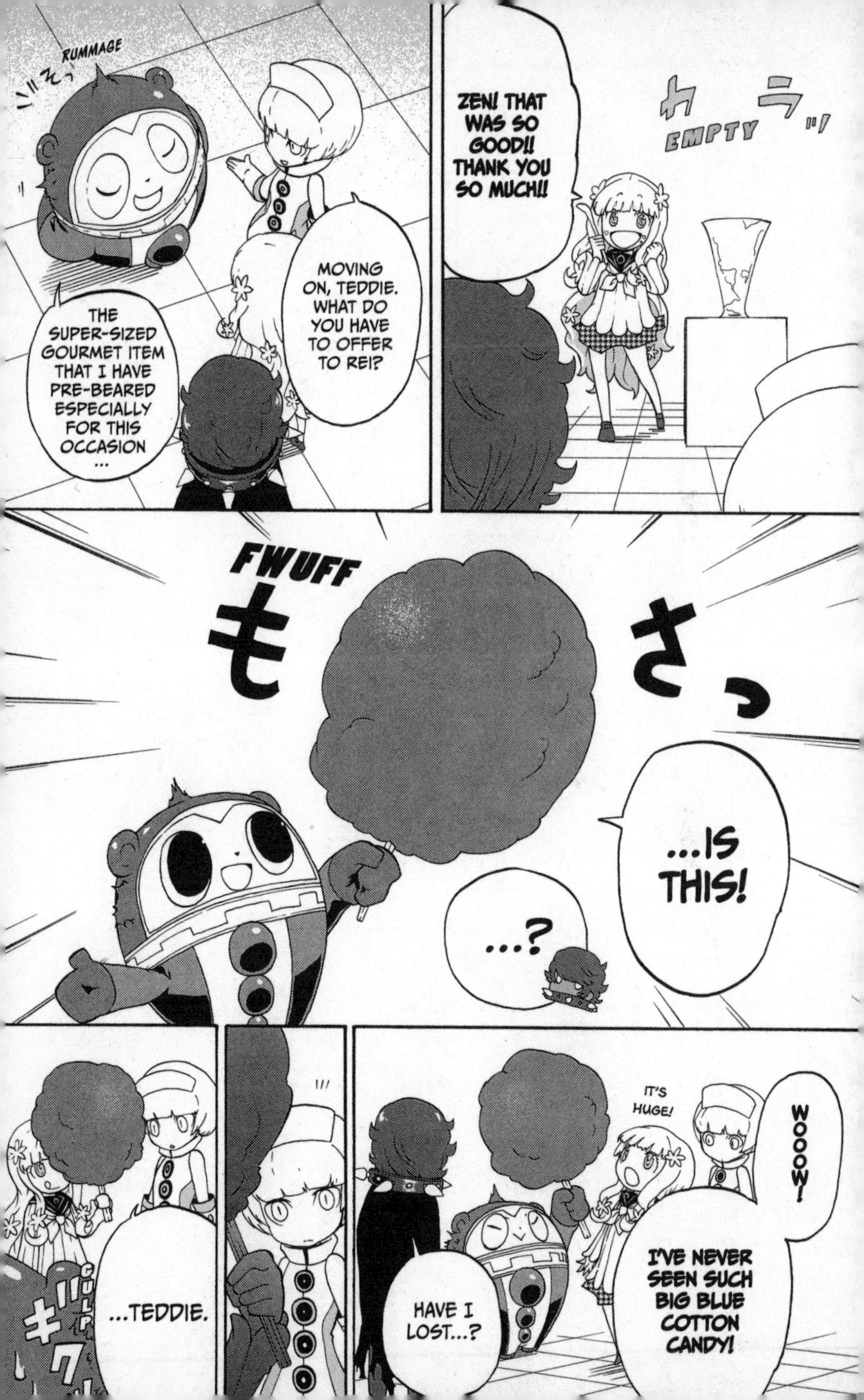
ZEN! THAT WAS SO GOOD!! THANK YOU SO MUCH!!
EMPTY
RUMMAGE
MOVING ON, TEDDIE. WHAT DO YOU HAVE TO OFFER TO REI?
THE SUPER-SIZED GOURMET ITEM THAT I HAVE PRE-BEARED ESPECIALLY FOR THIS OCCASION ...
FWUFF
...IS THIS!
...?
WOOOW!
IT'S HUGE!
I'VE NEVER SEEN SUCH BIG BLUE COTTON CANDY!
!!!
HAVE I LOST...?
...TEDDIE.
GULP

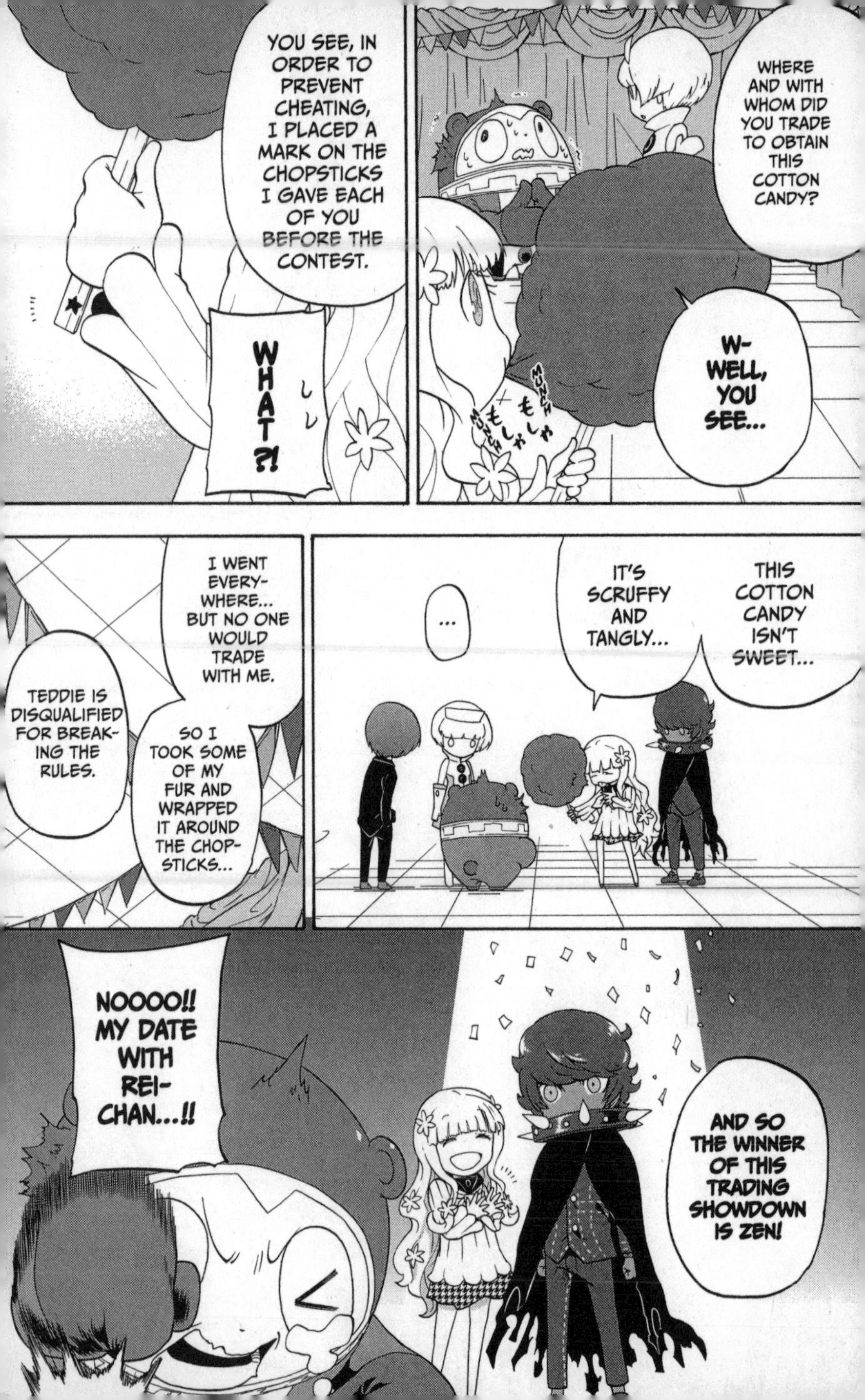
WHERE AND WITH WHOM DID YOU TRADE TO OBTAIN THIS COTTON CANDY?
W-WELL, YOU SEE...
MUNCH MUNCH
もしゃ もしゃ
YOU SEE, IN ORDER TO PREVENT CHEATING, I PLACED A MARK ON THE CHOPSTICKS I GAVE EACH OF YOU BEFORE THE CONTEST.
WHAT?!
THIS COTTON CANDY ISN'T SWEET...
IT'S SCRUFFY AND TANGLY...
...
I WENT EVERY-WHERE... BUT NO ONE WOULD TRADE WITH ME.
SO I TOOK SOME OF MY FUR AND WRAPPED IT AROUND THE CHOP-STICKS...
TEDDIE IS DISQUALIFIED FOR BREAK-ING THE RULES.
AND SO THE WINNER OF THIS TRADING SHOWDOWN IS ZEN!
NOOOO!! MY DATE WITH REI-CHAN...!!

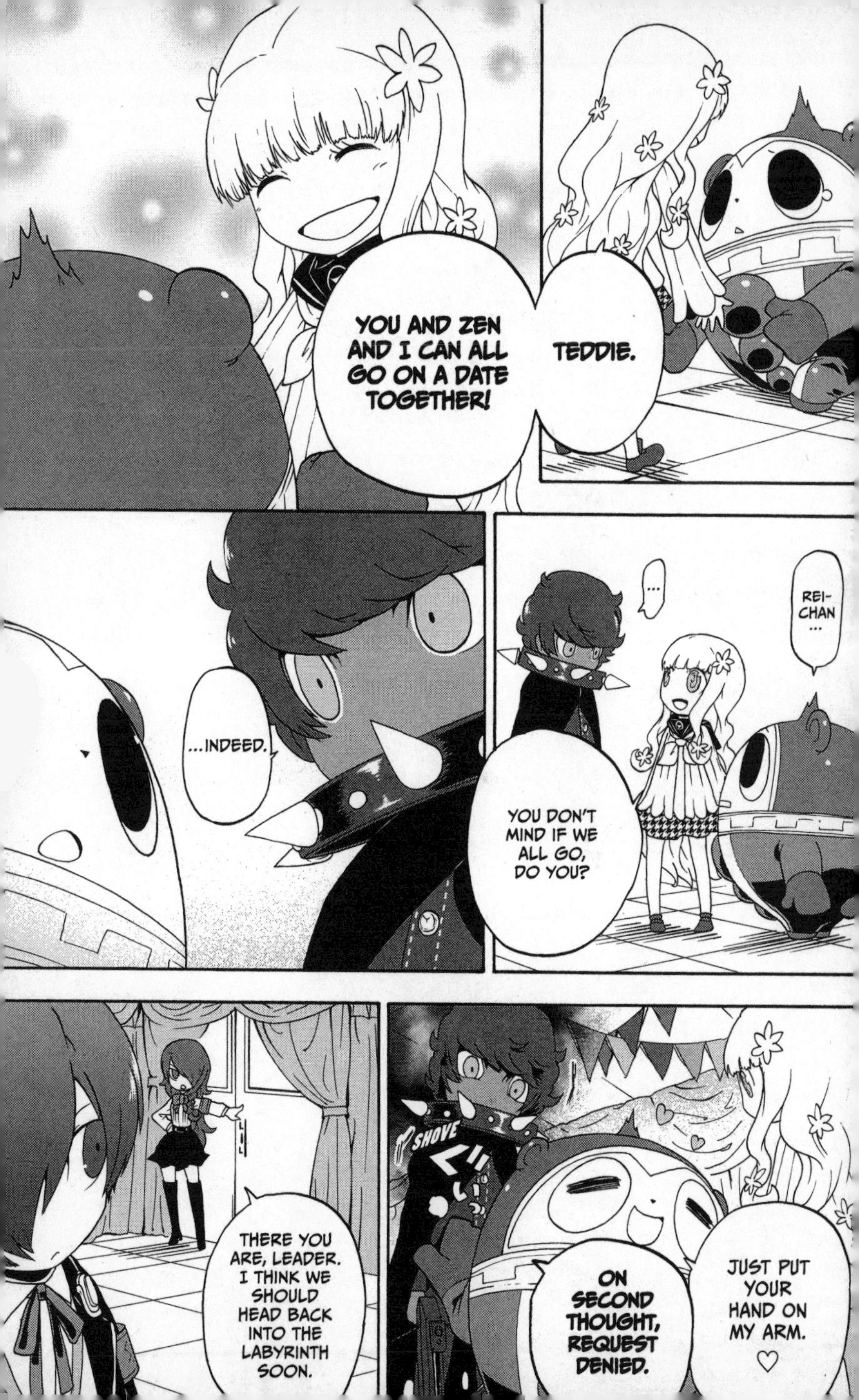
TEDDIE.
YOU AND ZEN AND I CAN ALL GO ON A DATE TOGETHER!
REI-CHAN...
...
YOU DON'T MIND IF WE ALL GO, DO YOU?
...INDEED.
JUST PUT YOUR HAND ON MY ARM. ♡
SHOVE
ON SECOND THOUGHT, REQUEST DENIED.
THERE YOU ARE, LEADER. I THINK WE SHOULD HEAD BACK INTO THE LABYRINTH SOON.

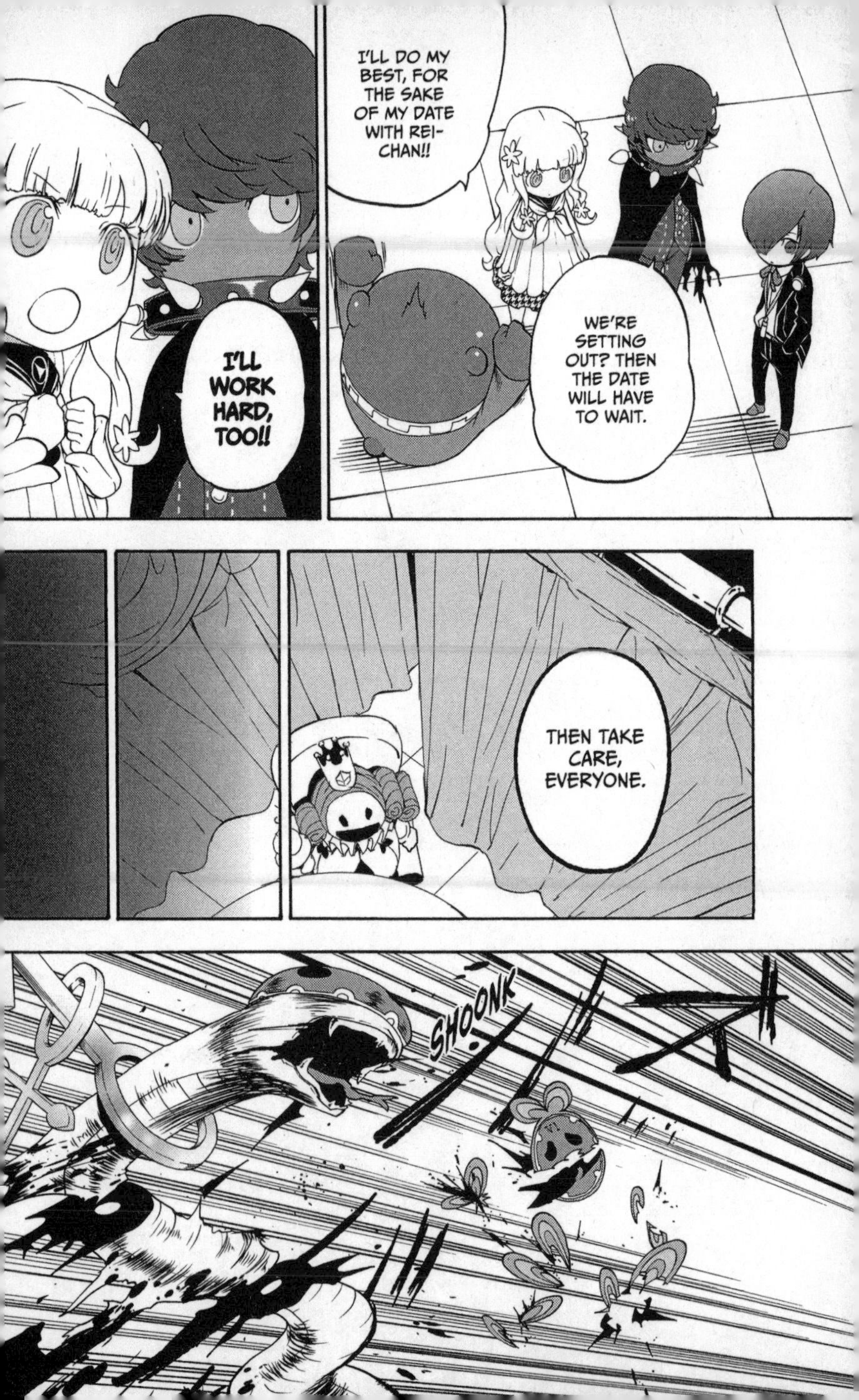
I'LL DO MY BEST, FOR THE SAKE OF MY DATE WITH REI-CHAN!!
WE'RE SETTING OUT? THEN THE DATE WILL HAVE TO WAIT.
I'LL WORK HARD, TOO!!
THEN TAKE CARE, EVERYONE.
SHOONK

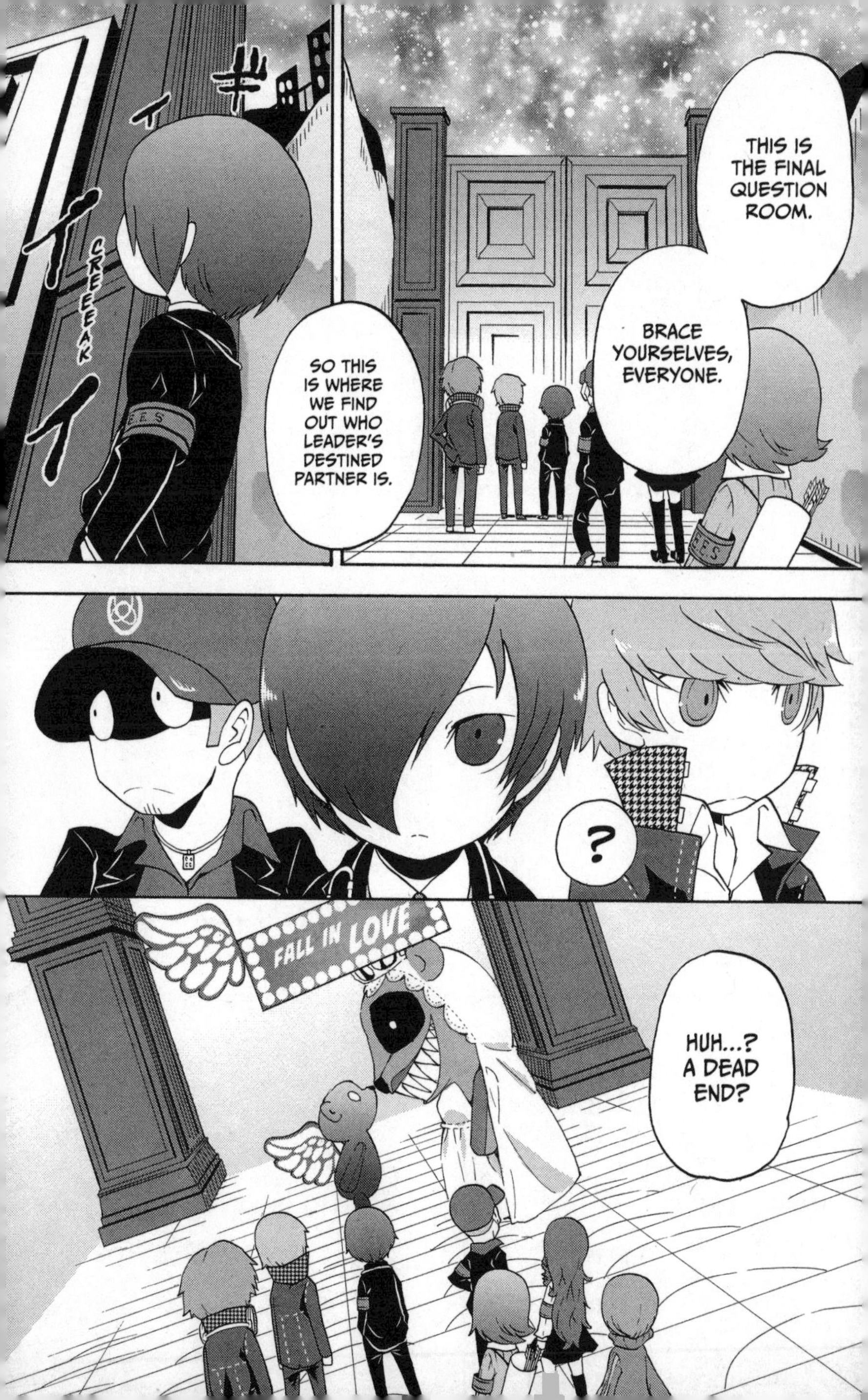

THIS IS THE FINAL QUESTION ROOM.
BRACE YOURSELVES, EVERYONE.
SO THIS IS WHERE WE FIND OUT WHO LEADER'S DESTINED PARTNER IS.
CREEEAK
?
FALL IN LOVE
HUH...? A DEAD END?

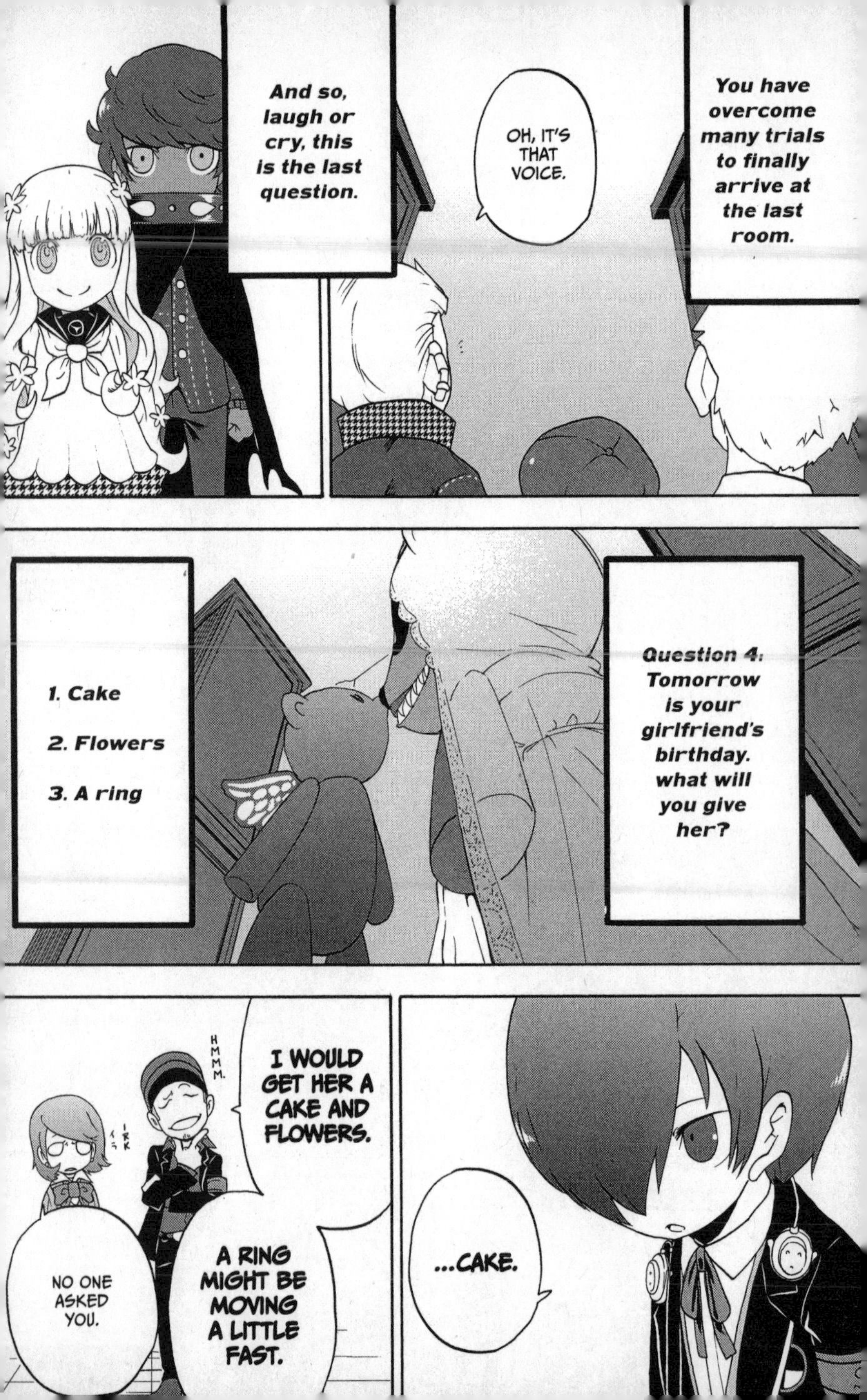
You have overcome many trials to finally arrive at the last room.
OH, IT'S THAT VOICE.
And so, laugh or cry, this is the last question.
Question 4: Tomorrow is your girlfriend's birthday. what will you give her?
1. Cake
2. Flowers
3. A ring
...CAKE.
I WOULD GET HER A CAKE AND FLOWERS.
HMMM.
IRK
A RING MIGHT BE MOVING A LITTLE FAST.
NO ONE ASKED YOU.

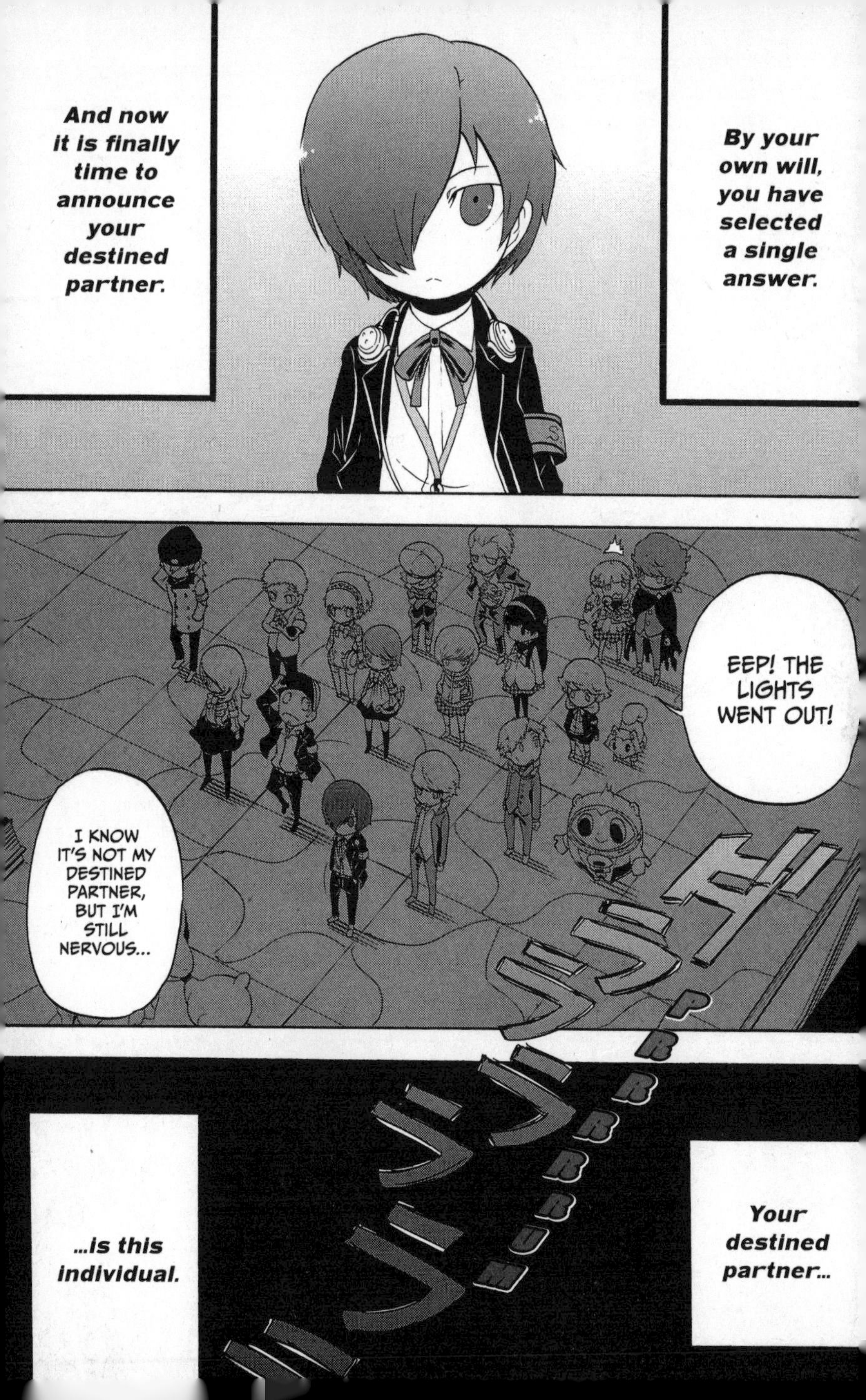
By your own will, you have selected a single answer.
And now it is finally time to announce your destined partner.
EEP! THE LIGHTS WENT OUT!
I KNOW IT'S NOT MY DESTINED PARTNER, BUT I'M STILL NERVOUS...
PRRRRUM
Your destined partner...
...is this individual.

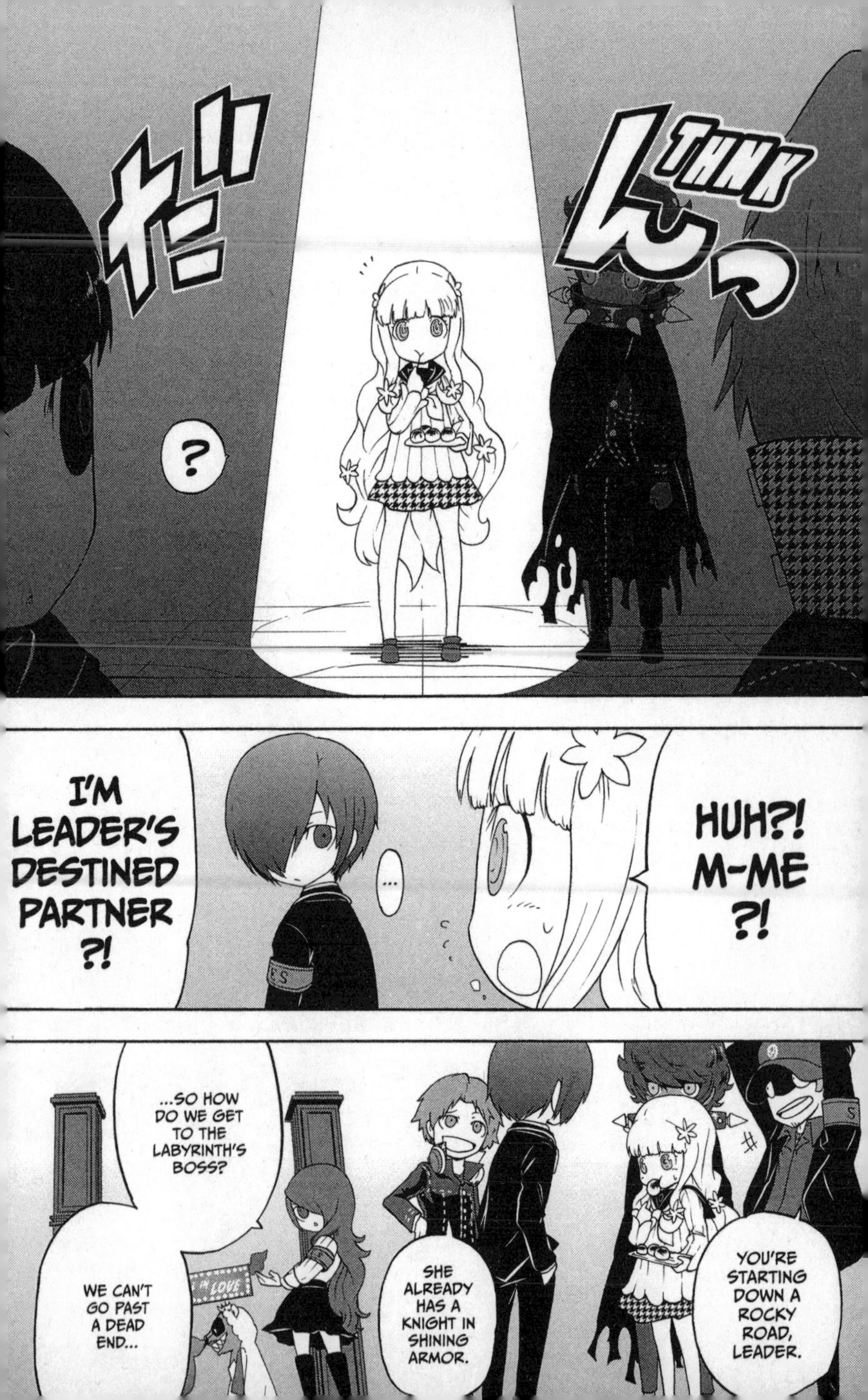

んっ
THNK
だ!!
?
HUH?! M-ME ?!
...
I'M LEADER'S DESTINED PARTNER ?!
YOU'RE STARTING DOWN A ROCKY ROAD, LEADER.
SHE ALREADY HAS A KNIGHT IN SHINING ARMOR.
...SO HOW DO WE GET TO THE LABYRINTH'S BOSS?
WE CAN'T GO PAST A DEAD END...

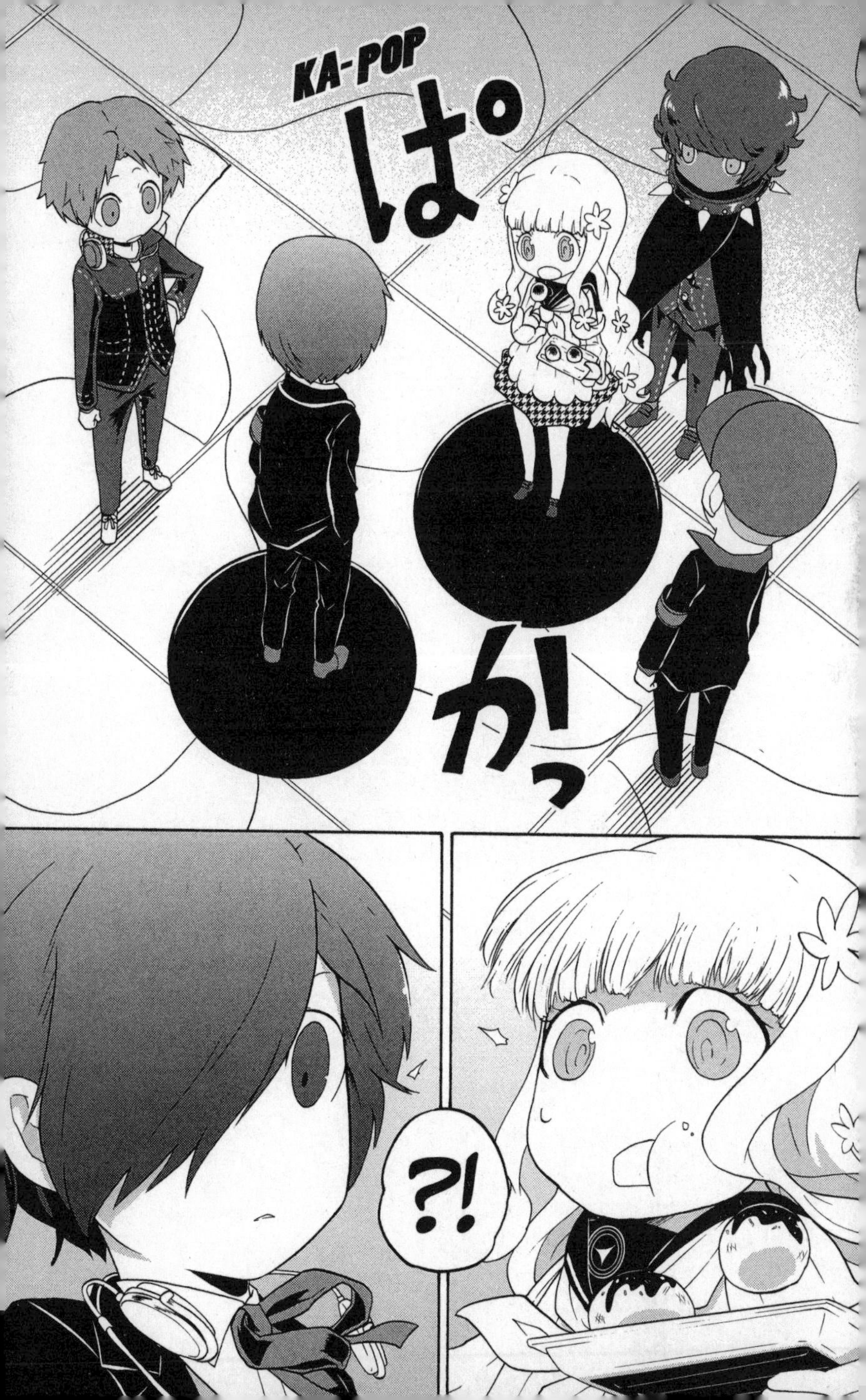
KA-POP
ぱ
かっ
?!

PERSONA Q
SHADOW OF THE LABYRINTH
side: P3

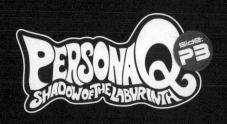

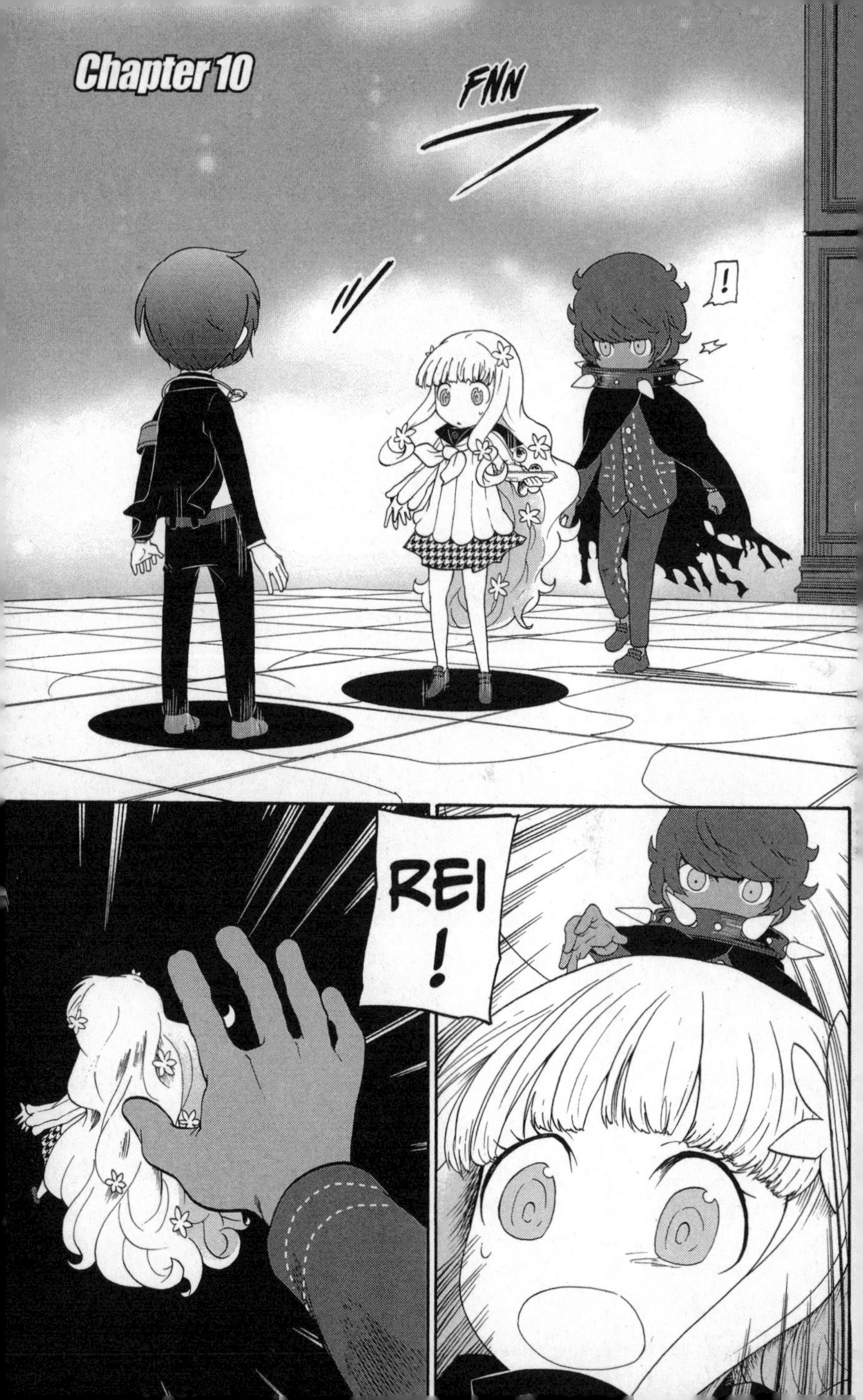
Chapter 10
FNN
!
REI!

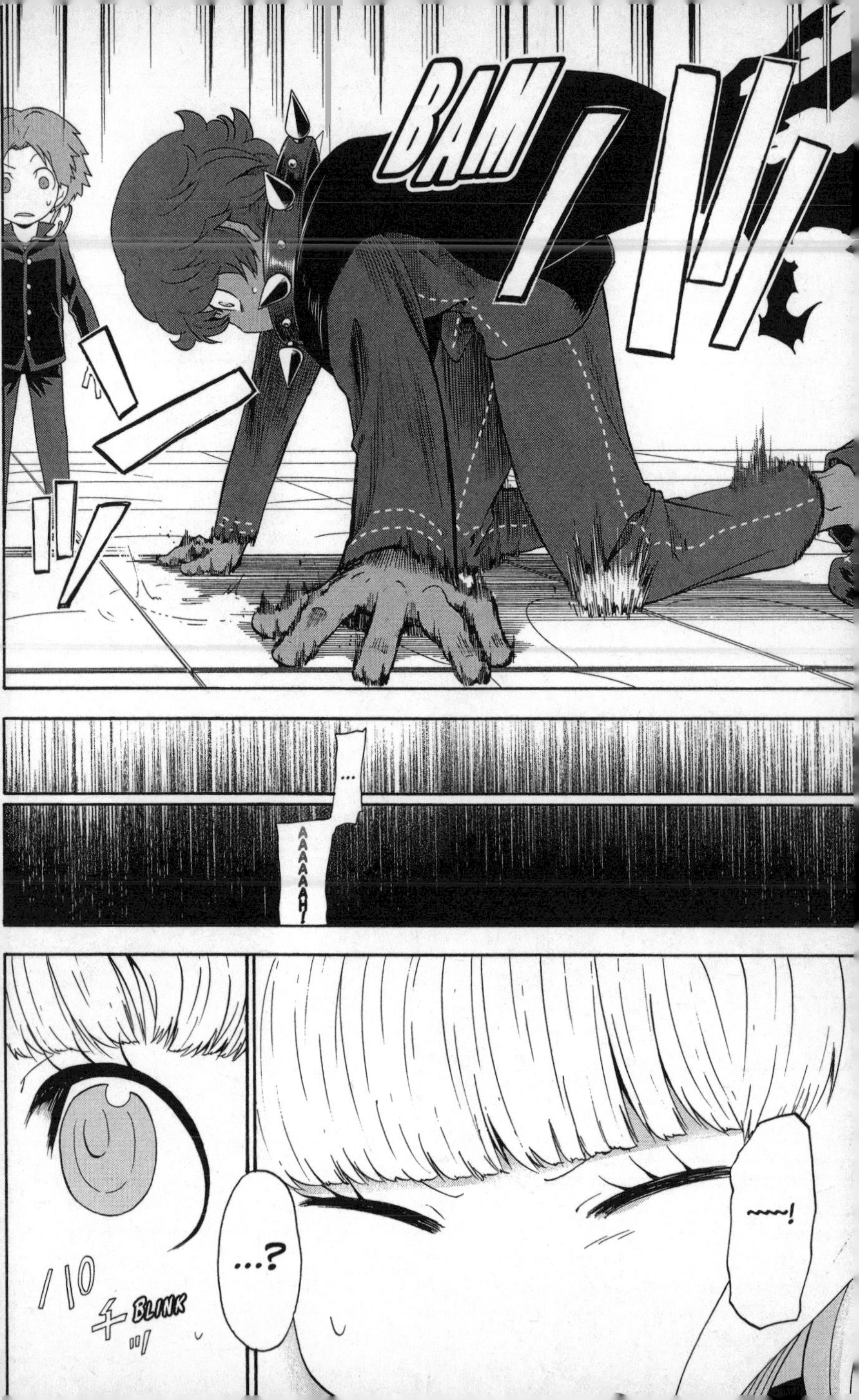
BAM
...
AAAAAAH!
~~~!
...?
BLINK
~~~

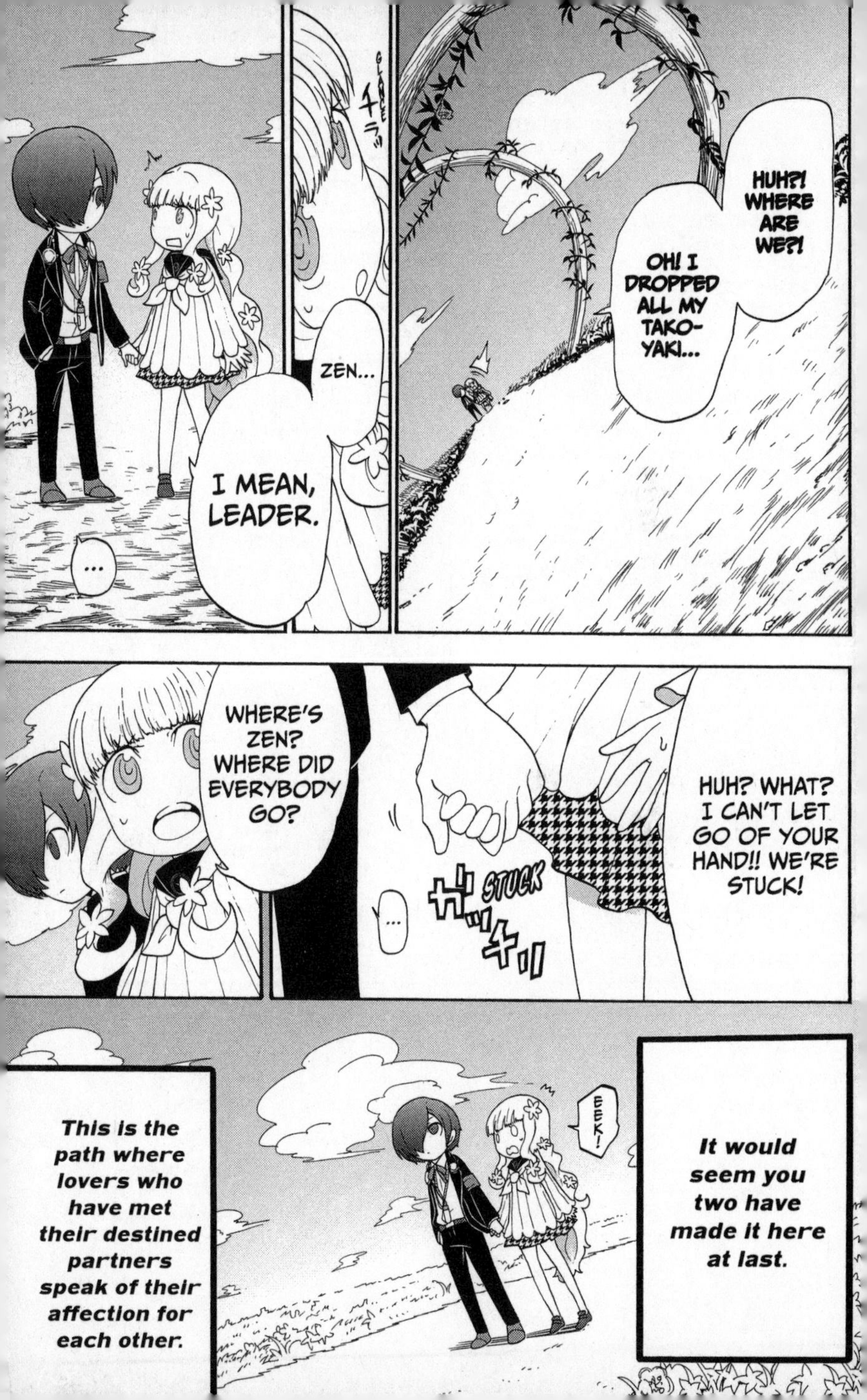
HUH?! WHERE ARE WE?!
OH! I DROPPED ALL MY TAKO-YAKI...
GLANCE
チラッ
ZEN...
I MEAN, LEADER.
...
HUH? WHAT? I CAN'T LET GO OF YOUR HAND!! WE'RE STUCK!
STUCK
...
WHERE'S ZEN? WHERE DID EVERYBODY GO?
It would seem you two have made it here at last.
EEK!
This is the path where lovers who have met their destined partners speak of their affection for each other.

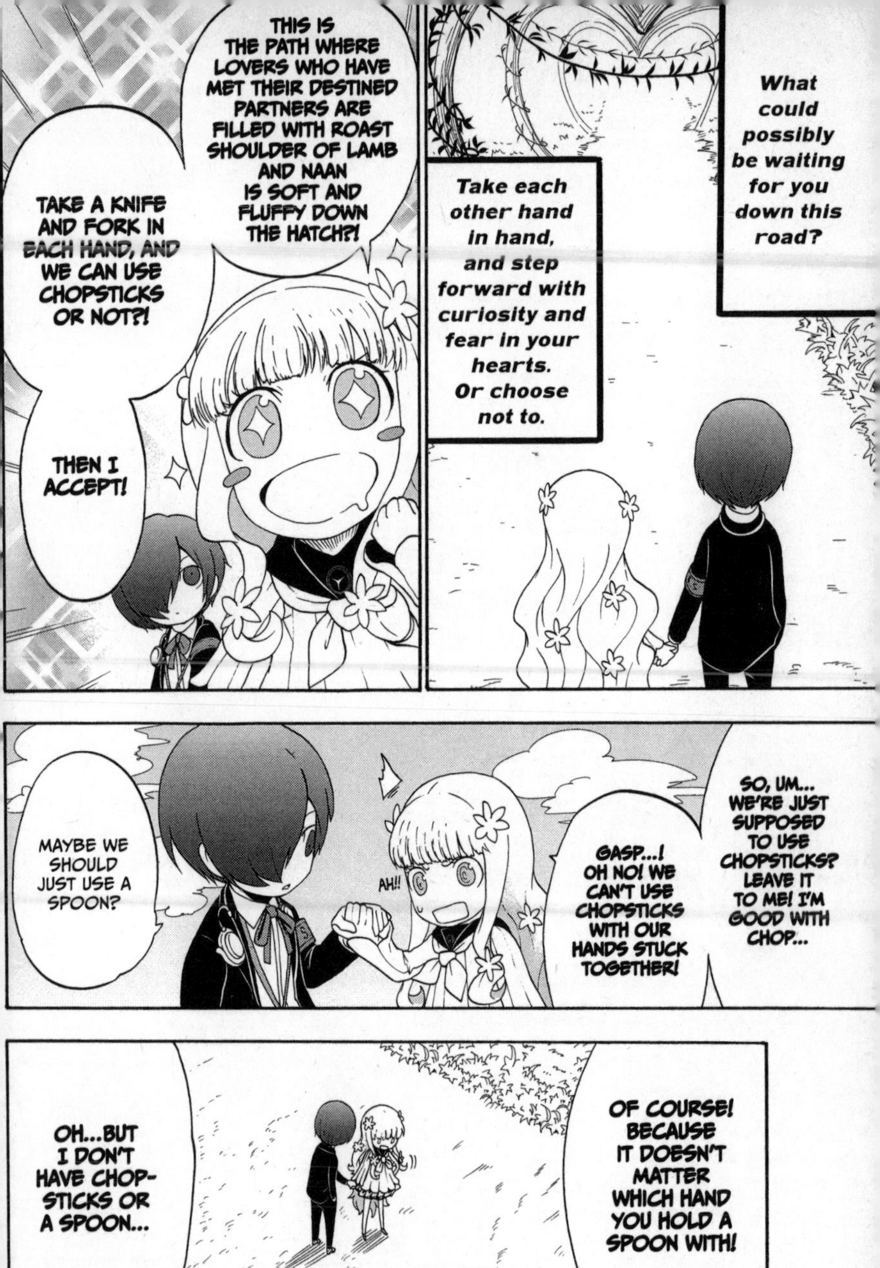
What could possibly be waiting for you down this road?
Take each other hand in hand, and step forward with curiosity and fear in your hearts. Or choose not to.
THIS IS THE PATH WHERE LOVERS WHO HAVE MET THEIR DESTINED PARTNERS ARE FILLED WITH ROAST SHOULDER OF LAMB AND NAAN IS SOFT AND FLUFFY DOWN THE HATCH?!
TAKE A KNIFE AND FORK IN EACH HAND, AND WE CAN USE CHOPSTICKS OR NOT?!
THEN I ACCEPT!
SO, UM... WE'RE JUST SUPPOSED TO USE CHOPSTICKS? LEAVE IT TO ME! I'M GOOD WITH CHOP...
GASP...! OH NO! WE CAN'T USE CHOPSTICKS WITH OUR HANDS STUCK TOGETHER!
AH!!
MAYBE WE SHOULD JUST USE A SPOON?
OF COURSE! BECAUSE IT DOESN'T MATTER WHICH HAND YOU HOLD A SPOON WITH!
OH...BUT I DON'T HAVE CHOP-STICKS OR A SPOON...

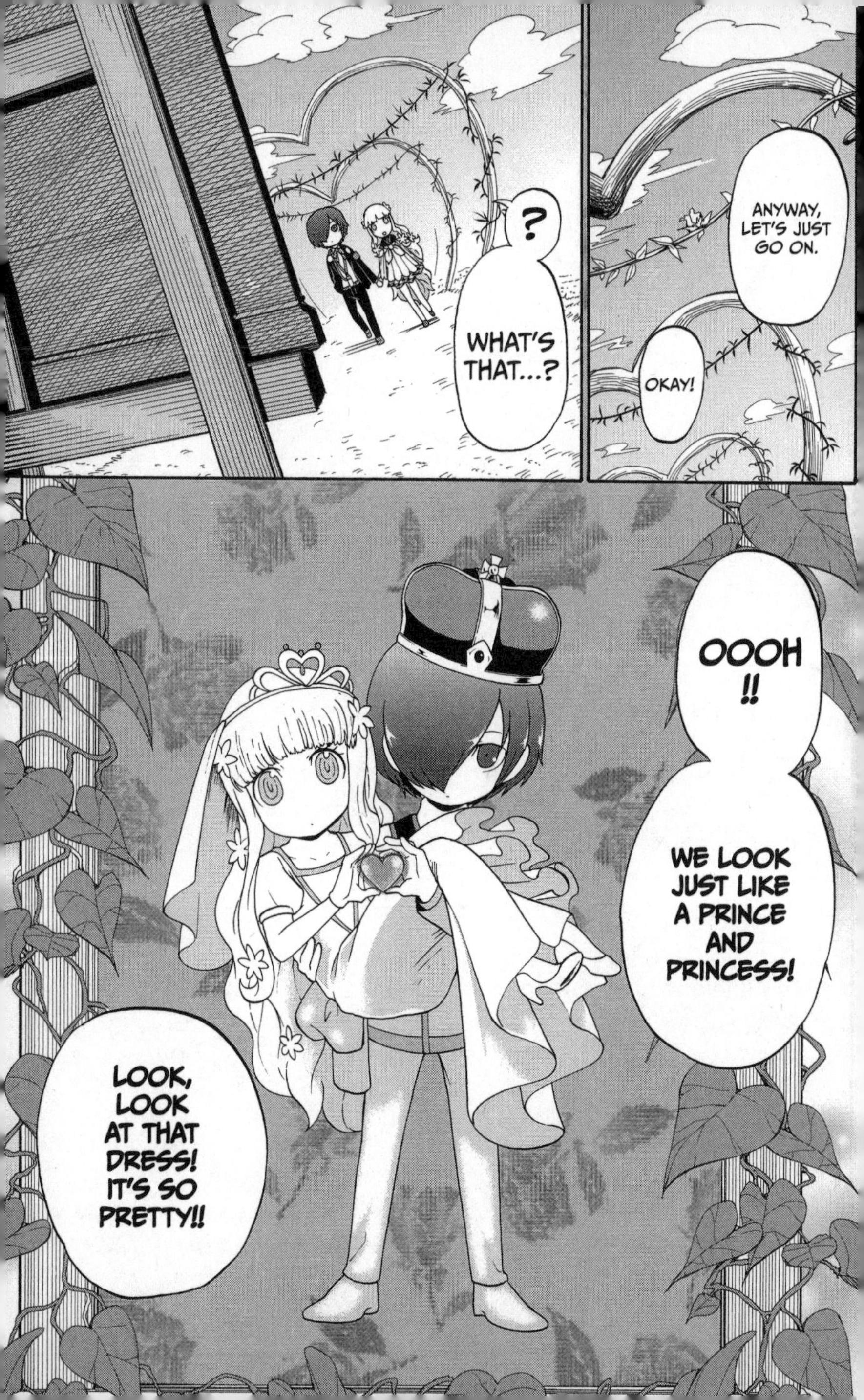
ANYWAY, LET'S JUST GO ON.
OKAY!
?
WHAT'S THAT...?
OOOH!!
WE LOOK JUST LIKE A PRINCE AND PRINCESS!
LOOK, LOOK AT THAT DRESS! IT'S SO PRETTY!!

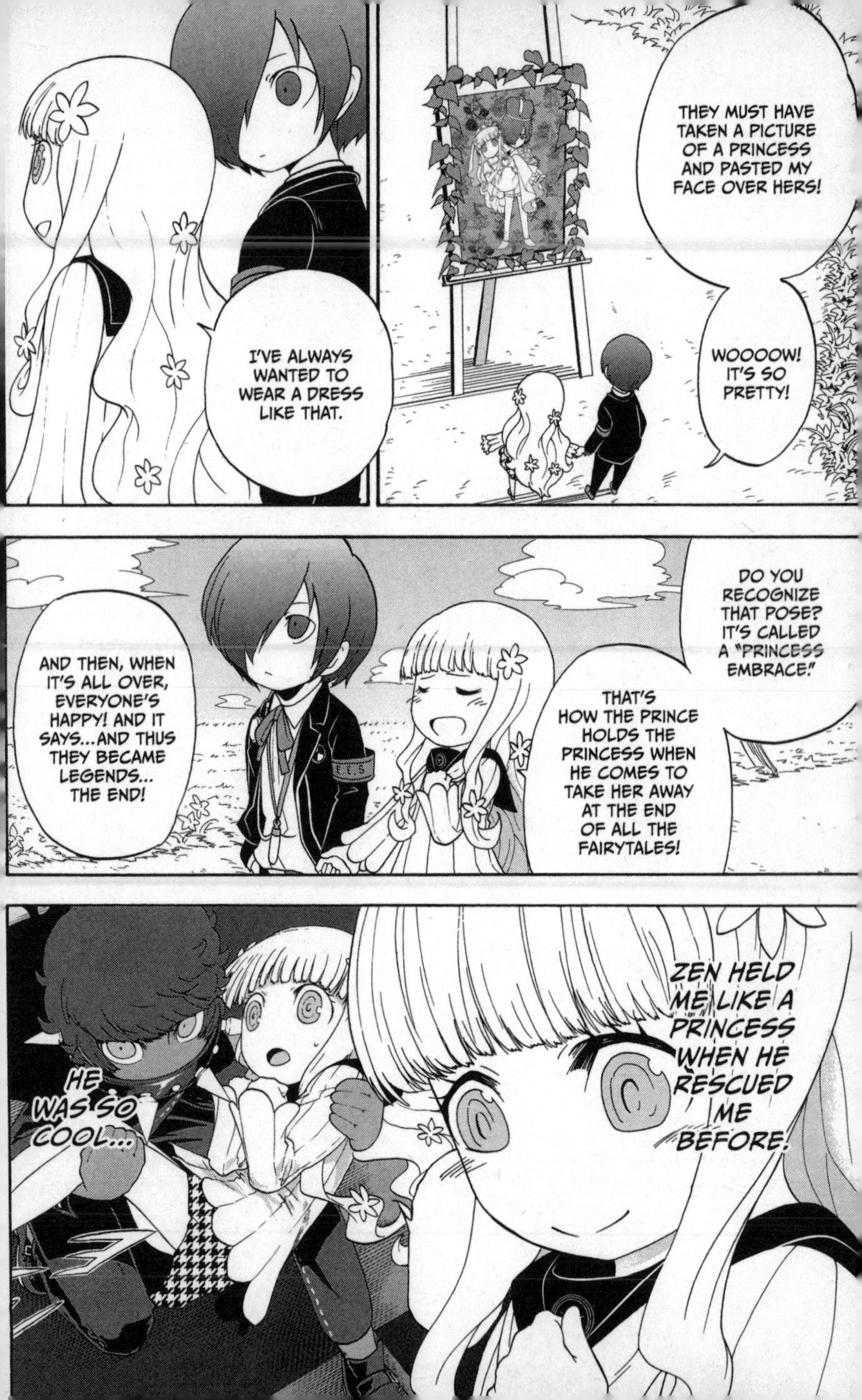
THEY MUST HAVE TAKEN A PICTURE OF A PRINCESS AND PASTED MY FACE OVER HERS!
WOOOOW! IT'S SO PRETTY!
I'VE ALWAYS WANTED TO WEAR A DRESS LIKE THAT.
DO YOU RECOGNIZE THAT POSE? IT'S CALLED A "PRINCESS EMBRACE."
THAT'S HOW THE PRINCE HOLDS THE PRINCESS WHEN HE COMES TO TAKE HER AWAY AT THE END OF ALL THE FAIRYTALES!
AND THEN, WHEN IT'S ALL OVER, EVERYONE'S HAPPY! AND IT SAYS...AND THUS THEY BECAME LEGENDS... THE END!
ZEN HELD ME LIKE A PRINCESS WHEN HE RESCUED ME BEFORE.
HE WAS SO COOL...

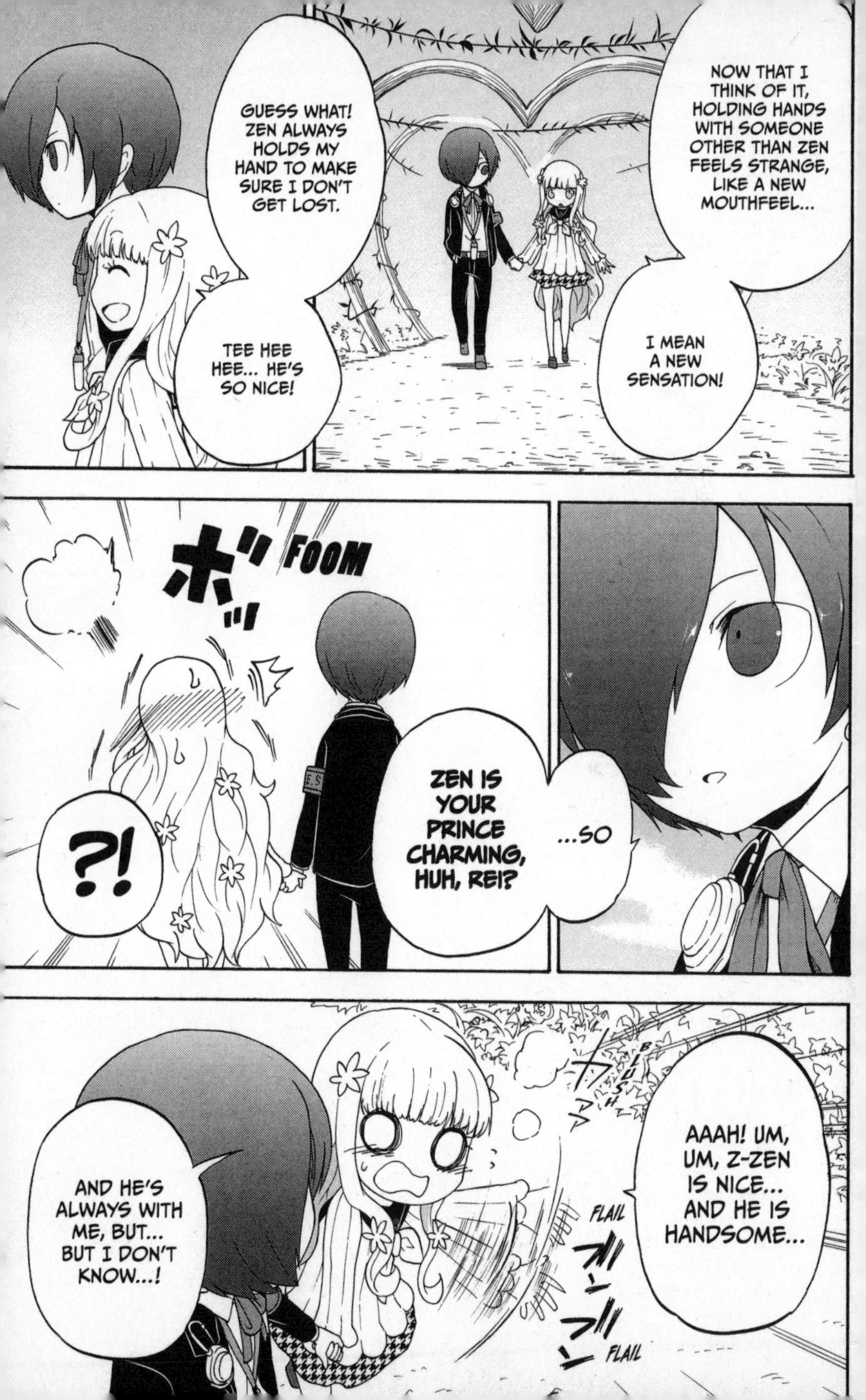
NOW THAT I THINK OF IT, HOLDING HANDS WITH SOMEONE OTHER THAN ZEN FEELS STRANGE, LIKE A NEW MOUTHFEEL...
I MEAN A NEW SENSATION!
GUESS WHAT! ZEN ALWAYS HOLDS MY HAND TO MAKE SURE I DON'T GET LOST.
TEE HEE HEE... HE'S SO NICE!
...SO
ZEN IS YOUR PRINCE CHARMING, HUH, REI?
FOOM
?!
BLUSH
AAAH! UM, UM, Z-ZEN IS NICE... AND HE IS HANDSOME...
FLAIL
FLAIL
AND HE'S ALWAYS WITH ME, BUT... BUT I DON'T KNOW...!

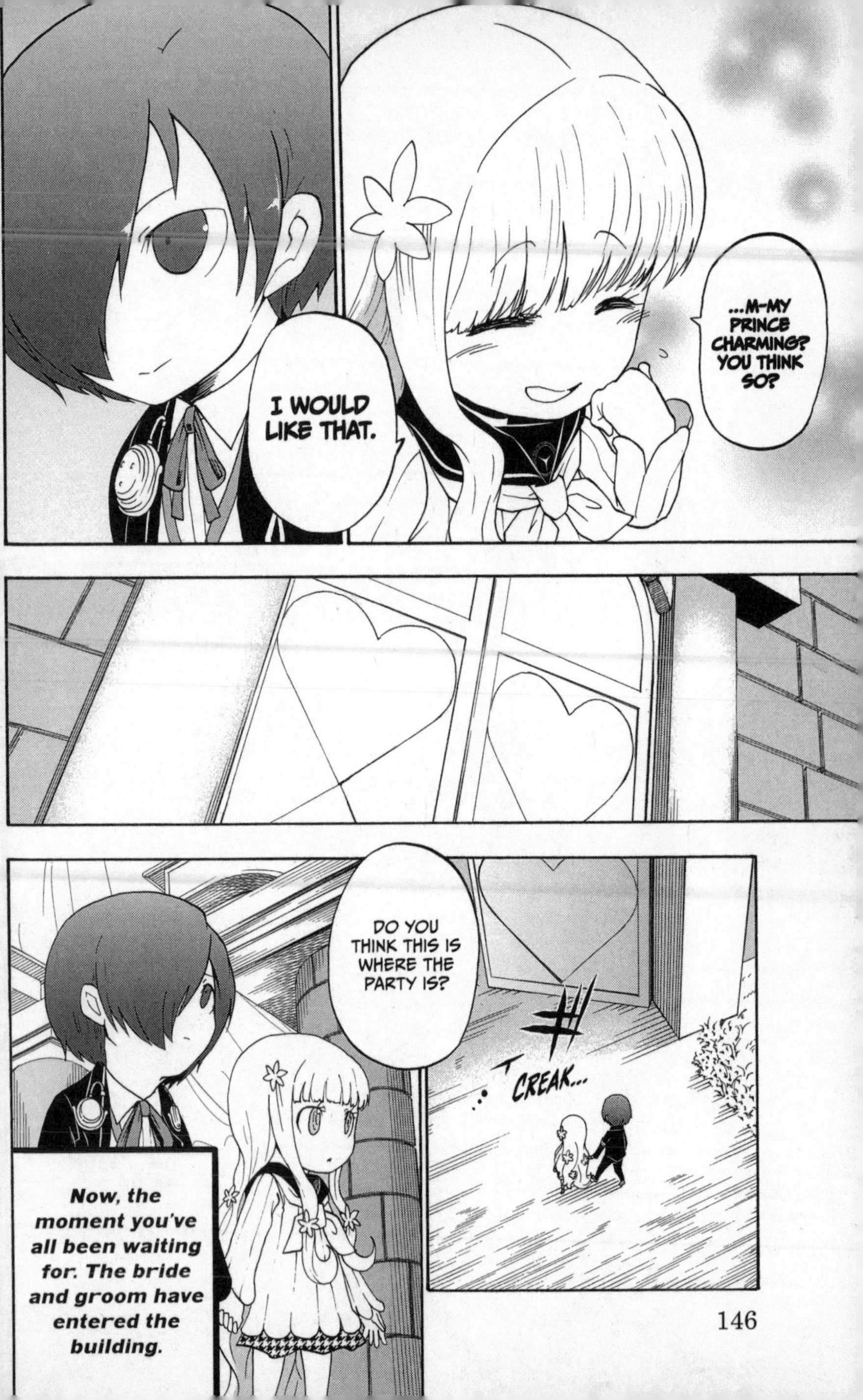
...M-MY PRINCE CHARMING? YOU THINK SO?
I WOULD LIKE THAT.
CREAK...
DO YOU THINK THIS IS WHERE THE PARTY IS?
Now, the moment you've all been waiting for. The bride and groom have entered the building.

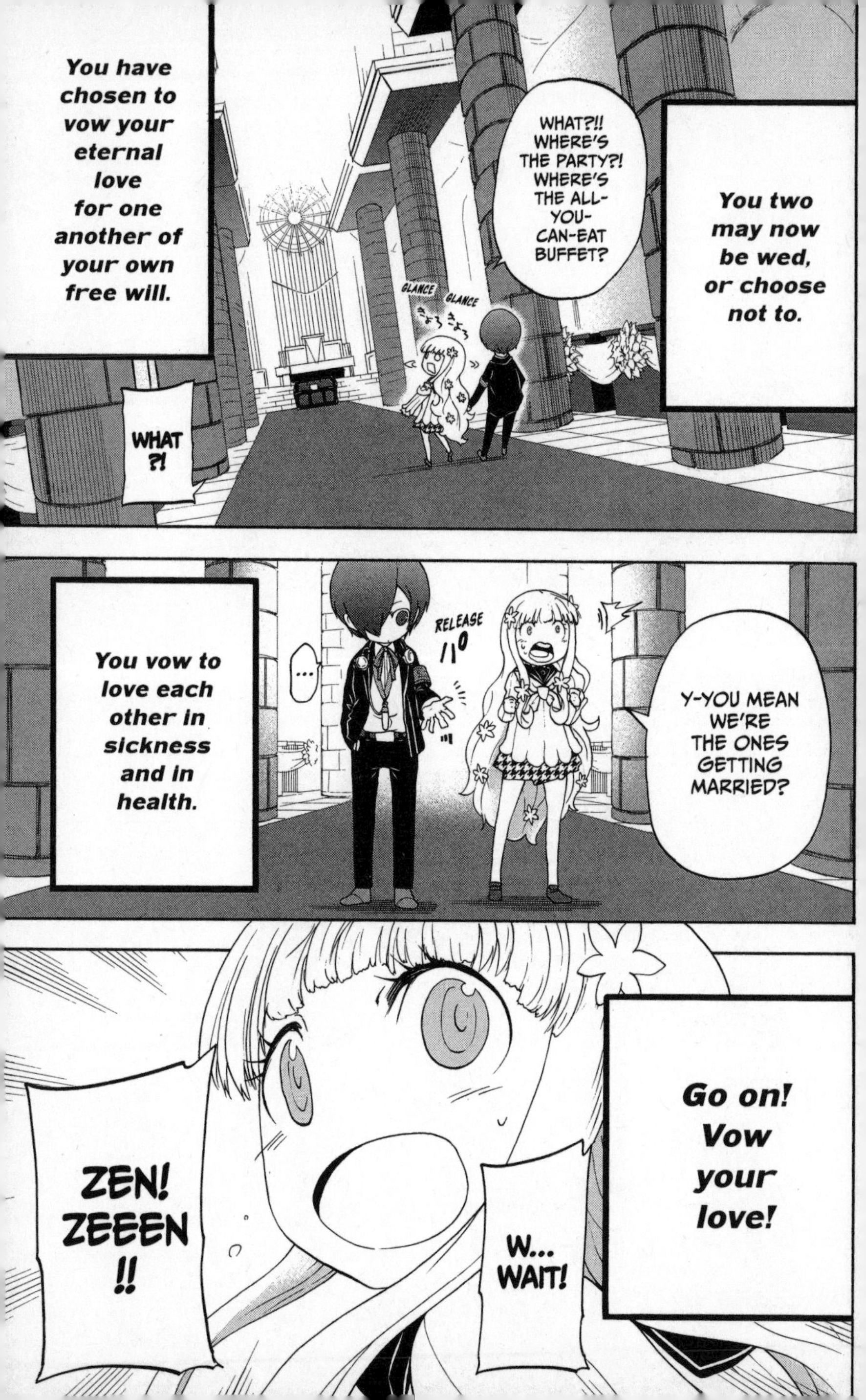
You two may now be wed, or choose not to.
WHAT?!! WHERE'S THE PARTY?! WHERE'S THE ALL-YOU-CAN-EAT BUFFET?
You have chosen to vow your eternal love for one another of your own free will.
GLANCE GLANCE
WHAT ?!
Y-YOU MEAN WE'RE THE ONES GETTING MARRIED?
RELEASE
...
You vow to love each other in sickness and in health.
Go on! Vow your love!
W... WAIT!
ZEN! ZEEEN !!

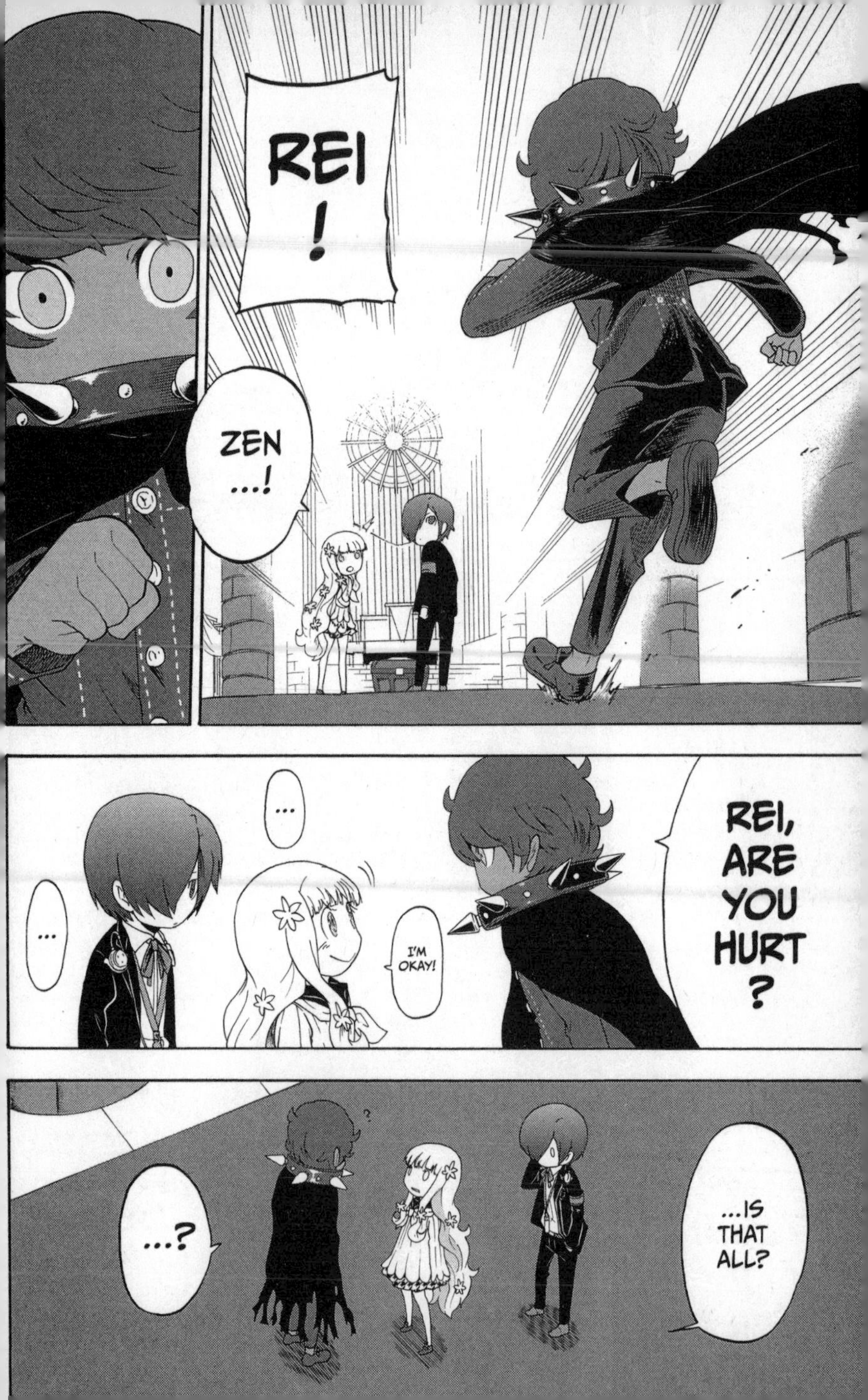
REI!
ZEN...!
REI, ARE YOU HURT?
I'M OKAY!
...
...
...IS THAT ALL?
...?

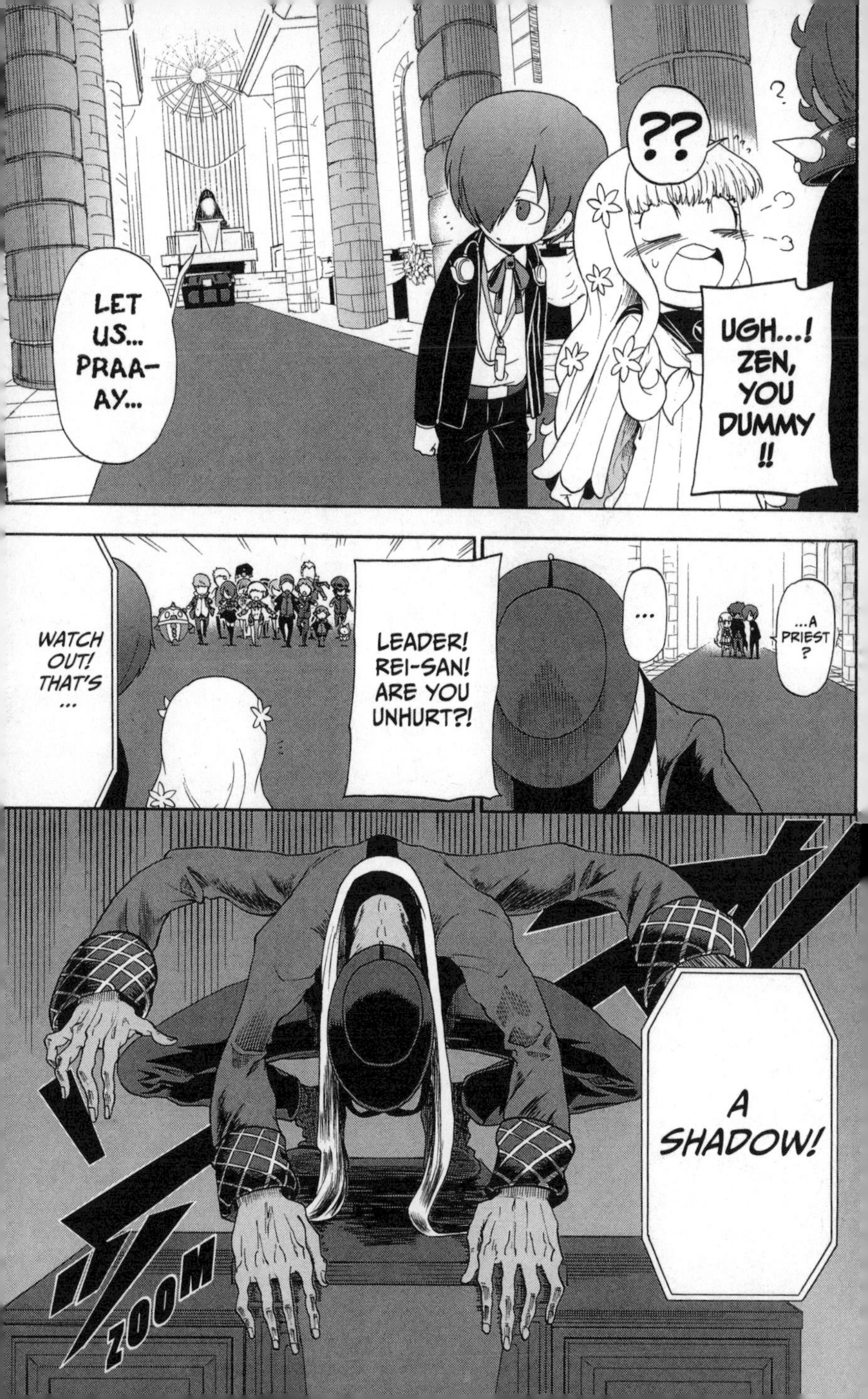
??
UGH...! ZEN, YOU DUMMY !!
LET US... PRAA-AY...
...A PRIEST ?
...
LEADER! REI-SAN! ARE YOU UNHURT?!
WATCH OUT! THAT'S ...
A SHADOW!
ZOOM

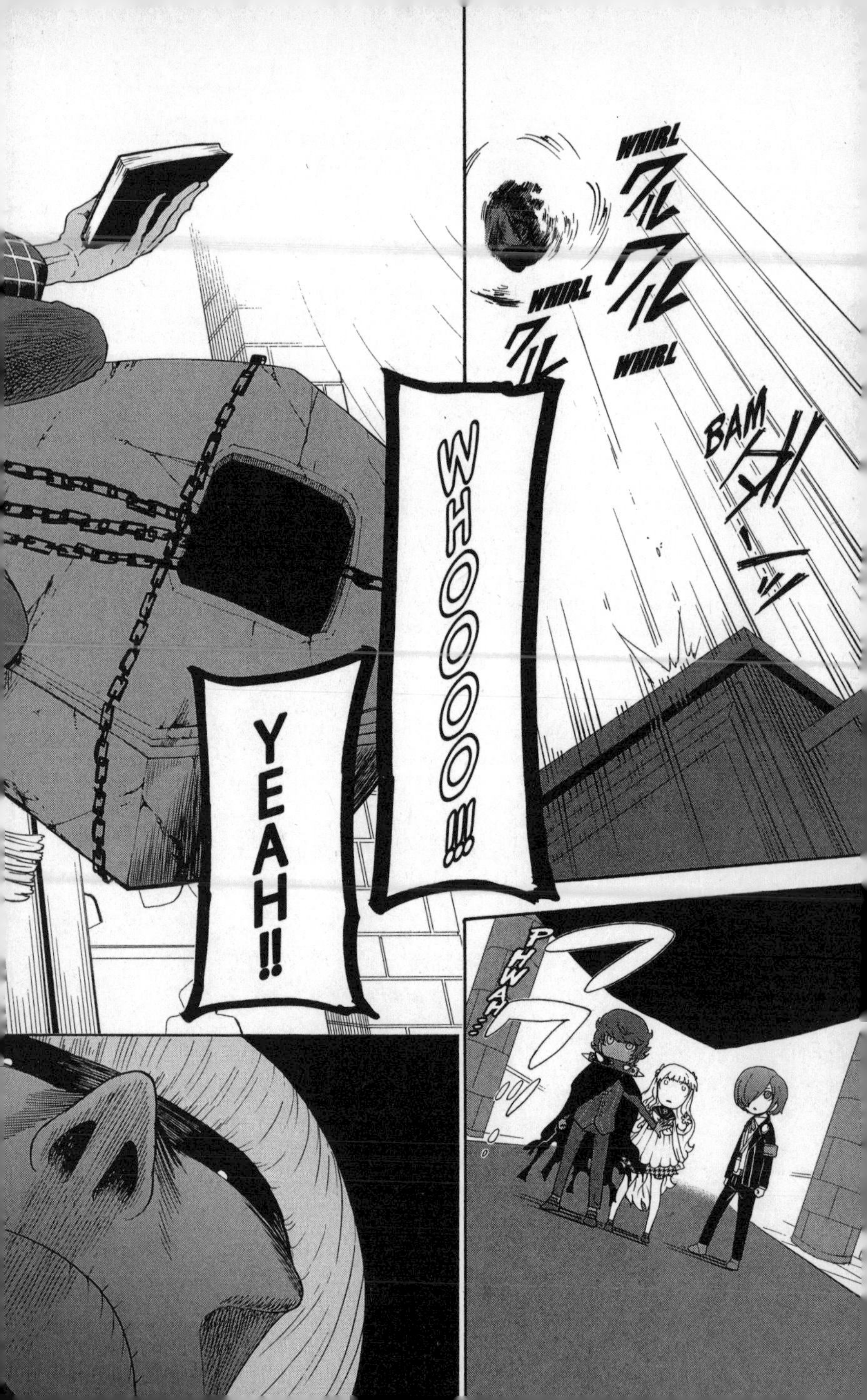
WHIRL
WHIRL
WHIRL
BAM
WHOOOOO!!!
YEAH!!
PHWAA...

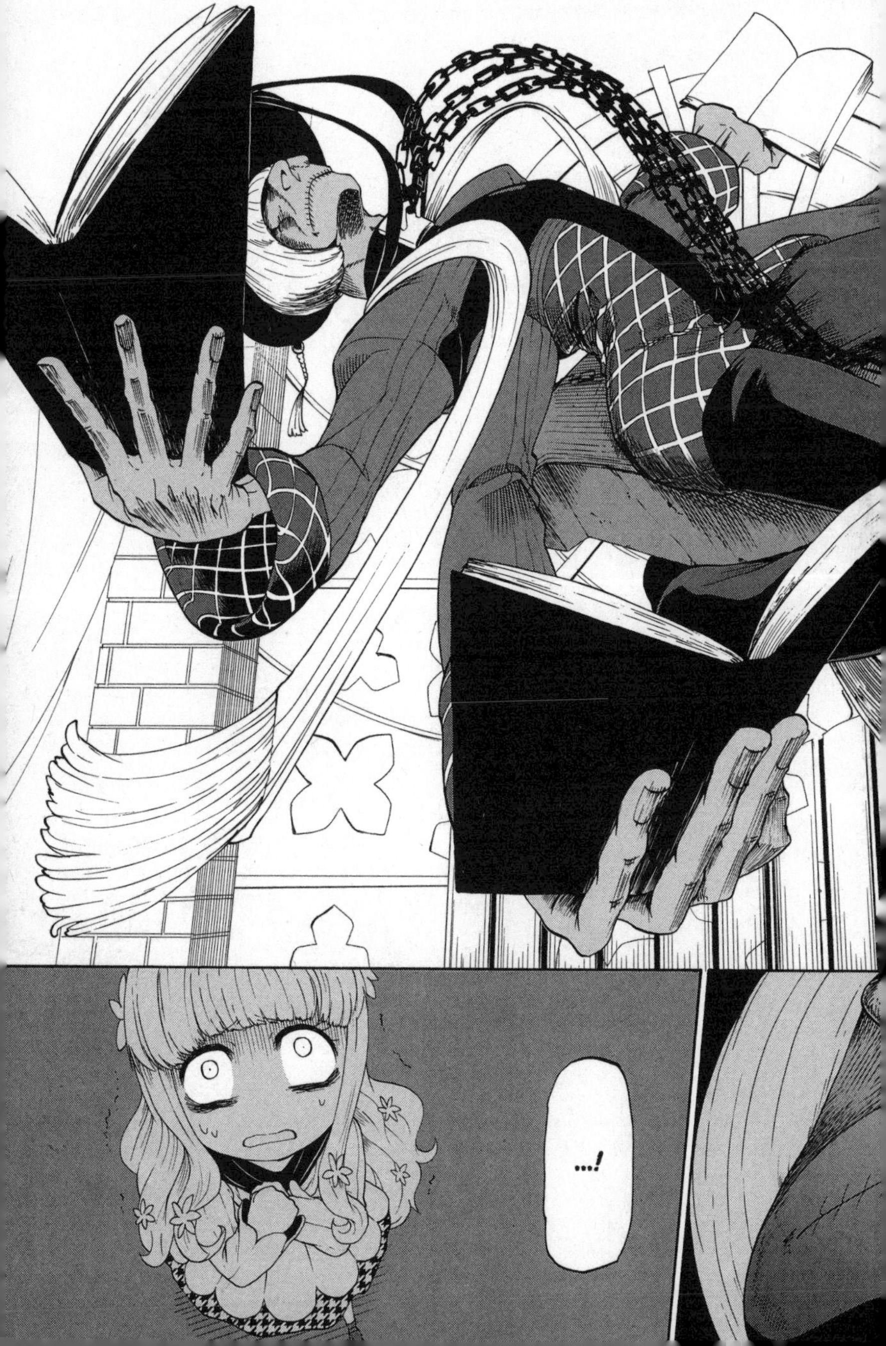
...!

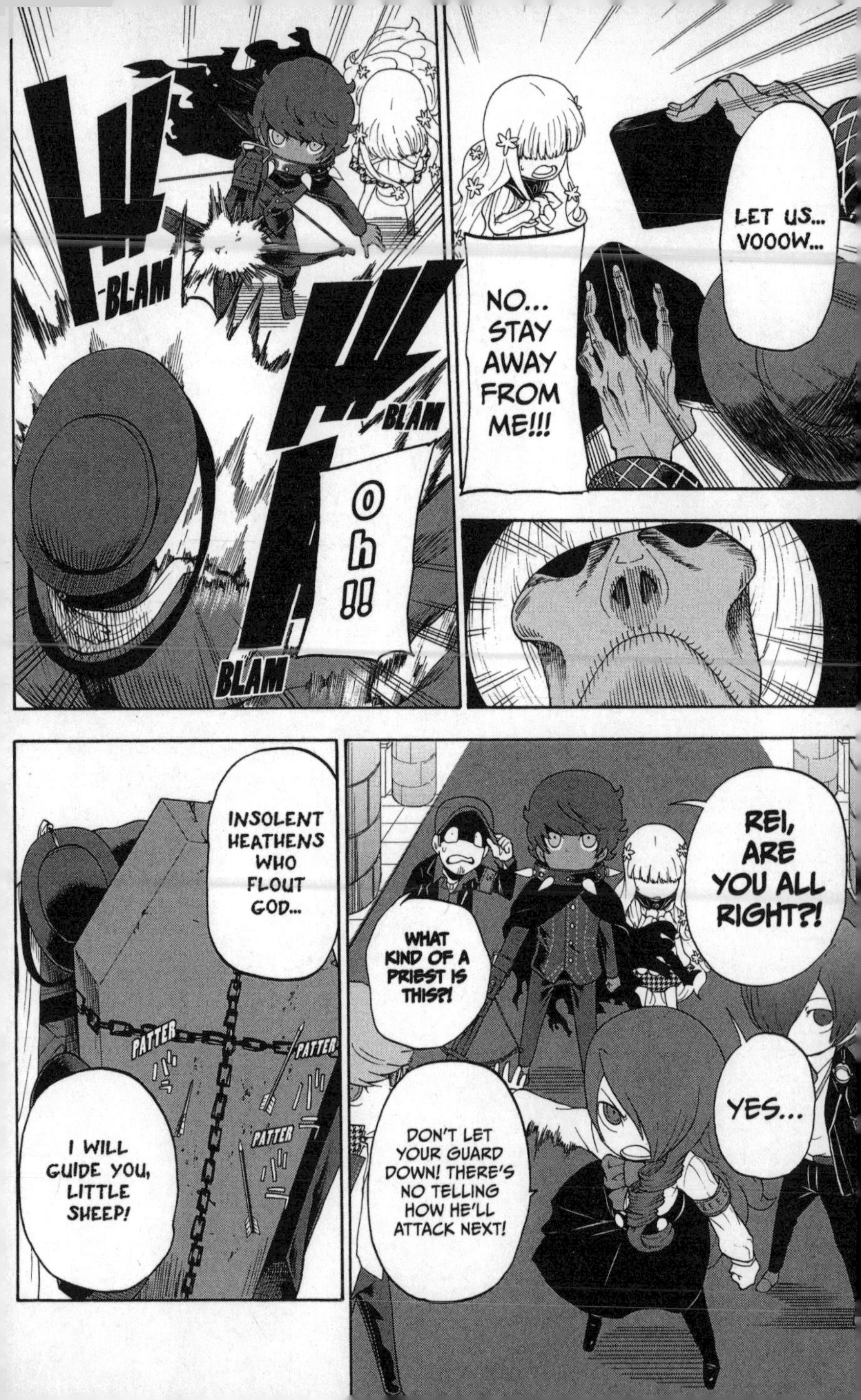

LET US... VOOOW...
NO... STAY AWAY FROM ME!!!
BLAM
BLAM
BLAM
Oh!!
REI, ARE YOU ALL RIGHT?!
YES...
WHAT KIND OF A PRIEST IS THIS?!
DON'T LET YOUR GUARD DOWN! THERE'S NO TELLING HOW HE'LL ATTACK NEXT!
INSOLENT HEATHENS WHO FLOUT GOD...
PATTER
PATTER
PATTER
I WILL GUIDE YOU, LITTLE SHEEP!

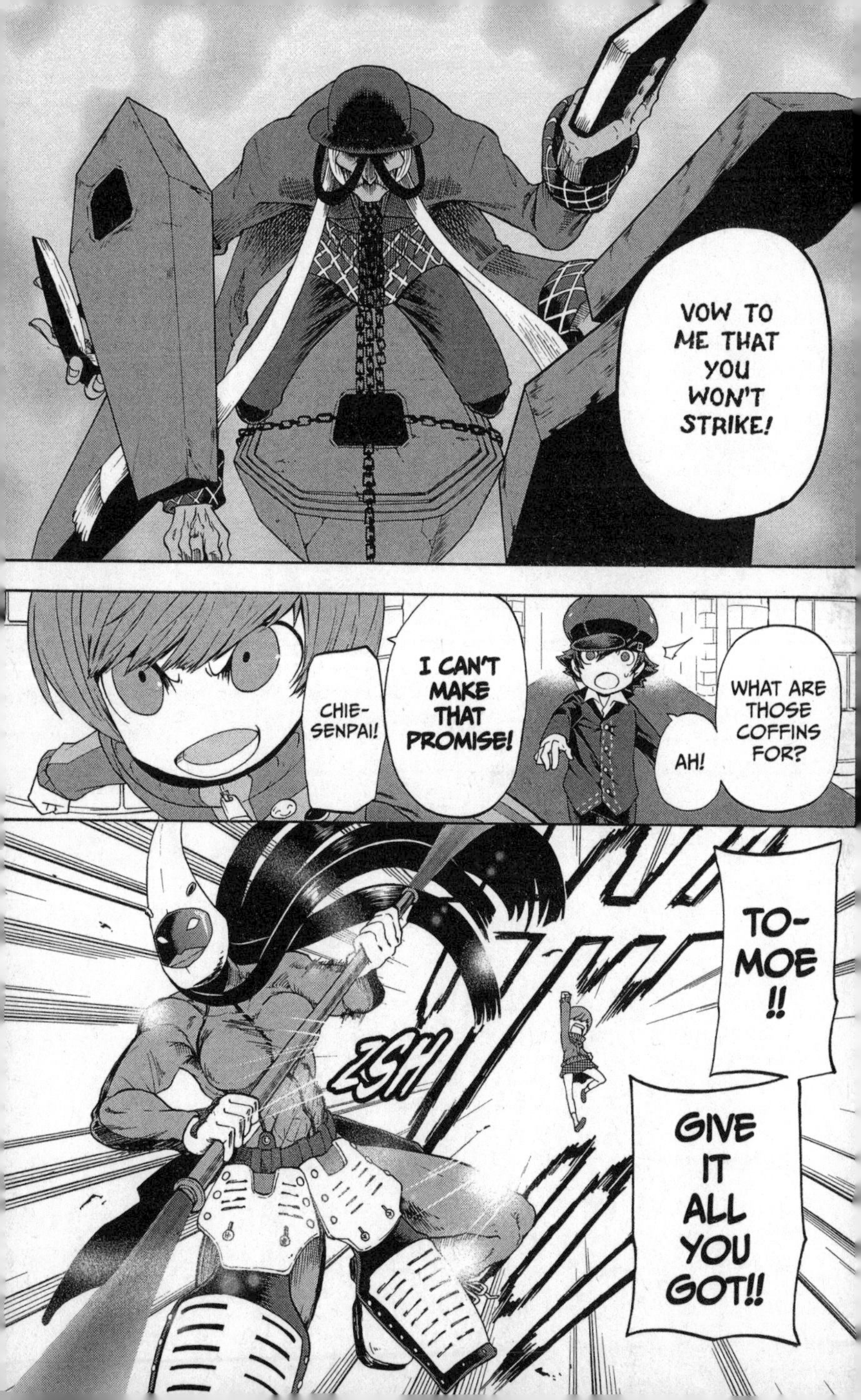
VOW TO ME THAT YOU WON'T STRIKE!
WHAT ARE THOSE COFFINS FOR?
AH!
I CAN'T MAKE THAT PROMISE!
CHIE-SENPAI!
TO-MOE!!
GIVE IT ALL YOU GOT!!
ZSH

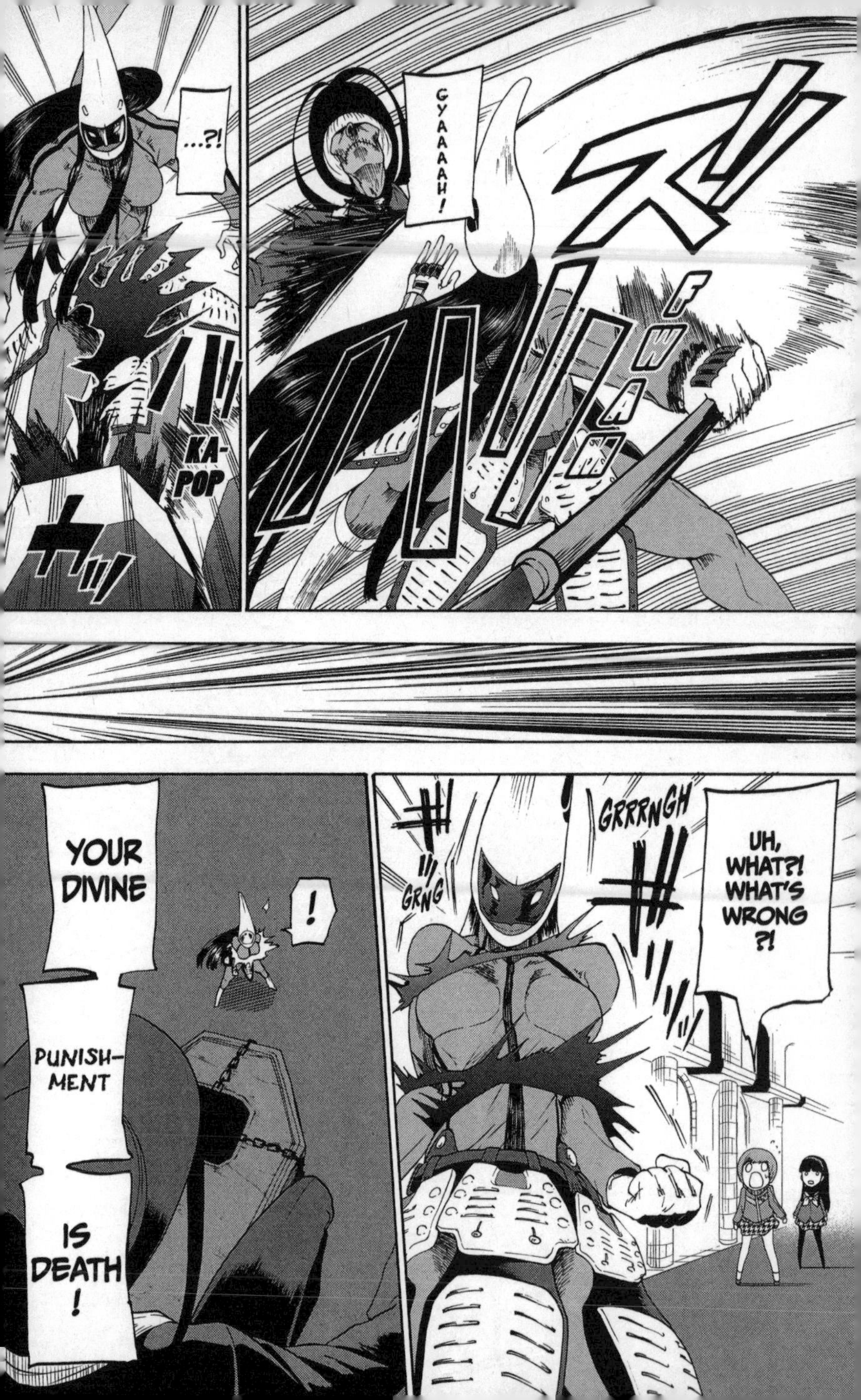
GYAAAAAH!
FWAM
...?!
KA-POP
GRRRNGH
GRNG
UH, WHAT?! WHAT'S WRONG ?!
!
YOUR DIVINE
PUNISHMENT
IS DEATH!

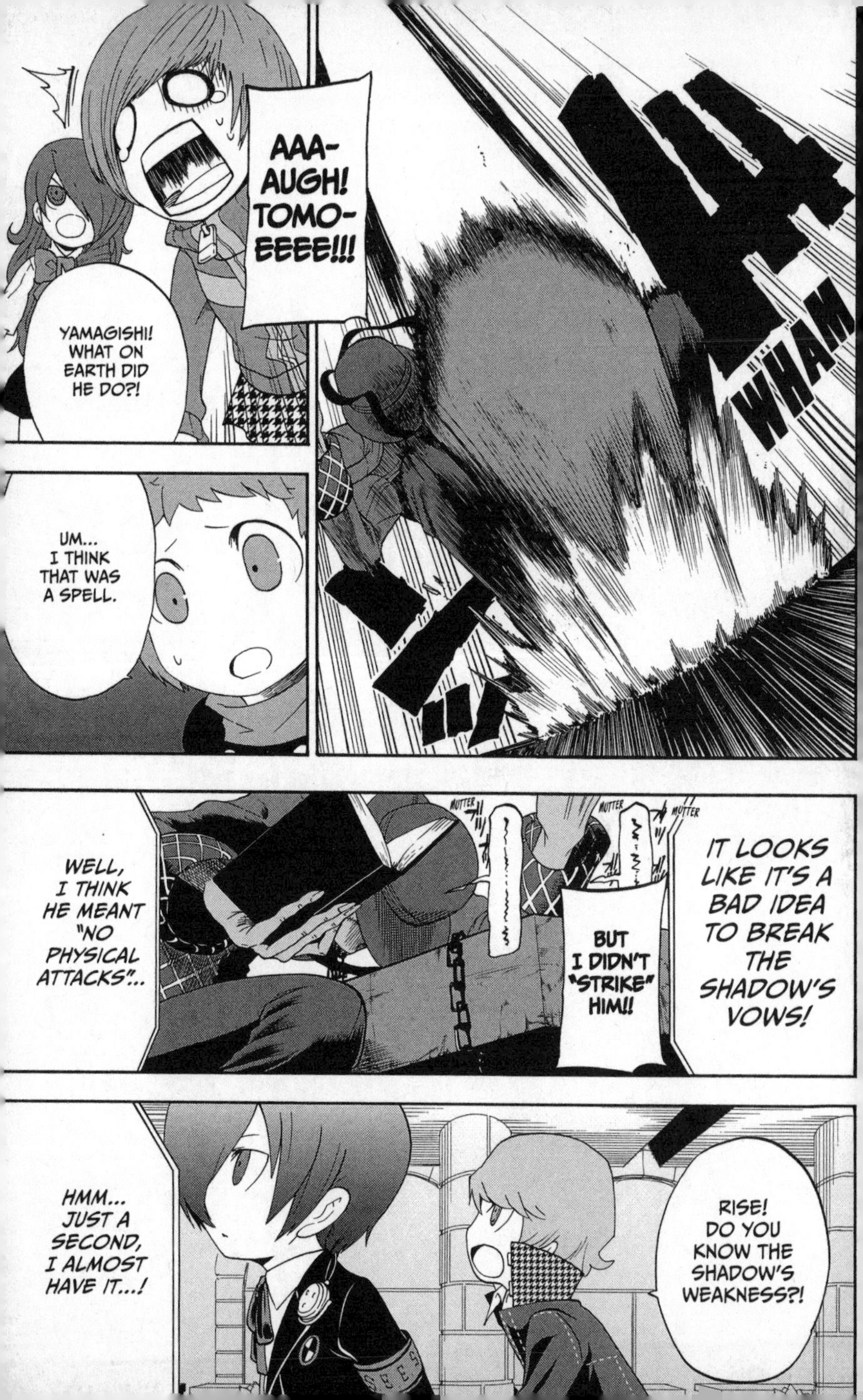
WHAM
AAA-AUGH! TOMO-EEEE!!!
YAMAGISHI! WHAT ON EARTH DID HE DO?!
UM... I THINK THAT WAS A SPELL.
IT LOOKS LIKE IT'S A BAD IDEA TO BREAK THE SHADOW'S VOWS!
MUTTER
MUTTER
MUTTER
BUT I DIDN'T "STRIKE" HIM!!
WELL, I THINK HE MEANT "NO PHYSICAL ATTACKS"...
RISE! DO YOU KNOW THE SHADOW'S WEAKNESS?!
HMM... JUST A SECOND, I ALMOST HAVE IT...!

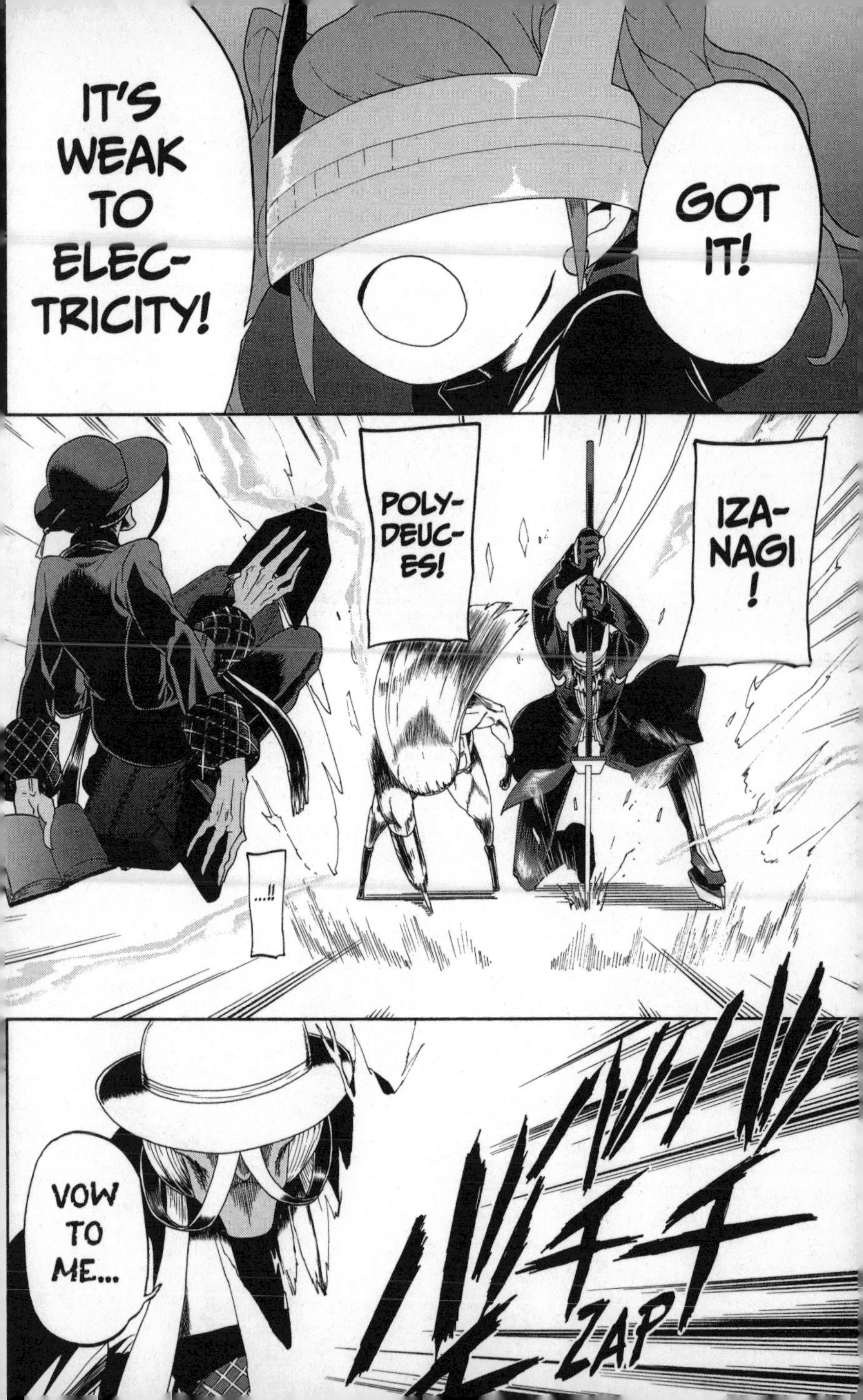
IT'S WEAK TO ELEC-TRICITY!
GOT IT!
IZA-NAGI!
POLY-DEUC-ES!
...!!
VOW TO ME...
ZAP

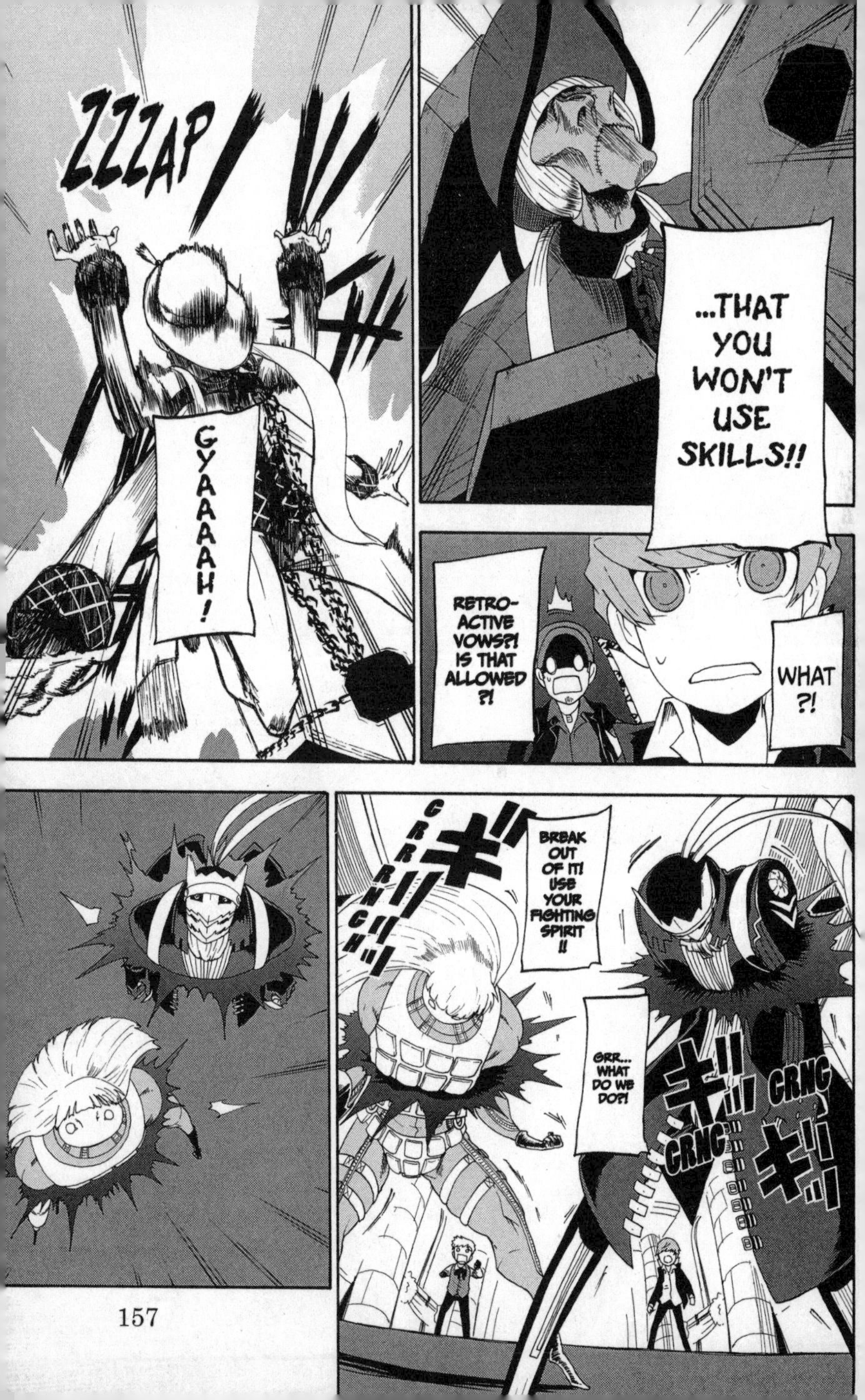
...THAT YOU WON'T USE SKILLS!!
WHAT?!
RETRO-ACTIVE VOWS?! IS THAT ALLOWED?!
ZZZAP
GYAAAAAH!
GRRRRNGH
BREAK OUT OF IT! USE YOUR FIGHTING SPIRIT!!
GRR... WHAT DO WE DO?!
CRNG
CRNG

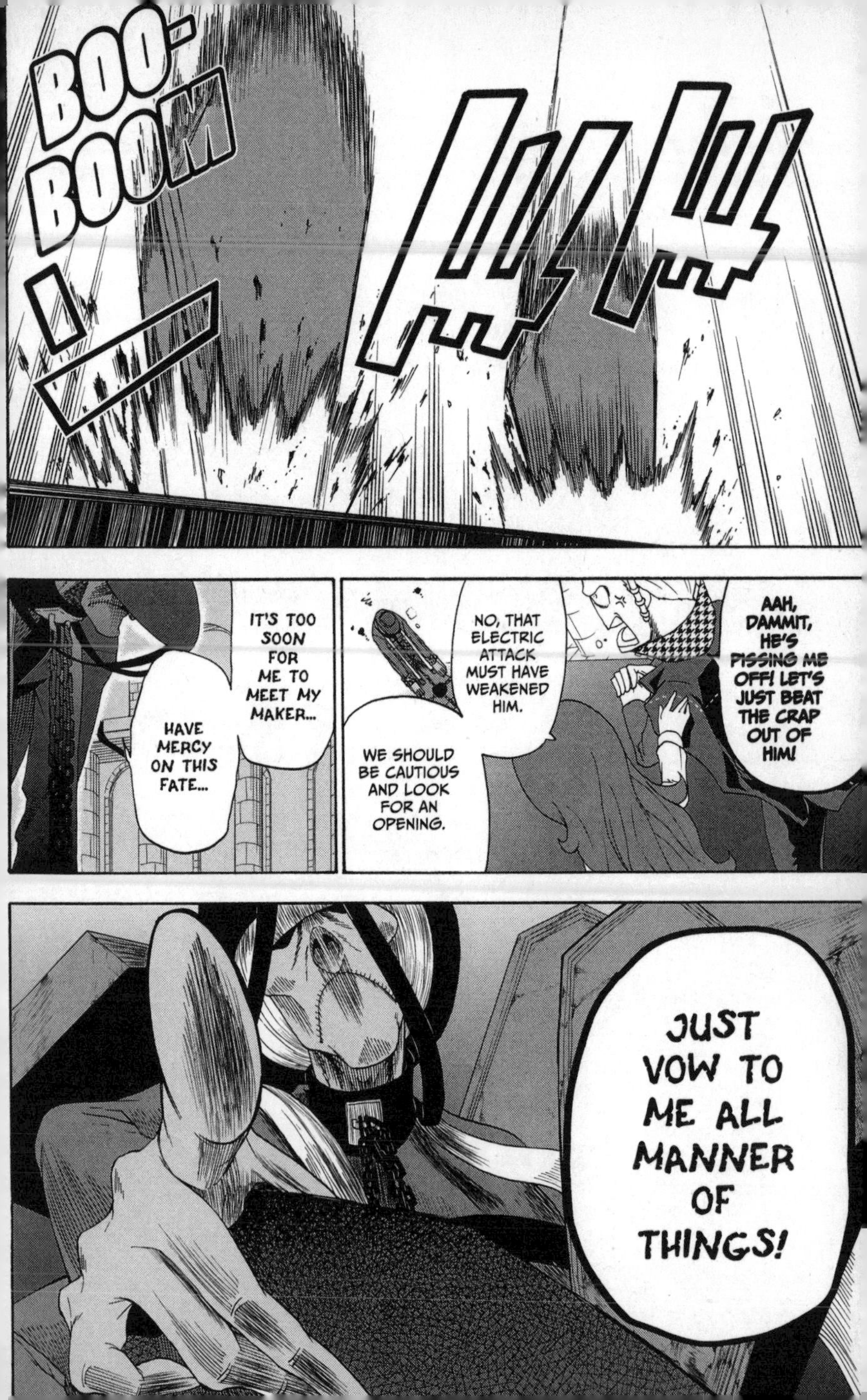
BOO-BOOM
AAH, DAMMIT, HE'S PISSING ME OFF! LET'S JUST BEAT THE CRAP OUT OF HIM!
NO, THAT ELECTRIC ATTACK MUST HAVE WEAKENED HIM.
WE SHOULD BE CAUTIOUS AND LOOK FOR AN OPENING.
IT'S TOO SOON FOR ME TO MEET MY MAKER...
HAVE MERCY ON THIS FATE...
JUST VOW TO ME ALL MANNER OF THINGS!

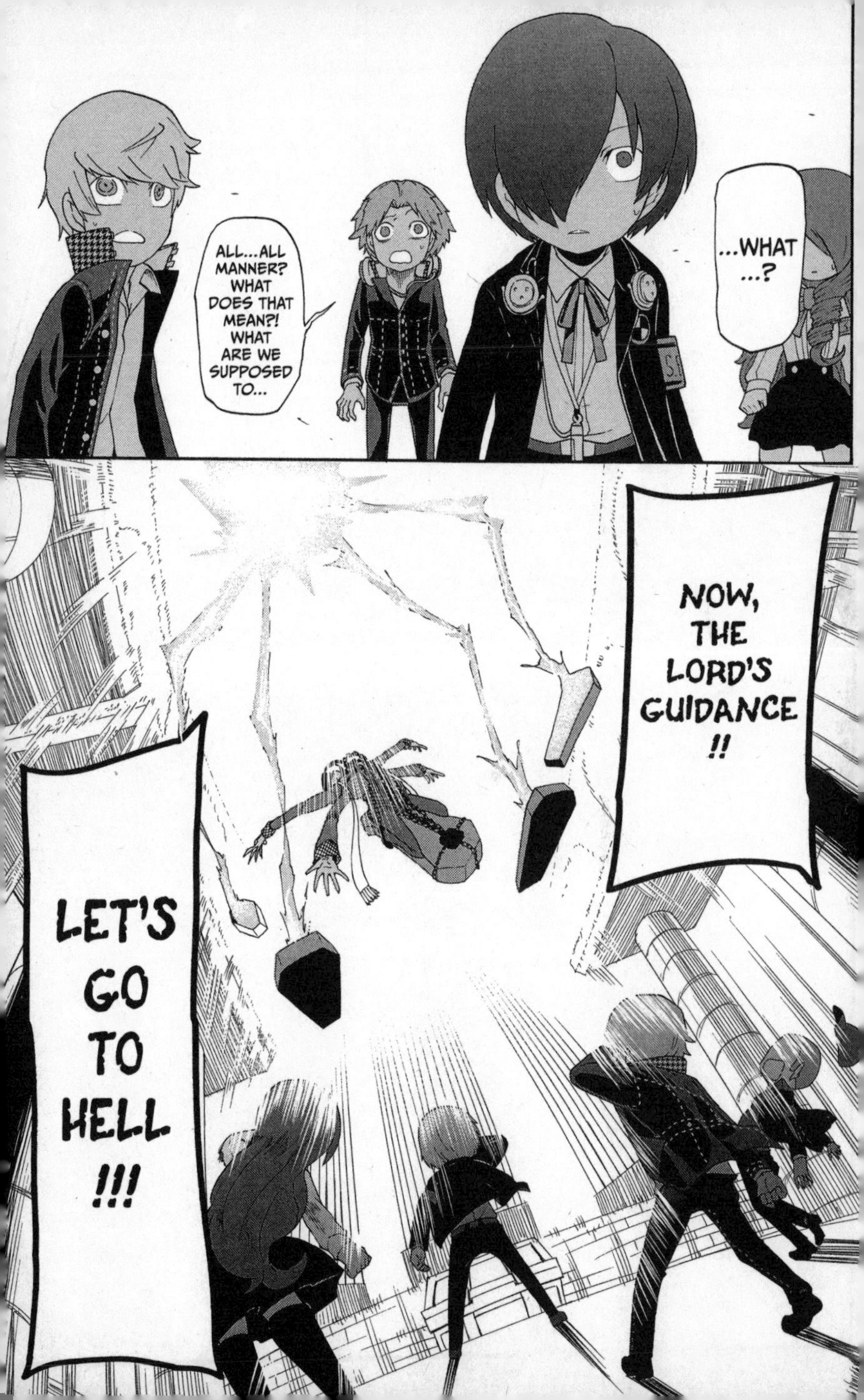
...WHAT ...?
ALL...ALL MANNER? WHAT DOES THAT MEAN?! WHAT ARE WE SUPPOSED TO...
NOW, THE LORD'S GUIDANCE !!
LET'S GO TO HELL !!!

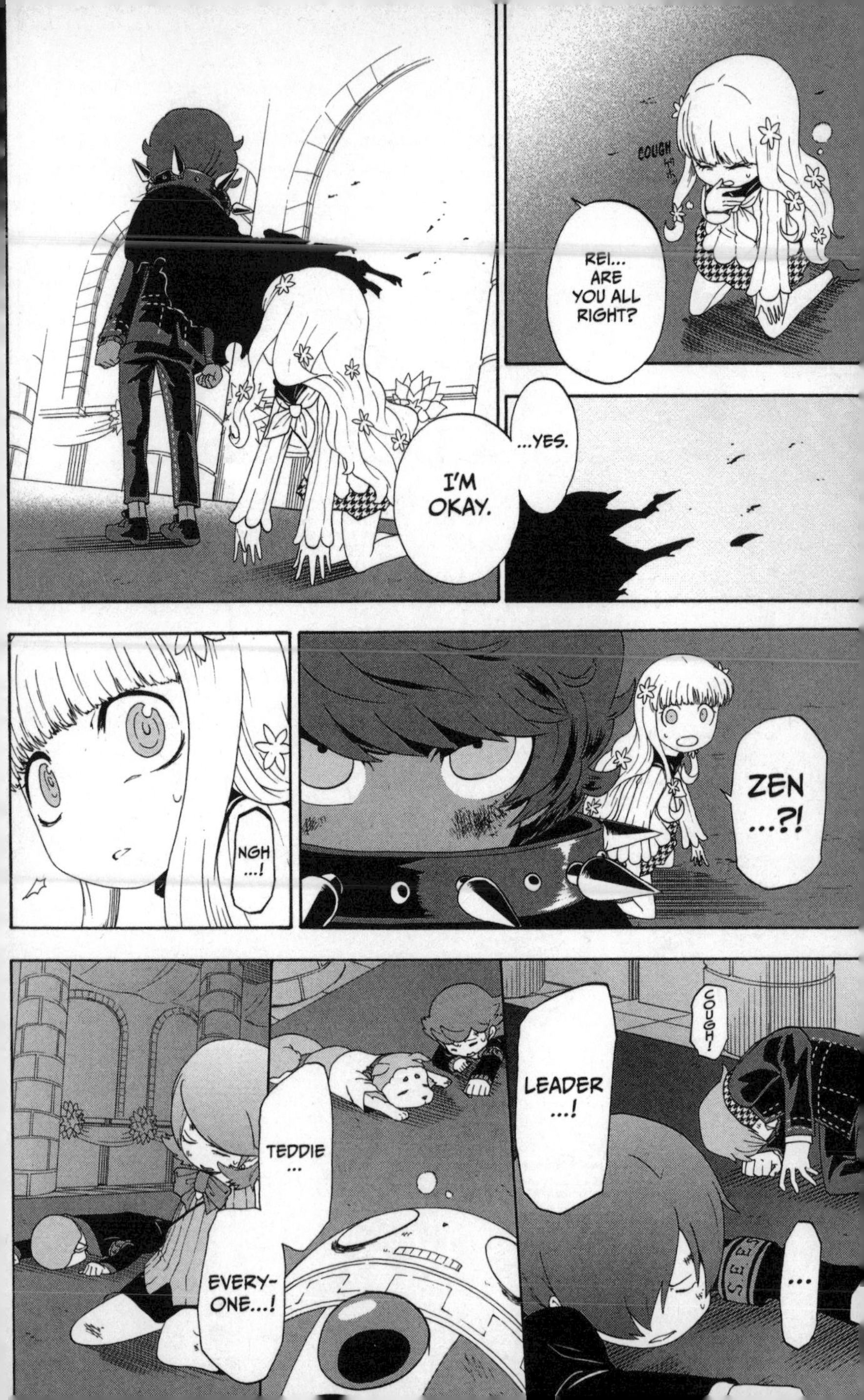
COUGH
REI... ARE YOU ALL RIGHT?
...YES.
I'M OKAY.
ZEN ...?!
NGH ...!
COUGH!
LEADER ...!
...
TEDDIE ...
EVERY-ONE...!

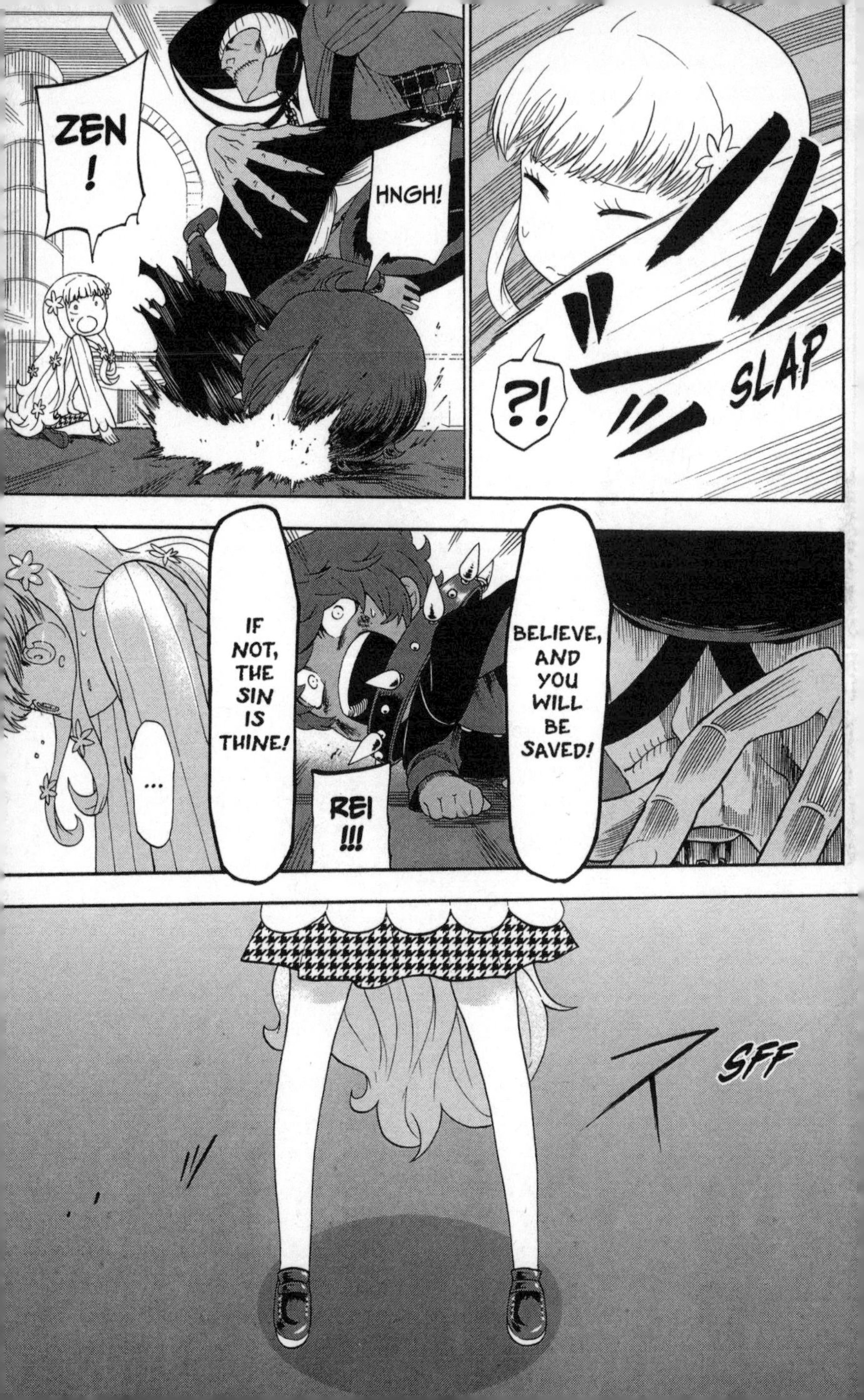
SLAP
?!
HNGH!
ZEN!
BELIEVE, AND YOU WILL BE SAVED!
IF NOT, THE SIN IS THINE!
REI!!!
...
SFF

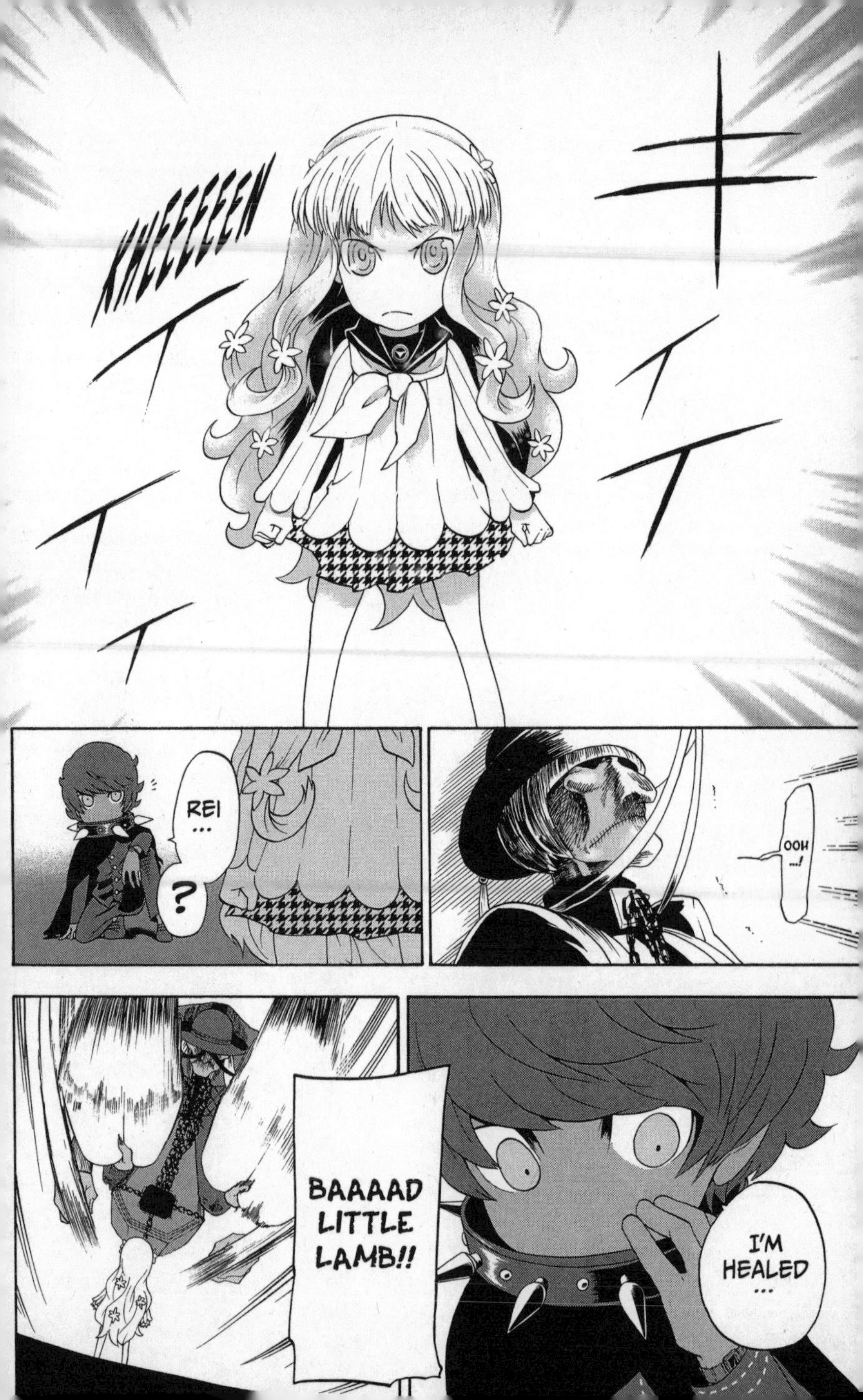
KHLEEEEEN
OOH ...!
REI ...
?
BAAAAD LITTLE LAMB!!
I'M HEALED ...

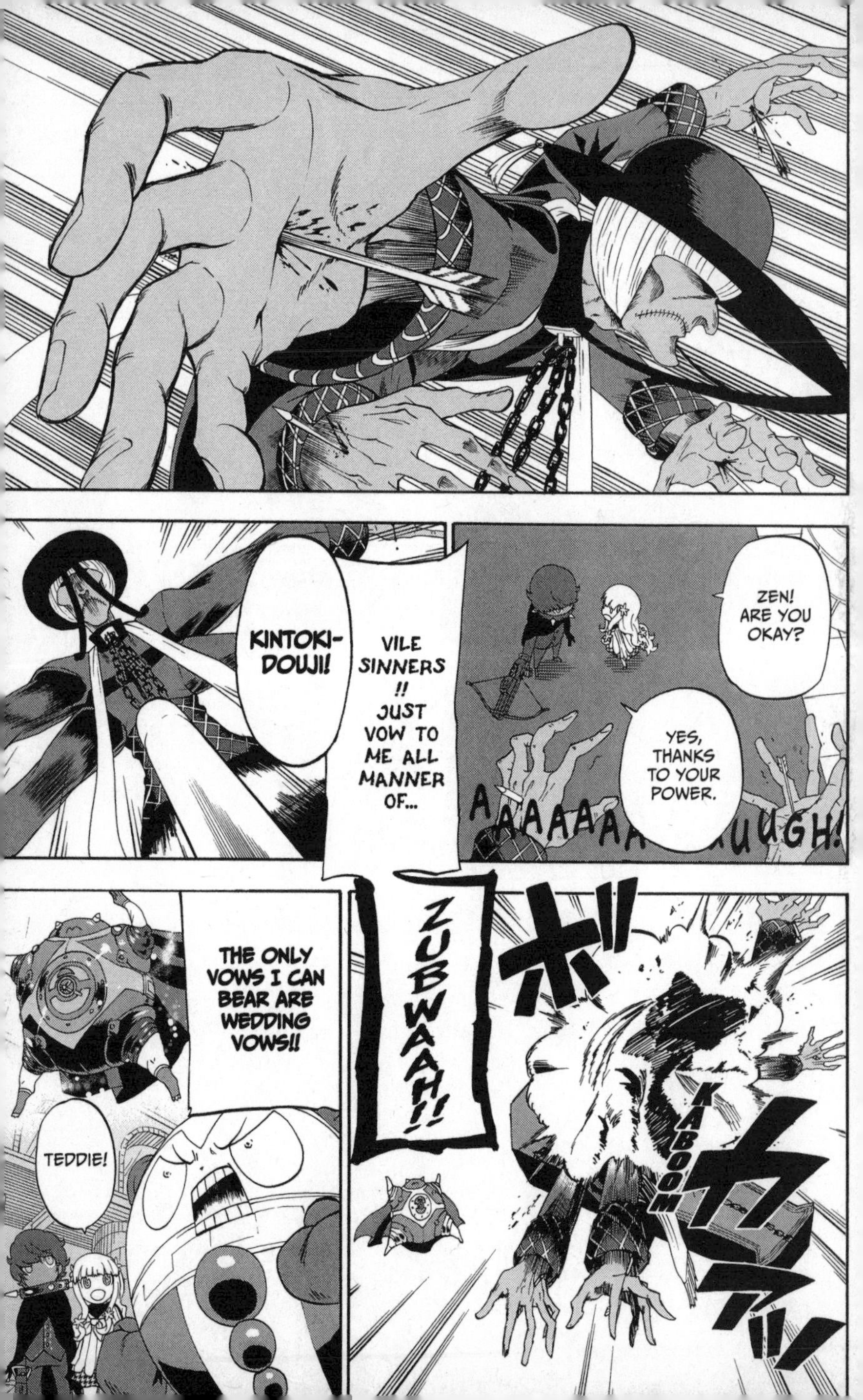
ZEN! ARE YOU OKAY?
YES, THANKS TO YOUR POWER.
AAAAAAAA UUUGH!
VILE SINNERS!! JUST VOW TO ME ALL MANNER OF...
KINTOKI-DOUJI!
ZUBWAAH!!
KABOOM
THE ONLY VOWS I CAN BEAR ARE WEDDING VOWS!!
TEDDIE!

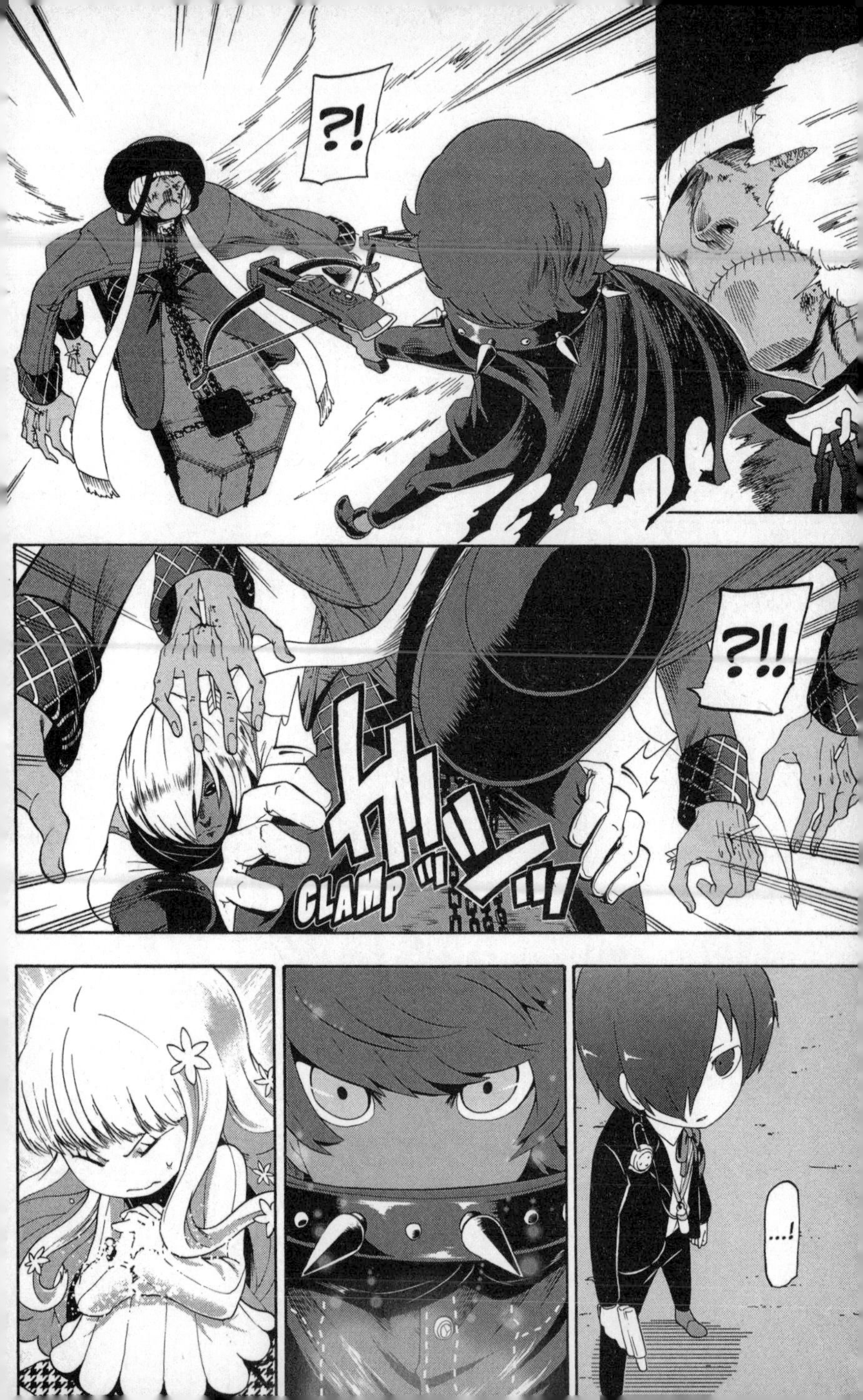
?!
?!!
CLAMP
...!

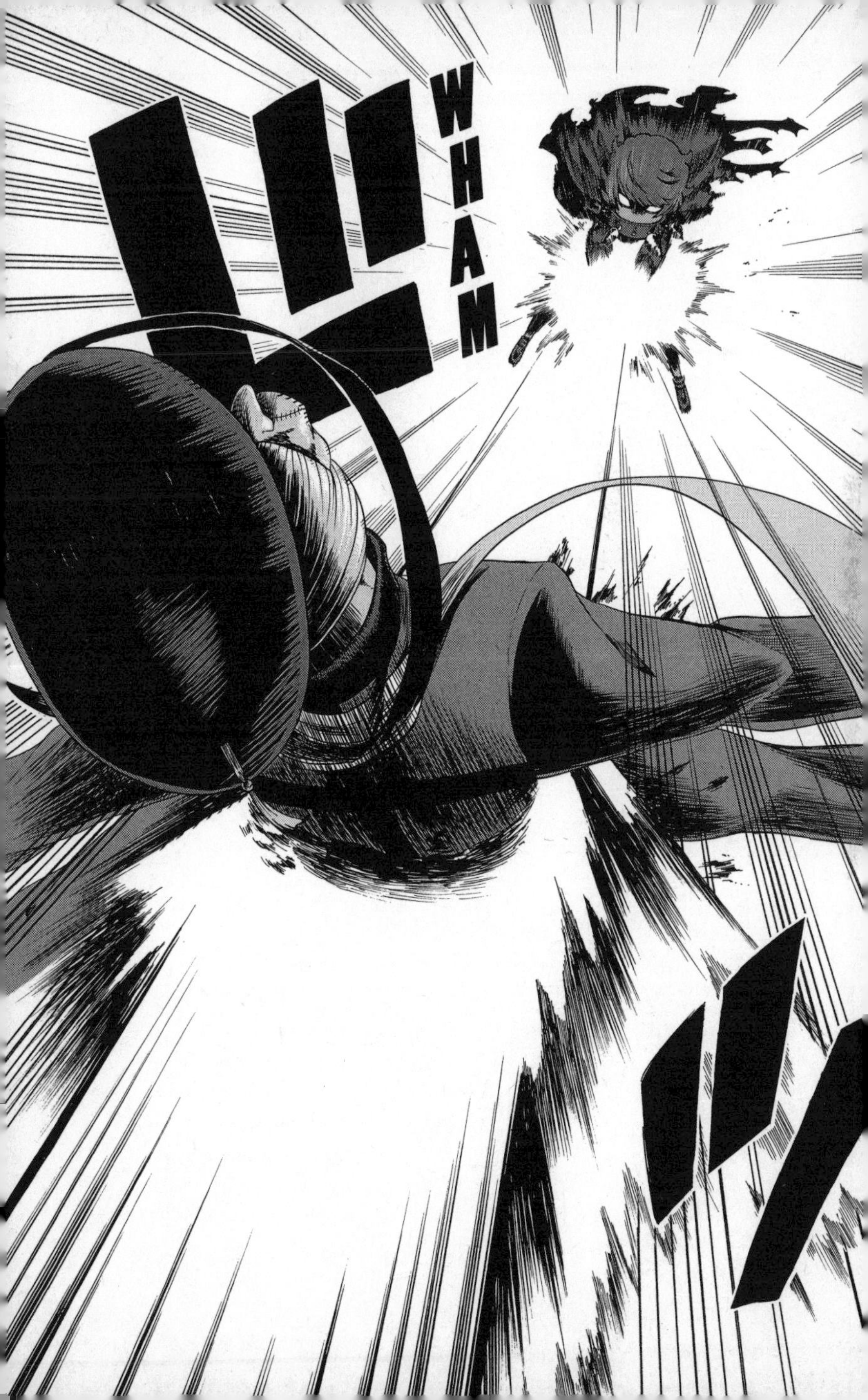
WHAM

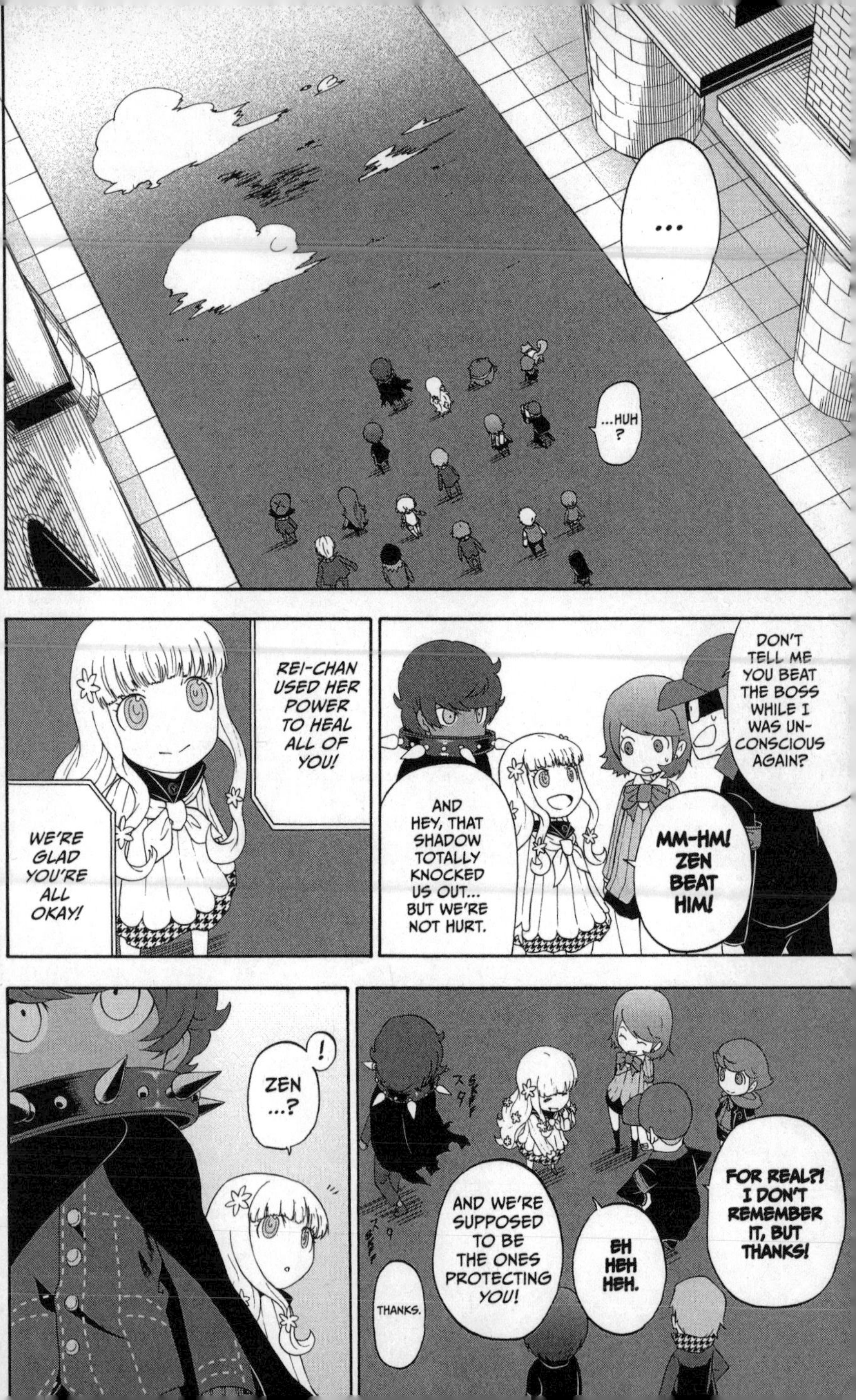
...
...HUH?
DON'T TELL ME YOU BEAT THE BOSS WHILE I WAS UN-CONSCIOUS AGAIN?
MM-HM! ZEN BEAT HIM!
AND HEY, THAT SHADOW TOTALLY KNOCKED US OUT... BUT WE'RE NOT HURT.
REI-CHAN USED HER POWER TO HEAL ALL OF YOU!
WE'RE GLAD YOU'RE ALL OKAY!
FOR REAL?! I DON'T REMEMBER IT, BUT THANKS!
EH HEH HEH.
AND WE'RE SUPPOSED TO BE THE ONES PROTECTING YOU!
THANKS.
!
ZEN ...?

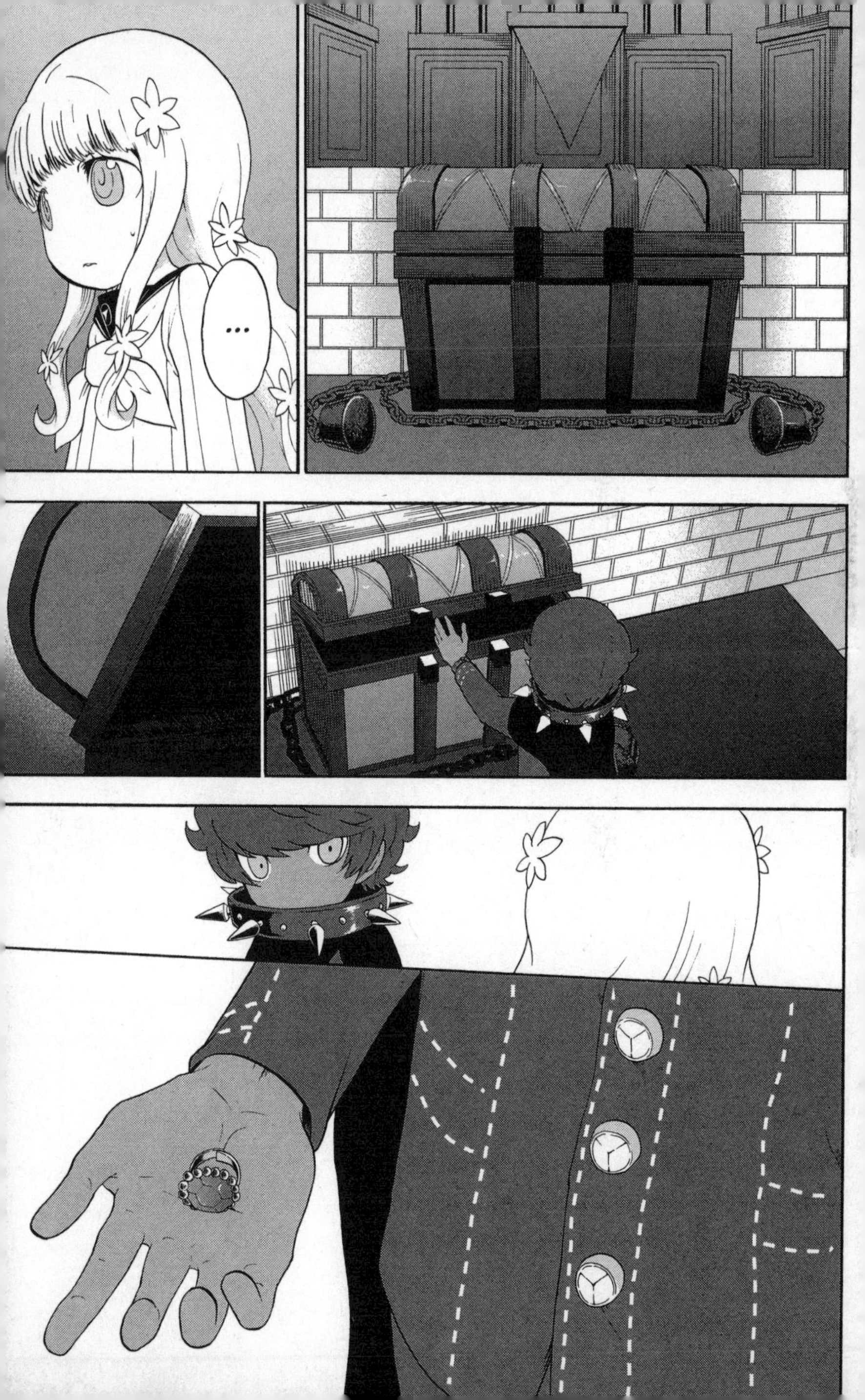
...

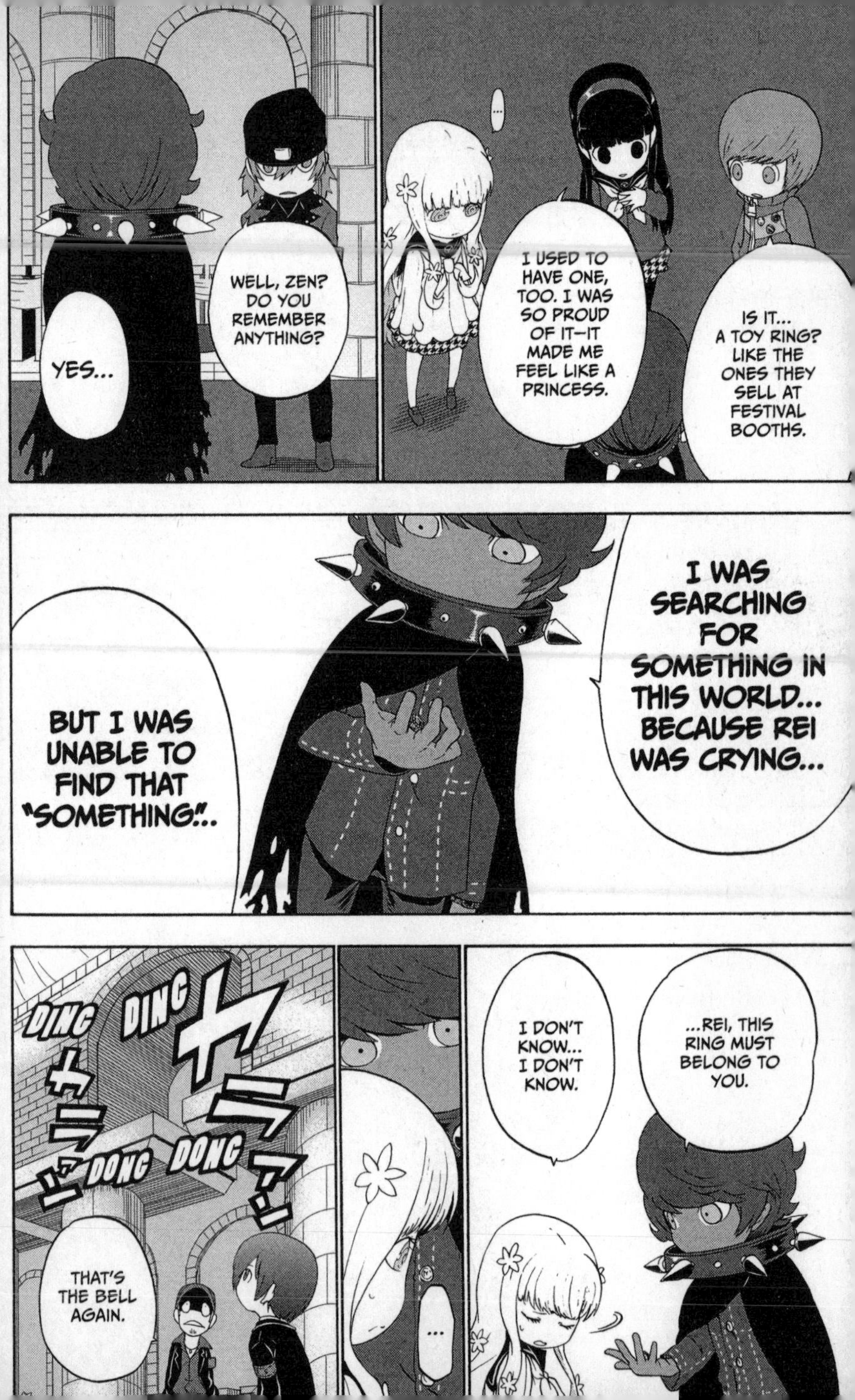
...
IS IT... A TOY RING? LIKE THE ONES THEY SELL AT FESTIVAL BOOTHS.
I USED TO HAVE ONE, TOO. I WAS SO PROUD OF IT—IT MADE ME FEEL LIKE A PRINCESS.
WELL, ZEN? DO YOU REMEMBER ANYTHING?
YES...
I WAS SEARCHING FOR SOMETHING IN THIS WORLD... BECAUSE REI WAS CRYING...
BUT I WAS UNABLE TO FIND THAT "SOMETHING"...
...REI, THIS RING MUST BELONG TO YOU.
I DON'T KNOW... I DON'T KNOW.
...
DING DING
DONG DONG
THAT'S THE BELL AGAIN.

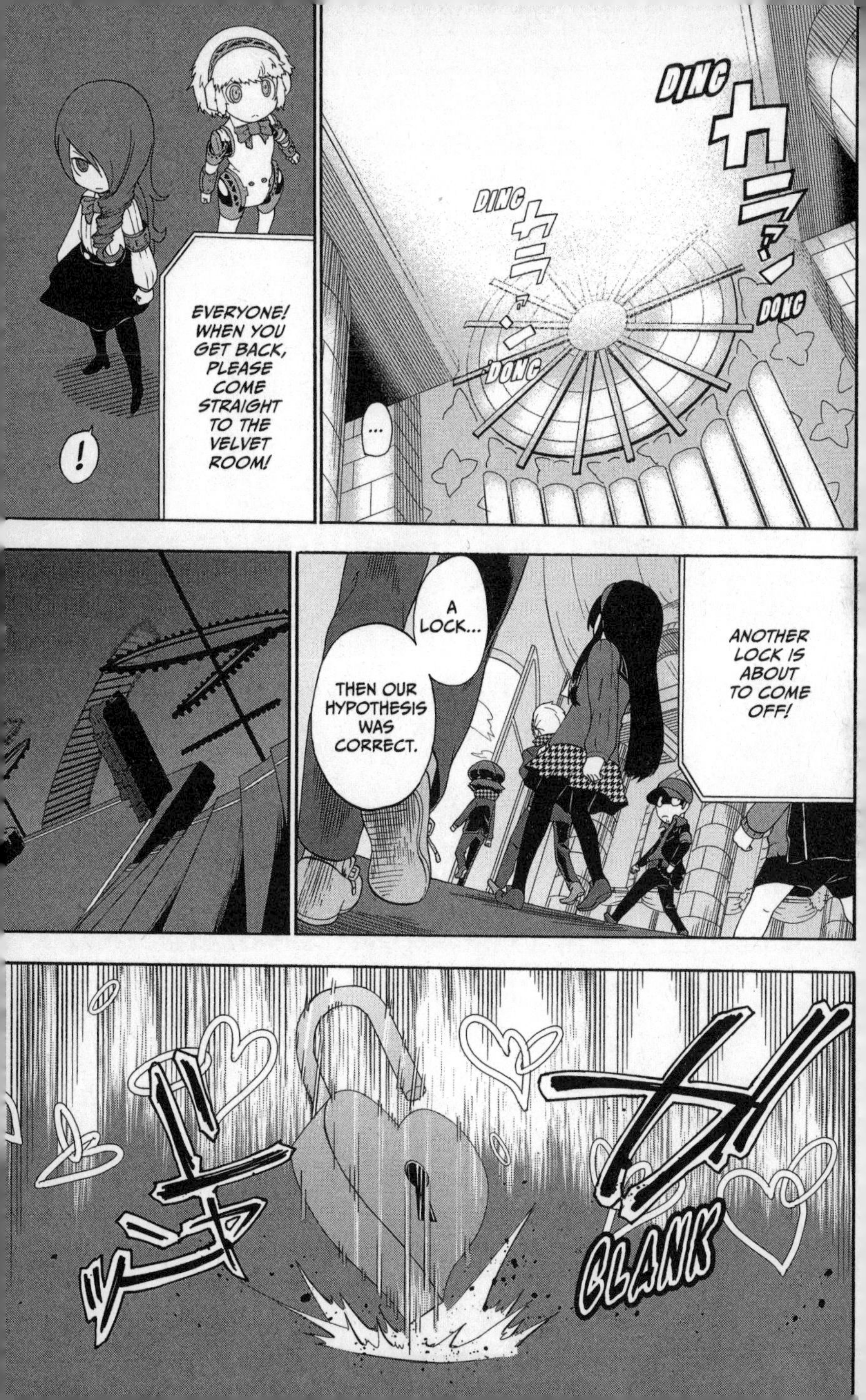
DING
DONG
DING
DONG
...
EVERYONE! WHEN YOU GET BACK, PLEASE COME STRAIGHT TO THE VELVET ROOM!
!
ANOTHER LOCK IS ABOUT TO COME OFF!
A LOCK...
THEN OUR HYPOTHESIS WAS CORRECT.
CLANK

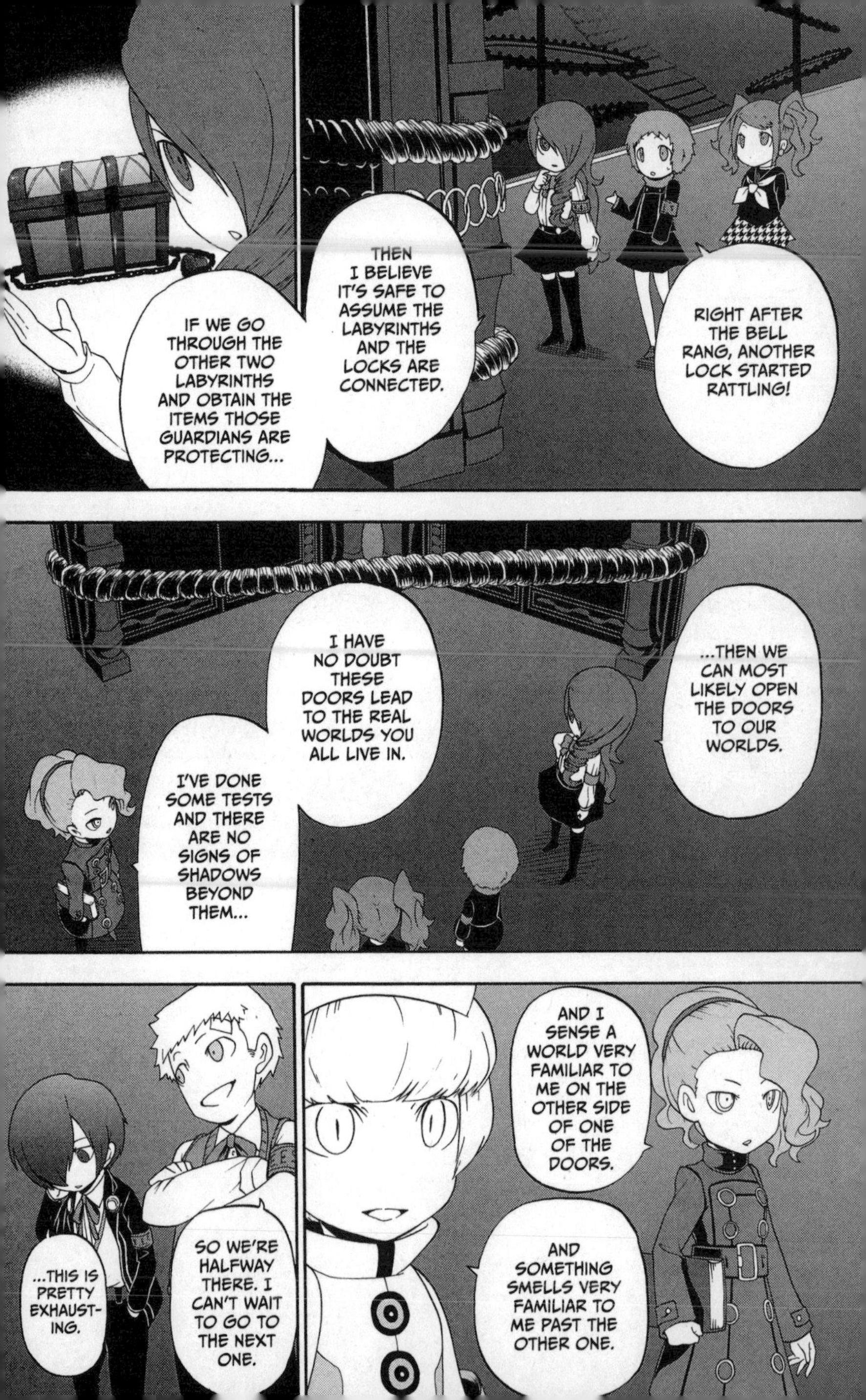
RIGHT AFTER THE BELL RANG, ANOTHER LOCK STARTED RATTLING!
THEN I BELIEVE IT'S SAFE TO ASSUME THE LABYRINTHS AND THE LOCKS ARE CONNECTED.
IF WE GO THROUGH THE OTHER TWO LABYRINTHS AND OBTAIN THE ITEMS THOSE GUARDIANS ARE PROTECTING...
...THEN WE CAN MOST LIKELY OPEN THE DOORS TO OUR WORLDS.
I HAVE NO DOUBT THESE DOORS LEAD TO THE REAL WORLDS YOU ALL LIVE IN.
I'VE DONE SOME TESTS AND THERE ARE NO SIGNS OF SHADOWS BEYOND THEM...
AND I SENSE A WORLD VERY FAMILIAR TO ME ON THE OTHER SIDE OF ONE OF THE DOORS.
AND SOMETHING SMELLS VERY FAMILIAR TO ME PAST THE OTHER ONE.
SO WE'RE HALFWAY THERE. I CAN'T WAIT TO GO TO THE NEXT ONE.
...THIS IS PRETTY EXHAUST-ING.

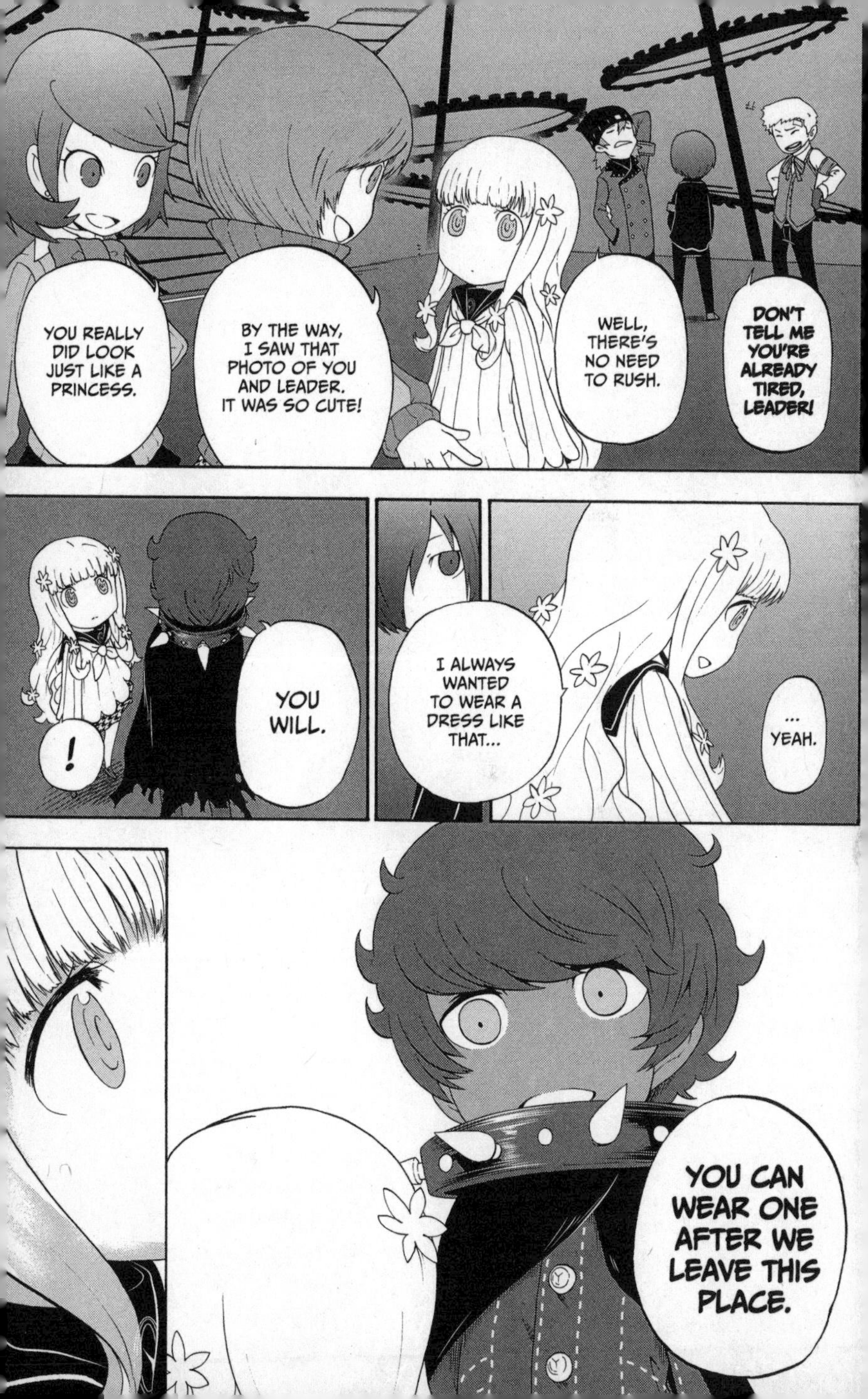
DON'T TELL ME YOU'RE ALREADY TIRED, LEADER!
WELL, THERE'S NO NEED TO RUSH.
BY THE WAY, I SAW THAT PHOTO OF YOU AND LEADER. IT WAS SO CUTE!
YOU REALLY DID LOOK JUST LIKE A PRINCESS.
... YEAH.
I ALWAYS WANTED TO WEAR A DRESS LIKE THAT...
YOU WILL.
!
YOU CAN WEAR ONE AFTER WE LEAVE THIS PLACE.

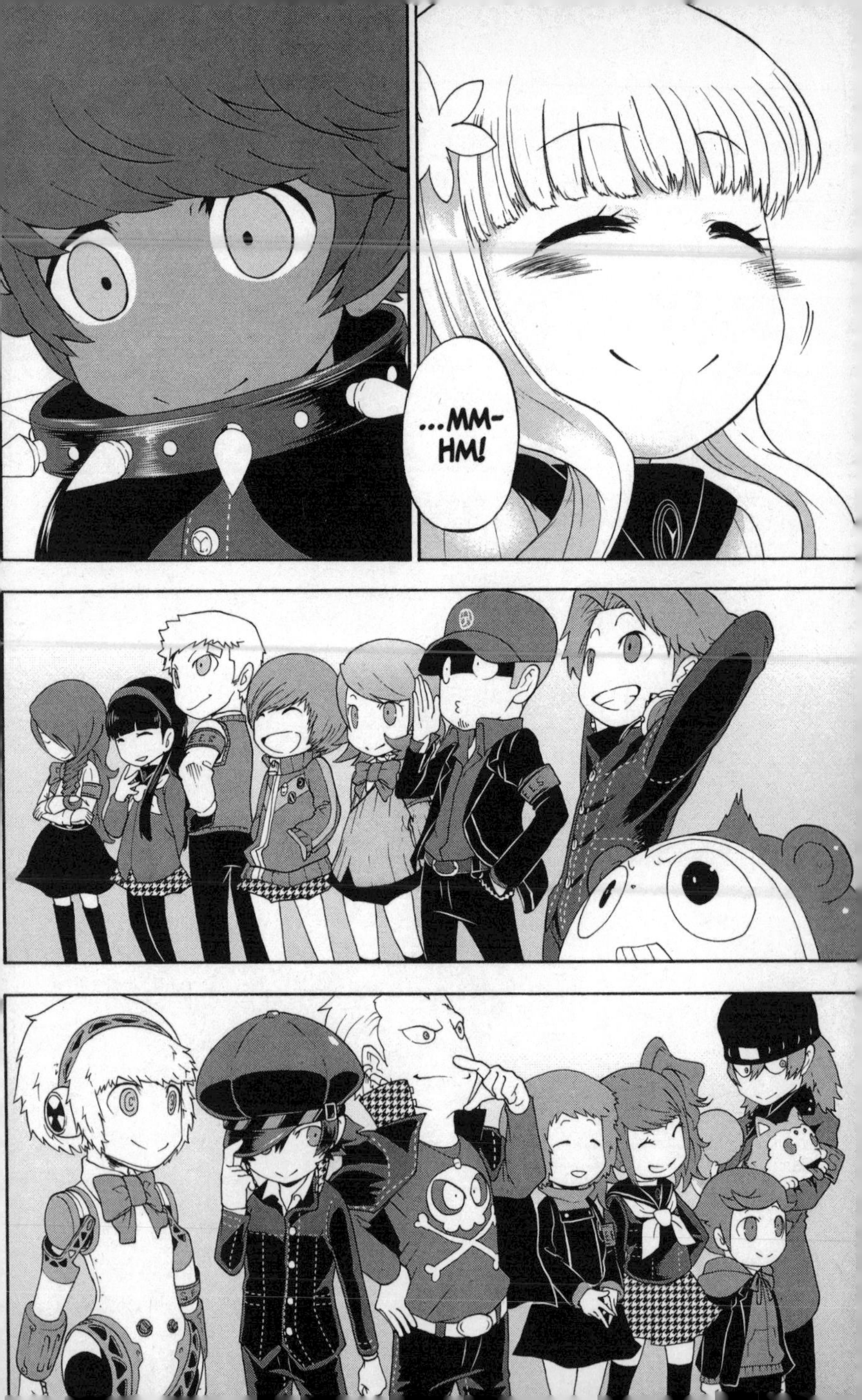
...MM-HM!

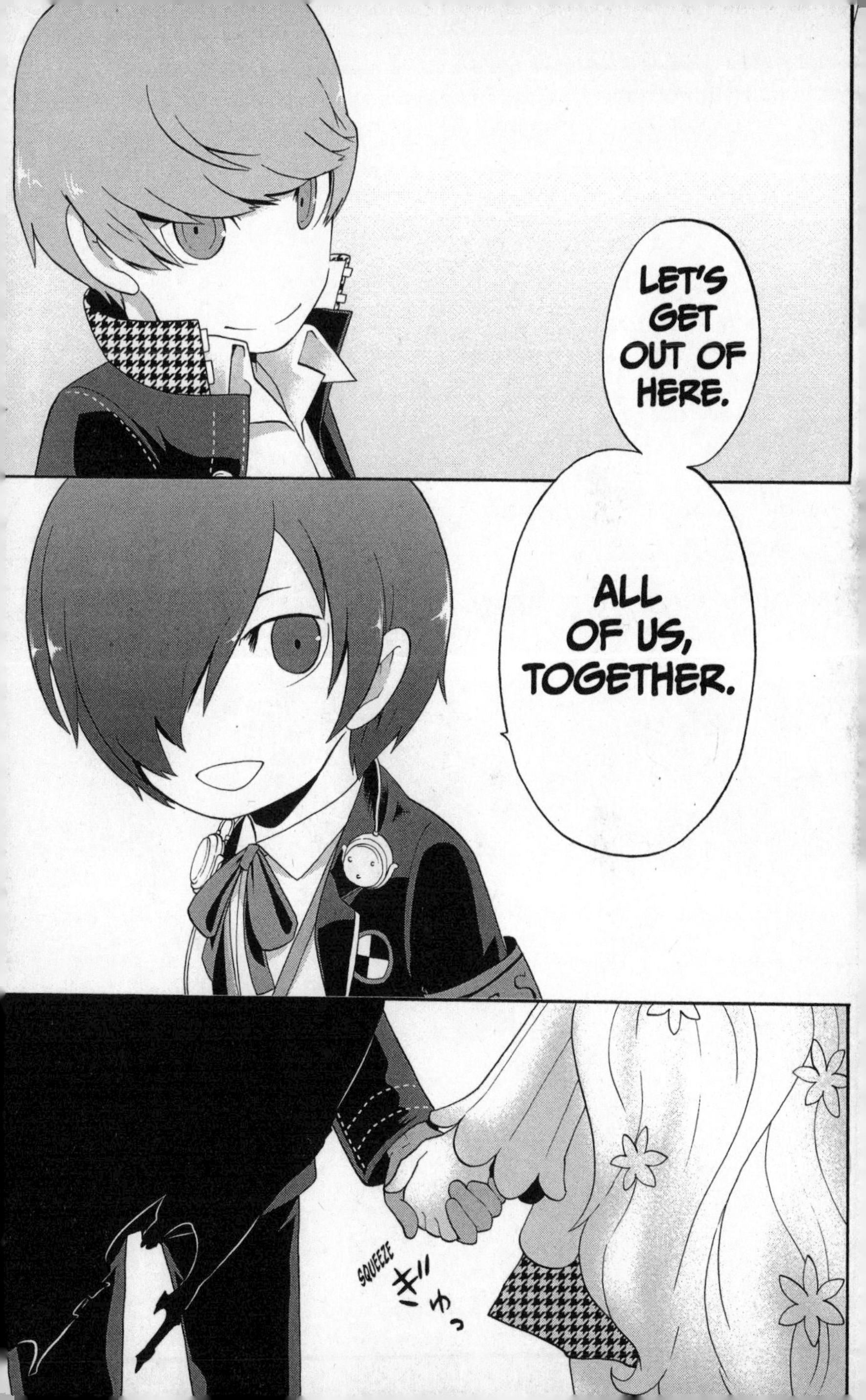
LET'S GET OUT OF HERE.
ALL OF US, TOGETHER.
SQUEEZE
ぎゅっ

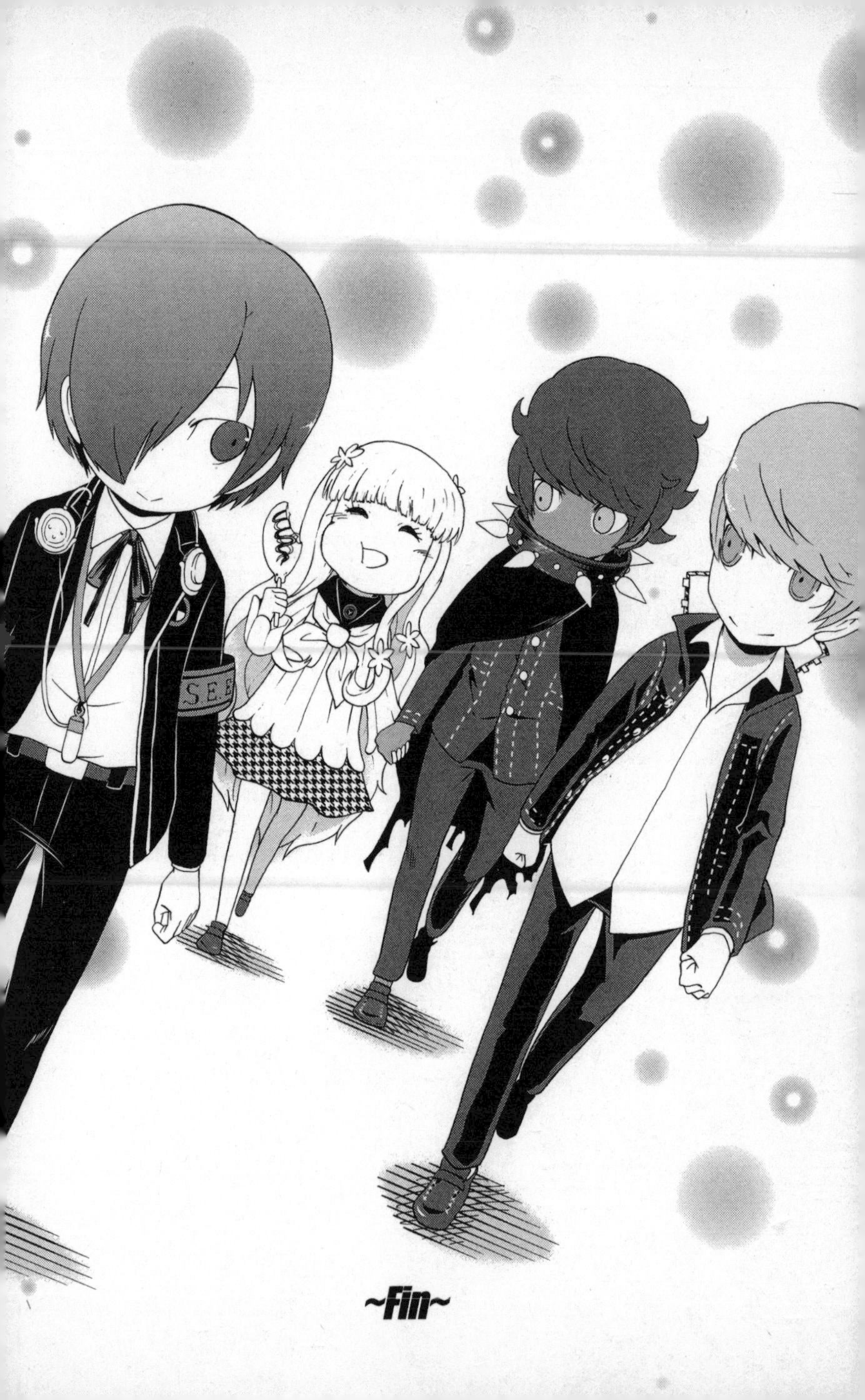
~Fin~

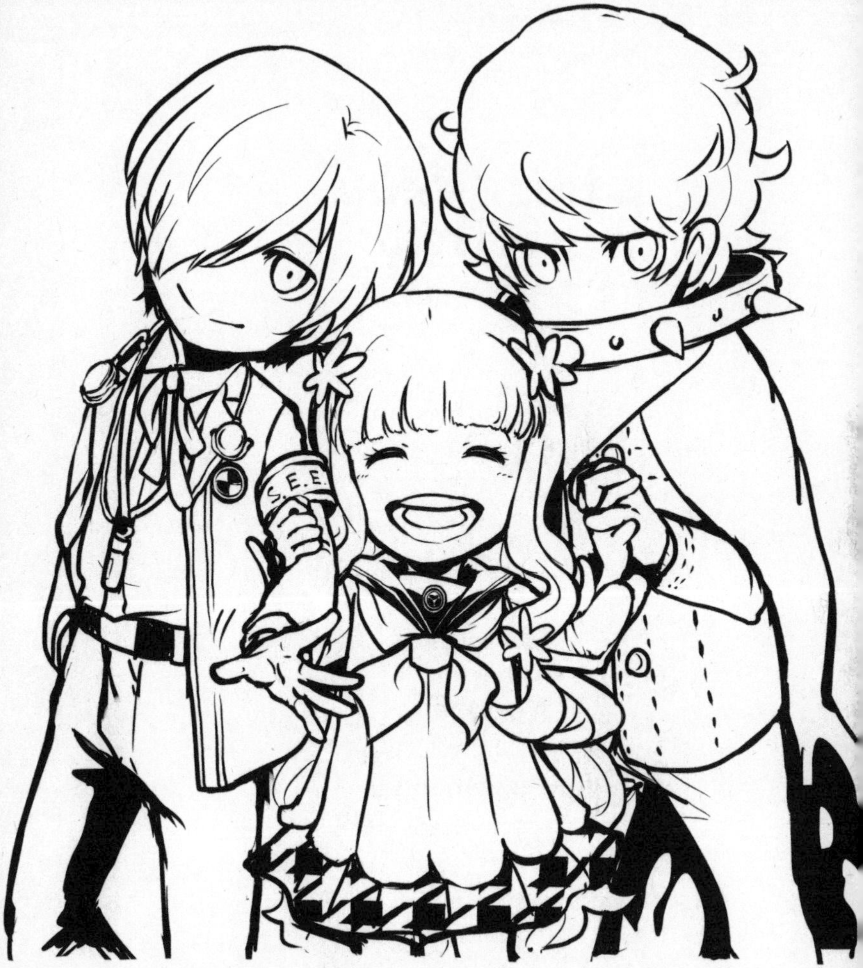
S.E.E.

I BELIEVE I'VE GROWN A LOT IN SO MANY WAYS THROUGH THE WORK I WAS ABLE TO DO ON THE MANGA VERSION OF THIS GAME. TO EVERYONE INVOLVED, EVERYONE WHO HELPED ME WITH THE ART, AND EVERYONE WHO READS THIS BOOK, THANK YOU VERY MUCH!

ART ASSISTANCE: KOTOBA INOYA, AMI FUSHIMI, CHIHIRO MASUDA, MIURA, TAKASHI MIZUMORI

A NOTE FROM THE AUTHOR, SO TOBITA

It's done!
It was really fun to
draw this manga.
Thank you very much!

TRANSLATION NOTES

Vincent, page 11

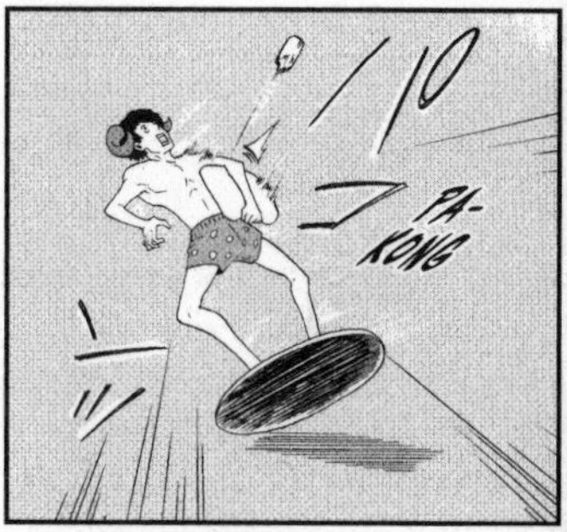
PA-KONG

The figurine that Mitsuru shoots at the shooting gallery is Vincent Brooks, the main character of the Atlus puzzle game *Catherine*. After meeting the "Catherine" of the game's title and spending the night with her, Vincent finds himself tormented by nightmares in which he must climb a tower and face his fears as they appear before him in sheep form.

Yo-yo tsuri, page 15

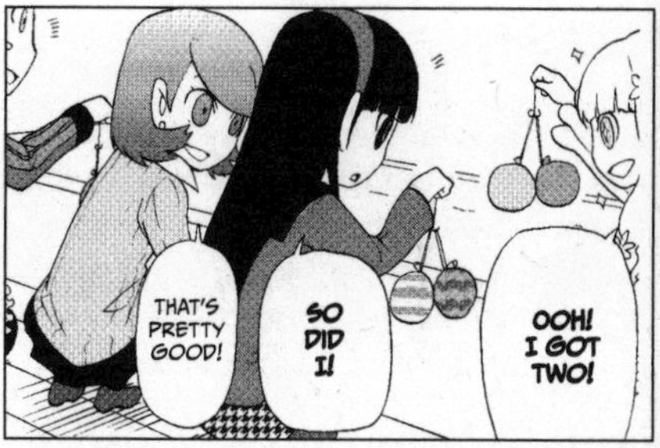
OOH! I GOT TWO!
SO DID I!
THAT'S PRETTY GOOD!

Here the *Persona* characters are playing a festival game called *yo-yo tsuri*, or "yo-yo fishing." As the picture demonstrates, they are fishing for water balloons that have elastic loops at the end, making them act like yo-yos. The "fishing rods" are hooks attached to twisted paper, which breaks easily when wet, making the game quite challenging, especially for beginners.

Red string of destiny, page 17

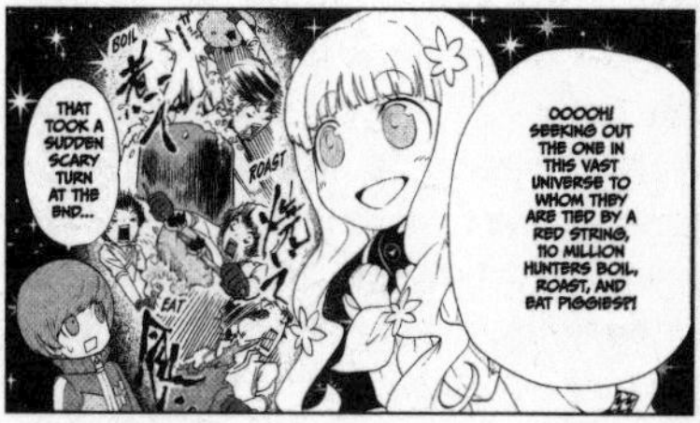
OOOOH! SEEKING OUT THE ONE IN THIS VAST UNIVERSE TO WHOM THEY ARE TIED BY A RED STRING, 110 MILLION HUNTERS BOIL, ROAST, AND EAT PIGGIES?!
ROAST
BOIL
EAT
THAT TOOK A SUDDEN SCARY TURN AT THE END...

The red string of destiny, or red string of fate, is an East Asian belief that originated in China. The idea is that a man and a woman who are destined to be married are tied together by a red string or thread. It's similar to the concept of soul mates.

Jack Frost, page 38

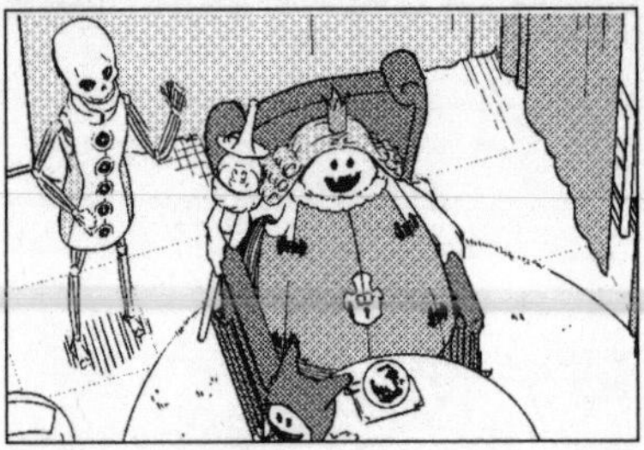

Anyone familiar with Atlus games should recognize this character as Jack Frost. He first appeared in *Persona's* parent series, *Shin Megami Tensei*, and has been gracing the screens of Atlus games ever since. Don't miss his major role in the *Devil Survivor* manga, hee-ho!

Poink, page 48

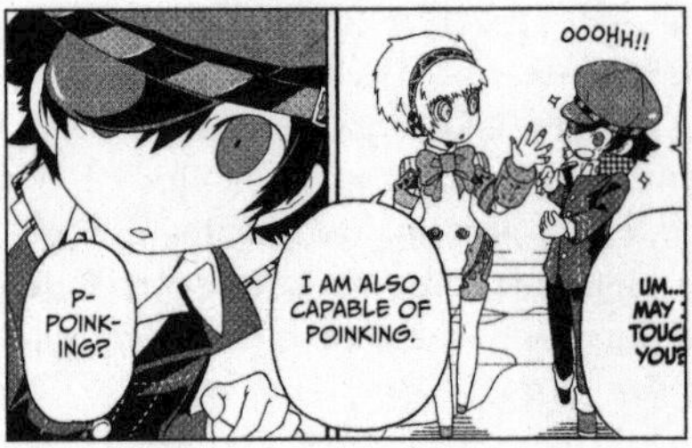
OOOHH!!
UM... MAY TOUC YOU?
I AM ALSO CAPABLE OF POINKING.
P-POINK-ING?

"Poink" is a translation of the Japanese sound effect, *porori*, which is the sound of something falling off, or falling out. What neither Aigis nor Rei seems to understand is that this sound effect is generally used to accompany a wardrobe malfunction.

Kusaya, page 73

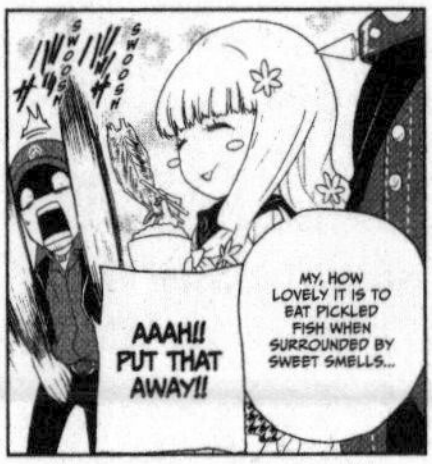
MY, HOW LOVELY IT IS TO EAT PICKLED FISH WHEN SURROUNDED BY SWEET SMELLS...
AAAH!! PUT THAT AWAY!!

Kusaya is a Japanese food that is made by taking a horse mackerel, letting it soak in salt water, then drying it in the sun. While it is certainly known for its powerful aroma, Rei is one of very few people who find its fragrance appealing.

The Straw Millionaire, page 122

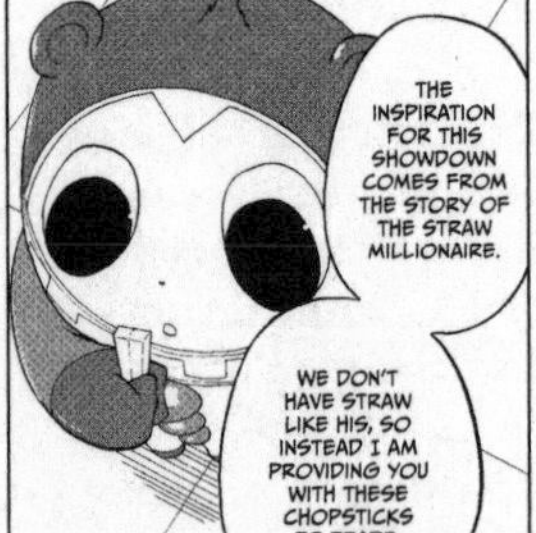
THE INSPIRATION FOR THIS SHOWDOWN COMES FROM THE STORY OF THE STRAW MILLIONAIRE.
WE DON'T HAVE STRAW LIKE HIS, SO INSTEAD I AM PROVIDING YOU WITH THESE CHOPSTICKS TO TRADE.

As indicated by the contents of the quest Elizabeth sends our heroes on, the tale of the Straw Millionaire is one of a poor man who eventually becomes a millionaire by trading. It starts with him praying to Kannon the goddess of mercy, who tells him to carry the first thing he touches west. That first thing is a piece of straw that he touched when he stumbles on his way out of the temple. He manages to trade the piece of straw for better and better things until he becomes a millionaire.

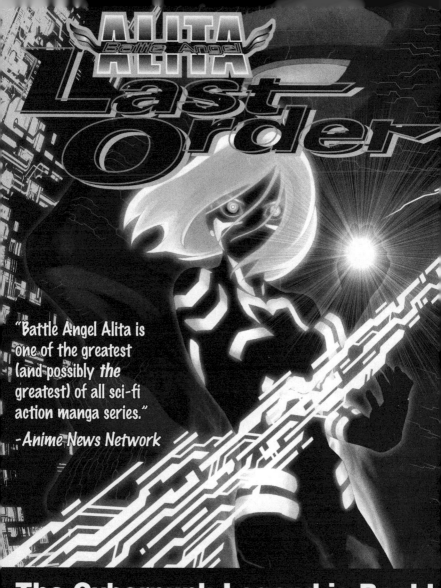

ALITA
Battle Angel ALITA
Last Order

"Battle Angel Alita is one of the greatest (and possibly *the* greatest) of all sci-fi action manga series."

-Anime News Network

The Cyberpunk Legend is Back!

In deluxe omnibus editions of 600+ pages, including ALL-NEW original stories by Alita creator Yukito Kishiro!

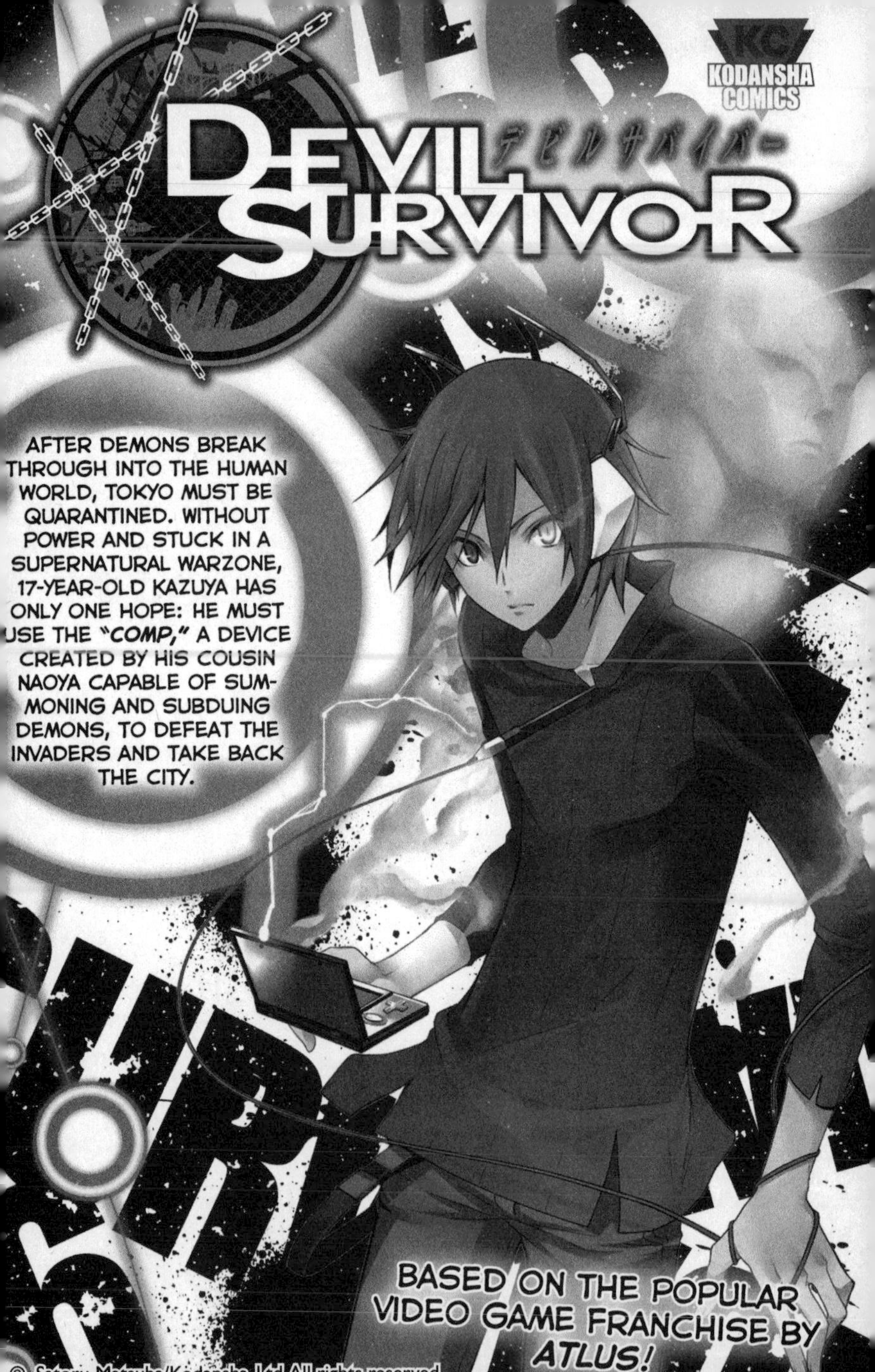
KC KODANSHA COMICS
DEVIL SURVIVOR
AFTER DEMONS BREAK THROUGH INTO THE HUMAN WORLD, TOKYO MUST BE QUARANTINED. WITHOUT POWER AND STUCK IN A SUPERNATURAL WARZONE, 17-YEAR-OLD KAZUYA HAS ONLY ONE HOPE: HE MUST USE THE "COMP," A DEVICE CREATED BY HIS COUSIN NAOYA CAPABLE OF SUMMONING AND SUBDUING DEMONS, TO DEFEAT THE INVADERS AND TAKE BACK THE CITY.
BASED ON THE POPULAR VIDEO GAME FRANCHISE BY ATLUS!

SWAPPED WITH A KISS?!

Class troublemaker Ryu Yamada is already having a bad day when he stumbles down a staircase along with star student Urara Shiraishi. When he wakes up, he realizes they have switched bodies—and that Ryu has the power to trade places with anyone just by kissing them! Ryu and Urara take full advantage of the situation to improve their lives, but with such an oddly amazing power, just how long will they be able to keep their secret under wraps?

Available now in print and digitally!

INUYASHIKI

A superhero like none you've ever seen, from the creator of "Gantz"!

Ichiro Inuyashiki is down on his luck. He looks much older than his 58 years, his children despise him, and his wife thinks he's a useless coward. So when he's diagnosed with stomach cancer and given three months to live, it seems the only one who'll miss him is his dog.

Then a blinding light fills the sky, and the old man is killed... only to wake up later in a body he almost recognizes as his own. Can it be that Ichiro Inuyashiki is no longer human?

Comes in extra-large editions with color pages!

A Kodansha Comics Trade Paperback Original.

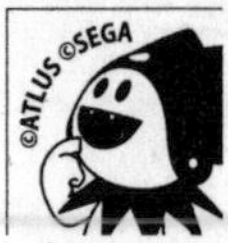
©ATLUS ©SEGA

Published in the United States by Kodansha Comics, an imprint of Kodansha USA Publishing, LLC, New York.

Publication rights for this English edition arranged through Kodansha Ltd., Tokyo.

First published in Japan in 2016 by Kodansha Ltd., Tokyo, as *Persona Q: Shadow of the Labyrinth, Side: P3* volume 2.

ISBN 978-1-63236-276-6

Printed in the United States of America.

www.kodanshacomics.com

9 8 7 6 5 4 3 2 1

Translation: Alethea Nibley & Athena Nibley
Lettering: James Dashiell
Editing: Ajani Oloye
Kodansha Comics Edition Cover Design: Phil Balsman